Palgrave Studies in Economic History

Series Editor
Kent Deng, London School of Economics, London, UK

Palgrave Studies in Economic History is designed to illuminate and enrich our understanding of economies and economic phenomena of the past. The series covers a vast range of topics including financial history, labour history, development economics, commercialisation, urbanisation, industrialisation, modernisation, globalisation, and changes in world economic orders.

More information about this series at
http://www.palgrave.com/gp/series/14632

Leonardo Caruana de las Cagigas ·
André Straus
Editors

Role of Reinsurance in the World

Case Studies of Eight Countries

Editors
Leonardo Caruana de las Cagigas
Faculty of Economics and Business
University of Granada
Granada, Spain

André Straus
Sorbonne University
Paris, France

ISSN 2662-6497   ISSN 2662-6500 (electronic)
Palgrave Studies in Economic History
ISBN 978-3-030-74001-6   ISBN 978-3-030-74002-3 (eBook)
https://doi.org/10.1007/978-3-030-74002-3

© The Editor(s) (if applicable) and The Author(s), under exclusive license to Springer Nature Switzerland AG 2021
This work is subject to copyright. All rights are solely and exclusively licensed by the Publisher, whether the whole or part of the material is concerned, specifically the rights of translation, reprinting, reuse of illustrations, recitation, broadcasting, reproduction on microfilms or in any other physical way, and transmission or information storage and retrieval, electronic adaptation, computer software, or by similar or dissimilar methodology now known or hereafter developed.
The use of general descriptive names, registered names, trademarks, service marks, etc. in this publication does not imply, even in the absence of a specific statement, that such names are exempt from the relevant protective laws and regulations and therefore free for general use.
The publisher, the authors and the editors are safe to assume that the advice and information in this book are believed to be true and accurate at the date of publication. Neither the publisher nor the authors or the editors give a warranty, expressed or implied, with respect to the material contained herein or for any errors or omissions that may have been made. The publisher remains neutral with regard to jurisdictional claims in published maps and institutional affiliations.

Cover illustration: North Wind Picture Archives/Alamy Stock Photo

This Palgrave Macmillan imprint is published by the registered company Springer Nature Switzerland AG
The registered company address is: Gewerbestrasse 11, 6330 Cham, Switzerland

Contents

1	**Introduction**	1
	Hugh Rockoff	
	1.1 What Is Reinsurance?	2
	1.2 Some Historical Examples	3
	1.3 Our Contributions	4
	1.4 Final Thoughts	11
	References	11
2	**The Core Countries in Reinsurance**	13
	Leonardo Caruana de las Cagigas and André Straus	
	References	21
3	**Reinsurance in America: Regulatory Regimes and Markets**	23
	Robert E. Wright	
	3.1 Introduction	23
	3.2 America Has Fewer World-Class Reinsurers Than Suggested by Its Large Insurance Market	24
	3.3 Relatively Costly and Inappropriate Regulations Forced Reinsurance into Other Channels	26
	3.4 America's Too Numerous State Insurance Regulators Treated Reinsurers as Direct Writers and Clung Tenaciously to the Monoline Model	28

	3.5	The Reinsurance Company of New York Case Shows the Difficulties Faced by American Reinsurers	33
	3.6	U.S. Reinsurance Regulation Remained Relatively Costly After World War II	35
	3.7	U.S. Reinsurers Trailed Market Leaders Based in Bermuda and Europe, Spurring Market-Based Innovations	36
	3.8	In the Future, ARTM May Displace Reinsurance as the Best Way to Spread Risk Globally	38
	References	39
4	**Reinsurance in the Netherlands from 1800 till 1950: A Failure?**	45
	Ben P. A. Gales	
	4.1	A Missed Opportunity?	45
	4.2	Co-Insurance and Reinsurance	48
	4.3	Between Germany and England	50
	4.4	Reinsurance and Life Insurance	59
	4.5	Networking and Unequal Exchange	67
	4.6	Collective Action and Nationalization	71
	4.7	Uncommon Risks as Exemplar	74
	4.8	Reinsurance Between the First and Second World War	77
	4.9	Life and Fire: A Summarily Comparison	79
	4.10	Assessment	80
	References	81
5	**The Rise and Fall of Swedish Non-Life Reinsurance**	89
	Mikael Lönnborg	
	5.1	Introduction	89
	5.2	The Early Reinsurance Business	92
	5.3	San Francisco and World War I	95
	5.4	Reorganizing Reinsurance After World War II and the Merger Waves	97
	5.5	Expansion of Reinsurance in 1970s and 1980s	100
	5.6	Closing Down the Reinsurance Business	104
	5.7	Conclusion	107
	References	111

6	**The Ups and Downs of French Reinsurance in the Twentieth Century** André Straus	115
	6.1 *The Reinsurance Market Between Two Worlds Wars*	116
	6.2 *French Reinsurance from the Second World War*	122
	References	146
7	**Currency Constraints, Risk Spreading Regulation, and the Corporate Demand for Reinsurance: A National Reinsurance Market in the Spanish Autarky (1940–1959)** Pablo Gutiérrez González and Jerònia Pons Pons	147
	7.1 *Introduction*	148
	7.2 *The Spanish Insurance Market in 1940 and the New Regulatory Framework for the Reinsurance Business*	150
	7.3 *Corporate Networks and Risk Management Strategies: A National Reinsurance Market in Spain?*	153
	7.4 *An Empirical Approach to the Actual Effect of Corporate Networks on the Performance of Insurance Firms*	161
	7.5 *The First Steps Toward the Liberalization and the Re-opening to the International Reinsurance Market*	165
	7.6 *Conclusions*	168
	References	169
8	**The Role of Foreign Reinsurance in the Setting of Insurance in Spain (1960–2000)** Leonardo Caruana de las Cagigas	173
	8.1 *Introduction*	173
	8.2 *The Relevance of Foreign Reinsurance Companies in the Development of Spanish Insurance Companies*	178
	8.3 *The Instituto Nacional de Industria*	180
	8.4 *The Insurance Company of INI: MUSINI*	183
	8.5 *Conclusion*	190
	Appendix	191
	References	194

9	Few and Small: The Reinsurance Industry in Italy in the Twentieth Century	197
	Giorgio Cingolani and Giandomenico Piluso	
	9.1 Introduction	197
	9.2 Few, Small and Subsidiary	200
	9.3 A Neglected Branch Within the National Insurance Industry	217
	9.4 Why Did the Reinsurance Sector Not Develop in Italy?	222
	9.5 Conclusion	225
	References	227
10	Government Intervention in Rural Insurance and Reinsurance Markets in Mexico: 1940–2000	231
	Gustavo A. Del Angel	
	10.1 Introduction	231
	10.2 Precedents of the Insurance Industry in Mexico	233
	10.3 Early Attempts at Rural Insurance in the Twentieth Century	234
	10.4 The Aseguradora Nacional Agrícola Y Ganadera (Anagsa)	239
	10.5 Financial Reform, State Reform, and the Creation of Agroasemex	247
	10.6 Concluding Remarks	252
	References	253
11	The Introduction of Life Reinsurance in Japan Before WWII	255
	Takau Yoneyama	
	11.1 Background and Research Questions	255
	11.2 'Spanish Flu' and Promotion of Life Reinsurance Business	257
	11.3 Reinsurance Plan of Munch Re and a Response of the Japanese Life Insurers	260
	11.4 Provisional Reinsurance Contract of a Japanese Life Insurance Company with a Foreign Insurer	262
	11.5 Introduction of Life Insurance for Substandard Risks	265
	11.6 Historical Lessons from the Introduction of Life Reinsurance Before WWII	267
	References	269

12	**Conclusions: Reinsurance, Politics, and Missed Opportunities**	271
	Niels-Viggo Haueter	
	12.1 Path Dependency	272
	12.2 Reinsurance Versus Alternative Risk Sharing	274
	12.3 Reinsurance and Autarky	275
	12.4 Politics and Limits of Insurability	279
	12.5 Free Markets	281
	12.6 Special Risks	283
	12.7 What Difference Did Reinsurance Make?	285
	12.8 Final Remarks	288
	Bibliography	289

Index 291

Notes on Contributors

Leonardo Caruana de las Cagigas is a Tenure at the University of Granada (Spain). Does research in insurance and reinsurance history. Has published *From Mutual to Multinational, Mapfre, 1933–2008* with Gabriel Tortella Casares and José Luis García Ruiz. About the internationalization of the Spanish Insurance the case of Mapfre in ICE with José Luis García Ruiz. Also the History of Spanish Insurance with Gabriel Tortella Casares, Alberto Manzano Martos, Jerònia Pons Pons and José Luis García Ruiz. About Corporate Forms has published in Oxford University Press edited by Robin Pearson and Takau Yoneyama. Recently has published with André Straus (eds.) *Highlights on Reinsurance History*, Peter Lang, Bruxelles, 2017.

Giorgio Cingolani is a Lecturer for Modern History and Economic History at the Faculty of Economics «G. Fuà» of the Università Politecnica delle Marche, Ancona, is author of *The Adriatic-Bakan Area from Transition to Integration* (with G Canullo and F. Chiapparino, 2011), *Nationalism and Terror* (with P. Adriano, 2018) and *Le assicurazioni private in Italia* (2019). He participated in various international research projects.

Gustavo A. Del Angel is Professor and Chair of the Department of Economics at CIDE (México City). He is specialized in financial history and contemporary banking regulation.

He also is the President of the Mexican Association of Economic History Gustavo has been visiting researcher at the Centro Espinosa Yglesias; National Fellow at the Hoover Institution in Stanford University; Professeur visitant at Université de Paris; and researcher at UC San Diego. He also worked at the Banco de México, the Mexican central bank.

Ben P. A. Gales recently retired as Lecturer at the Faculty of Economics of the University of Groningen, The Netherlands. He taught economic history, economic growth, methodology and philosophy of science and managed the training of Ph.D.'s of the national N.W. Posthumus Institute.

Ben P. A. Gales has two main fields of interest. He researches long-term developments of energy, the evolution of mining and its externalities. He was involved in a national project on sustainability in a historical perspective. In the mid-1980s, he wrote a business history of AEGON, one of the major Dutch insurance companies. He continued to work on insurance history and the evolution of risks to life and limb. This is his second field. He published also about poverty and the rise of social security and about the emergence of multinationals and peculiar organizations as free-standing companies. At the moment, he is working on occupational hazards.

Pablo Gutiérrez González is an Assistant Professor at the Department of Economics and Economic History of the University of Seville (Spain). The focus of his research is the role of reinsurance in the development of the Spanish insurance market since nineteenth century. He has published the results of his research as a book in the *Economic History Red* series of the Spanish Central Bank, and separate works in *Enterprise and Society*, *Business History* and *The Economic History Review*.

Niels-Viggo Haueter is Head of Swiss Re's Corporate History unit and the company's historical archives. He was a guest lecturer at Hitotsubashi University in Tokyo and serves as deputy Chairman of the Academic Council at the European Association for Banking and Financial History in Frankfurt.He co-edited World Insurance—The Evolution of a Global Risk Network, published by Oxford University Press (OUP) in 2012 and Managing Risk in Reinsurance—From City Fires to Global Warming (OUP, 2017).

Mikael Lönnborg is a Professor at Södertörn University, Department of Social Sciences, School of Business Studies, Enter Forum, Stockholm,

Sweden. His most recent publications are: '"Same Same but Different". Trust, Confidence and Governance Among Swedish Mutual Insurers' (2019) (with Mats Larsson), in: Alexius, S. & Furusten, S. (eds.) *Managing Hybrid Organizations. Governance, Professionalism and Regulation* (Palgrave Macmillan, Cham), and *Unplanned. The Transformation of States and Financial Markets in 'Transition' Countries* (2019) (co-edited with Mikael Olsson and Michael Rafferty) (Dialogos, Stockholm). Lönnborg are currently researching about internationalization of the dairy industry, the insurance industry, entrepreneurship and cooperatives and financial crises.

Giandomenico Piluso, Ph.D. in Economic and Social History (Bocconi University, Milan), is currently an Associate Professor of Economic History at the University of Siena. He has been Jemolo Fellow at Nuffield College, University of Oxford, in 2015 and Jean Monnet Fellow at the European University Institute in 2016–2017. His research interests range from business history to financial history, from insurance history to the history of central banking. His latest publications include *Adjusting to Financial Instability in the interwar period. Italian Financial Elites, International Cooperation, and Domestic Regulation, 1919–1939*, in Y. Cassis and G. Telesca (eds.), Financial Elites and European Banking, Oxford, OUP, 2018.

Jerònia Pons Pons is a Full Professor of Economic History at the Department of Economics and Economic History of the University of Seville (Spain). For the last 25 years, she has researched in the field of private and public insurance in Spain in the nineteenth and twentieth centuries. She has published the results of this research in the *Economic History Review, Business History Review* and *Journal of European Economic History*. In addition, she has contributed to collective books edited by Robin Pearson, The development of international Insurance, and by Peter Borscheid and Niels-Viggo Haueter, World Insurance.

Hugh Rockoff received his A.B. from Earlham College in 1967 and his Ph.D. from Chicago in 1972. He began teaching (mainly U.S. economic history, money and banking, and history of economic thought) at Rutgers in 1971. His primary research interests include the history of price controls, the U.S. economy in World War II, and U.S. monetary history. He has published in Cambridge University Press and in the top journals of economic history, he is a Distinguished Professor.

André Straus is a researcher at the CNRS, where he is Directeur de recherches Emeritus and Professor at University Paris1 Panthéon Sorbonne. Its main topics of research are in economic and financial history nineteenth to twentieth centuries, notably the history of banking, financial markets, insurance and reinsurance. Among his recent publications, International reinsurance in the 1920s, in André Straus, Leonardo Caruana de Las Cagigas, (eds.) *Highlights on Reinsurance History*, Peter Lang, Bruxelles, 2017. Les négociations franco-soviétiques sur les emprunts russes, in Laure Quennouëlle-Corre, Gérard Béaur, Les crises de la dette, CHEFF/IGPDE 2019. Insurance and Regulation Modes in France and Spain from the End of the Nineteenth Century until the End of World War Two, in Jerònia Pons y Robin Pearson (eds.) (2020), *Risk and the Insurance Business in History*, Madrid, Fundación Mapfre.

Robert E. Wright (Ph.D. History, SUNY Buffalo, 1997) has taught business, economics, history, and public policy courses at Augustana University, Georgia College and State University, New York University, Temple University, and the University of Virginia and consulted for the American Institute for Economic Research, the Property and Environment Research Center, and the Winthrop Group. He is the author of 19 books, including, with George Smith, *Mutually Beneficial, a history of mutual life insurer the Guardian Life Insurance Company of America*. He is also the author of scores of articles and book chapters, including a quantitative study, with Christopher Kingston, of antebellum U.S. insurance companies (*Business History Review* 2012) and an historical overview of America's insurance industry for *Encuentro Internacional Sobre la Historia del Seguro* (2010) edited by Leonardo Caruana.

Takau Yoneyama is an Emeritus Professor at Hitotsubashi University. In Tokyo Keizai University, where he takes a professorship on Business History. His research covers topics from Business History of Insurance to Enterprise Risk Management. He was a chair of the Study Group for Solvency Margin and the related regulations, FSA, and joined the Legislative Council on Insurance Law as a member. He was a president of the Asia-Pacific Risk and Insurance Association in 2012/2013. He has been presidents of the Japan Society of Household Economics, and the Japanese Association of Risk, Insurance and Pensions. He was Chief Editor of Japanese Business History, and an editor-in-chief of *JAVCERM Journal*. He edited *History of Insurance*, 8 volumes (2000) with David Jenkins, and A Commentary on the Insurance Act in Japan (2010, in

Japanese) with Tomonobu Yamashita. He edited *Corporate Forms and Organizational Choice in International Insurance* (2015) with Robin Pearson.

List of Figures

Fig. 4.1   Insurance capital paid-in (guilders) (*Source* Schuddebeurs [1928, p. 14], Vereeniging voor de Statistiek in Nederland [1882], Ministerie van Financiën [1861–1904], Centraal Bureau voor de Statistiek [1905–1920] and Smits et al. [2000])   47

Fig. 4.2   Share of premiums reinsured in gross premiums and share of capital reinsured in production (percent) (*Source* Vereeniging voor Levensverzekering; Verzekeringskamer)   65

Fig. 6.1   1997 premiums (billion of francs) (*Source* Association des Réassureurs Français)   140

Fig. 7.1   The corporate group of *La Unión y el FénixEspañol* (*Source* Anuario Financiero y de Sociedades Anónimas de España, 1942–1952)   157

Fig. 7.2   The Rosillo brothers and the Split of '*La Equitativa*' (*Source* Anuario Financiero y de Sociedades Anónimas de España, 1942–1952)   158

Fig. 7.3   Catalonian insurance and the new reinsurers (*Source* Anuario Financiero y de Sociedades Anónimas de España, 1942–1952)   160

Fig. 7.4   The network around *Compañía Hispano Americana (CHASYR)* (*Fuente* Anuario Financiero y de Sociedades Anónimas de España, 1942–1952)   161

xviii LIST OF FIGURES

Fig. 7.5	Direct insurance premiums over Spanish risks, reinsurance in Spain and reinsurance abroad, in all branches (million pesetas, 1951 price-level) (left axis) and total percentage of reinsurance over premiums underwritten (right axis) (1942–1957) (*Source* Memoria de la Dirección General de Banca e Inversiones, 1953; Revista del Sindicato Nacional del Seguro, 1943–1958; AGA (12) 1.14 Libro 473 Top. 65/79101; ABE, Departamento Extranjero, IEME, Comité Oficial de Reaseguros, Caja 85, Estadísticas y Memorias Anuales del Comité Oficial de Reaseguros, años 1946–1955 y libros 113–115, Libro de Registro del Impuesto del 1% [Caballero Sánchez1960])	166
Fig. 8.1	Percentage of direct insurance related to reinsurance (*Source* Anuario Español de Seguros 1951–1995)	180
Fig. 9.1	The size of the Italian market: life and non-life premiums as a share of GDP, 1921–2014 (*Source* Istat, *Serie storiche*, Life premiums and non-life premiums, Tab. 19.4, 1921–2014; GDP estimates provided by Banca d'Italia 2017)	200
Fig. 9.2	Top 20 insurance companies, insurance and reinsurance companies, purely reinsurance companies in Italy, by total assets, 1903–2000 (*Source* Assonime, *ad annos* [1903–1960]; Ania, *ad annos* [1970–2000] [our calculations])	206
Fig. 11.1	Rate of actual death against expected death, 1902–1920 (*Source* The 19th Annual Report of the Dai-ichi Mutual Life 1920, pp. 19–20)	259

List of Tables

Table 4.1	The *Dordrecht:* Profits by life insurance activity and region (guilders)	70
Table 6.1	French reinsurance companies in 1927	119
Table 6.2	Premium collected between 1930 and 1937	122
Table 6.3	French reinsurance companies premiums between 1948 till 1954	124
Table 6.4	Largest reinsurance companies in the world	128
Table 6.5	Distribution of the different currencies in France	128
Table 6.6	Comparing the French companies with the Germanic companies	129
Table 6.7	Distribution of the premiums of SCOR in the world	130
Table 7.1	Ranking of companies reinsuring Spanish risks, in Life, Fire, and Marine branches (1943–1951)	155
Table 7.2	Typology of the sample: Reinsurers and direct insurers authorized to reinsure in Spain (1943–1952)	162
Table 7.3	Corporate networks and their effect on the reinsurance market (1943–1952). Random-effect regression models	164
Table 9.1	Insurance companies, insurance and reinsurance companies, purely reinsurance companies in Italy, 1903–2000	203
Table 9.2	Top 20 insurance companies and reinsurance companies in Italy, by total assets, 1903–1927	208
Table 9.3	Top 20 insurance companies and reinsurance companies in Italy, by total assets, 1938–1950	212

xx   LIST OF TABLES

Table 9.4	Top 20 insurance companies and reinsurance companies in Italy. by total assets. 1950–1990	214
Table 9.5.	Reinsurance in some European countries in 1927. (premiums in Italian lire)	220
Table 9.6	Reinsurance in Italy in 1927 (premiums in Italian lire)	221
Table 10.1	Operation of mutual benefit societies. Data in Hectares (Has) and millions of current pesos	237
Table 10.2	Operation of the private *Consorcio*. Spring–Summer and late summer agricultural cycles. Data in Hectares (Has) and millions of current pesos	238
Table 10.3	Operation of ANAGSA. 1964–1969. Data in Hectares (Has)	241
Table 10.4	Operation of ANAGSA. 1970–1989. Data in Hectares (Has) and millions of current pesos	242
Table 10.5	Transfers of the federal government to the state-owned rural financial institutions. Millions of pesos, inflation adjusted 1992=100	246
Table 10.6	Crop coverage Agroasemex, rural insurance funds and private insurance companies. 1990–2000. Data in millions pesos (current and inflation adjusted 1990 = 100)	250
Table 10.7	Cattle coverage Agroasemex, rural insurance funds and private insurance companies. 1990–2000. Data in millions pesos (current and inflation adjusted 1990 = 100)	251
Table 10.8	Profit and Losses of Agroasemex. 1990–2000. Millions of current pesos	251
Table 11.1	Percentage of actual deaths compared with expected deaths in 1919	258
Table 11.2	The cause of policyholders' death in 1919	259

CHAPTER 1

Introduction

Hugh Rockoff

The papers presented here were originally presented in a session devoted to the history of reinsurance organized by Leonardo Caruana de las Cagigas, University of Granada, and André Straus, Sorbonne University Paris 1, for the World Economic History Conference held in Boston in the summer of 2018.

The papers describe and analyze the growth of reinsurance in the twentieth century in what might be called the advanced periphery of the reinsurance industry. The center of the industry was to be found in Germany, Switzerland, Britain. To be more specific, some of the major players were Munich Re, Swiss Re, and the British firms Royal Insurance and Lloyds, all familiar names today. The first three were conventional reinsurance companies. Lloyd's on the other hand, is famously, a mysterious mixture of syndicates, a form of organization that still reflects, to some extent, its origins in a seventeenth-century coffee house. The second chapter describes the origins of the reinsurance industry in the core countries. The following chapters then tell the stories of, to go in the order

---

H. Rockoff (✉)
Rutgers University, New Brunswick, NJ, USA
e-mail: Rockoff@econ.rutgers.edu

© The Author(s), under exclusive license to Springer Nature Switzerland AG 2021
L. Caruana de las Cagigas and A. Straus (eds.), *Role of Reinsurance in the World*, Palgrave Studies in Economic History,
https://doi.org/10.1007/978-3-030-74002-3_1

1

they appear, the United States, the Netherlands, Sweden, France, Spain, Italy, Mexico, and Japan.

1.1 What Is Reinsurance?

Many readers will already be familiar with the basics of reinsurance, but some will be approaching these essays without specific knowledge of the industry, perhaps as an outgrowth of an interest in international economics or finance. For them a few words are in order to provide a basic framework from which to start.

We can begin with the familiar. As individuals we buy life insurance to protect our heirs against the risk that we will suffer an early death. We may also buy insurance to protect ourselves against the risk of ill health; and we may insure our homes against the risk of fire or theft, and our automobiles against damages from collisions. Likewise, businesses buy insurance to protect themselves against a wide range of risks.

Normally, the companies who sell these insurance policies experience a regular flow of claims that they pay from their liquid reserves which they replenish regularly with the income from their current operations and their investments. But insurance companies in turn must think about the risks they face. A pandemic, for example, might lead to a sudden surge in the amount of life insurance claims that must be paid, a surge that might leave the company illiquid and possibly insolvent. An earthquake, a fire, a hurricane, and so on, any of these might create financial difficulties for an insurance company.

There are various ways that an insurance company can protect itself against extreme risks of this sort. Obviously, they will start by diversifying and limiting the risks they take on. But there are other methods available to them. One is coinsurance. One potential buyer of insurance might face risks that no single insurance company would want to take on. But two or more companies might provide adequate insurance by each selling a policy that covered part of the potential loss. In Chapter 4 Professor Gale tells us about a contract according to which a trading firm in Rotterdam that suffered losses from a fire in 1903 was compensated by thirty insurance companies, 13 Dutch, 6 colonial, and 11 foreign.

What then is reinsurance? As a matter of linguistics, the term could be and at times has been used in a variety of circumstances. For example, it was once common in the Netherlands, as professor Gale tells us, for members of the working class to take out several funeral insurance policies to protect themselves against the failure of one of the insurance companies. It could be said that the individual had "reinsured" the risk that their family would not have sufficient resources for an appropriate funeral.

Reinsurance as it is understood by business today, however, is something different and more specific: A direct insurance company sells all or part of a policy to another company. For example, a life insurance company may have sold a policy insuring someone's life for $5 million. But it may view this policy as too risky for it to keep on its balance sheet because of the large amount of the final payout. Therefore, it may protect itself by "reinsuring." For example, suppose the original policy called for a premium of $10,000 per year for the $5 million of insurance. The direct insurer might then reinsure, say, $2 million with another company for, say, $4,000 per year. The direct insurer would net $6,000 per year and be responsible for paying a claim of $3,000,000. The reinsurer would receive $4,000 per year, and be responsible for paying $2,000,000. Then, in the terminology normally used, we would say that the direct insurer had "ceded" part of the policy to the reinsurer.

1.2   Some Historical Examples

A few historical examples will help to clarify the concept of reinsurance. It appears that the first recorded reinsurance contract that we now have dates from the year 1370 when an underwriter named Guilano Grillo contracted with Goffredo Benaira and Martino Saceo to reinsure a ship on part of its voyage from Genoa to Bruges (Kopf 1929, 26). Grillo offered to retain the risk on the voyage through the Mediterranean and to cede to Benaira and Sacco the risk from Cadiz through the Bay of Biscay and along the French coast. When reading accounts of this contract, incidentally, one can't help but think that Antonio, the hero of Shakespeare's *Merchant of Venice*, who is ruined when his ships are lost at sea, and who soon after faces the threat of having Shylock cut away a pound of his flesh would have saved himself a good deal of trouble if he had availed himself of marine insurance!

The rational for reinsurance is clearly illustrated, moreover, by natural disasters. In 1861 a terrible file destroyed the town of Glarona in Switzerland. Local fire insurance companies were faced with claims that far exceeded their reserves. Two years later Swiss Re, as explained in Chapter 2, was founded, today one of the world's reinsurance giants. Another disaster that left a major imprint on the industry was the San

Francisco earthquake of 1906. The earthquake produced a fire that destroyed the city and had severe consequences for several European fire insurance and reinsurance companies. Indeed, the outflow of gold from England to pay for claims in San Francisco was so great that the Bank of England felt compelled to protect its reserve by raising its discount rate. And this action was an important cause of the severe international financial panic of 1907 (Odell and Weidenmier 2004). Some European insurance companies abandoned the West Coast of the United States after the earthquake. But others, companies that had fully paid their claims, took advantage of their enhanced reputations and the withdrawal of their rivals to expand.

1.3 Our Contributions

In the essays that follow our authors analyze the successes and failures of reinsurance in their chosen countries. Each author, as will become abundantly clear when one dives into the essays, is an expert on the industry in the country he is writing about. A key theme addressed in all of the papers is the role played by the state in hindering or encouraging the growth of the reinsurance industry through regulation or some form of financial backing. But the authors take note of many other influences on the industry including the roles played by individual entrepreneurs, industrialization, and chance.

Although the focus of the volume is on the growth of the reinsurance industry in the advanced periphery, one can't fully grasp this story without an understanding of the development of the industry in the core countries of Britain, Germany, and Switzerland. This is provided in Chapter 2, "The Core Countries in Reinsurance" by Leonardo Caruana de las Cagigas and André Straus. It is a absorbing story. The British part starts with marine insurance contracts negotiated at Edward Lloyd's coffee house. There we see not only the first beginnings of the industry, but also some of the earliest regulation. In 1745 the Marine Insurance Act was intended in part to address an ongoing problem. Owners would insure <u>after</u> they learned that their ship had been lost or damaged, a real danger in a world where information traveled slowly. In Germany, a country with a much smaller marine presence than Britain, the reinsurance industry grew out of the fire insurance industry. One particular event to which Leonardo Caruana de las Cagigas and André Straus draw attention was a fire in Hamburg that began on May 5, 1842, that left many people homeless and several-fire insurance companies in great difficulty. This tragedy led to the formation of Cologne Re that became a major reinsurance company with a major international presence. The final member of the triumvirate, Switzerland, lacked the economic heft of Britain or Germany. However, it made up for it with its strong currency, and the reputation of its workers and managers for prudence and competence. World War I and II also helped Switzerland's reinsurance industry because it allowed Swiss firms to take business from German firms.

In addition to fleshing out the stories of the core reinsurance countries, Leonardo Caruana de las Cagigas and André Straus also discuss some of the key contributors to the theories of reinsurance and reinsurance administration. The references they supply will take readers who want to pursue these any of these issues into the academic literature.

Chapter 3, "Reinsurance in America: Regulatory Regimes and Markets" by Robert E. Wright begins with a paradox. The United States has been the world's largest economy for over a century. A vast amount of insurance is written by American companies. Yet the United States has never developed reinsurance companies that play a major role in world markets. Indeed, the European giants, Swiss Re, and Munich Re still dominate the American market. Why?

A major part of the answer Wright explains starts with the fact that in the United States insurance has always been regulated at the state level. And these regulators have created enormous ongoing barriers to nationwide reinsurance. The full story, as Wright explains, includes a good deal of parochial concerns and misunderstanding. The result has been a hobbled industry. The United States has developed, however, what are sometimes known as alternative risk transfer mechanisms such as insurance-linked securities to substitute for reinsurance. He draws an interesting parallel here with the American banking industry. Commercial banking in the United States was also hobbled by state regulations in the nineteenth and a good part of the twentieth centuries. For one thing, interstate branching was strictly prohibited. To allow branch banking would have limited the power of state legislators and banking authorities. Banks were often too small and unstable to provide capital for industrialization. As a result, the United States was forced to develop highly liquid securities markets as an alternative way of raising and allocating capital. Professor Wright's emphasis on the role of regulation which plays such a clear and important role in the American case provides a useful introduction to a major theme in many, but not all, of the chapters that follow.

In Chapter 4, "Reinsurance in the Netherlands from 1800 till 1950: A Failure?" Ben P. A. Gales starts with a paradox similar to the one that Wright identifies at the beginning of his essay on the United States. Why did the Netherlands which has had a long and successful tradition of direct insurance fail to develop major international reinsurance companies? But in the case of the Netherlands, unlike that of the United States, it would appear that regulation was a secondary factor. Rather, it appears that in the Netherlands the success of other methods of diversifying insurer risks worked well from the early days of the industry. For example, some mutual insurance companies issued policies with claims that that would be indexed to the financial condition of the company. Or to take another example the *Hollandsche Societeit*, established in 1807, which was the first Dutch limited liability life insurance company, followed a policy of controlling its risks by placing limits on the maximum amount it would insure. Later events only served to continue limited Dutch presence in the international reinsurance market.

One factor that Professor Gales notes, one that must have seemed like nothing more than an interesting historical curiosity when the paper was presented at the time of the World Economic History Conference in 2018, but is now front and center in the minds of all of us, was the industry's response to the Spanish Flu pandemic that hit at the end of World War I. The death rate was high in the Netherlands, but the insurance industry was able to meet its claims successfully. Thus reinforcing the belief held by Dutch insurers that they did not need to go heavily into the international reinsurance market. I hasten to add that this was only one factor among many, one that I have raised because of its current interest. To get the whole of this story and a broad-based view of the history of Dutch reinsurance one must read Professors Gale's thorough account.

Chapter 5, "Swedish Reinsurers in the Non-life Sector" by Mikael Lönnborg tells a very different story from those encountered in Chapter 2 on the United States or Chapter 3 on the Netherlands. In those cases, the historical question was why there was so little reinsurance. But to the contrary, reinsurance was long an important part of the Swedish insurance scene. The story behind the relatively important role played by reinsurance in Sweden is complex. Regulation although not crucial, played a role. But unlike the United States where Professor Wright finds that the fragmented structure of American insurance regulation stifled the development of reinsurance, Professor Lönnborg finds the opposite in Sweden: the fact of one regulatory authority contributed to the growth of reinsurance. That some regulations seemed to hamstring the direct insurance industry also contributed, paradoxically, to the growth of reinsurance. The requirement, for example, that all profits from the sale of life insurance to Swedes be returned to policy holders—a requirement that would have seemed a form of extreme socialist regulation in the United States—encouraged the search for other sources of profit. Reinsurance turned out to be one of them.

But chance also played a role both in encouraging and discouraging reinsurance. *Skåne*, a major Swedish player in the international reinsurance market suffered severe losses in the San Francisco and Valparaíso earthquakes of 1906. This led Skåne to withdraw from the American markets and focus instead on the Russian market where they lost again after the Revolution.

After WWII Swedish reinsurance faced a host of challenges. The industry was buffeted by the merger movement of the 1960s, efforts to refocus its international business on the United Kingdom and the United States, inflation, deregulation, Hurricane Andrew in the United States in 1989, the Swedish financial crisis of 1991–1992, the entrance of Sweden into the European Common Market in 1995, scandals, and other factors. The net result was a withdrawal of the Swedish companies from the international reinsurance market. It is a complex and interesting story, told clearly but in detail by Professor Lönnborg.

In Chapter 6 "The Ups and Downs of French Reinsurance in the Twentieth Century" by André Straus we meet still another case, similar in the early part of the twentieth century to that of the United States, where one might have expected on the basis of the size of the economy and level of development more reinsurance activity. In France, however, a noneconomic and nonpolitical factor enters the story, a factor that Professor André Straus refers to as cultural. The French, evidently, showed relatively little interest in reinsurance in part because reinsurance was regarded as an inherently international industry. That attitude was to change, however, in 1970 when a French reinsurance company, SCOR (Société Commerciale de Réassurance) was created with the backing of the French government. There were many challenges, and many stumbles, along the way, but by 2017 SCOR was the fourth largest reinsurance company in the world. How it reached this level is discussed in detail by Professor André Straus, and cannot be summarized here. It's a complicated story, but readers will undoubtedly be interested to learn that part of its success was the firm's recognition, early on, of the importance of establishing offices in the Asia-Pacific region.

In Chapter 7, "Currency Constraints, Risk Spreading Regulation and the Corporate Demand for Reinsurance: A National Reinsurance Market in the Spanish Autarky (1940–1959)" by Pablo Gutiérrez González and Jerònia Pons Pons one views the reinsurance industry developing in a very different state-private-sector environment from those analyzed in many of the other chapters.

International reinsurance had been an important part of the Spanish industry during the first third of the twentieth century. But the Civil War and the autarkic policies of the long Franco regime put an end to its role. One of the key principles of the Franco regime was that the government had to strictly control any potential outflows of domestic currency. Signal events were the creation of the Official Committee on Marine Insurance in 1942 which was empowered to authorize all international marine reinsurance contracts and its transformation in 1945 into the Official Committee on Reinsurance, which supervised all international reinsurance.

The Spanish industry responded by creating a domestic reinsurance industry. Gutiérrez González and Pons Pons have done yeomen work in puzzling out how these domestic reinsurers operated. Their work will be of interest, not only to specialists in insurance, but to business and economic historians looking for models of how to explore the effects of corporate networks and interlocking directorates.

Professor Leonardo Caruana de las Cagigas then carries the Spanish story forward in Chapter 8, "The Role of Foreign Reinsurance in the Setting of Insurance in Spain (1960–2000)." One of the distinctive features of the Spanish push for industrialization and modernization during the Franco regime was the establishment of the Instituto Nacional de Industria (INI) in 1941. It was modeled to some extent on the Italian state holding company the *Istituto per la Ricostruzione Industriale* established in 1933. By the 1960s INI had become the most important industrial conglomerate in Spain. Spanish insurers were anxious to do business with it because of the safety provided by its size and its special role as a state-sponsored holding company with access to the taxpayer's money. Not surprisingly, the Spanish insurers did well from their contracts with INI subsidiaries. Indeed, they did so well that in 1966, partly to lower the cost of insurance, INI launched its own insurance company *Mutualidad de Seguros del Instituto Nacional de Industria* (MUSINI). The goal was to provide insurance for all of the subsidiaries of INI, but that meant, especially at the start, of relying heavily on reinsurance.

Munich Re was one of the reinsurers, and their connection with INI illustrates another dimension of the advantages of international reinsurance, one documented at length in this chapter: Munich Re provided more than risk diversification. It also provided Spanish insurance companies with new tools for assessing risk and Spanish industrial companies with technical expertise on accident prevention developed in more advanced industrial countries. Providing this information was at once, self interest and public interest, and proved an important start for the subsequent modernization of this dimension of industry in Spain. Professor Leonardo Caruana de las Cagigas develops this theme in detail, and it is well worth reading about this often neglected benefit from the globalization of reinsurance.

Chapter 9, by Giorgio Cingolani and Giandomenico Piluso carries one of those rare but wonderful titles that capture the essence of its story: "Few and small: The Reinsurance Industry in Italy in the Twentieth Century." The reinsurance industry in Italy indeed consisted of a few small firms at the beginning of the twentieth century. And reinsurance remained a relatively small part of the relatively small Italian insurance industry through the whole of the twentieth century. Indeed, the largest reinsurance companies in Italy were partly central European in origin and became fully Italian only with the annexation of Trieste in 1918. To document their theses Professors Cingolani and Piluso have compiled a new set of quantitative data on the firms in the industry that will undoubtedly be valuable to other students of Italian insurance.

They then explore the key determinants of the size and volatility of the industry. These determinants include economic factors, most importantly the low level of Italian income per capita compared with more economically advanced countries especially Italy's European neighbors. The list of influences also includes political factors such as the pressures exercized by the Mussolini government from the 1920s through WWII, and later state-backed welfare programs that in some measure provided alternatives to private insurance. Also important were the structure of the industry (the overwhelming position of the largest firms) and the first-mover advantages of the Italian reinsurance industry's competitors in Switzerland, Germany, and Britain. The relative importance of these factors, their interactions, and their evolution over the course of the "long" twentieth century, is the substance of the story well told in Chapter 9.

Chapter 10, "Government Intervention in Rural Insurance and Reinsurance Markets in Mexico: 1940–2000" by Gustavo A. Del Angel tells the complex story of the government's attempts to provide insurance for Mexican agriculture. Although the government's involvement is loosely analogous to some of the developments in Spain as outlined in Chapters 7 and 8, and Italy in Chapter 9, the Mexican story is unique. Agriculture was one of Mexico's most important industries and the source of livelihood for many poor Mexicans. After a long series of attempts to provide credit and insurance for poor farmers, the government created a state-owned monopoly Anagsa in 1961. Much of the Mexican story then centers on this firm, which was liquidated in 1990, and its successor, Agroasemex.

The history of both companies, laid out clearly in Chapter 10 with qualitative and quantitative data drawn from primary sources, can only be described as troubled. Both firms were constantly in financial difficulties. The basic problem was that Mexican governments saw insurance as a way of subsidizing poor Mexican farmers. It was a policy motivated by humanitarian and political concerns. But inevitably this meant losses for the insurance companies.

Chapter 11, "The Introduction of Life Reinsurance into Japan Before WWII" by Takau Yoneyama tells a story that is in some ways very different from those recounted in previous chapters. Chapter 10 tells a story in which the industry was slow to develop as a result of a unique combination of political and economic constraints reflecting a national vision of a Japan taking its place in the world economy.

A particular part of the story covered in Chapter 11, is the response of the Japanese life insurance industry to the Spanish Flu epidemic of 1919–1920. The story in Japan was similar to the story told by Professor Gale in Chapter 3 about the Netherlands. Deaths from the Spanish Flu were substantial in Japan, but the Japanese life insurance companies were able to successfully meet their obligations. So the pandemic did not lead to an immediate adoption of reinsurance. Part of the reason for their strong performance in the pandemic was that the Japanese life insurance companies were not insuring substandard risks. But it was clearly in the interest of the industry and of Japan itself that insurance be provided for such risks. Eventually, recognition of this need led to the launching of the Kyoei Life Reinsurance Company, Ltd. in 1936 for the purpose of reinsuring life policies for substandard risks. The story of how and why this firm was started is laid out in Chapter 10. It is a fascinating and informative discussion.

1.4 Final Thoughts

As one can see from these brief summaries the book is of first importance to anyone interested in insurance or reinsurance. But the lessons developed here will be of value to a much broader audience. Anyone interested in the effect of government interventions in a market economy and anyone who wants to understand the impact of the increasing (most of the time) integration of international financial markets will find much to chew on.

And, if I may be allowed a personal note, I enjoy reading many forms of economic history. I enjoy reading authors who build grand theories they defend with passionate rhetorical flourishes. I even enjoy reading attempts to explain history with elegant mathematical models. But even more I enjoy reading authors who have carefully studied the facts in a particular case and have carefully built defensible generalizations. In other words, I enjoy reading authors who really know what they are talking about! And for that reason, if your tastes are like mine, you will enjoy reading the papers that follow.

References

Kopf, Edwin W. 1929. "The Origins and Development of Reinsurance". *Proceedings of the Actuarial Society*: 16–33.

Odell, Kerry A., and Marc D. Weidenmier. 2004. "Real Shock, Monetary Aftershock: The 1906 San Francisco Earthquake and the Panic of 1907." *The Journal of Economic History* 64 (4): 1002–1027.

CHAPTER 2

The Core Countries in Reinsurance

Leonardo Caruana de las Cagigas and André Straus

To better understand the reinsurance world, we add briefly the core countries. Nevertheless, this is not the main purpose of the book. The aim of this research is to analyze eight countries in depth that had obviously important contact with the core countries. These are only three, as we explain in this chapter. Those countries are the United Kingdom, Germany and Switzerland.

Searching the chronology of the birth of reinsurance we can go back several centuries. However, the origin is not clear. That is so because managing risk had different methods, not only European systems. Peter Borscheid shows that insurance and reinsurance were European invention that spread throughout the world at the end of the eighteenth century (Borscheid 2013, pp. 23–47). With the advantage that insurance was created as suitable for any country and culture. It does not matter if the life assured is Chinese, British, or Brazilian. It is a solution that will

L. Caruana de las Cagigas (✉)
Faculty of Economics and Business, University of Granada, Granada, Spain

A. Straus
CNRS-Université Paris1 Panthéon Sorbonne, Paris, France

© The Author(s), under exclusive license to Springer Nature Switzerland AG 2021
L. Caruana de las Cagigas and A. Straus (eds.), *Role of Reinsurance in the World*, Palgrave Studies in Economic History,
https://doi.org/10.1007/978-3-030-74002-3_2

prevail in managing risk everywhere in the world. Not as the only one, but eventually it will be dominant. Maybe it is not the best, nevertheless the insurance methods, and its techniques slowly but steadily introduce its way, rules, and even specific standards that were present on the five continents. It was not always easy and had hybrid models, nevertheless the effort to introduce rational systems, with actuarial calculation in a global business with a judicial regulation, had its origin in the eighteenth century.

The European culture created in several countries' new methods and networks in insurance and reinsurance that followed the outstanding growth that generated the Industrial Revolution. The effort to introduce rational choice to manage risk had in William Stanley Jevons one of the great theorists (Grüne-Yanoff 2012, pp. 499–516). Risk is everywhere, and one particular risk was fire with excessive disasters as the great fire in London in 1666, which needed a satisfactory solution. The houses were of wood, and accidents were common. Insuring houses seemed necessary and several companies emerged. But they had great risk to insure, so the next step for the companies was coinsurance and reinsurance. Anyway, reinsurance developed slowly as one solution out of several possibilities to solve the problem of risk, especially for fire insurance companies, and became one of the best solutions in the eighteenth century. A century after the great fire of London.

More recently, in human decision-making, Paul Romer had one main question: "why was progress ... speeding up over time? It arises because of this special characteristic of an idea, which is if [a million people try] to discover something, if any one person finds it, everybody can use the idea" (Kiernan and Sugden 2018). The question in insurance and reinsurance would be why use up economic resources in an insurance policy? And then for the companies that accept the fire risk, how can they manage with so many to insure? With reinsurance? The companies to cover the risk assume offer premiums with a price that should cover the risk. Still, sometimes it does not happen and they increase capital for the bad moments, but to improve the management of risk, they have coinsurance and reinsurance, which is another option.

Daniel Kahneman has developed an additional aspect of the same issue with behavioral economics (Kahneman and Tversky 1979). In each society, they have different attitudes about assuming risk. In the old days, God desired a fire in a building (a feeble explanation but very popular). However, another solution or better said a possible solution was eventually buying a policy. This possible solution came to be a habit in many societies but not for others in the eighteenth century. Slowly in Britain, France, Germany, and several other countries, people insured their houses. Rare in centuries before. We can see that it was a habit for people or companies to have ensured a building in some societies, and they see it as a necessity. But in the Mediterranean countries with houses built of stone or brick was uncommon. Both Nobel prizes show different efforts to rationalize the economy, and one of the solutions most important to Europeans was to manage risk with insurance and reinsurance. Initially, the insurance industry was organized mainly in mutual societies and later came stock companies, both functioning today. As we said, in addition to the story of the development of reinsurance in eight countries, we add here the development in a concise way in those countries that can be considered the core countries in its growth. Those countries are United Kingdom, Germany, and Switzerland. A prominent place was Britain for a long time because it started the Industrial Revolution and developed the British Empire that spread in all the continents. The branches with a more significant economic impact were marine insurance, fire insurance, and life insurance.

In England, it will be outstanding in maritime insurance with a famous coffee house owned by Edward Lloyd in London as early as 1688. Modern insurance started in the eighteenth century and particularly modern reinsurance in the nineteenth century. The coffee house became first a place of marine trade information that develops in the long run into one of the most important markets in which autonomous insurance underwriters join in syndicates to sell insurance, mostly through brokers, under the canopy of Lloyd's. From 1734 they introduce a list of Ships arriving or leaving London or the main British ports, name Lloyds List. In 1774 the corporation office moved to the Royal Exchange, founded by Thomas Gresham in 1571 (Marcus 1975, pp. 192–195). As Robin Pearson points out, practically one-fourth of European ships were British just before the French Revolution and before the Industrial Revolution (Pearson 2012, p. 68). The mighty of the British Empire will grow substantially since the battle of Trafalgar and will last until the end of the First World War. This prominent position facilitated trade and commerce worldwide and managed the risk with insurance, coinsurance, and reinsurance with a dominant role in maritime insurance with Lloyds.

The British government, as early as 1745, regulated the insurance market with the Marine Insurance Act. Its introduction specified that the know-how learned by experience, made possible the insurance market. They did limit the risk assume in the policy to avoid pernicious practices. One of the problems in those days was that many ships, with their cargoes, have been fraudulently lost or destroyed. Legislation approved in 1746 wanted to control moral hazard and gambling. The aim was to identify what was illegal to insure without an insurable interest and banned reinsurance. The reason to ban reinsurance was that sometimes the ship owners first had the information of a loss and after reinsured. It was probably very common, so they decided directly to ban it (Kingston 2007, p. 381). Even if it was only for marine insurance, it did extend to other branches, not developing reinsurance. The main branch that develops reinsurance in Britain, fire insurance, did not reinsure until the 1820s, that is over 70 years, and the main reason was the doubts or uncertainties of English company law (Pearson 1997, p. 244). The government and the general opinion in England about reinsurance were negative. It was considered contrary to the public interest, inducing speculation in premiums and promoting gambling. That is why all reinsurance contracts, with few exceptions, were prohibited, and this was not removed until 1864 (Vance, p. 670). Over a century after.

Summing up: reinsurance in England had a difficult start. The reason was mainly that it was considered dishonest, and even worse a game (Straus and Caruana 2017). Harold James argues that they did not need reinsurance as much as other countries because Britain had a dominant political and economic situation (James 2013, p. 9). An author of the period, Millar (1787), explained that it was common that the ships first did not underwrite reinsurance. If the vessel was not arriving on time, they immediately subscribe the reinsurance premium. This fraudulent behavior triggers all the alarms for a business in its early stages and introduces a ban that had clear consequences for its development in Britain. That is why central Europe had more say at the start, although in the second half of the nineteenth century, Britain regained its position and was one of the core places for reinsurance. Even if the law was repealed in 1864, foreign companies run the reinsurance business without the competition of British companies for over 120 years. The first UK reinsurer was the Reinsurance Company Limited, established in 1867.

Another country that will be a leader in reinsurance was Germany. Germany did not have as big a fleet as Britain at the start of the nineteenth century, nor did it experienced an Industrial Revolution, and the GDP per person was clearly less than in France or the UK. However, they started modern reinsurance in this century and basically in fire risk. Germany, or better said, the territories that finally will be Germany January 18, 1871, developed reinsurance slowly in the first half of the nineteenth century as the economy of Prussia and the other several nations that end up in the German state. Probably necessity made reinsurance advance because the amounts of buildings assured were so significant that the insurance companies were assuming too many risks, and they had to find solutions to limit their commitments. Also, they had the organization's problem that at first were mutual and could appeal to the members of the mutual policyholders for emergencies if they had a significant loss to sort it out. But with stock companies, this was not possible, and they had to find other solutions. The normal answer was coinsurance, and the insurance firms shifted part of the risk to other insurance companies. Another solution was the Reinsurance Treaty. We can trace since 1825, the contract between "Vaterlandische Feuerversicherungs Gesellschaft" in Elberfeld with the "Compagnie Royale d'Assurances Contre L'Incendie," in Paris (Kopf 1929, p. 28). And Robin Pearson indicates 34 contracts of reinsurance between 1820 to 1850 of German, British, French, Belgium, what would be Italy, Russian and Austrian firms. And of all of them, 65 percent were German contracts that indicate a more common tendency for this type of solution in this country than in the others (Pearson 2017, p. 72).

What is outstanding in that period the contracts done between companies of different nations, because in those days they had a mentality and even habit or culture protectionist. Coming from Colbert was the commercial idea of building their domestic economies at other nations' expense. The business should always be sorted out in their own country. Slowly in Germany, they had more reinsurance contracts, mainly between German insurance firms. However, they had a serious problem that the competitors new about what your firm was doing. Breaking the norms and traditions of the moment, they partially solved the problem by signing reinsurance contracts with foreign companies that did not do business in their country in direct insurance. That was done by 47% of the contracts in Germany. In reinsurance, it is a turning point in the middle of the century. It is also for the general development of the Industrial Revolution that was expanding in several countries in a relatively fast way. Western Europe more than doubles its GDP between 1820 and 1870. In Germany, it multiplies by 2.7, Britain 2.8, and United Stated by 7.8 (Maddison 2006, p. 259).

In the early years' reinsurance business was done mainly by German direct-writing firms. That had the inconvenience already stated, that when signing this type of contract, the other German insurance company can only do it only if they had full information of the risk assumed. That meant that the other company knew many aspects of the management of the other company that was a competitor in Fire insurance. So, for the first company, this was not the best solution. Another solution was to search in the international market, and mainly in Germany's case, they sign reinsurance contracts with French insurance companies.

Fire insurance became more challenging with the increase in risk introduced by the Industrial Revolution: machines, factories, boilers, etc. This triggered the demand for more reinsurance. Under the Prussian government, they regulated this new situation, in a relatively early law of May 8, 1837. This made it compulsory that foreign firms needed official approval to do business in the country. Also was regulated the maximum amount that one company could assume in one contract: 10,000 thalers. This restriction reduced the presence of foreign companies in Prussia. Fewer insurance companies in the country also increased the demand for reinsurance to make manageable the risk assumed. In this situation, what would make for significant change in the development of reinsurance was a big catastrophe, the terrible fire in Hamburg that began on May 5, 1842, and lasted for three days leaving 20,000 people homeless. The buildings were mostly insured. The leading insurance company, Hamburg Fire Fund, founded in 1667, was in serious financial problems. The fire insurance stock corporation, Fünft e Hamburgische Assekurranz-Compagnie, which was the only early German insurance company that remained on the market for a long time, became insolvent (Müssener 2008, p. 37).

The demand of the German market for more reinsurance was clear. It is the crucial moment that was founded the first reinsurance company: Cologne Re. However, it took time for the first contract because although it was founded on April 8, 1846, its first official agreement was written in 1852. The two main problems were the difficult economic and political situation that ends in the revolution of 1848 and the lack of capital that was sorted out by the Rothschilds in Paris and French capital (Bähr 2016, p. 19). One of the questions is why Cologne re and not Hamburg re? the probable answer is that the initiative came from several influential Rhenish bankers. And between them was Simon, baron von Oppenheim born in that city and was president of the Chamber of Commerce of Cologne from 1833 and his father founded his own bank, Sal. Oppenheim. Also, the person that had the idea of promoting the reinsurance company was from the region, as a politician and entrepreneur, Gustav von Mevissen. Both burgers were promoted to von for their achievements in German society.

As was common in any nation, they wanted reinsurance in Germany to stay in Germany and not go to France or Belgian firms (Golding 1927, pp. 100–103). The name of the company was German; however, the capital was French! Another important aspect was that from the start, it had already business in Austria, Switzerland, Belgium, Holland, and France (Kopf 1929, p. 30). This company was one of the most important companies in reinsurance in the world. Rank the third company in net premiums for 1938 (Review 1939, pp. 1067–1068). The company will last for a long time, till 1994, when the American company General Re buys Cologne Re. However, it will take a long time for its final disappearance Cologne Re becomes General Reinsurance AG from July 2010.

The often forgotten "second company" that started reinsurance, Aachen Re, started differently because it depended on another company Aachen and Munchener Fire Insurance Company, and was its subsidiary founded in 1853. The Review put Aachen Re as the tenth reinsurance company in the world in net premiums in 1938 (Review 1939, pp. 1067–1068). Another American company, Employers Re bought the company in 1995. The following companies' founder in Germany was Frankfurter Re (1857) and Magdeburger Re (1862). Frankfurter Re was bought by Employers Re the same year as Aachen Re. Shortly later, ten professional reinsurance companies were founded. It was the moment that many entrepreneurs thought that it was time to gain money with reinsurance (Gerathewohl 1982 p. 701; Kopf 1929, p. 31). Though at last, few survive because of the terrible financial crisis of 1873.

Another essential management achievement was the possibility that the reinsurance company or the insurance companies that signed reinsurance contracts can do retrocession to a third company. This allows the reduction of the risk of the second company because another company manages it. This particular type of business will develop significantly in the twentieth century. We can see this type of agreement back in 1854 when Le Globe Compagnie d'Assurance Contre L'incendie ceded fire business to Riunione Adriatica (Carter 1979, p. 16).

In the German case, the most important company is Munich Re (Münchener Rückversicherungs-Gesellschaft AG, from now MR) that is one of the leaders in the world today. Among the company's founders, there is one of the most important persons in reinsurance, Carl von Thieme. The company started late because it was already over 30 years later than Cologne Re in 1880. It is significant to establish the place Munich. Is the capital of the Bavarian state. It was a Kingdom that joins the German Empire in 1871 with great autonomy of its own government. The company will have a significant say in the develop of Alliance that also has its headquarters in this capital. The success of the company MR is related to the capital of the banking house Merck, Finck & Co. and of Freiherr von Cramer-Klett one of the richest persons in Bavaria. And the human capital was mainly of Carl Thieme that out of the founders was the person that had the know-how in insurance. He had been working before in the insurance company Thuringia where his father already worked, learning from the mistakes done by the reinsurance division of this company. In addition, the economic cycle when MR started was excellent in Germany and benefited the management of the company. The special capacities of this man in organization and his incredible ability to understand the market made the company a leader not only in his own country but in the world. One of the key explanations of the success of MR is that since the start they internationalize the business. MR ceded in a great way, so it was possible to assume more risk, but at the same time as it was extremely widespread in its undertakings the risk for the company was not so great. The other great success that in many ways was difficult and risky was to introduce the company in the highly regulated market of the United States. This country changed in a unbelievable way, thanks to the success in the development of the Industrial Revolution but also the large number of immigrants that intensively arrive in the last decades of the nineteenth century and the beginning of the twentieth century. If France multiply by four its economy since 1820 to 1913, or Britain 6.2 or Germany 8.5, the case of the United States is incredible, because it is 41.2 times (Maddison 2006, p. 639). Of course, the population also grew extremely rapidly, from 9,981,000 to 97,606,000 that is 9.8 times. In France it was 1.3, Britain 2.1 and Germany 2.6 (Maddison 2006, p. 636). The country for the people that had no future in Europe, mainly peasant became the most powerful country in the world. Its insurance market grew rapidly bolstered by the lack of a welfare state.

The last country that is a core country for reinsurance is small, lacks a direct connection to the ocean, and is the most mountainous country in Europe: Switzerland. It has the other big company in reinsurance Swiss

Re, founded on December 19, 1863. The start was not easy and practically ended then. The company assumes large risks at the beginning and practically disappears after five years. The critical situation was solved by developing business in foreign countries as the Swiss market was insufficient. In business, the five first years are crucial, and many do not make the sixth year. One would say that although it was difficult, as had from the start excellent companies that supported Swiss Re. From a financial point of view, it had the support of very important banks: Kreditanstalt and Handelsbank. Also, the Helvetia insurance supported the new reinsurance company. Nevertheless, the management's capability at the start was not able to reduce the risk and was on the verge of making the new company disappear.

Also, maybe we can say no one is a prophet in their own land. The economic cycle of expansion and globalization at the end of the nineteenth century and the beginning of the twentieth century was brilliantly managed by the company. In the expansion, they managed to put a foot in the challenging and difficult American market by opening in New York a crucial office. The prestige of the Swiss, capable, and highly qualified employers, made them perfect reinsurers in the growing American insurance market. Also, in many important markets in Europe. Switzerland's characteristics, a neutral, peaceful country and with trustworthy institutions and hard currency, the Swiss franc, made them ideal for many insurance companies in many developing countries (Straumann 2013, p. 239). Finally, the last significant advantage of Swiss Re was that it is not German. Germany lost Two World Wars that for the reinsurance business mean losing the American market and many other markets during both wars. In the 20s, the company was the world leader; they had the expertise, know-how, and trust that made many insurance companies change from MR to Swiss Re in France, UK, or the US. Since then, the two leading companies in the world have been both in the reinsurance market.

References

Bähr, Johannes, and Christopher Kopper. 2016. *Munich Re: The Company History 1880–1980*. Munich: C. H. Beck.

Borscheid, Peter. 2013. "Global Insurance Networks". In *The Value of Risk*, ed. Harold James, et al. New York: Oxford University Press.

Carter, Robert L. 1979. *Reinsurance*. Brentford, Middlesex: Kluwer Publishing Limited.

Golding, Cecil E. 1927. *A History of Reinsurance with a Sidelight on Insurance*. London: Waterlow & Sons.
Gerathewohl, Klaus. 1982. *Reinsurance Principles and Practice*, trans. John Christopher La Bonté, vol. II. Karlsruhe: Verlag Versicherungswirtschaft e. V. Underwriter Printing & Pub Co.
Grüne-Yanoff, Till. 2012. "Paradoxes of Rational Choice Theory". In *Handbook of Risk Theory*, ed. Sabine Roeser, Rafaela Hillerbrand, Per Sandin, and Martin Peterson, 499–516. Dordrecht: Springer.
Harold, James, Peter Borscheid, David Gugerli and Tobias Straumann. 2013. *The Value of Risk*. New York: Oxford University Press.
James, Harold, et al. 2013. *The Value of Risk*. New York: Oxford University Press.
Kahneman, D., and A. Tversky. 1979. "Prospect Theory: An Analysis of Decision Under Risk". *Econometrica* 47: 263–291.
Kiernan, Paul, and Joanna Sugden. 2018. *The Wall Street Journal*, October 8.
Kingston, Christopher. 2007. "Marine Insurance in Britain and America, 1720–1844: A Comparative Institutional Analysis". *The Journal of Economic History* 67 (2): 379–409.
Kopf, Edwin W. 1929. *Notes on Origin and Development of Reinsurance*. New York: Globe Printing Company.
Maddison, Agnus. 2006. "The World Economy, 1–2001 AD". OECD. http://www.ggdc.net/maddison/oriindex.htm.
Marcus, Geoffrey J. 1975. *Heart of Oak: A Survey of British Sea Power in the Georgian Era*. Oxford: Oxford University Press.
Müssener, Alexander. 2008. *Die Entwicklung der Aachener Feuer-Versicherungs-Gesellschaft im 19. Jahrhundert*. Hamburg: 436 Seiten.
Millar, John. 1787. *Elements of the Law Relating to Insurance*. Edinburgh: Printed for J. Bell, Parliament-Close.
Pearson, Robin. 2012. "United Kingdom: Pionerrig Insurance Internationally". In *World Insurance*, ed. Peter Borscheid and Niels Viggo Haueter, 67–97. Oxford: Oxford University Press.
Pearson, Robin. 2017. "The Evolution of the Industry Structure". In *Managing Risk in Reinsurance*, ed. Niels Viggo Haueter and Geoffrey Jones. New York: Oxford University Press.
Review, November 24, 1939.
Straus, André, and Leonardo Caruana. 2017. *Highlights in Reinsurance*. Brussels: Peter Lang.
Pearson, Robin. 1997. "Towards an Historical Model of Services Innovation: The Case of the Insurance Industry, 1700–1914". *The Economic History Review*, New Series 50 (2): 235–256.
Vance, William R. 1902. "The Contract of Reinsurance". *The Virginia Law Register* 7 (10): 669–679.

CHAPTER 3

Reinsurance in America: Regulatory Regimes and Markets

Robert E. Wright

3.1 Introduction

The importance of reinsurance to our American commercial civilization is as yet little appreciated. -- William H. Hotchkiss (1914, p. 168).

Although its economy has been one of the world's most important over the last two centuries or so, and despite its predilection, surpassed perhaps only by that of Japan, for suffering large property losses due to natural (avalanches and landslides, earthquakes, floods, wildfires, extreme wind events, and so forth) and man-made catastrophes (arson, blackouts, bridge, and dam failures, civil disturbances, terrorism, etc.) (Cummins 2007, p. 215; Ayling 1982, pp. 2–10; Kobrak 2012, p. 274), the United States of America has domiciled only a handful of world-class reinsurers (Haueter and Jones 2017a, b, p. 11, pp. 14–15). It is, instead, an undisputed leader in market-based approaches to insurance, and ARTM,

---

R. E. Wright (✉)
American Institute for Economic Research, Great Barrington, MA, USA

© The Author(s), under exclusive license to Springer Nature Switzerland AG 2021
L. Caruana de las Cagigas and A. Straus (eds.), *Role of Reinsurance in the World*, Palgrave Studies in Economic History,
https://doi.org/10.1007/978-3-030-74002-3_3

or alternative risk transfer mechanisms, including insurance exchanges (Pearson 2017, p. 86) and, more recently, markets for ILS, or insurance-linked securities like cat(astrophe) and death (XXX) bonds (Jarzabkowski et al. 2015).

The parallel with America's banking and securities market history is striking and probative. Until the regulatory reforms of the 1990s lowered the cost of interstate branching and allowed commercial banks to engage in investment banking activities, the United States also had relatively few banks in the top global rankings by asset size (Anon. 1980). Policies that favored small unit banks over large branch banks, like those in neighboring Canada (Calomiris and Haber 2014), induced the relatively rapid development of America's corporate securities markets (White 2010, pp. 66–69). Similarly, U.S. insurance regulations favored the development of markets for facultative coverage and reciprocal reinsurance treaties and, eventually, ARTM and ILS, over the formation of globally important reinsurers (Haueter and Jones 2017a, b, p. 12, pp. 323–24).

The lesson for this book appears to be that insurance industry development requires some form of reinsuring risks, but that does not necessarily mean that large, domestic reinsurers must arise because direct writers can insure each other (reciprocal), reinsure with specialized foreign professional reinsurers (Werner 2007, p. 113; Ayling 1982, pp. 1–2; Lencsis 1997, p. 39), and/or develop risk markets that meet the same functional goals, though perhaps at a higher cost. Direct writers, or insurance companies that cover the risks facing individuals, businesses and NGOs, and governments, themselves need insurance for various reasons. Reinsurance and retrocession, in the words of one of their earliest historians, "keep insurance companies out of the 'mortuary chapel' (Kopf 1929, p. 25)." Direct writers naturally seek out the least costly way of avoiding failure and that is not necessarily by reinsuring through domestic professional reinsurers if they are inappropriately regulated.

3.2 America Has Fewer World-Class Reinsurers Than Suggested by Its Large Insurance Market

As Welf Werner showed a decade ago, reinsurers domiciled in the United States have never come close to dominating the global reinsurance industry in terms of quality or size rankings (2007, pp. 112–28). Of the 275 professional reinsurance companies formed globally between 1840 and 1936, only 30 were chartered in the U.S. That number was second only behind Germany (with 71) but much smaller countries, like Denmark (29), were close behind, and over two-thirds of the U.S. count (21) began operations in the 1920s, with only 6 formed before 1920 (Haueter and Jones 2017a, b, p. 301). The first specialized U.S. reinsurer, Reinsurance Company of America, was shuttered in 1890. Most of the newer companies managed to survive until 1930, though Pilot Life Re, which incorporated in 1928, was liquidated in 1929 without a significant book of business (Kopf 1929, p. 61, p. 65). Clearly, the 1920s were an aberration, America's rather late entrance into reinsurance fads or bubbles like those that had plagued European countries in the nineteenth century (Pearson 2017, pp. 76–77).

Moreover, America's reinsurers were relatively small. In the 1920s and 1930s only a handful of the top 15 global reinsurers were American and two of the largest, Rossia and European General, had European origins, as did North American Re, which was established in 1923 by Swiss Re to write business in the U.S. and Canada (Kopf 1929, pp. 65–66; MacGregor and Boyco 1988, p. 14, p. 34). All were dwarfed by global leaders Munich Re and Swiss Re. In 1929, the top U.S. reinsurers earned only 15.6% of the total premiums earned by the global top 15 reinsurers. By 1938, their share had dropped to a mere 10.5% (Haueter and Jones 2017a, b, p. 303).

World War II took its toll on European reinsurers such that by 1952 American reinsurers held 6 of the top 15 spots and 28% of the big 15's total net premium. By 1965, however, the number of American global reinsurers leaders had shrunk back to 3 and even though American Re and General Re held the number 3 and 4 slots, they were so dominated by Swiss Re and Munich Re that the Americans' share of the market had shrunk to 18.2% (Haueter and Jones 2017a, b, p. 304). Competition from foreign reinsurers became even stiffer in the 1970s. By 1977, U.S. insurers ceded to foreign reinsurers $400 million more than they assumed from foreign insurers (Kobrak 2012, p. 299).

By 1980, 5 American reinsurers were in the global 15, including General Re in the third spot, but their combined market share of net premiums increased only slightly, to 18.7%. A decade later (1990), only 3 American reinsurers remained in the top 15 and their market share had dropped to 16.8%. That year, like every year since data was compiled beginning in 1949, and undoubtedly in all the years prior and since, the U.S. ran a reinsurance trade deficit, meaning that American insurers ceded more business to foreign reinsurers than American reinsurers earned from foreign cedents (Werner 2007, p. 115). In 1996, 4 American reinsurers made the top 15 and their market share, thanks to the 1994 merger of General Re and Cologne Re, jumped back to 22.3%. Reinsurance, however, continued to be "European led" (Kobrak 2012, p. 302) as American professional reinsurers in 1998 supplied only 22% of reinsurance worldwide although the United States itself represented slightly more than 30% of the global market (Anon. 1998).

In 2000, America's Berkshire Hathaway Reinsurance Group was the third largest reinsurer in the world but its net premiums written was not much more than half those of either of the top two, a situation that persisted throughout the first decade of the twenty-first century (Anon. 2002, p. 27; Anon. 2007, p. 65). In 2005, 5 American reinsurers were in the top 15 and their market share stood at 24.9% (Haueter and Jones 2017a, b, pp. 305–6). That might seem somewhat impressive but two-fifths to half of the premiums ceded worldwide came from North American insurers (Haueter and Jones 2017a, b, p. 310). Those top 5 were essentially America's reinsurance industry because in 2005 no other U.S.-domiciled reinsurer made the top 35 non-life reinsurers globally and most of the remaining smaller players were bound to exit (Cummins 2007, pp. 179–220, p. 185). Moreover, more than half of total reinsurance premiums ceded by U.S. insurers went to non-U.S. reinsurers, almost half to reinsurers based in Bermuda (Cummins 2007, p. 187, pp. 215–16; Cummins 2008, Fig. 6.1). Several large U.S. reinsurance companies exited via merger, including GE Global Insurance Holdings, which Swiss Re acquired in 2006 (Haueter and Jones 2017a, b, p. 307). So in the past decade only three U.S. reinsurance groups, Berkshire (Hathaway) Re, which in 1998 bought the combined General Re-Cologne Re, Reinsurance Group of America (RGA), and Transatlantic Holdings (TransRe, Putnam Re, and TransRe Zurich), regularly made global rankings by reinsurance premiums and other key financial measures (Haueter and Jones 2017a, b, p. 17).

3.3 Relatively Costly and Inappropriate Regulations Forced Reinsurance into Other Channels

Why have American reinsurers failed, for the most part, to develop into global leaders despite America's large economy and insurance sector? The failure is largely self-reinforcing, of course. Because America has few important professional reinsurers, few Americans regulators, scholars, or voters even know about the industry, much less care about it. Unsurprisingly, the best research on reinsurance comes from the Continent and Britain (Ayling 1982, F1–F4). The chapter on reinsurance and retrocession in Peter Lencsis's 1997 survey of American insurance regulation, for instance, is only four pages long (about three percent of the book), including notes (100–104)!

But why did Americans not seize the reinsurance market in the nineteenth century, as they did so many other industries? In short, a changing menu of insurance regulations have stymied the development of reinsurers in America. In Europe, reinsurance was long considered a distinct line within the insurance business and was allowed to develop as such (Kopf 1929, p. 25). In the U.S., regulators wedded to the concept of monoline insurance would not countenance the development of all lines reinsurers and regulated reinsurers as if they were direct writers. After the slow, grudging acceptance of multiline insurance finally came to fruition in postwar America, domestic reinsurers began to thrive until regulators saddled them with new burdens, including Regulation XXX (Kobrak 2012, pp. 277–278, p. 294). This story can of course be told in a more detailed and nuanced fashion, which is the goal of this paper.

One of the first histories of reinsurance noted that "in tracing the development of reinsurance from its earliest days, there is necessarily much of conjecture, for written records are scanty" (Golding 1931, p. 25). As far as has been ascertained, reinsurance began in Europe in the fourteenth-century marine insurance industry on a facultative basis between direct writers. It began to take on more modern forms, like automatic treaties, in the continental fire insurance industry in the early nineteenth century. At first, domestic direct writers reinsured each other but competitive pressures led them to reinsure with direct writers in nearby countries and specialized captive reinsurers and, eventually, with independent professional reinsurers (Kopf 1929, pp. 25–30).

Following early European precedents, American marine and fire insurers at first engaged in coinsurance (i.e., they split large policies into smaller ones with each directly writing each piece), reinsured the policies of direct writers as they exited the market (i.e., took over part or all of an existing book of business), and employed facultative reinsurance (i.e., direct writers reinsured specific large risks with other insurers) or reciprocal reinsurance treaties (i.e., direct writers shared each other's excess losses on various negotiated terms). American direct writers continued those practices, which spread their risks over time and space at a time when citywide conflagrations were common, even after specialized reinsurers began to form, starting in Germany in the 1840s and other advanced continental economies in the 1850s and 1860s (Kopf 1929, pp. 27–28, 58; Golding 1931, pp. 40–42; Pearson 2017, p. 71).

To help direct writers to reinsure each other's risks, reinsurance bureaus, like those in New York state and Illinois, and reinsurance associations, like that for farm fire insurance mutuals in Iowa, formed (Kopf 1929, pp. 62–63), and plans for a reinsurance "league" to help reduce farm insurance costs were drawn up (Anon. 1922, pp. 502–10). Congress explicitly exempted marine insurers that formed an association to "apportion among its membership the risks undertaken by such association" from antitrust regulations (Udell 1957, p. 51). Advocates of professional reinsurance, however, disdained such arrangements as uneconomical and inconvenient (Hotchkiss 1914, p. 170).

When arrangements between direct writers seemed too costly or inadequate, American direct writers reinsured through Lloyd's (Haueter and Jones 2017a, b, p. 12; Hotchkiss 1914, p. 169; Kobrak 2012, p. 286) or rising European reinsurers like Munich Re, United Fire Reinsurance Company of Manchester, or Societe Anonyme de Re-assurances de Paris (Kopf 1929, p. 32, p. 36, pp. 60–61). Much of the business was not officially authorized by U.S. insurance regulators but was conducted nonetheless (Hotchkiss 1914, p. 175). Those and other reinsurers, with help from a new breed of specialized reinsurance brokers like A. F. Pearson and Company (later merged with Sterling Offices Limited), scoured the globe for clients to ensure broad diversification (Golding 1931, pp. 123–38; Ayling 1982, p. 2–2). In a market where even large British fire insurers could not compete, U.S. fire insurers, which were relatively numerous but typically small and fragile, were unlikely global entrants (Pearson 2017, pp. 73–77).

3.4 America's Too Numerous State Insurance Regulators Treated Reinsurers as Direct Writers and Clung Tenaciously to the Monoline Model

In America, reinsurance was considered just another type of insurance and hence was regulated state by state, largely as direct writers were. After an initial period before the U.S. Civil War when multiline insurers were countenanced under special incorporation laws (Kingston and Wright 2012), insurers were subjected to general incorporation laws that largely mandated single-line business, a policy that regulators in most states defended (Kopf 1929, p. 61). Some state laws did not reference reinsurance at all, while the laws pertaining to reinsurance in other states, like New York and Massachusetts, were sparse or difficult to comprehend (Hotchkiss 1914, p. 168). Insurance commissioners therefore applied the old "practice of segregating insurance powers by lines or groups of lines" to reinsurers, which of course limited their size and their ability to diversify, which increased their retrocession costs and hence their risk-adjusted profitability (Kopf 1929, p. 71).

Many small direct writers, including fraternals and mutuals on the assessment plan, did not reinsure at all (Report of the Examination of the Loyal Protective Association of Boston, Mass. 1903). That worried Zeno M. Host, Wisconsin's insurance commissioner, who urged out-of-state insurers doing business in Wisconsin to instruct their mortgage borrowers to insure mortgaged properties with stock companies instead of "local mutual fire companies, which operate upon the assessment basis" (Report of the Supreme Ruling Fraternal Mystic Circle of Philadelphia, Pa. 1903). The dearth of reinsurance coverage rendered small direct writers more vulnerable to shocks but also allowed them to avoid the wrath of regulators largely uninterested with such small concerns, many of which were run by "men of honor" who received no compensation for their toils but who often made silly mistakes, like booking internal fund transfers as income (Fraternal Reserve Association 1905).

As insurers grew larger and hence important to more constituents, insurance regulators paid more attention to their reinsurance strategies, if only because of the tricky taxation issues involved. In 1908, for example, United States Lloyd Marine Insurance Underwriters of New York ran into difficulties with Wisconsin regulators because it took "credit for unauthorized reinsurance" (Subscribers at United States Lloyd Marine Insurance Underwriters 1908). Aachen and Munich Fire Insurance Company's branch in New York and a number of other foreign insurers also ran afoul of the insurance commissioners in Madison by reinsuring with companies, including Munich Re, not authorized to do business in Wisconsin (U.S. Branch of the Aachen and Munich Fire Insurance Company of Germany 1909; Royal Exchange Assurance Company of London 1908). If readers' heads are spinning, so too were those of insurance regulators, who admitted that "there are a great many difficulties in the distribution of premiums, on marine business, among the different states" (Subscribers at United States Lloyd Marine Insurance Underwriters 1908), while complaining that the victims of the complicated tax system treated them in a "discourteous" manner (U.S. Branch of the Aachen and Munich Fire Insurance Company of Germany 1909).

Reinsurance was an especially sticky issue for companies that were not required to post significant collateral, usually in the form of bonds or high-quality mortgages, with state officials, due to the risks they could pose for policyholders in the event of unexpectedly large losses or other shocks (Policy Holders of the Northwestern National Life Ins. Co. of Minneapolis, Minn. 1903). Regulators regularly praised direct writers that responsibly reinsured, like United American Fire Insurance Company of Milwaukee, which by 1905 enjoyed a capital and surplus of over $140,000 and acted as both cedent and reinsurer (United American Fire Insurance Company 1905). Nevertheless, insurance commissioners allowed much larger insurers, like Indiana Millers Mutual Fire, to avoid reinsuring so long as their affairs were "carried on in a methodical and systematic way" on both sides of the balance sheet by respected businessmen (Indiana Millers Mutual Fire Insurance Company 1905). Northwestern Mutual Life of Milwaukee was huge for its day and so well conducted, especially compared to the big New York insurers lambasted during the Armstrong Investigation, that regulators did not criticize it for not ceding (Northwestern Mutual Life Insurance Company 1905).

Insurers in a "very unsatisfactory" condition, by contrast, had their reinsurance arrangements most carefully scrutinized, though usually more basic problems like inadequately addressing adverse selection and moral hazard, as well as sloppy accounting practices, were at the root of the regulators' critiques (Northwestern Casualty Company 1903; Western Relief Association 1903). "A great many accounts and details of the business," one regulator complained of the Merchants & Bankers Mutual Fire Insurance Company of Beloit, Wisconsin in 1911, "are kept on slips of paper which have been mislaid or lost. ... The entire books of the company consisted of a policy register and a ledger" (Merchants & Bankers Mutual Fire Insurance Company of Beloit 1911).

In response to the lack of reinsurance, a consortium of ten mutual fire insurers formed the Wisconsin Town Mutual Reinsurance Company (WTMRC) in 1931. Growth was slow at first but business picked up considerably after regulators allowed Wisconsin's so-called "town mutuals" (O'Donnell 2006) to write windstorm and hail coverage, and 92 out of 173 elected to do so (Equity Town Mutual Reinsurance Agreement n.d.). Clyman Town Mutual Fire Insurance, for example, applied to WTMRC in 1965 to cover its aggregate excess windstorm and hail exposure, provision of which its policyholders had approved by a vote of 33 to 5 (Clyman Town Mutual Fire Insurance Co., Windstorm and Hail Reinsurance Agreement n.d.). Established in 1873, Utica Mutual Fire Insurance Company of Omro also reinsured with WTMRC. It also reinsured individual risks on a facultative basis up to 50% (Utica Mutual Examination Reports n.d.). In 1964, Auburn Mutual Insurance Company, nee the Auburn German Mutual Fire Insurance Company of Campbellsport, Wisconsin, reinsured with WTMRC but also with another tiny Wisconsin mutual, Midland Union of Juneau, which assumed all of its windstorm risk in exchange for a 70% of Auburn's premium income (Auburn Mutual Reinsurance Agreement n.d.). For a time, Auburn also had a reinsurance agreement with Campbellsport Mutual Insurance Company (Auburn Mutual Examination Report n.d.).

After the entrance of Munich Re into the American market in 1898, specialized reinsurance began to grow. The number of professional reinsurers authorized to do business in New York, one domestic and the balance foreign, grew from 10 in 1909 to 23 by 1913 and their combined premium income jumped from $18.34 million to $38.32 million over that same short period. At the same time, Wisconsin regulators were content to allow the captive reinsurers of foreign direct writers admitted to do business in Wisconsin, like Frankona Re of Germany, Warsaw Fire of Russia, and L'Abeille Fire of France, to function, but domestic professional reinsurers remained subject to the same rules as direct writers (L'Abeille Fire Insurance Company 1911; Phoenix Fire Insurance Company 1911; Frankona Reinsurance Company 1912; Warsaw Fire Insurance Company 1912). Wisconsin regulators by then believed that "a purely reinsurance business" was "very simple" to understand and they believed that European reinsurers had by then figured out how to make "the law of average" work "out well for their protection" and "large profit" (Warsaw Fire Insurance Company 1912). They saw little need to encourage the formation of domestic reinsurers, however, because they were also convinced that, even in Russia or Spain, U.S. citizens or insurance companies could effectively sue to protect all of their contractual rights (Van Iderstine to Fester et al. 1911).

In 1914, failed legislative reforms in New York, Massachusetts, and New Jersey induced three former and current state insurance commissioners to lay out the costs and benefits of the American monoline system. Two of them came out strongly in favor of maintaining the status quo for both direct writers and reinsurers and the third admitted that any change would cause a "great shock ... that would unsettle the insurance business for a number of years" (Hotchkiss 1914, pp. 169–72, p. 176).

Frank Hasbrouck, New York's Superintendent of Insurance and hence arguably the most powerful insurance regulator in the country, argued that the division of insurance into six main categories, to wit fire and marine; life; casualty; title; securities guaranty; and credit guaranty, was imperfect but ultimately a workable classification system because it recognized "that marked differences exist in the character and hazard of the various kinds of insurance business" (1914, 161). Life insurers were fundamentally different because they were essentially fiduciary in nature. Other insurers differed in the knowledge and skills required to successfully operate. Moreover, unwinding the affairs of a failed multiline insurer "would be seriously complicated," as would their prudential supervision in general (165). For prudential reasons, he continued, "the statutory limitations of the direct writer should be equally applicable to the reinsurer" (166) so mixing lines in a reinsurer would be too complicated and would serve as an "opening wedge for the direct company to enter into all fields." Besides, "every direct company by the very nature of the business is more or less a reinsurer," so there was no clear need for specialized reinsurers in his view and certainly no reason to favor them even though they did not deal directly with consumers (166). Foreign entrants from Germany and elsewhere that allowed multiline reinsurers may enter the U.S. market by organizing "separate domestic corporations with independent capital and surplus." Monoline restrictions, Hasbrouck added, also prevented the "concentration of the insurance business in the hands of a few mammoth corporations," a perpetual fear of Americans (167).

Former New York insurance commissioner William H. Hotchkiss, by contrast, wanted to adopt a "policy that will make scientific reinsurance as general in the United States as it is and long has been abroad" (1914, p. 169). In addition to being more efficient, specialized reinsurance and retrocession companies aided small companies by allowing them to compete with larger ones for large risks. Without professional reinsurance, he predicted, many small insurers would be forced to exit through bankruptcy or merger, leading to the creation of the mammoth insurers that Hasbrouck so feared (174). But even Hotchkiss believed that "so long as we continue to believe in the classification or single field system, as distinguished from the multi-field system abroad, any uniform reinsurance law should deny to reinsurance companies multi-field powers" (176).

In the early 1920s, Congress dabbled with the idea of establishing a farm reinsurance "league" that would "transact the business of insurance of every nature whatsoever, sell indemnity against any and every contingency, to negotiate reinsurances of risks and companies." The league, however, would have to "maintain a separate department for each class of business done by it" and "segregate the assets, capital, surplus funds, and receipts of each department." True to its name, in other words, the league would not have been a single diversified insurer but rather an umbrella brand under which several distinct companies would have operated. It would also have been a direct writer with reinsurance powers rather than a professional reinsurer (Anon. 1922, pp. 502–3).

3.5 The Reinsurance Company of New York Case Shows the Difficulties Faced by American Reinsurers

Given the hard line taken against diversified insurers, it is unsurprising to learn that before World War II only one U.S. reinsurer, First Reinsurance Company of Hartford, did a general, multiline reinsurance business (Strauman 2013, p. 264). Formed in 1912 by Munich Re, the company tried and failed to induce more states to allow multiline reinsurance (Hotchkiss 1914, p. 173). During the Great War, the Alien Property Custodian seized and sold much of its stock to ten domestic insurers. Rossia Insurance, the American offspring of an Imperial Russian reinsurer of the same name, secured majority control of First Re in 1925 and began selling off its life and fire books, rendering it a strictly monoline casualty reinsurer by 1926 (Kopf 1929, p. 70, p. 73). Other early U.S. professional reinsurers were monoline, though by the late Depression era at least one, the Reinsurance Corporation of New York (RCNY) could lawfully reinsure both inland marine and fire risks, though its participation in the former was limited to "a small participation in the American Marine Insurance Syndicates," which covered only hulls, and only in peacetime (Reinsurance Corporation of New York Annual Reports).

By the time the U.S. developed a reinsurance industry of its own in the 1910s and 1920s, Munich Re and Swiss Re had established their dominance and the duopoly managed to maintain their first mover advantages despite the twentieth and early twenty-first centuries' great economic, geopolitical, and insurance shocks (Strauman 2013, pp. 236–352). Swiss Re, for example, filled much of the non-life reinsurance gap left by the exit of Munich Re from the U.S. market during the world wars (Haueter and Jones 2017a, b, p. 13), including its dramatic decline during and after the Great War (Kopf 1929, p. 33; Strauman 2013, p. 274; Kobrak 2012, pp. 290–91). On the life side, Metropolitan Life formed a separate reinsurance department after the Alien Property Custodian asked it to take over the business of two German reinsurers, Prussian Life and Mercury Re. (Kopf 1929, p. 65).

This is not to say that RCNY did not try to capitalize on the disruptions caused by the world wars and the Great Depression. RCNY, which began operations in December 1936, considered itself a "pioneering venture to provide and develop an American market for admitted reinsurance of fire and allied lines of the classes that, heretofore, have been largely placed abroad." To win both participating but especially excess of loss treaties, which generally went to Lloyds or continental reinsurers, it brought in personnel "with experience gained both here and in the London market" and pushed its relative stability "in these times of political uncertainty in Europe," along with the advantages of doing business with an admitted reinsurance carrier, namely "being able to take full credit for premium and loss reserves" in the states where regulators only counted reinsurance made with admitted carriers. (Certain tax breaks were available in some states as well [Anon. 1924].)

Those tactics worked to some extent as RCNY had written 70 fire insurance contracts by the end of 1937, its first full year of operation. "The constantly increasing number of reinsurance contracts issued by" the company in subsequent years pointed to the desire of some U.S. direct writers to deal with domestic reinsurers. RCNY, however, was a captive in the sense that its sole underwriting manager, the Excess Management Corporation, was controlled by a dozen or so prominent fire insurers, which constituted the bulk of its business by revenue. Even before Pearl Harbor, RCNY learned that catastrophes, like the large fire in Fall River, Massachusetts in 1941, could damage profits. After the outbreak of war, losses climbed yet higher; 1943 witnessed a 21% increase in fire losses. Another 11% increase followed in 1944, thanks in part to the Great Atlantic hurricane, "which reached catastrophic proportions" (Reinsurance Corporation of New York 1941, p. 1).

By the mid-1960s, RCNY was in trouble. It lost $1.35 million in 1964 on top of almost $1.9 million in 1963. The following year, 1965, was disastrous as tornadoes ripped through the Midwest on Palm Sunday, a twister hit Minneapolis in May, riots devastated Los Angeles in August, and Hurricane Betsy beat up Florida and New Orleans in September (Reinsurance Corporation of New York1941). Unable to recover, RCNY merged with another reinsurer and went private in 1968. The private owner, Piedmont Management Company, had to make two capital infusions totaling $26 million in 1994–1995 (Scott 2001, p. 3).

3.6 U.S. Reinsurance Regulation Remained Relatively Costly After World War II

Many other domestic U.S. reinsurers suffered similar fates. Despite low formal entry barriers into the reinsurance business, the dominance of the two big continental reinsurers continues to this day (Haueter and Jones 2017a, b, p. 16). Their dominance, however, was only relative as coinsurance and reciprocity again rose to prominence globally in the aftermath of the Great War and the other megashocks of the twentieth century, including the dissolution of fixed exchange rates like the gold standard and Bretton Woods systems, depression, hyperinflation, stagflation, exchange controls, nationalization, or state monopolization of reinsurers, and war (Kobrak 2012, p. 299). The sea change in business practices away from relational toward transactional also disrupted traditional reinsurance markets (Pearson 2017, pp. 79–81).

After World War II, reinsurance premiums grew faster than direct premiums but profits did not due to increased competition from U.S. and U.K.-based reinsurers and losses in the rapidly growing automobile reinsurance line and even in the traditional fire reinsurance line. U.S. reinsurers stuck largely to the home market, which they found easier to tap once rules forcing monoline insurance began to be loosened in the 1950s (Haueter and Jones 2017a, b, p. 14).

But regulatory reforms came slowly and were never complete. According to a marketing report by Stevenson and Kellogg written for M&G, a Swiss Re subsidiary operating out of Canada and looking to expand, the U.S. insurance market was "fiercely competitive" in the 1960s but it required a high level of service quality and speed because "direct writers are very concerned about the amount of paperwork required to operate. They are looking for help in finding a solution." M&G also learned that securing licenses in states, some of which did not yet have reinsurance-specific licenses or regulations, and hence still treated reinsurers like direct writers, was "a long and tedious process." Moreover, insurance regulators in some states, like Michigan, could not conceive of a British reinsurer, operating in Canada but ultimately owned by Swiss Re, wanting to enter the U.S. market. To make headway, M&G learned to wine and dine regulators in some states while in others it discovered that making powerful friends who would coerce regulators into action was a faster and cheaper method of gaining entry (MacGregor and Boyko 1988, pp. 39–43). To this day, matters have not substantively improved as entry remains relatively costly and slow, especially compared to offshore regulatory and tax havens such as Bermuda (Cummins 2008, p. 1; Kobrak 2012, p. 276).

Starting in the 1960s, technological and climate change increased demand for reinsurance as businesses sought cover for nuclear power plants, oil supertankers, passenger jets, and as insurers sought to mitigate the risks of more destructive and numerous storms and floods. Upticks in earthquakes, terrorism, and long-tail pollution and health risks, like asbestos, also helped to spur demand for professional reinsurance while causing the reinsurance industry to gyrate through soft and hard cycles like those experienced by direct writers (Pearson 2017, pp. 83–89). The number of domestic reinsurers doubled to 137 between 1979 and 1982, for example, but higher-than-expected losses and downward pressure on premiums led to the quick slaughter of many of the new, inexperienced entrants (Meier 1988, pp. 91–92).

3.7 U.S. Reinsurers Trailed Market Leaders Based in Bermuda and Europe, Spurring Market-Based Innovations

In the 1980s and 1990s, asbestos and other product liability claims constituted a major crisis (Kobrak 2012, pp. 300–2) that drove even more U.S. reinsurers to Bermuda, a 20.5 square mile island almost 900 miles east of South Carolina. A British Overseas Territory of about 60,000, Bermuda long served as a tax shelter and after World War II became an offshore haven for captives and its own insurers (Duffy 2004). Over time,

Bermuda attracted a significant amount of human capital but the enormous financial capital flight to this dot in the North Atlantic is proof positive of the importance of proper regulatory and tax policies to the reinsurance industry. By 2008, 12 of the top 40 global reinsurers were based in Bermuda, more than any other jurisdiction (Cummins 2008, i–ii).

The loss of both reinsurance capital and know-how reduced America's ability to reinsure its own direct writers. In 2016, for example, American insurers ceded 60% of their reinsured risks to foreign-owned reinsurers, 90% if one counts the parent companies of U.S.-based reinsurers, essentially leaving the nation in the familiar position of a net importer of non-reciprocal reinsurance (Haueter and Jones 2017a, b, p. 15). The U.S. life reinsurance market also remains dominated by European reinsurers Munich Re and Swiss Re. In recent years, for example, the continental duopoly has captured almost three quarters of America's total group life premiums.

Their dominance is unsurprising. In Bermuda and the EU, reinsurers are still relatively lightly regulated, though a distinct trend toward more regulation in the latter is evident (Cummins 2007, p. 201). As Milos Vec has argued, global reinsurance "is a unique, normative order, formed, above all, by the relationships between reinsurers and the reinsured," not regulators. It is a "B2B" industry after all (Reinsurance Corporation of New York 1941, p. 1), and hence not subject to the same sorts of populist political strains or even court decisions because disputes are usually handled privately, by arbitration if necessary (Vec 2017, p. 2065).

Reinsurance regulation in America, by contrast, has been relatively "more intrusive ... outmoded and counter-productive," according to insurance economist J. David Cummins (2007, p. 201). Reinsurance brokers, including excess and surplus line brokers, for example, are more heavily regulated in the U.S., partly due to malfeasance by some reinsurance intermediaries in New York and New Jersey in the 1970s (Lencsis 1997, pp. 76–78). As recently as the late 1990s, U.S. insurance regulators in many states still considered professional reinsurers as just another type of insurer (Lencsis 1997, p. 100). Worse, relationships between insurers and the nation's 51 insurance regulators (52 if one includes Puerto Rico) are, in Cummins' words, "often conducted on an adversarial basis" (2008, p. 1).

Regulation of direct writers also favor ARTM and coinsurance or reciprocity over professional reinsurance. The widespread regulation of the premiums that direct writers can charge policyholders create large market inefficiencies, including rate compression (subsidization of the highest risk policyholders by lower risk ones) and rate suppression (too low to pay claims and remain profitable, leading to exit of the best insurers first), that adversely affect reinsurers. Some direct state intervention in insurance markets, like Florida's Hurricane Catastrophe Fund, are mandatory or heavily subsidized and hence crowd out private reinsurers (Cummins 2007, pp. 202–5).

On the other hand, ARTM, especially ILS, has met relatively little resistance from U.S. securities regulatory bodies, which are splintered into competing but not completely overlapping jurisdictions, none of which directly cover markets for exchanging risks. Berkeley professors Bob Goshay and Richard Sandor helped along the development of ARTM in the early 1970s by publishing papers about the workings of a reinsurance futures market. Goshay took the idea to Lloyd's, which rejected it, much to the surprise and chagrin of Sandor, who thought "it paradoxical that those who were willing to underwrite nontraditional risks would not consider new risk management tools." The idea sat dormant for almost two decades until being resuscitated by the Chicago Board of Trade in 1990 in response to a string of large and increasingly expensive natural catastrophes. Insurance catastrophe futures began trading on the CBOT in late 1992. The initial contract failed but after modifications and a learning period for traders, insurers and other investors caught on and the rest, as they say, is history (Ayling 1982, p. 2–9, pp. 2–10; Sandor 2012, pp. 239–51).

3.8 In the Future, ARTM May Displace Reinsurance as the Best Way to Spread Risk Globally

Today, ARTM, not specialized reinsurance, appears to represent the future of risk spreading, both for direct writers and some of the world's largest and financially most sophisticated non-insurers. Gone are the days of double digit annual growth in global non-life and life reinsurance premiums (Haueter and Jones 2017a, b, p. 308). Life reinsurance premiums in the U.S., for example, have plummeted by more than half since 2005 due in part to a global slowdown in the global reinsurance market growth measured in real dollars and in part to the growth of coinsurance induced by the adoption of Regulation XXX in 2000 (Sebastian 2016, pp. 10–14). Regulation XXX (and the similar AXXX for universal life policies) significantly increased statutory reserve requirements for term life insurers writing in the U.S., causing capital strain that induced many insurers to establish captives in which blocks of policies (term or UL) could be ceded under coinsurance treaties (Lash and Wang 2005, pp. 18–22).

While it is unlikely that the largest or most efficient reinsurers will exit anytime soon, they may continue to lose market share to ARTM, in much the same way that industrial life insurance slowly gave way to group insurance in the U.S. after World War II, to the point that reinsurers become analogous to investment bankers and earn most of their profits from design and the placement of ILS. In mid-2017, for example, Hannover Re placed about a billion dollars worth of ILS for three U.S. catastrophe insurers and bragged about the attractive and low-risk margins that it earned on the deals (Anon. 2017).

In sum, direct writers need to be able to reinsure some risks (and reinsurers need retrocession). In the right regulatory environment, large, domestic professional reinsurers will arise to meet that need but where regulatory costs are too high, as in the United States throughout much of its history, insurers will turn to each other, foreign reinsurers (captive or not), and/or market-based alternatives, like catastrophe and death bonds, to meet their reinsurance needs.

References

Printed Sources

Anon. 1922. *Agricultural Inquiry: Hearing Before the Joint Commission of Agricultural Inquiry*. Washington: GPO.
Anon. 1924. *Digest of State Laws Relating to Taxation and Revenue, 1922*. Washington, GPO.
Anon. 1980. "Top 20 World Banks, 1980." *The Banker*.
Anon. 1998. "Global Reinsurers Mirror U.S. Consolidation Trend." *BestWeek Special Report*.
Anon. 2002. "Standard & Poor's Top 25 Reinsurance Groups." *Risk & Insurance*.
Anon. 2007. "Swiss Re Takes Top Global Reinsurer Slot." *Best's Review*.

Anon. 2017. "Hannover Re Complete ILS Deals for Florida, Massachusetts, and Texas Catastrophe Risks." *Captive Insurance News.*
Ayling, David E. 1982. "An Investigation into the Underwriting of Excess of Loss Reinsurance." Ph.D. Diss., University of Aston, Birmingham.
Calomiris, Charles, and Stephen Haber. 2014. *Fragile by Design: The Political Origins of Banking Crises and Scarce Credit.* Princeton: Princeton University Press.
Cummins, J. David. 2007. "Reinsurance for Natural and Man-made Catastrophes in the United States: Current State of the Market and Regulatory Reforms." *Risk Management and Insurance Review* 10, 2.
———. 2008. "The Bermuda Insurance Market: An Economic Analysis." *Wharton and Fox Schools of Business, Working Paper.*
Duffy, Catherine R. 2004. *Held Captive: A History of International Insurance in Bermuda.* Toronto: Oakwell Boulton.
Golding, C.E. 1931. *A History of Reinsurance, with Sidelights on Insurance*, 2nd ed. London: Waterlow & Sons.
Hasbrouck, Frank. 1914. "Should We Abandon the American Restrictions Upon the Lasses of Insurance Written Both (a) by a Company Doing Direct Writing and (b) by a Company Doing Reinsurance?" *Proceedings of the National Conventions of Insurance Commissioners.* Columbia, S.C.: The State Company.
Haueter, Niels Viggo and Geoffrey Jones. 2017a. "Risk and Reinsurance." In *Managing Risk in Reinsurance: From City Fires to Global Warming*, edited by Niels Viggo Haueter and Geoffrey Jones. New York: Oxford University Press.
Haueter, Niels Viggo and Geoffrey Jones, Eds. 2017b. *Managing Risk in Reinsurance: From City Fires to Global Warming.* New York: Oxford University Press.
Hotchkiss, William H. 1914. "Reinsurance and Retrocession as Affecting and Affected by Our American Insurance System," *Proceedings of the National Conventions of Insurance Commissioners.* Columbia, S.C.: The State Company.
Jarzabkowski, Paula, Rebecca Bednarek, and Paul Spee. 2015. *Making a Market for Acts of God: The Practice of Risk-Trading in the Global Reinsurance Industry.* New York: Oxford University Press.
Kingston, Christopher and Robert E. Wright. 2012. "Corporate Insurers in Antebellum America." *Business History Review* 86: 447–476.
Kobrak, Christopher. 2012. "USA: The International Attraction of the US Insurance Market." In *World Insurance: The Evolution of a Global Risk Network*, edited by Peter Borscheid and Niels Viggo Haueter, New York: Oxford.
Kopf, Edwin W. 1929. "The Origins and Development of Reinsurance." *Proceedings of the Actuarial Society,* 16–33.

Lash, Steven D. and Rebecca Kao Wang. June 2005. "Demystifying Life Insurance Securitization: XXX and AXXX Securitization Issues and Considerations." *The Financial Report* 61: 18–22.

Lencsis, Peter M. 1997. *Insurance Regulation in the United States: An Overview for Business and Government*. Westport, Conn.: Quorum Books.

MacGregor, Malcolm, and Lydia Boyko. 1988. *Mercantile & General Reinsurance: Life in North America*. Toronto: Mercantile and General Reinsurance Co.

Meier, Kenneth J. 1988. *The Political Economy of Regulation*. Albany: State University of New York Press.

O'Donnell, James. 2006. *The Town Mutuals: Wisconsin's Grass Roots Insurance Industry*. Wisconsin: Trafford Publishing.

Pearson, Robin. 2017. "The Evolution of the Industry Structure." In *Managing Risk in Reinsurance: From City Fires to Global Warming*, edited by Niels Viggo Haueter and Geoffrey Jones. New York. Oxford University Press.

Reinsurance Corporation of New York. 1941. *Report to Stockholders, The Reinsurance Corporation of New York*.

Reinsurance Corporation of New York. 1943. *Report to Stockholders, The Reinsurance Corporation of New York*.

Sandor, Richard L. 2012. *Good Derivatives: A Story of Financial and Environmental Innovation*. New York: John Wiley and Sons.

Scott, Barrington. 2001. *Report on Examination of the Insurance Corporation of New York as of December 31, 1999*.

Sebastian, Harindra. 2016. "Results of the 2015 Life Reinsurance Survey." *Reinsurance News*.

Strauman, Tobias. 2013. "The Invisible Giant: The Story of Swiss Re, 1863–2013." In *The Value of Risk: Swiss Re and the History of Reinsurance*, ed. Harold James. New York: Oxford University Press.

Udell, Gilman G. 1957. *Antitrust Laws with Amendments, 1890–1956*. Washington: GPO.

Vec, Milos. 2017. "Reinsurance Law as an Autonomus Regulatory Regime?: Resistance to Codification and Avoidance of State Jurisdiction in the Twentieth Century." In *Managing Risk in Reinsurance: From City Fires to Global Warming*, ed. Niels Viggo Haueter and Geoffrey Jones. New York: Oxford University Press.

Werner, Welf. 2007. "International Reinsurance Trade Between the U.s. and Western Europe, 1949–1989," In *Internationalisation and Globalisation of the Insurance Industry in the 19th and 20th Centuries*, ed. Peter Borscheid and Robin Pearson. Zurich: Philipps-University.

White, Eugene. 2010. "Regulation and Governance: A Secular Perspective on the Development of the American Financial System." In *State and Financial Systems in Europe and the USA: Historical Perspectives on Regulation and*

Supervision in the Nineteenth and Twentieth Centuries, ed. Stefano Battilossi and James Reis. Burlington, Vermont. Ashgate.

Archival Sources (State Historical Society of Wisconsin Archives, Madison, Wisconsin)

"Auburn Mutual ... Reinsurance Agreement." n.d. Insurance Department, Examining Division, Records of Merged, Withdrawn or Liquidated Insurance Companies, 1869–, Box 5, Series 1027.

"Auburn Mutual Examination Report," n.d. Insurance Department, Examining Division, Records of Merged, Withdrawn or Liquidated Insurance Companies, 1869–, Box 5, Series 1027.

"Clyman Town Mutual Fire Insurance Co., Windstorm and Hail ... Reinsurance Agreement." n.d. Insurance Department, Examining Division, Records of Merged, Withdrawn or Liquidated Insurance Companies, 1869–, Box 12, Series 1027.

"Equity Town Mutual ... Reinsurance Agreement." n.d. Insurance Department, Examining Division, Records of Merged, Withdrawn or Liquidated Insurance Companies, 1869–, Box 18, Series 1027.

"Frankona Reinsurance Company," January 26, 1912. "Examination Reports, Domestic Companies, 1911–1912," Insurance Department, Examining Division, Box 3, Series 1049.

"Fraternal Reserve Association." September 15, 1905. "Examination Reports, Domestic Companies, 1903–1907." Insurance Department, Examining Division, Box 1, Series 1049.

"Indiana Millers Mutual Fire Insurance Company." June 27, 1905. "Examination Reports, Domestic Companies, 1903–1907," Insurance Department, Examining Division, Box 1, Series 1049.

"L'Abeille Fire Insurance Company," June 3, 1911. "Examination Reports, Domestic Companies, 1911–1912," Insurance Department, Examining Division, Box 3, Series 1049.

"Merchants & Bankers Mutual Fire Insurance Company of Beloit." November 29, 1911. "Examination Reports, Domestic Companies, 1911–1912," Insurance Department, Examining Division, Box 3, Series 1049.

"Northwestern Casualty Company." April 18, June 23, 26, 1903. "Examination Reports, Domestic Companies, 1903–1907," Insurance Department, Examining Division, Box 1, Series 1049.

"Northwestern Mutual Life Insurance Company." March 6, 1905. "Examination Reports, Domestic Companies, 1903–1907," Insurance Department, Examining Division, Box 1, Series 1049.

"Phoenix Fire Insurance Company," June 3, 1911. "Examination Reports, Domestic Companies, 1911–1912," Insurance Department, Examining Division, Box 3, Series 1049.

"Policy Holders of the Northwestern National Life Ins. Co. of Minneapolis, Minn." April 9, 1903. "Examination Reports, Domestic Companies, 1903–1907," Insurance Department, Examining Division, Box 1, Series 1049.

"Report of the Examination of the Loyal Protective Association of Boston, Mass." February 11, 1903. "Examination Reports, Domestic Companies, 1903–1907." Insurance Department, Examining Division, Box 1, Series 1049.

"Report of the Supreme Ruling Fraternal Mystic Circle of Philadelphia, Pa." February 20, 1903. "Examination Reports, Domestic Companies, 1903–1907." Insurance Department, Examining Division, Box 1, Series 1049.

Robert Van Iderstine to Messrs. Fester, Douglas & Folsom. March 8, 1911. "Examination Reports, Domestic Companies, 1911–1912," Insurance Department, Examining Division, Box 3, Series 1049.

"Royal Exchange Assurance Company of London." October 28, 1908. "Examination Reports, Domestic Companies, 1908–1910," Insurance Department, Examining Division, Box 2, Series 1049.

"Subscribers at United States Lloyd Marine Insurance Underwriters." November 6, 1908. "Examination Reports, Domestic Companies, 1908–1910," Insurance Department, Examining Division, Box 2, Series 1049.

"U.S. Branch of the Aachen and Munich Fire Insurance Company of Germany." January 20, 1909. "Examination Reports, Domestic Companies, 1908–1910." Insurance Department, Examining Division, Box 2, Series 1049.

"United American Fire Insurance Company." July 17, 1905. "Examination Reports, Domestic Companies, 1903–1907," Insurance Department, Examining Division, Box 1, Series 1049.

"Utica Mutual ... Examination Reports." n.d. Insurance Department, Examining Division, Records of Merged, Withdrawn or Liquidated Insurance Companies, 1869-, Box 46, Series 1027.

"Warsaw Fire Insurance Company," April 18, 1912, "Examination Reports, Domestic Companies, 1911–1912," Insurance Department, Examining Division, Box 3, Series 1049.

"Western Relief Association." June 8, 1903. "Examination Reports, Domestic Companies, 1903–1907," Insurance Department, Examining Division, Box 1, Series 1049.

CHAPTER 4

Reinsurance in the Netherlands from 1800 till 1950: A Failure?

Ben P. A. Gales

4.1 A Missed Opportunity?

Insurance, both life and non-life, is a time-honored activity in the Netherlands; dedicated reinsurance much less so. Was this a missed opportunity? Some contemporaries worried and some historians are likely to answer the question positively. Let's first trace the evolution of insurance. Figure 4.1 shows the evolution between 1800 and 1920 of capital paid-in of limited liability companies. That is a partial indicator, but it traces the evolution of a major part of the main insurance sectors—sea, fire, life—taken together. Schuddebeurs collected the data about limited liability companies from the government gazette (Schuddebeurs 1928, p. 14). Tax data provide a second series (Vereeniging voor de Statistiek in Nederland 1882; Ministerie van Financiën 1861–1904; Centraal Bureau voor de Statistiek 1905–1920). The gap in the level before 1880 is an enigma,

---

B. P. A. Gales (✉)
Faculty of Economics, University of Groningen, Groningen, the Netherlands
e-mail: b.p.a.gales@rug.nl

© The Author(s), under exclusive license to Springer Nature Switzerland AG 2021
L. Caruana de las Cagigas and A. Straus (eds.), *Role of Reinsurance in the World*, Palgrave Studies in Economic History,
https://doi.org/10.1007/978-3-030-74002-3_4

but both series portray a consistent evolution.[1] The insurance business accelerated after 1840, to be followed by a remarkable crash after 1865. The second phase of growth from the 1890s onwards was nominal, for capital invested in insurance companies remained a stable percentage of national wealth.[2] The level did return after the bubble to the plane of the early nineteenth century.

The ups and downs of insurance is usually analyzed as institutional failure; the stagnation behind the simulacrum of growth is commonly overlooked. Historians neglect reinsurance in this debate of real or imagined failure of the bubble. Contemporaries, however, considered reinsurance, trying to make sense of the perplexing evolution. Some suggested that reinsurance was a missed opportunity. A domestic reinsurance business was the dream not achieved. Reality could and should have been different. There was an "insurance question" or affair and reinsurance was twice a piece of the controversy.

Just before the peak of the insurance boom, an upcoming politician, Heemskerk, suggested that there was still one weakness to fix: the lack of domestic reinsurance (Heemskerk 1854, p. 149).[3] He intervened in an acrimonious debate about liberalizing maritime insurance. In his eyes, Heemskerk identified a market failure. Supply of capital obviously was not the problem. There even were voices talking about an oversupply of capital. Heemskerk lamented that the boom had not attracted foreign business and that Dutch sea insurance was fragmented. Reinsurance should make good for the many units whose capacity to underwrite was exhausted soon and charm business from abroad. Reinsurance was not only a compensation for the existing market structure, it was foremost the mechanism to bring back the golden age, when "*not only natives, but*

---

[1] Schuddebeurs contacted the Dutch Central Bureau of Statistics, but the gap between both series before 1880 could not be explained.

[2] Smits et al. estimated national wealth from the inheritance tax (Smits et al. 2000, pp. 207–9). I extended the series from 1914 till 1920, using the estimates of Bonger, but choosing the level of Smits et al. (Bonger 1915, p. 228; Bonger 1923, p. 8).

[3] The "insurance question" of those days was the government pondering to self-insure more in the state-controlled trade with the East Indies. This would end exuberance among insurers, attracted by favourable conditions. Heemskerk, a moderate liberal, sided with insurers opposing liberalization.

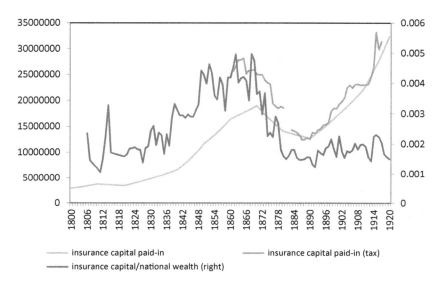

Fig. 4.1 Insurance capital paid-in (guilders) (*Source* Schuddebeurs [1928, p. 14], Vereeniging voor de Statistiek in Nederland [1882], Ministerie van Financiën [1861–1904], Centraal Bureau voor de Statistiek [1905–1920] and Smits et al. [2000])

also strangers prefer to insure here [in Amsterdam] *above in their own cities* (Le Moine de l'Espine 1753, pp. 39–40)".[4]

The golden age remained an era of the past. Even the "natives" increasingly looked elsewhere: both major transport and fire risks were underwritten in London or Berlin. In that context a second insurance affair popped up in 1904. The remaining Dutch transport insurers, in particular, were targeted as missing "the organization of reinsurance contracts". Firms still had enough capital and reserves, they did reinsure, but they were easy prey. The press highlighted that reinsurance forced Dutch firms to cooperate with foreign ones. British and German underwriters dominated the Dutch Association of Fire Insurance. The word Dutch in the name was deceitful, but the raison d'être of the cartel was more worrying. Was the association not created to increase premiums on

---

[4] Reprinting of Le Moine de l'Espine's book from 1694 stopped by 1800, but this kind of literature still set the level of aspiration during the 1850s.

industrial risks, particularly big warehouses in Amsterdam and Rotterdam (S. 1904; B. 1904)?[5] In the early 1900s, reinsurance had become a straightjacket for a weak domestic insurance industry.

So, reinsurance was perceived as a missed opportunity in any circumstance. As the missed opportunity to attract foreign business. As the missed opportunity to avoid foreign business. As the missed opportunity to achieve competitive strength. In short as the missed opportunity to create a national insurance industry of international standing. Was reinsurance truly an opportunity foregone?

4.2 Co-Insurance and Reinsurance

Reinsurance is a mechanism to manage the risks accepted by insurers. It allows a first insurer to accept more risk than he would do on his own. Already in 1370, Giuliano Grillo, the insurer who had issued a policy for a ship's voyage from Genoa to Sluys near Bruges, reinsured the more hazardous part from Cadiz to the Low Countries with Di Benavia and Maruffo. A broker had intermediated (Golding 1927, p. 20; Mossner 2012, pp. 28–34). Without the option, Giovanni Sacco might have found his ship not insurable. In a wide sense reinsurance in the Netherlands goes back a long time. An ordinance of the city of Amsterdam mentioned reinsurance for the first time in 1707. Manifest circulation of knowledge could be traced to that period as well. The year 1707, however, is late. One might even question whether this ruling truly aimed at reinsurance (Teding van Berkhout 1866, p. 27).[6] Since, archival traces have been found. The oldest is a cargo policy signed in 1592. These early traces are usually co-insurance, in this case of two individuals and as the third

---

[5] The association consisted of 34 foreign firms, 33 Dutch ones and 7 from the colonies. Rumour was that several of the Dutch members were in foreign hands. The existing standard warehouse policy limited the control of insurers. For the contracts lasted thirty years; furthermore, certificates on the value of goods circulated as money. Insurers underlined that premiums in the Netherlands were low, less than half of those on warehouses in Hamburg. The owners of warehouses focused upon declining damages. A negotiated solution ended the uproar. In 1923, something similar happened. The English fire insurers and reinsurers pushed through the so-called English tariff for industrial risks. They failed with simple fire risks in the 1930s.

[6] Teding van Berkhout observed that the regulation of 1707 might deal with reinsurance, but more likely dealt with taking a second policy, after the first one had been canceled or the insurer had gone bankrupt.

party an association, *Reynier de Loeker & Company* (Go et al. 2016, p. 5). Co-insurance expanded in tandem with the depth of the capital market. In the seventeenth century, big values could be insured and reinsured in Amsterdam. Complex contracting was normal; so, reinsurance was an integral part of bottomry since the late sixteenth century (Winkelman 1983, p. L–LI).

Co-insurance is the alternative to reinsurance proper: it is a contract underwritten by several risk-takers. Co-insurance was practiced in insurance exchanges. It remained long the dominant form of distributing risks. Over time, ships and cargoes or industrial risks would be underwritten by many more names than the three of 1592 and increasingly by firms. In 1903, thirty firms compensated a trading firm in Rotterdam for its stock of tobacco lost in a fire. The crowd consisted of 13 Dutch companies, 6 colonial ones and 11 firms from abroad. The foreign share in the risk was 60%. The Dutch firms had underwritten, on the average, 7000 guilders, the colonial offices a bit less, but the foreign companies 18,000, with the British firms reimbursing 24,000 guilders ("Brand" 1903).[7] The co-insurance environment was flexible enough to combine mobilization of a crowd for a wide range of sums to be insured on the one hand with on the other substantial variation in the preference for risk. And claims were paid without fuss, usually.

The contract of Grillo was "true" reinsurance by chance: it was a lucky circumstance that the trip could be parcelled. In a "true" reinsurance contract the reinsurer will have no relation with the insured. The insured only has a bond with the first or direct insurer (Mossner 2012, p. 44). Reality usually is complex. In many legal texts and historical works is the concept at first sight used misleadingly: reinsurance is confused with credit insurance (Ehrenberg 1885, p. 1). However, if inappropriate use is normal, then this practice should at least be considered, as we will do (Dooren de Jong 1929, pp. 81, 105).[8] A common alternative to the legal approach is to consider the layered spreading

---

[7] Not allocated to a specific firm was 12% of the reported damage.

[8] Ehrenberg already choose insuring against insolvency of an insurer as the very example of credit insurance wrongly labelled as re-insurance. The label, however, was common historically. Besides credit insurance, there were other practices with the insured "re-insuring". A Belgian court had to judge an insured who had "re-insured" his fire policy underwritten by Belges Réunis with Securitas. The intention was that Securitas would continue the insurance, when the first contract lapsed. The court deemed the transaction between the insured and his next insurer licit "re-insurance" (Overloop and Bastiné 1857).

of risks as a function of the risk to be covered. In this light Cummins and Weiss do distinguish four sets (Cummins and Weiss 2000, p. 164). Reinsurance is the domain of globally insurable risks, in contrast to the field of insurers specializing upon locally insurable risks. Tornadoes in the American Midwest and in Australia are big, but independent risks and thus insurable globally. However, insurability is not only a matter of the inherent properties of risk and scale. Very uncommon risks were insurable locally, while other common, but infrequent risks remained uninsurable: flooding in the Netherlands. Mutuality on a national level was enough for revolution insurance, as national pooling would be for reinsuring terrorism in the 2000s (Pot 1984; Haensel 1965; Organisation for Economic Co-operation and Development 2005).[9] Furthermore, historically reinsurance was a phenomenon within the domain of already insurable risks: it was an aspect of transport, fire or life insurance. That is the evolution to be sketched here.

4.3 BETWEEN GERMANY AND ENGLAND

The contrast between Britain and the German-speaking world is most characteristic of the evolution of reinsurance. Britain, the world's center of insurance, did not develop a major independent reinsurance industry. Haueter and Jones refer to the ban on marine reinsurance between 1746 and 1864 as the frequently invoked cause of the missed chance (Haueter and Jones 2017, p. 12). Both authors deem, rightly, the competitive strength of Lloyds more important; they, furthermore, stress the thriving co-insurance practices and the large size of British fire insurers. Reinsurance was not a technique superior all over. Other techniques, pricing based upon interaction within a community, were as good; possibly better. Using the famous concepts of R. Ehrenberg, opinion premiums were superior to experience premiums (Ehrenberg 1901, p. 378). Optimal risk sharing theory implies more generally that mutual trade, pooling, is optimal and the involvement of specialized reinsurers not (Borch 1962). Other factors of production than information were at work as well. Pure

---

Den Dooren de Jong argued that wrong, but common usage showed that the motivation for reinsuring had changed.

[9] Revolution or sabotage insurance became fashionable in the wake of the First World War. It was a kind of molest insurance. Employers insured the risk by mutual apportionment.

companies did not necessarily have an advantage in gathering risk capital; exchanges might do or arrangements between firms. The foregoing assessment is perhaps too simple. Admitting that it was economically rational for the British insurers with their comparative advantage to ignore reinsurance as a specialized business, Robin Pearson thinks it was after all a mistake not to seize a slice of a developing market. The British condemned themselves to the role of consumer in the niche. That was "*a relative failure*" (Pearson 1995, pp. 570–71). Still, a relative failure raises, as well as an absolute failure, the question whether and why opportunities were not seen.

France initially looked like the world's leader for reinsurance, but in the long run the German-speaking world dominated the world's markets. Of the 143 reinsurance firms active in Europe by the First World War, 58 were domiciled either in Germany or Austria. The German–Austrian share of sales was larger: almost half (Mailluchet 1917, pp. 93–94).[10] In 1913, premium income of the seven largest non-German reinsurance companies, including two Austrian ones and *Swiss Re*, was around 70% of the income of *Munich Re* alone. It was 40% of the four biggest German firms. Two-thirds of the premiums received in Germany came from abroad (Kißkalt 1924, p. 45; Umbach 2008, p. 346).

International leadership was the outcome of national specifics. The domestic German and Austrian insurance markets were heterogeneous; in particular, fire. These heterogeneous markets were filled by small enterprises heavily dependent upon reinsurance. Not characteristics of risks shaped the evolution, but characteristics of markets, in combination with a path-dependent evolution. The latter is a process with a start, often a coincidence, which vigorously shapes outcomes much later. Supply did not change much over 170 years, once reinsurance had been brought into being. Still, path-dependent processes can be disrupted. During the First World War, "a country as (apparently) unlikely as Denmark" became the number two worldwide in the export of reinsurance (Haueter and Jones 2017, pp. 12–13).[11] Contemporaries thought a new pattern was

---

[10] The German–Austrian share was in reality bigger. The Russian companies, covering 20% of European business, were controlled by German ones.

[11] Haueter and Jones stress that defection of Russian reinsurers helped the rise of Denmark. At the time, Denmark was a sensitive benchmark in the Netherlands. Performing as Denmark stood for performing as one could expect of a small, agricultural economy without colonies. The Netherlands should do better.

emerging, mistakenly. Dutch insiders expected to emulate the Danish "revolution", with some French help: a miscalculation, though not fully (Grossmann 1918).

The Netherlands was and is an economy in between the British and German world. The insurance industry had some German characteristics. Insurance business was intensely fragmented. Many small firms were active in just one branch. Composite offices, combining fire and transport insurance or life and non-life, were rare. Over time, market leaders emerged, but their market shares were hardly impressive. Entry remained easy and the business crowded. Practices, however, were Anglo-Saxon. An illustration is the bookkeeping custom noticed in the world of international reinsurance: Dutch non-life firms matched underwriting reserves and actual requirements. Surplus funds went into general reserves. The continental tradition was to use surpluses to increase underwriting reserves ("Dutch Insurance Conditions" 1940).[12] Practices were embedded in an institutional setting. As in Britain, insurance exchanges were old and prominent. As in Britain, pure reinsurance virtually did not exist in the Netherlands. That is, reinsurance did not exist as a separate, national business.

Not much is known about early practices other than co-insurance. Cession of an accepted risk to other direct insurers might have arisen in the periphery, say Rotterdam instead of Amsterdam. The first publicly quoted company doing transport (and some fire) insurance, the *"Maatschappij van assurantie, discontering en beleening der stad Rotterdam"* of 1720, ceded West-Indian risks to London in 1726. It was a case of regret about existing policies: the first hostilities of the English–Spanish war changed the mind. This was a common motive at the time, but not the regular reinsurance of later. The company did not start accepting risks from fire insurers till 1865 (Dooren de Jong 1929, p. 112; Laar and Vleesenbeek 1990, pp. 45–46, 56, 67–68). In Antwerp, another minor center, a company ceded and accepted risks of other insurers regularly and internationally after the mid-eighteenth century (Couvreur 1936, p. 167). Running reinsurance—transfer no longer confined to individual risks each with facultative acceptance—was first attempted in

---

[12] "The custom did not necessarily make profits transparent. Dutch companies concealed profits in working reserves ("Dutch insurance companies" 1929).

Brussels in 1821 (Golding 1927, pp. 44–46; Koch 1978, p. 138).[13] At this time, Belgium and the Netherlands were an united kingdom. The contract was partially a case of completely reinsuring a portfolio in liquidation, again a special case of reinsuring. The French company involved had insured fire risks before it had been allowed to do business in the Netherlands and thus had a problem when entry was refused (Mossner 2012, p. 88–89).[14] This explains the transborder nature of the contract, while the just established Belgian *Compagnie des Propriétaires Réunis* sought a senior partner. There are hardly any data about common facultative and obligatory treaty-based reinsurance, so it is hard to fathom the evolution. One factor is easily observed. While the insurance business expanded in the Netherlands and even more in the Belgian south, organizational choice stunted diffusion of reinsurance. Many companies were created as mutual and a mutual did not venture easily or at all in reinsuring before the 1860s.[15]

The pure reinsurance business emerged in the western parts of Germany. In 1837, foreign direct insurers in fire were expelled from the Prussian market. The policy resulted in "insurance distress". French and Belgian, but also British offices had captured a substantial market share, especially in the Rhineland. In 1822, top officials had characterized Düsseldorf "a war-theatre of foreign insuring" (*Aachener und Münchener* 1925, pp. 11–12).[16] Domestic insurers could not cope easily with

---

[13] Mossner underlines that the treaty in Brussels created an institutional bond, but that it was not truly obligatory, as older literature claims (Mossner 2012, p. 91).

[14] Kyrtsis wrongly identifies the *Compagnie Royale d'Assurance contre l'Incendie* as Dutch. It was a French major. Kyrtsis neglects the role of the state: the French company was refused entry after it had started (Kyrtsis 2006, p. 153). Regulation was policy, not law. Dutch historians assume that the prohibition of foreign activity was a dead letter and not known (*Gedenkboek ter gelegenheid* 1957, p. 342). This is not accurate. Dutch contemporaries, however, were uncertain. In the 1830s, the insurers of Amsterdam organized a pressure group to engineer a formal prohibition; the administration preferred policy.

[15] Insurance companies were often not integrated and that complicates the matter. The bylaws of the *Onderlinge Brandwaarborg-Maatschappij* of 1809, a major provincial, allowed reinsuring on behalf of the mutual since 1864. Previously, the firm managing the mutual, an autonomous unit, had reinsured on its expense. The managing firm was active on the exchange and in transport since the early 1820s (*De Onderlinge Brandwaarborg-Maatschappij* 1909, pp. 204, 208–9).

[16] The Rhineland had been part of France between the 1790s and 1814 and had kept the Napoleonic legal system.

demand after 1837. They had to cede part of their risks abroad, which was tolerated by the authorities. The gap also induced organizational innovation: dedicated reinsurance institutions.

This organizational innovation happened very close to the Dutch border, was even inspired by what happened on the Dutch side. In 1842 the *Rückversicherungsverein* was created by the *Niederrheinische Güter-Assekuranz-Gesellschaft* in Wesel, 50 km from the frontier. The transport-insurance company had already established an internal reinsurance association among its shareholders two years earlier. The company of Wesel had intended to reinsure a third of its portfolio in Paris, but negotiations failed (Borscheid 2006, p. 50).[17] This reinsurance firm was a running mate or captive of an established direct insurer.[18] The *Aachener-Rückversicherungs-Gesellschaft* dates formally from 1853, but the roots go back to 1842. This daughter company of the *Aachener und Münchener Feuer-Versicherungs-Gesellschaft* from 1825 was domiciled within walking distance of the Dutch border. The first independent reinsurer was the *Kölnische Rückversicherungs-Gesellschaft*, an initiative of the Colonia and, in particular, of a manager who had come from Wesel. The *Kölnische Rück* was established in 1843, but was not operational before 1852.[19] Transport and fire were the preferred domains of reinsurance. Already in the 1850s reinsurance companies showed an interest in life insurance, but the *Kölnische Rück* abandoned the field in 1860, because there was no demand (Hollitscher 1931, p. 172).[20] Contacts between Wesel, Aachen and Cologne on the one hand and the Netherlands on the other were intimate. The "land without frontiers" was economically integrated and knowledge about experiments in insurance was readily available everywhere. However, the very border of 1816 seems a line dividing two areas

---

[17] In February 1841, the *Companie d'assurances générales* of Paris was allowed to operate in Rhineland.

[18] In June 1840, stockholders were asked to participate in an internal association. The associated "stockholders" would get one third of the net premiums against one third of the potential damages. The association was formed for a year and the experiment was prolonged for another one. In December 1842, the association was transformed into a captive business with stock and the captive was approved by the state a year later.

[19] The company of Wesel was and still is referred to as the first professional reinsurance company in the world; the one of Cologne as the first independent reinsurance company. This is also the traditional view in Dutch literature (Niemeijer 1926, p. 9).

[20] Swiss Re was the only reinsurance firm active in life between 1865 and 1880.

differing in how insurance markets worked. To the east, one adopted specialized reinsurance, and none on the western side.

The line did not mark a difference in capacity to innovate. The origin of the experiments even lay in the west, but Dutch promoters also turned to the east. The company of Wesel of 1842 was an emulation of the *Nederlandsche Algemeene Verzekering Maatschappij* of 1837. This company was the captive of a Dutch fire-insurance firm, which had been established in Tiel in 1833. The provincial town was a harbour at the main branch of the Rhine, not far from the border.[21] The Dutch company was to become one of the "provincial" majors in fire. In its early years, however, the firm diversified in insuring sea and river transport (Schuddebeurs 1928, pp. 68–70). Its captive daughter for transport insurance inspired the creation of the *Niederrheinische Güter-Assekuranz-Gesellschaft* in the late 1830s (*100 Jahre Kölnische* 1953, p. 12; Gerathewohl 1979, p. 738, n. 165). Less known is that the company from Tiel established the *Nederlandsche Algemeene Verzekering Societeit tegen Zee- en Rivierschade* early in 1840. This society could underwrite sea risks, but it would only accept river-transport risks as reinsurance of the company of 1837 ("Naamlooze Vennootschappen" 1840).[22] This was an even earlier example of running mate reinsurance than the initiative in Wesel.

Reinsurance might have been something of a "collective" effort. Umbach mentions that both the company from Tiel and the one from Wesel entered a joint venture in 1840. The Dutch company left its agents in Rhineland to its partner, while the latter transferred half of the business generated by those agents to Tiel, cemented by a reinsurance treaty (Umbach 2006, p. 422). I did not find corroboration. In any case, the joint venture did not last. The Dutch company expanded along the Rhine and reached Bavaria in 1841, just after the company from Wesel ("Niederländische Versicherungsgesellschaft" 1854). More tellingly, the company of Tiel soon found another partner. In 1845, the company of 1837 became the partner of the *Düsseldorfer Allgemeine Versicherungs Gesellschaft*. It paid half of the share capital and an association was created with treaty reinsurance. Reinsurance in transport would become

---

[21] The sandbars in the river made Tiel notorious in the Rhineland. Till 1850, the risk of transporting over the Rhine was higher than sea transport. Compare *De Stad Rotterdam* and *Wed. Van Bosse*, assuming these firms represent sea respectively Rhine, in Horlings' thesis (Horlings 1995, p. 434).

[22] The press brought the news before the Official Gazette ("Binnenland" 1840).

a specialty of the *Düsseldorfer* (Schuddebeurs 1928, p. 42; "Allerhöchste Bestätigung" 1846).[23]

Partnerships seem a less intense kind of operating in a foreign country, a half retreat, but that impression would be misleading. The company from Tiel was itself active in Germany during the birth of specialized reinsurance. Already in 1841, the Dutch firm had been the foreign participant in a group, which agreed to work with the same conditions and premiums in Cologne. Soon, in 1843, the group manifested itself as the *Association of Insurance Companies of Rhineland*. The press speculated whether this was a reinsurance group. In the end, trade newspapers thought this unlikely: legal identities should prevent institutionalised solidarity (Gothein 1916, p. 441).[24] The *Niederrheinische* of Wesel stayed outside the Association in contrast to *Colonia*, the leader in Cologne and later promotor of *Kölnische Rück*. Was pooling perhaps an alternative to the Wesel option of a dedicated institution? The skeptical reception of pooling explains the focus upon specialization and independence in the next phase of experimenting in Cologne. The promotors of reinsurance around *Colonia* concluded that a dedicated firm was more likely to be accepted (Koch 2012, p. 86; Bähr and Kopper 2015, p. 19). Independent enterprise could better cope with the fear that valuable information might leak to competitors.[25]

The later evolution of the companies reflected national patterns. The general insurance company of Tiel remained foremost a direct insurer. The company abandoned transport insurance in 1882 at the latest and

---

[23] The association probably had to guarantee continued entry to the Prussian market. For the company from Tiel itself was not registered as a foreign company with approved agents. However, the combination was labelled as active in 1849 ("Versicherungen gegen Gefahr" 1853, pp. 539–40; Koch 2012, pp. 79–80).

[24] On the association and whether it had any surplus value above the participants insuring individually, see "Vereinigung Rhein. Versicherungsgesellschaften" (1843). The newspaper argued that the Dutch member could not be taken seriously, for foreigners only could start legal procedures in the Netherlands with difficulty. This is correct. Still in 1864, a suitcase of the *Rheinschiffahrt Assecuranz-Gesellschaft* of Mainz against a Dutch partner was judged inadmissible. The firm from Mainz was a foreign limited liability company without royal approval. The supreme court decided otherwise two years later.

[25] The birth of the Kölnische Rück took so long, because it looked an ancillary of Colonia. See also on the information externalities and on disciplining direct insurers: *100 Jahre* Kölnische (1953, pp. 15, 23, 34, 60, 64).

concentrated successfully on fire.[26] The German companies located in Wesel and Düsseldorf remained both transport insurers and reinsurers of repute, with a "global" presence till the First World War.

The contrasts between both sides of the border and between the trajectories were not a consequence of knowledge or entrepreneurship, but might be caused by the environment. Capital was less abundant in Germany than in the Netherlands. Interest was lower in the Netherlands till the end of the nineteenth century. Mercantilist notions of preserving capital and profits for the domestic economy motivated contemporaries, even in such an open city as Cologne. Insurers even called for a German National Reinsurance Association (Bähr and Kopper 2015, pp. 18–19; Bühlmann and Lengwiler 2006, p. 128).[27] The fear for information leaking suggests that trust and reputation worked less well as mechanisms to cope with information externalities in the Rhineland (and the German-speaking world) than in the regions to the west. Were traders and insurers in Amsterdam and London perhaps more homogeneous communities than those in the Rhineland or Germany? Heterogeneous societies fail in providing public goods.

These commonly invoked factors are, however, problematic. How seriously should the patriotic motive be taken, except that it was convenient to market ideas, as would be the case again after 1918? The scarcity of capital for infrastructure and industrialization, first in the Rhineland, later the Ruhr, is not as convincing as it looks. Indeed, in 1844, both the company from Tiel and the one from Wesel participated in the flotation of the *Rheinpreußisch Niederländischen Dampfschleppschiffahrtsgesellschaft*, a new company for steam tugboats. This was an example of mobilizing capital through insurance. However, investment was not allocated exclusively to companies of capital-scarce Prussia; it did go to Dutch companies as well (Schawacht 1973, p. 138, 161).[28] Furthermore, Cologne was defined as capital-abundant (or as one lacking investment options) at the very moment the appropriate share capital of the *Kölnische Rück* had to

---

[26] The last reference I found about the Tiel-based running mate reinsuring river transport dates from the mid-1860s. The mother left the field in the 1870s.

[27] In 1842, the founding fathers of the Kölnische Rück limited the potential world of their reinsurance business to German and Austrian financial centers (*100 Jahre Kölnische* 1953, p. 25).

[28] R. Tilly argued that insurance companies substituted for (investment) banks in the Rhineland (Tilly 1966, pp. 121–26).

be defined (*100 Jahre Kölnische* 1953, p. 50; Tilly 1980, p. 267). More generally, was the gap in the level of interest or were the frictions in the capital market so big that it explains the varying paths taken?

The beginning of reinsurance was determined by institutional shocks more than by insurance ones.[29] As we saw, protectionism created insurance distress in Germany. Supervision also imposed a demand for capital higher than in the Netherlands.[30] A cultural difference in cooperating informally might have been a factor with lasting impact upon organizational choice. For it entailed a feedback mechanism: why change, if co-insurance works smoothly? And it will work smoothly, if it is habitual.[31] Other aspects of trust are hard to accept as a factor explaining the contrast between the Netherlands and western Germany. Was the Rhineland a society with another level of trust than the communities to the west? Lastly, composition matters, but is hard to trace. In marine, but also in (non-provincial) fire insurance, the Dutch specialized gradually upon intermediation instead of underwriting.[32] Indicative is the company of Tiel leaving, in 1877, the Berlin-based association of transport insurers (Frenzl 1924, p, 136).[33] The big and the special risks were intermediated to Lloyds. Foreign and in particular German underwriters had a substantial market share in the ports of Rotterdam and Amsterdam and the First World War and hyperinflation did not change this (Gales and Gerwen 1988, pp. 57–60; Kracht 1922; Umbach 2008, pp. 275–76). In the present context it is important that this shift to intermediation diminished the demand for reinsurance in Holland.

---

[29] The fire of Hamburg in 1842, supposedly stimulating reinsurance, is presented as proof that people only learn by burning themselves first (Ferguson 2008, p. 186).

[30] The insurance company from Tiel had 80% of shares *not* paid in; the Düsseldorfer had to collect 80% before it could start (Masius 1846, p. 669). There are counter examples to the pattern. In 1839, the company of Wesel could start with 10% capital paid-in, the *Kölnische Rück* with 20%. In Cologne, the absolute sum was a matter of contention (*100 Jahre Kölnische* 1953, pp. 49–56).

[31] An insider wrote, that the exchange was to the Dutchman what the alehouse was to the German (Mees 1871, p. 13).

[32] It was not different in Hamburg (Kiesselbach 1901, pp. 72, 76, 86–87, Anlage 8). However, German transport insurers were very profitable around 1880 (Frenzl 1924, p. 31, 149; Umbach 2006, p. 418).

[33] The Dutch company had been a member of the association since its start in 1874.

4.4 Reinsurance and Life Insurance

Can we say more about reinsurance activity in absence of a domestic reinsurance business? I will concentrate upon life insurance, though it was not the niche most alluring to reinsuring. Life gradually became the most important branch in the Netherlands and its business practices are relatively well documented.

In this sector too, reinsurance was frequently used wrongly, but the habit signals what the culture of risk looked like. Besides reinsurance by the insurer, the "proper" idea, handbooks also identified "return-insurance" of the insured. Return-insurance was insuring the solvency of one's insurer. A second insurance was taken. It was credit insurance labelled as reinsurance. This practice was stimulated by the tontine format of much early life insuring. Tontine constructions were coupled with "re-insurance" of the premiums. The solvency of the insurer was not the concern, but the loss of capital paid. Tontines were a common, if not the most common kind of life contracts till well into the nineteenth century. They were also the most important product of the first life insurance offices. The tontine tradition lasted, even when tontine groups as such had been phased out by the companies. The query reinsurance in the database of Dutch historical newspapers, Delpher, is indicative. Most hits refer to the advertisement of the *Hollandsche Societeit* of 1807, highlighting its *"widow- and orphans-insurance with or without reinsurance of premiums or capital paid"*. The *Victoria* of Berlin let readers know that for each premium paid yearly, the insured would get *"an unassailable proof of reassurance"* (Delpher 2020).

Why was such a proof necessary? Insurance implied that customers had a claim, but the long spacing between payment and benefit was worrisome. A double—or triple—security had to be used to increase trust. The need for "re-insurance" signaled also that the dreaded overstretch had been addressed. The insured felt uneasy about insurers accepting risks without limitation. Much insurance practice consisted of signaling restraint and creating constraint. The insured themselves tended to partition stakes. Perhaps more so when income was low, for the custom is documented more for industrial than ordinary life. Within funeral insurance, the insured with two or more policies increased. Testimonies indicate that these were issued by different companies.[34] It must have been a strategy of a minority, though. Movement from one fund to the other was the common strategy to insure against the default of the insurer. Still, by 1900 there were more policies than clients; not much later, there were more than the total population. Quietly some people co-insured themselves.

The function of proper reinsurance was to let an insurer go beyond his self-imposed constraints. That option was rarely needed in life. To start with, because the internal constraints were also the public ones. The first funeral funds would insure just one sum or a specified service in kind. Variation was a market phenomenon. Growth both increased the number of identical units and led to mutation. Institutions chose their niches; different niches allowed potential customers to choose. Separate institutions underwrote different sums. Occasionally, there was some in-house variation, but it was limited. A fund offered a choice between a big and a small "box". The risks were, furthermore, only specified with uncertainty. Funds could change the benefit or the premium in the light of the times and their financial state. This was the contractual flexibility peculiar to mutual insuring: unalterable commitments weighed less. The bigger funds, however, constrained their flexibility: emergency measures as a reduction of the benefit could only last for three months.

From the 1840s onwards, some companies selling industrial insurance became national organizations. The local format worked also for mass business. Risk management was therefore not radically different. The big industrial insurers offered a range of insurable sums, three, six or twelve classes. Some homogenized risks using geographical units: an Amsterdam section and a country-side one. Classes and the bigger geographical scope increased the minimum efficient scale of spreading risk. Still, statutes and habits defined maxima for policies. Limited liability companies in particular were bound by regulation by the state, at least till 1881.[35] Life insurers outside the scope of the state's supervision could change bylaws

---

[34] This kind of behaviour by the insured was not necessarily strategic, but was occasionally framed so by observers (Staatscommissie 1892, p. 81). The Royal Commission argued also that double insuring was more prevalent under Catholics and tried to explain why.

[35] In life, supervision by the state implied that the statutes were officially checked and a company then was approved. The procedure was a choice, in that sense one could choose to use limited liability or not.

with less hassle, but had to cope with the received wisdom of the public and, foremost, of intermediaries.

Business evolved gradually, so did revealed risk preference, though new markets might produce jumps. Take the example of the *Dordrecht*, one of the more enterprising companies. In 1836, a family head of a middle-class family had become agent of a funeral fund for the town of Dordrecht. The eldest son created a fund of his own in 1862. With relatives, he setup an office of administration a decade later. The prime intention was to add a life-insurance company: *the Dordrecht*. Institutional change was also an evolution in risk taking. The funeral fund insured sums between 46 and 81 guilders. The new company initially considered benefits between 50 and 500 guilders. As a limited liability company, the projected *Dordrecht* had to seek official approval and management learned much in this tedious process. In turn, knowledge raised ambitions. An indication was the rise of the insurable maximum to 1000 and in the end to 10,000 guilders. Those 1000 guilders—around three times the yearly average wage—was not unusual as a maximum among the larger industrial insurance companies. The 10,000 guilders signaled the ambition to enter ordinary or big life insurance. The maximum of 10,000 guilders was frowned upon by the government's advisor. However, the applicants, management, prevailed. Evolution did not end when *the Dordrecht* entered the market in 1874 as an approved company. After a few years, the reference to a maximum insurable sum was taken out of the bylaws. The company could now insure any sum, provided the risk was not more than 2.5% of the capital paid-in. This defined the sum retained. In the 1880s, that was 25,000 guilders. In practice, the company initially used 10,000 guilders, then 12,500 as a limit. In the 1890s, acceptable risk varied between 12,500 and 25,000 guilders. Management, however, promised itself, "*not to be zealous*"; it thus opted in principle for the lower bound. In 1896 the company went to the (statutory) 25,000 guilders as a norm. Management underlined in 1902 that this was not "scientific". For the norm had no relation whatsoever with characteristics of the portfolio insured. Management regularly struggled with perceived frictions between (actuarial) science and practice—it hired prominent actuarial advisors—but the top management decided to stick with practice.

Reinsurance matches the gap between acceptance and retention of risks. Unlimited acceptance thus created room for reinsurance and stimulated this business. The possibilities for reinsuring varied. The kind of market was a factor, also the market position of the individual company and, of course, the choice between either limiting beforehand the risks to be accepted or trusting upon cession after acceptance. All this created a complex dynamic. Industrial insurers stuck to the funeral fund tradition of limiting risks. These firms did not engage at all in reinsurance or the level was minimal, say one percent of gross premiums. In time, industrial insurance gradually overlapped with ordinary or big life insurance, both the products and the firms, but the sector remained a world apart till well into the twentieth century.

In ordinary life, reinsurance was more substantial, but not from the start. The *Hollandsche Societeit* was the first Dutch limited liability company in life. It was established in 1807. Reinsurance was discussed at the start, but partners were not easily found. Transferring risks abroad or to exchanges was not an option for the founders, though they were well connected with the financial world. It was the period of the Napoleonic wars, foreign markets were thin anyway and transactions with "lives" easily smacked of illicit speculation. Prudent acceptance was the alternative, made more transparent, in 1818, with placing maxima on individual policies. The trend of the maxima was initially downwards. From 1818 onwards, the *Hollandsche Societeit* worked with 25,000 guilders, half of its first policy. In 1848, this maximum was reduced to 10,000 for the Indies and for Europe to 20,000 in 1852. Insurable sums only became indefinite later in the century, though constrained by the companies' capital (*Gedenkboek ter gelegenheid* 1907, pp. 77–78, 117). By then reinsurance must have become an option. The company histories, however, are silent on the topic, though they reveal that formal rules did not fully determine practice. In the early 1920s, amidst a severe crisis in life insurance, the company discouraged intermediaries from bringing in big applications. Management wanted to minimize its dependence upon others through reinsurance (*Gedenkboek ter gelegenheid* 1957, p. 65).

Older companies generally saw less of a need to reinsure, though age might just be primogeniture and market strength. The *Nillmij* of 1859 had a dominant position in "big" life in the East Indies. This company started to reinsurance fifty years after its birth (*Gedenkboek 1859–1909* 1909, pp. 163–64). The common dynamic in ordinary life was an opposite life cycle, in combination with a level determined by the products on offer. The switch from industrial to ordinary life, implied instantaneously that *the Dordrecht* engaged more in reinsurance. Reinsurance was then more important during the early years of building up the ordinary life portfolio. Reinsurance required one percent of gross premiums in 1885, but 17 in 1890. After this peak, the number dropped.

Did expansion abroad stimulate the demand for insurance? Haueter and Jones suggest that in this context "piggybacking" was likely. Insurance companies going abroad were interested in information about foreign markets. They could collect it efficiently by profiting from other insurers' ventures in new markets or from the (foreign) partner contracted in the market envisaged. This was why and how British companies used reinsurance outside Britain (Haueter and Jones 2017, p. 12). The *Dordrecht* experienced something like piggybacking in the early 1890s. In France, substantially more large policies were insured directly after the company acquired a better position in reinsuring French companies.[36] Agents could perhaps identify better local possibilities, once they had tapped into the reinsurance of partner competitors. However, the use of information externalities must have been limited. Domestically, where the externality should have existed too, the mechanism—or the perception that such mechanism existed—was a hurdle for attempts to set up reciprocal reinsurance between competitors of the same nationality. In the context of internationalization, piggybacking on either domestic firms internationalizing or on foreign firms confronted with entry, must have met a similar hurdle. An entrant from elsewhere did not differ from a domestic competitor in this respect. A game between internationalizing firms of the same nationality was not likely to occur. The number of Dutch insurers going abroad, in life, but also fire, was small and each firm had its own foreign market.

There was one exception: entering the Dutch East Indies was an ambition several companies shared. Here, obligatory sharing was preferred, at least initially. In the late 1880s, the *Dordrecht* and the *Eerste Nederlandsche* contacted each other about their plans. In a contract they promised mutually to reinsure half of the new policies. Quota sharing reduced risk in a simple way. In 1894, having learned that the market was not that risky, both companies switched to the normal reinsurance practice of passing on the surplus above retention. Bonds were loosened, because companies expected to profit by generating growth independently. Identical constructions were used in non-colonial contexts. Even more often,

---

[36] I do not specify the documents kept in the AEGON archive. Information about the *Dordrecht* was mainly collected from the so-called "*Geheim Verslag*"; about the *Vennootschap Nederland* from the "*Notulen van de commissarissen*".

a company interested in entering a new market abroad teamed up with one determined to remain an outsider. The *Royal Belge* approached the *Vennootschap Nederland* about projects in Denmark and Italy in 1886. The *Vennootschap Nederland* did not intend to set up a business of its own in these countries. But the company was interested in the indirect business of taking over half of the contracts and to participate in the costs of establishment, through exclusive provisions. The *Royal Belge* was a special case, a quasi-relative. This was certainly not the *Nationale Levensverzekerings Bank*. Aiming to conquer the Scandinavian market in 1902, it offered the *Vennootschap Nederland* a sharing contract identical to the one made for the Dutch Indies between the *Dordrecht* and the *Eerste Nederlandsche*.

Before companies tried to find partners, they had to consider the implications for their own organization of expanding abroad. The acceptable level of risk possibly had to be increased. Companies could change bylaws or increase capital paid-in. They, however, stayed aloof from capital markets and rarely changed articles of association. It is therefore to be expected that formal retention changed with internationalization. When the *Vennootschap Nederland* was setting up a branch in the United States, the level of risk-taking was internally a major issue of contention (Gales 2007, p. 87–90). At the onset of the venture in 1893, management proposed to increase own risk from 50,000 to 250,000 guilders. The vote of the board of directors was divided equally. Thereupon, the maximum was put at 100,000. As usual, these numbers were theoretical. In practice, the company retained 5000 guilders and it had only increased the level to 10,000, shortly before the American project popped up. It is unknown whether the gap between theoretical and practical retention decreased under the impact of the dramatic events in the United States. The project was in the end a painful failure due to excess growth. Overall, there was not a strict relation between risk keeping and going international. The impact of globalization upon reinsurance was therefore ambiguous.

Coming back to the *Dordrecht*, actual retention was increased at one stroke from 12,500 guilders to 25,000 in 1896, the statutory level. There is no clear link with the international activities of the company. That was so with the next major change too. In 1912, management of the *Dordrecht* doubled retention, only to undo this in 1913. The background for this reversal was failed talks followed by successful ones with competitors about cooperation, perhaps merging. All in all, internationalization had no substantial impact upon reinsurance.

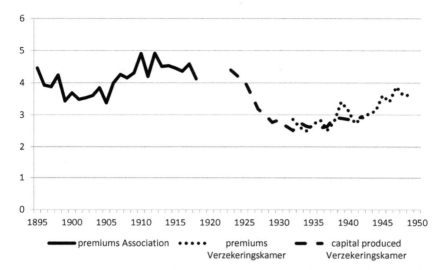

Fig. 4.2 Share of premiums reinsured in gross premiums and share of capital reinsured in production (percent) (*Source* Vereeniging voor Levensverzekering; Verzekeringskamer)

The *Association for Life Insurance* published data of its members in a common format (Vereeniging voor Levensverzekering 1890–1921).[37] The share of reinsurance of 26 (out of 27) companies in gross premium income was 4.6% in 1913. Reinsurance here is limited to outgoing reinsurance. Variation was big. Five companies reinsured one percent of premium income or less, three 19 to 20%. Figure 4.2 shows the evolution over time of premiums reinsured (or the reinsured production of capital) as percentage of gross premiums (total production). The data of the association were linked with those of the Board for Insurance for the interwar years (Verzekeringskamer 1924–1950).[38] In life, the demand for reinsurance was stable. Entry and expansion around 1900 exerted a slight upward movement. The financial crisis of the early 1920s brought the level somewhat down. It is not obvious that reorganization and reduced concentration were the causes. The retreat from foreign markets did on

---

[37] There are several problems, the major one that the population of companies changed.
[38] The Board's indicator 'premium reserve reinsured' is not reported here.

its own increase the level, because the *Algemeene*, by far the biggest international, reinsured very little. It is hard to establish any cross-sectional pattern. In 1913, size mattered, but statistically not enough. The impact of age was weak, but more noticeable: younger companies reinsured more. Reinsurance thus eased entry into the market. The weight of reinsurance also varied significantly between "globalizers", between 1 and 6% of gross premiums received by the two companies with big and old foreign portfolios; between 0 and 10%, if another two with a small portfolio abroad are included. One might think that the option to reinsure would be negatively related to the sums rejected by the direct insurers. The sign was in fact positive. This too should be labelled chance, the more so because there is no compelling reason to think that medical selection and reinsurance should be linked.[39]

International comparisons show that the level of outgoing reinsurance in the Netherlands was both relatively low and stable. Belgian companies reinsured three, four times more. Premiums paid were between 13 and 15% of gross premiums in the late 1930s (Dievoet 1940, pp. 272–74).[40] In Switzerland the level was rather stable at 9% between 1901 and 1929. In Norway levels doubled from 6 to 9% around 1900 to more than 20 by the start of the interwar period. In international comparisons as well, it is hard to see a pattern. Hollitscher proposed an interesting hypothesis: life reinsurance signaled that pure reinsurance companies had successfully fenced in markets. The international growth in life reinsurance was a matter of market power and it had to be so, because under normal conditions the demand was very small. A comparison with Germany, the country with the most market power, might then be most telling. Hollitscher argued that *Munich Re* first got a grip on German firms and then commanded the foreign ones. Primarily those in Austria-Hungary, but Dutch firms were targeted too. The (relative) importance of reinsurance should be a first indicator of this market power. In 1900, the German level was at 2% lower than the Dutch one. However, it increased gradually and the gap disappeared during the war years. If there was market power, then it was hardly spectacular. After 1924, a quarter or more of the premiums received in Germany were reinsured. This high level—and

---

[39] Kader et al. found that investment substituted for reinsurance in Swedish fire insurance during the interwar years. The database of Dutch life around 1913 used here is imperfect, but this factor was the weakest one (Kader et al. 2010, pp. 278–79).

[40] I did not include the foreign companies active in Belgium.

the high ones observed in some other countries–probably can be better explained by the war, by postwar uncertainty and domestic particularities. Market power did, in any case, not impact structurally the Dutch level (Hollitscher 1931, pp. 172–73, 182; Statistischer Teil pp. 13, 43–44, 58).[41]

4.5 Networking and Unequal Exchange

Reinsurance was a network activity among insurers. The Dutch *Vennootschap Nederland* was approached by a Belgian company, the *Royal Belge* in the 1880s. International contacts were remarkable then, but this one was not: It was the path-dependent outcome of birth. Both companies had been creations of the "*Napoleon of financiers*", A. Langrand Dumonceau. He had established more institutions which survived the collapse of his empire, like the Austrian *Der Anker*. These companies operated as an informal collective, sharing and distributing markets. That remained so after the spectacular undoing of Langrand Dumonceau. After the first contacts about internationalization, the *Vennootschap Nederland* hoped to specialize in reinsuring on behalf of the *Royal Belge*. Old networks so enabled a firm to tiptoe into new ones. For acting as the preferred reinsurer of the *Royal Belge*, the *Vennootschap Nederland* hoped to become partner of the *Assicurazione Generali*.

It is not easy to find solid and more general information about the networks. For example, it is hard to know whether the *Vennootschap Nederland* was representative in its preference for reinsuring abroad. The network of the *Dordrecht* suggests at first sight that internationalization was not preferred. The *Dordrecht* started with contacting national companies. It first ceded a surplus to the *Eerste Nederlandsche*; the internationally active *Vennootschap Nederland* was the sixth in the row of companies to contact. It is hard to see a clear pattern in the ranking: neither size nor international orientation were dominant factors. Personal or path-dependent contacts probably mattered most. Some companies were hard to get. In the 1890s, the *Hollandsche Societeit* of 1807, was

---

[41] The market-power idea was inspired by the participations of *Munich Re*. An eminent Dutch insurer commented positively on the creation of large, composite offices by mergers under guidance of German reinsuring companies (Holwerda 1924, p. 404). This road was not taken in the Netherlands at the time. Foreign guidance was considered, as we saw earlier, a failure: the second insurance affair.

coveted as the oldest and most solid Dutch life company, one that only accepted risks on its own premium and conditions. It forced as it were a new insurance instead of negotiating a deal. The *Hollandsche Societeit* did therefore not belong to the domestic network of the *Dordrecht*. Revealed preference was an indicator of what would later happen during the first wave of mergers. In the wake of the First World War, the domestic portfolio of the *Dordrecht* was acquired by the *Eerste Nederlandsche*. Reinsurance contracts lasted long, fed upon reputation, and that eased takeovers.

The strategy of the Dordrecht was in all likelihood not representative; the predilection of the *Vennootschap Nederland* for foreign business was. For the *Dordrecht* started to cede its surplus across borders from 1897 onwards. It created a relation with the *Swiss Re* and *Kölnische Rück*. It did so, though management saw this as second best. The problem was that the other Dutch companies had not much to offer. They traditionally reinsured abroad. The aversion of the top management of the *Dordrecht* to be forced to work with specialized, foreign reinsurers was noticeable till the First World War. This constitutes an interesting conundrum. The *Dordrecht* belonged to the small group of truly international companies. These internationals in particular preferred a domestic reinsurance network. The nationals, the majority, tended to go abroad, though hard, overall data are lacking and the share of reciprocal domestic insurance versus transborder activity of this group is unknown. All we know is that variation was substantial. Still, the conumdrum suggest that there was a balance problem.

It is important to differentiate between direct business, incoming reinsurance or acceptations, and outgoing reinsurance. Cessions made reinsurance a search for independent risks. Ceding abroad contributed to a better spread of risk; as did accepting from elsewhere. Indirect insuring was also interesting, because the costs were low. Profits might be low too, but were steady. Indirect business acquired a reputation similar to industrial insurance: both were good to build up financial strength. So, the *Vennootschap Nederland* focused upon indirect business as a means to recover from its American adventure of the early 1890s. However, matching problems plagued reinsuring. Observers thought that companies did not eagerly accept persons living in an area in which the firm was not active. This then was a countervailing force to spreading risks internationally. Furthermore, life insurers combining direct and indirect business operated in a reciprocal setting. Incoming reinsurance was supposed to be matched by outgoing reinsurance, which in turn was a function of direct business. That, for example, constrained the strategy of the *Vennootschap Nederland*. Management continuously feared that insurers would cancel contracts, as the stagnating company would not generate a stream sufficient to keep the partners happy. In the end, a takeover was a better solution than acquiring financial strength slowly and precariously. The combination of direct and indirect insurance created problems for expanding companies as well. In this context, qualities were important. Did the quality of the incoming stream match the outgoing one?

The *Dordrecht* is an interesting case. It had less ambition to develop its indirect business, nevertheless the company engaged above average in reinsurance. The incoming stream of reinsurance was bigger than the outgoing one. From the start management hoped it could end reinsuring as a business, but it did not dare to do so. Solace was offered by the belief that over time reinsurance would become less important. All this was combined with the hope that incoming reinsurance would meanwhile generate an easy and steady stream of profits. The hope was faulty, though the belief was sensible. Outgoing reinsurance peaked in 1890 and then declined. Indirect business followed a similar trajectory; it was about 8% of capital insured in 1900 and 6% in 1913. From 1910 onwards, outgoing insurance surpassed the incoming stream. Despite expectations becoming true, the ambitious top management of the expanding company looked at reinsuring as an unwanted stepdaughter. The expected easy profits did not materialize. Why?

The problem the *Dordrecht* experienced with reinsuring was one of proportionality. This problem was troublesome, as its direct business was marginal. Foreign business was structurally loss making (Table 4.1).[42] Negative figures could be acceptable; they were often interpreted as growth pains. The question was how long these had to be endured. Furthermore, reinsurance was a worry, despite indirect insuring compensating for losses out of direct insuring abroad. The proceeds were less than expected; less than outgoing reinsuring, the cost of reinsuring the company's own portfolio at home and abroad. That was disappointing for a line of business pursued actively. Management so labelled incoming reinsuring the most worrisome phenomenon it had to cope with.

---

[42] The data from 1913 onwards are not comparable, due to the introduction of Zillmer-accounting.

Table 4.1 The *Dordrecht:* Profits by life insurance activity and region (guilders)

		1899/1900	1906	1912	1898–1912
Direct business	Netherlands	30,943	103,534	79,287	71,591
	Dutch Indies	55,218	41,463	24,124	54,051
	Abroad	−74,463	−159,061	−106,256	−118,764
	Total	11,698	−14,064	155	6,878
Indirect business	Netherlands	24,429	32,217	−14,658	13,923
	Abroad	10,601	−50,141	51,830	6,745
	Total	35,030	−17,924	37,162	20,668
Result outgoing reinsurance	Total	−23,053	−5,701	−51,567	−25,419
Insuring	Total	23,675	−37,689	−14,250	2,127
Non-insurance benefits		50,353	176,719	196,738	137,155
End result		74,028	139,030	182,488	139,282
Sums insured (1900 = 100)		100	156	251	

Source AEGON Archive, Dordrecht, Geheim Verslag

Management of the *Dordrecht* found it difficult to extract a cause from available information. It strongly believed that reinsurance originating from the Netherlands was better than reinsuring foreign risks. Colleagues asked, had the same impression; the insurance press too. The speculation about why self-selection had this effect, reminds one of the arguments brought forward in the 1840s during the birth of reinsurance companies. Then the issue was why foreign companies accepting German reinsurance profited at the expense of direct insurers. The answer: big risks of a better kind of people were reinsured, as well as city risks, and not countryside dangers (*100 Jahre Kölnische* 1953, p. 21). In the 1900s, life risks offered from abroad were big and were credit operations. The *Dordrecht* speculated that the lives were actually persons with a history of pecuniary embarrassment. The insurers even contemplated the possibility that the lives insured might be persons whose future was made more worrisome by the financial help of insurers. This groping for an understanding was informed by general rumors that health and longevity decreased with wealth or that nervousness was the killing disease of the well-to-do.

Entrepreneurial common sense, however, might have been a casualty of information. Managerial views were based upon profit-loss accounting, but exercises using mortality tables gave a positive impression (Moll

1912, pp. 103–4).[43] Managers, however, did not embrace the actuaries' view, for national statistics too showed that life reinsurance was unprofitable in Germany and Austria. However, they also showed that reinsurance was not integrated internationally, for Swiss business was profitable (Hollitscher 1931, pp. 182–83). The analysis that good risks were offset by incoming bad ones from abroad should have been a stimulus to act. Management of the *Dordrecht* felt constrained; possibly by its direct portfolio and because incoming Dutch reinsurance could be unprofitable too. Collective, national action therefore got precedence.

4.6 Collective Action and Nationalization

The *Dordrecht* started to advocate mutual reinsurance by Dutch life companies around 1900. This was actually an old and more general idea. In 1887 the *Vereeniging voor Levensverzekering* was established, an informal club of twenty-five managers. The first meeting was dedicated to conveying what such a society was all about. Similar associations in Britain, Germany, France, Austria-Hungary, and Scandinavia were described. Prominent attention was given to the *Rückversicherungsverband Deutscher Lebensversicherungs-Gesellschaften* of 1877 (Blankenberg 1893, pp. 11–18). The next year, another manager of the biggest and most international company, the *Algemeene*, discussed reinsurance as "*a kind of partnership*" (Schevichaven 1893, p. 100). Reinsurance was becoming more common, but all this happened out of trust and ad-hoc. General rules binding partners were lacking. In 1891, the talks resulted in a model contract for reinsurance (Vereeniging voor Levensverzekering 1893).

The *Algemeene* stood for modernization, thus explicit contracting and formalized reinsurance instead of the customary practices. More important was a nationalistic motive, cherished by the most international life insurer of the Netherlands. The aim was to expand national business over large risks: sums between 50,000 and 75,000 guilders. Foreign insurers would be involved, if huge but very rare risks, 200,000 guilders, had to be accepted. The German reinsurance association of 1876, a mutual club

---

[43] Moll analyzed Austrian contracts offered to the *Algemeene* (*Niederländische* in Austria) to test managerial ill-feeling. The insolvency report later sketched the activities of the *Algemeene* in Austria and Hungary as costly and dubious. Moll was not employed by the Algemeene, but by *Netherlands of 1845*, a newcomer in life insurance.

of around ten companies, had been created to allow acceptance of "the highest sums" on lives. Organizing reinsurance nationally was a kind of import substitution of a financial service. More elements are important, but only can be mentioned. Commissions, up to a 100% at the beginning, were a force countervailing the outflow of premiums. States increasingly regulated against the export of premium reserves, in the Netherlands in the 1920s.

Internationalization was a channel which diffused national projects. One learnt from abroad. There was a second mechanism. Internationals joined associations in host countries, like information exchanges.[44] Reinsurance, however, was more than exchanging information about rejections, which perforce was locally valuable. Is it then not paradoxical that international companies in particular pressured for nationalizing a segment of the industry?[45] Market power of dedicated reinsurers might have been an issue; at least the perception that reinsurers might force direct insurers. Nevertheless, market power was a weak force.[46] There was a more potent motive. Nationalization of reinsurance was a battle about savings. Reinsurance was foremost quota sharing. The reinsurer received also a part of the savings included in the premium, which in life was substantial. The service was unbalanced, for reinsurance basically had to do with risk. An important, but not explicit, part of the debate was to restrict financial streams to the risk premium. Reinsurance solely based upon risk became normal after the First World War.

Already in 1887, Schevichaven, the manager of the *Algemeene*, had argued that a national reinsurance company had to be established. He, however, did not believe that the association of life insurers could go beyond a model contract. A company should be the initiative of the big offices (Schevichaven 1893, pp. 106, 119). In 1906 the *Dordrecht* launched proposals identical to those of the 1880s and1890s, but in another group: an alliance set up by seven big life companies. The alliance

[44] The *Kosmos* did not join the German *Rückversicherungsverband*, but was involved in the *Verband der gegenseitigen Mittheilung abgelehnter Risiken* of 1869. The *Algemeene* participated in the Austrian *Mittheilungs-Verband der Lebensversicherungs-Gesellschaften* of 1883, which led to a reinsurance association later, which the *Algemeene* did not join.

[45] Since 1900, mutuality of local or regional institutions within social security was seen as a blueprint for organizing national reinsurance ("II Séance" 1912).

[46] The business history of *Munich Re* tells that having an impact upon life was more difficult than upon non-life (Bähr and Kopper 2015, pp. 43, 91, 93).

was intended to become a trust, which would swallow up many of the small companies. That did not happen. The club worked also at a common actuarial basis. The grouping of the big firms failed to establish an internal consensus. An actuarial focus did not guarantee common views. The scheme to organize reinsurance nationally met no success. Agreement about premiums and conditions turned out to be infeasible. The plan for reinsurance stalled in 1907. The priority of actuarial matters did not work for reinsurance either. In fact, actuarial knowledge ran counter to established wisdom. The safe sums estimated actuarially were much lower than the maximal retentions in use. The procedure of the famous Dutch actuary Landré had the lowest outcome (Meidell 1912, p. 85). Insurers concluded that that established practice could not be wrong (Holwerda 1930, p. 6; Visser 1953, pp. 5–6).

All in all, the scope for enlarging the market by national, collective reinsuring was small. The lesson of the German—and Austrian—example was that there was no major business case.[47] Diverging interests and distrust were the main causes.[48] The *Eerste Nederlandsche* represented the nationally oriented companies, which reinsured relatively much of the business. In contrast, the Algemeene had big international interests, but reinsured little. Its incoming business was special, if not dubious.[49] The latter company advocated nationalizing acceptances, while the *Eerste Nederlandsche* was not keen upon receiving foreign cessions from domestic partners with international portfolios.[50] To some extent this was the same problem the *Dordrecht* struggled with. One group produced good

---

[47] The market in the Netherlands was small too. The sums targeted in the debate were considerably above normal levels of retention. In 1909, only two companies went beyond 25,000 guilders (Moll 1912, p. 102).

[48] The German reinsurance association was dissolved in 1898 (Manes 1931, p. 294; Gerathewohl 1979, p. 770). On the Austrian *Lebensversicherungs-Teilungsverein* of 1886: (Grömansperg and Prenger 1988, pp. 873–74).

[49] Reinsurance did not figure in the analysis of the insolvency of the *Algemeene*. The exception was the secret Russian daughter set up in 1899. The *Algemeene* profited from the reinsurance contract with the *Generalnoie*. The daughter, however, had to be subsidized continuously and was a huge financial drain (Sleutelaar 1922, pp. 11, 12, 16, 23, 24, 59).

[50] Matching of currencies was not an issue. Institutional factors were the cause, besides the gold standard. So did German supervision deal with both the German and Dutch portfolios of the *Kosmos* and prescribed the exchange rates. The company did reinsure in marks risks, originally insured in guilders, and vice versa (Brakel 1922, pp. 2–3).

reinsurance, the other bad. The problems did not necessarily arise due to a difference in quality between national and international policies. The German and Austrian insurers' associations had not been viable, because firms could not match satisfactorily supply and demand within the country (Radtke 1903, p. 34). Participants underlined most the traditional externality problem. Reinsurance might give an idea of where good quality big contracts could be found. Who was to profit? The question continued to be raised (Verzekeringskamer 1935, pp. 30–32). The answer was known, though not easily realized nationally: outsourcing reinsurance to specialized institutions at arm's length.

Just before the First World War, the hurdles were overcome. It is not clear what broke the deadlock: possibly a game of increasing retentions and an increased interest in colonial business, due to a new assessment of tropical risks. The seven big companies of the *Alliance to further Life Insurance* agreed to reinsure mutually up to 120,000 guilders. The companies also separated savings and risk. This was internationally early and induced Kopf to underline, that the risk premium system of life reinsurance had "*been regularly in effect in Holland since 1914*" (Kopf 1929, p. 55). Centralized outsourcing and intermediation helped to solve the problem of combining the circulation of information with competition. The problem of selection between companies was delegated to an outsider. The companies interested notified the Alliance's central office of their surpluses. The office assigned these to one or more companies. After the First World War, a reduced number of companies would opt for pooling cessions. There are no statistics giving an idea of the balance between the outgoing and incoming stream of reinsurance and the impact of the shift to reciprocal reinsuring in 1914 cannot be observed either. The rough impression was that the Netherlands had a small import-surplus of reinsurance coming from Germany (Hollitscher 1931, pp. 178–79).[51] As we will see later, the opposite was true at the end of the interwar period.

4.7 Uncommon Risks as Exemplar

Within a rather special niche, 'substandard risks', "cooperative" reinsurance emerged more easily. It is unlikely that this was due to actuarial innovation, though that is the common suggestion for other countries.

---

[51] Hollitscher does not specify whether the impression pertains to 1914 or to the 1920s.

In the Dutch case it was all about institutional change.[52] In 1905, the alliance of big life insurance companies established *Hope* [*de Hoop*], a life insurance company. It was an initiative of a manager of *Vennootschap Nederland*. Supposedly he had gotten the idea in the mid-1890s, forgot it, but by accident snatched the file, because a lamp in the vault broke at just the right moment. The anecdote is fine, but the moment was more importantly right, because the future of *Vennootschap Nederland*, stagnating due to its American adventure, looked bleak (Nierstrasz 1924; Niemeijer 1926, pp. 43–44).

The ambition was to make persons insurable who had been rejected after medical examination. The participating life insurers could fully reinsure the rejected with *Hope*. The company also had a few direct contracts, because the *Algemeene* refused a contractual relationship with refused applicants.[53] *Hope* would assess medical reports anew and worked with premiums and surcharges specific for each person. Pricing was informed roughly by outdated mortality tables. Pooling increased the market; the procedure resulted in contracts. At the same time, *Hope* made visible how risky substandard insuring was. A large proportion of the accepted died within three years from the illness identified. Many candidates did not accept the contract offered, illustrating the gap between preference and willingness to pay. The broadening of the market was limited. Nevertheless, the Dutch companies embraced "the rejected" early. The German industry only did go in a similar direction in 1915 and underlined big time their idealistic motivation. War-invalids was given a chance to look after the future of their families.[54]

---

[52] Bühlmann and Lengwiler stress the actuarial analysis of uncommon risks, particularly by Hunter and Rodgers of New York Life after 1900, and the development of a collective theory of risk, mainly since 1930 (Bühlmann and Lengwiler 2006, pp. 128–29). In the Netherlands, Hunter and Rodgers did not play a role, though they were appreciated for their assessment of tropical risks (Braun 1916, pp. 76–78).

[53] The *Algemeene*, reinsuring very little of its portfolio, had the highest rejection rate.

[54] The German insurers saw a separate company created by their own initiative primarily as a negotiation chip for the expected post-war initiatives in the realm of social policy. The company was established before the relevant statistical information was available; it was expected to become the vehicle to generate that information ("Deutschland Geschichte des Jahres" 1916, pp. 148–50). M. Roloff argues against the position I take, for the Austrian counterpart. The association failed because a theory of "inferior lives" lacked (Roloff 1988, p. 360).

Hope still exists; more or less as it was established in 1905 (Verbaan 2012). Insuring substandard risks became a substantial—at times the most substantial—type of reinsurance within life (Verzekeringskamer 1943, p. 18). The *Hope* established the pattern followed later by reinsuring domestically large sums. The company was a "collective department" of the participants, but the companies involved did outsource decisions about acceptance and premiums to the institution. "Nothing scientific about the Hope", the managing director stated in 1924 and joked about the "insurance-medical system", which *Hilfe*, the German counterpart, had offered at its dissolution in 1923. The Dutch refused to pay for the system. This was the path-dependent outcome of entering the market of substandard risks without solid foundation for assessment and finding it too costly to acquire empirical knowledge. This culture was not confined to the company. Within firms, the staff did not think much about standardization of substandard risks and they operated ad-hoc (Nierstrasz 1924, pp. 1–2; Nolen et al. 1925, pp. 344–45). The *Hope* is an example of the insurance institution coming first and the statistics coming second and with a long delay.[55]

Cooperation on "substandard" risks was easier than with large sums. Why? Transfer to *Hope* was an exceptional case of reinsurance without retention. At least this was the type envisaged, for companies could opt for a surplus treaty. The share holding companies and experts presented *Hope* as "idealistic" reinsurance. Insuring without a stake was in principle undesirable. Idealism then should signal initiative and commitment beyond normal business dealings. Still, *Hope* produced a collective good: it was a central check upon cumulation of risk by candidates going from one firm to another. At the same time, concentration of, say, epileptics implied that a group too small for each insurer separately could be treated actuarially fair. The initiative was also a move in institutional competition. The first Dutch company insuring without medical examination—an idea introduced by *Sun Life* in Britain around 1890—had entered the

[55] In his contribution, managing director Nierstrasz was not fully consistent. In the end, he did plea for a mortality table of substandard risks (Nierstrasz 1924). It was a wish in the international debate among medical advisors since 1901. Direct insurers collected material and some participated in a Statistical Office of Substandard Risks set up in 1916. The office was an example of suspended animation: the first output came in the late 1930s. The material of this—and other—initiatives was burned during the Second World War. In 1958, a more fruitful attempt to analyze uncommon risks was undertaken, involving *Hope* (Overbeeke 1970, pp. 194–95; Horstman 1996, pp. 177–85).

market. This soon was a failed innovation, at least in the Netherlands, for the protagonist shifted its endeavor to France. Lastly, Hope contributed perhaps to standardization of daily practice. Rejection rates of companies varied considerably. Still, there was no swift convergence. In 1913, rates varied from 1 to 13% among the three companies existing 50 years. The companies might have profited otherwise, even when they had outsourced non-standard information. Some medical advisors developed a more analytic approach to medical examining.

4.8 Reinsurance Between the First and Second World War

The debate over whether a national reinsurance business was viable and important and, more generally, to what extent contracts should be national or international, continued in the interwar years. The early 1920s seemed a watershed. War and hyperinflation changed drastically the international setting. Dutch life insurance had its own existential crisis. The most international companies went out of business. Still, the national structure remained the same. The industry had become frozen in the institutional setup of, say 1913, and that only changed in the 1960s. Of course, there was a nationalistic backlash ending the first wave of globalization. Nationalist initiatives within insurance and reinsurance, however, went back to the late nineteenth century and had a moderate impact after 1918. As nationalism generally had been on the rise in the Netherlands from before 1900, but did not dominate later.

After 1918, reinsurance with foreign companies was presented with even more urgency as an unnecessary export of scarce capital. Catastrophes like the flu epidemic of 1918 fed optimism: it showed that the Netherlands was big enough to spread risks adequately. The international environment, however, had become riskier and that impacted transborder activity. Monetary problems made experts focus upon the unwanted possibility, that reinsurance turned the direct insurers' loss into a gain: a payment in marks was more than compensated by the reimbursement in guilders. Experts were also impressed by puzzling new realities, as currencies once pegged, therefore not specified in contracts, and now having a path of their own: the Dutch-Indies guilder and Dutch guilder (Niemeijer 1926, pp. 28, 71–72). These were new, but solvable contractual issues. Common sense was that a mix of reinsuring domestically and abroad was optimal and this remained common sense.

The weight of the Dutch component in life reinsurance increased. A more autarkic world helped, but the change would have occurred anyway. As we saw, the biggest companies agreed to reinsure with some preference amongst themselves in 1913. The composition of the group—and the ranking of the firms—changed due to the postwar crisis. But the agreement remained in existence: it only became *the Pool*. Why was pooling preferred? More formality might simply substitute for informality due to time, but the *Pool* also reflected changes in the environment of reinsurance. Direct life insurance had become more volatile. The shift to a risk basis should make reinsurance more volatile as well. On the one hand, volatility increased the demand for reinsurance, on the other pricing became more difficult and reinsurance proper generated losses (Hollitscher 1931, pp. 180–84).[56] Pooling is a better mechanism to cope with uncertainty.

The *Pool* captured about half of the market. In 1935, the total reserve for reinsurance was 28.1 million guilders, of which 13.7 was reinsured abroad, thus 49%. This number included the Dutch Indies. Variation was substantial. Companies, which still had a foreign portfolio, reinsured more than 80% of their liabilities with foreign companies; the domestic (big) life offices 39% and industrial life firms merely 16%. In terms of all their liabilities, the percentages were 2.6, 1 and 0.4% respectively. These numbers reaffirmed the picture of Fig. 4.2: within life, reinsurance abroad and in total was a threadlike phenomenon (Verzekeringskamer 1935, pp. 30–32). In the international literature, the Netherlands figured as an economy acquiring a position in international reinsurance, similar to Denmark. In Belgium, the outgoing stream was three, four times bigger than domestic reinsurance. This balance was not changed much by reinsurance coming from abroad (Dievoet 1940, p. 272). Change in the Netherlands was, however, minute. Dutch success—a change of a few percent relative to 1913—was not the result of a new competitive advantage. It reflected the scope of a nationalist reflex in autarkic times on top of a domestic market which remained fundamentally open (Meyer 1936, p. 50).[57]

---

[56] As noted, before, Hollitscher underlines that German business was already loss making before 1914.

[57] After 1945 reinsurance became both more important and national, and recent globalization brought no change. Nowadays, Dutch direct insurers reinsure most nationally. In the rest of the world, also in Europe, the opposite is true (Lelyveld et al. 2011, p. 197).

4.9 LIFE AND FIRE: A SUMMARILY COMPARISON

The evolution of life reinsurance was specific. Still its history was representative enough for insurance generally. The evolution in provincial fire insurance was not very different, though levels of reinsurance were higher and practices reflected this. So came obligatory reinsurance earlier and was more prevalent. Introduced in the late 1870s, it reduced transaction costs of the bigger firms. A short overview of some similarities and contrasts.

Treaty reinsurance became normal even among the small local mutuals during the last quarter of the nineteenth century. The involvement of the general public was peculiar. The clientele of local fire funds—competitive and preferred institutions—found it increasingly difficult to accept the uncertainty of traditional mutuality: the distribution of realized costs instead of a premium based upon expected costs. The locals therefore signaled in the press and elsewhere that they had concluded reinsurance contracts with domestic societies. Or the mutuals created fixed premium companies, which reinsured with the mutual (*Gedenkschrift* 1920, pp. 27–29).[58]

The larger, so-called "provincial" fire companies learned from internationalization that they did not have a comparative advantage in reinsuring. By the mid-1880s, foreign turnover of the *Nederlanden van 1845* surpassed domestic business; it was 75% by the mid-1890s. Incoming reinsurance then counted for half of the business. The American portfolio was unprofitable over decades, but was kept because of its standing for the rest of the world. Other foreign business was not so bad, because the Dutch companies profited from price agreements abroad (Barendregt and Langenhuyzen 1995, pp. 43–47, 58, 60–62, 66–67, 71, 129, 135–136). Reinsurance was unavoidable, but not loved by direct fire offices.

Fire reinsurance by specialized firms was attempted in the early 1860s. Companies did not start in reality or switched soon to direct business,

---

The contrast is highlighted in the unpublished thesis of Kampman, which preceded the article.

[58] Occasionally life firms commercialized their reinsurance contracts, but not in reaction to the insured preferring stability. A case is the *Algemeene*, when it still was a regional mutual. In this case, advertising contacts with solid reinsurers targeted the well-to-do and reminds of the fears addressed by "re-insurance" as credit insurance (Otterloo and Crans 1873).

finding indirect business too risky.[59] Promoters of dedicated reinsurance were hurt by the highly publicized failure of a new direct insurer due to ambitious reinsuring.[60] The first lasting fire reinsurance companies date from the end of the nineteenth century: a series running mates of the *Netherlands of 1845*. In the late 1920s, the three daughters established a pool, almost at the moment that life reinsurance was pooled too. In short, similarities between fire and life outweigh dissimilarities: the pattern sketched for life was the one of the Dutch insurance industry overall.

4.10 Assessment

Reinsurance was an important, but modest addition to the instruments used to spread risks. That was so in life insurance as well in the other major branches, though levels varied. Reinsurance proper was long ignored, for it was not really needed. There existed other options equally efficient: traditional co-insuring and exchanges, embedding locals in a geographically wider framework, pooling. And when demand for reinsurance grew it did not change the business fundamentally. Reinsurance eased the switch from limited acceptance to unlimited acceptance and it eased entry in the market by incumbents. Reinsurance eased internalization of business, but it did not make insuring outside the Netherlands more solid. It was direct business that made internationalization problematical, but reinsurance came with matching problems. Matching of transborder activity was a problem during that very international area of the late nineteenth century. Domestic matching was almost as difficult. It was only on the brink of the First World War that problems of collective action within the Netherlands were solved, somewhat. Reinsurance in the form of national pooling was a successful mechanism of substituting for capital export in times of deglobalization. Still, the Netherlands had little interest in protectionism and the "nationalization" of reinsurance was, all in all, of little importance.

---

[59] Reinsurance was mentioned the first time in the name and bylaws of *de Nederlandsche Herverzekering Compagnie* created in 1862 (Schuddebeurs 1928, pp. 30, 83). One should consult also the Official Gazettes of 14 June 1862 and 22 July 1863. The company was non-life, but management of Kosmos, a life company, was involved in its foundation.

[60] *Ultrajectum*, established in 1859 and liquidated in 1865. The government considered in 1865 to forbid members of the cabinet or high-ranking civil servants from getting involved in insurance business. A supreme judge had to appear in court in Berlin in a quarrel about the security of Ultrajectum deposited in Germany.

References

"II Séance, Mardi 3 Septembre 1912: 'La Réassurance dans l' assurance vie' (Suite)." 1912. In *Septième Congrès International d'Actuaires. Amsterdam 2 au 7 Septembre 1912. Rapports, Mémoires et Procès Verbaux.* Tome Seconde: Procès Verbaux, 480–483. Amsterdam: s.n.

100 Jahre Kölnische Rückversicherungs-Gesellschaft. 1953. Köln: Dumont Schauberg.

Aachener und Münchener Feuer-Versicherungs-Gesellschaft. Denkschrift zur Hundertjahr-Feier 1825–1925. 1925. Aachen: Aachener Verlags- und Druckerei-Gesellschaft.

"Allerhöchste Bestätigung des Associations-Vertrages vom 6. Mai v.J., welchen die Düsseldorfer Allgemeine Versicherungs-Gesellschaft für See-, Fluß- und Land-Transport mit der Niederländischen Allgemeinen Versicherungs-Gesellschaft zu Tiel abgeschlossen hat." 1846. In *Amtsblatt der Regierung zu Düsseldorf Jahrgang 1846*, Nr. 57, 31. Oktober 1846, Nr. 1172, 487–490. Düsseldorf: J.C. Dänzer'schen Buchdruckerei.

B. 1904. "De assurantie-quaestie." *Algemeen Handelsblad*, January 20.

Bähr, Johannes, and Christopher Kopper. 2015. *Munich Re. Die Geschichte der Münchener Rück 1880–1980.* München: C.H. Beck.

Barendregt, Jaap, and Ton Langenhuyzen. 1995. *Ondernemend in risico: Bedrijfsgeschiedenis van Nationale-Nederlanden.* Amsterdam: NEHA.

"Binnenland." 1840. *Algemeen Handelsblad*, May 6.

Blankenberg, J.F. Louis. 1893. "De Inrichting en Werking van de in Europa bestaande Vereenigingen van Directiën van Levensverzekering-Maatschappijen. Voordracht gehouden in de Vergadering van 14 November 1887." In *Bijdragen over levensverzekering. Bundel van Voordrachten en andere Geschriften uit de jaren 1887–1891*, ed. Vereeniging voor Levensverzekering, 1–89. Amsterdam: P.N. van Kampen & Zoon.

Bonger, Willem A. 1915. "Vermogen en inkomen in Nederland (II. 1908–1913)." *De Nieuwe Tijd.* 20: 226–249, 269–291.

Bonger, Willem A. 1923. *Vermogen en inkomen in Nederland gedurende den oorlogstijd (1913–1920). Een statistische studie.* Amsterdam: Boekhandel en Uitgevers-Maatschappij 'Ontwikkeling'.

Borch, Karl. 1962. "Equilibrium in a Reinsurance Market." *Econometrica* 30: 301–329.

Borscheid, Peter. 2006. "Systemwettbewerb, Institutionenexport und Homogenisierung. Der Internationalisierungsprozess der Versicherungswirtschaft im 19. Jahrhundert." *Zeitschrift für Unternehmensgeschichte* 51: 26–53.

Brakel, Simon van. 1922. *Verslag van den Rechter-Commissaris in zake de Verzekeringsbank "Kosmos" te Zeist.* Utrecht: s.n.

"Brand van het tabakspakhuis 'Zeevaart' te Rotterdam." 1903. *Algemeen Handelsblad*, March 24 Evening.
Braun, Heinrich. 1916. "Die Behandlung von Auslandrisiken durch die holländischen Lebensversicherungs-Gesellschaften." *Assekuranz-Jahrbuch begründet von A. Ehrenzweig*. 37 II. Teil: 69–109.
Bühlmann, Hans, and Martin Lengwiler. 2006. "Calculating the Unpredictable: History of Actuarial Theories and Practices in Reinsurance." In *Managing Risk in Reinsurance. From City Fires to Global Warming*, ed. Niels V. Haueter and Geoffrey Jones, 118–143. New York, Oxford: Oxford University Press.
Centraal Bureau voor de Statistiek. 1905–1920. *Statistiek der rijksinkomsten over het jaar [1903–1928]*, 's-Gravenhage.
Couvreur, Louis. 1936. "De eerste verzekeringscompagnie te Antwerpen (1754–1793?)." *Tijdschrift voor Economie en Sociologie*. 2: 145–174.
Cummins, David J., and Mary Weiss. 2000. "The Global Market for Reinsurance: Consolidation, Capacity, and Efficiency." *Brookings-Wharton Papers on Financial Services* 2: 159–209.
Delpher. 2020. https://www.delpher.nl/nl/kranten.
"Deutschland Geschichte des Jahres." 1916. *Assekuranz-Jahrbuch begründet von A. Ehrenzweig*. 37 III. Teil: 125–185.
Dievoet, Emiel Van. 1940. *Het verzekeringswezen in België. Economische en sociale gegevens, het bestaande recht, de voorgestelde hervormingen, Tweede Deel*. Antwerpen, Zwolle: De Sikkel, Belinfante.
Dooren de Jong, Elie L.G. den. 1929. "Bijdragen tot de geschiedenis der Zeeverzekering II. Reassurantie in de zeeverzekering 1500–1800." *Het Verzekerings-Archief* 10: 81–112.
"Dutch Insurance Companies." 1929. *The Review*, November 22.
"Dutch Insurance Conditions." 1940. *The Review*, January 12.
Ehrenberg, Richard. 1901. Studien zur Entwicklungsgeschichte der Versicherung. *Zeitschrift für die Gesamte Versicherungswissenschaft* 1: 368–379.
Ehrenberg, Victor. 1885. *Die Rückversicherung. Festschrift der Rostocker Juristen-Facultät*. Hamburg, Leipzig: Leopold Voss.
Ferguson, Niall. 2008. *The Ascent of Money. A Financial History of the World*. New York: The Penguin Press.
Frenzl, Margareta. 1924. *Fünfzig Jahre Internationaler Transport-Versicherungs-Verband*. Berlin: R. Boll.
Gales, Ben P.A., and Jacques L.J.M. van Gerwen. 1988. *Sporen van leven en schade. Een geschiedenis en bronnenoverzicht van het Nederlandse verzekeringswezen*. Amsterdam: NEHA.
Gales, Ben P.A. 2007. "Odds and ends. The problematical first wave of internationalization in Dutch insurance during the late 19th and early 20th centuries." In *Internationalisation and Globalisation of the Insurance Industry*

in the 19th and 20th centuries, ed. Peter Borscheid and Robin Pearson, 84–111. Marburg, Zürich: Philipps-University, Swiss Re Corporate History.

Gedenkboek ter gelegenheid van het honderdjarig bestaan der Hollandsche Societeit van Levensverzekeringen 1807–1907. 1907. Amsterdam: Hollandsche Societeit van Levensverzekeringen.

Gedenkboek ter gelegenheid van het honderdvijftigjarig bestaan der Hollandsche Societeit van Levensverzekeringen N. V. 1957. Amsterdam: Hollandsche Societeit van Levensverzekeringen.

Gedenkboek 1859–1909. Nederlandsch-Indische Levensverzekering- en Lijfrente-Maatschappij. 1909. Amsterdam: Nederlandsch-Indische Levensverzekering- en Lijfrente-Maatschappij.

Gedenkschrift bij het honderd-jarig bestaan van de Onderlinge Brandwaarborg-Maatschappij aan de Zaan opgericht anno 1819 gevoerd onder de Firma "Koning & Boeke" gevestigd te Zaandijk 1820–1920. 1920. Zaandijk: s.n.

Gerathewohl, Klaus. 1979. "Geschichte der Rückversicherung." In *Rückversicherung. Grundlagen und Praxis, Band 2*, ed. K. Gerathewohl, 697–858. Karlsruhe: Verlag Versicherungswirtschaft.

Go, Sabine, Karel Davids, and Timon Schultz. 2016. *Zekere zaken. Mijlpalen uit de geschiedenis van de coassurantiemarkt*. Rotterdam: Vereniging Nederlandse Assurantiebeurs.

Golding, Charles E. 1927. *A History of Reinsurance with Sidelights on Insurance*. London: Sterling Offices.

Gothein, Eberhard. 1916. *Die Stadt Cöln im ersten Jahrhundert unter Preußischer Herrschaft 1815 bis 1915, Erster Band, I. Teil. Verfassungs- und Wirtschaftsgeschichte der Stadt Cöln vom Untergange der Reichsfreiheit bis zur Errichtung des Deutschen Reiches*. Cöln: Verlag von Paul Neubner.

Grömansperg, Heide, and Christian Prenger. 1988. "Rückversicherung in der Monarchie (1874–1918)." In *Versicherungsgeschichte Österreichs. Band 2 Die Ära des klassischen Versicherungswesens*, ed. Wolfgang Rohrbach, 859–919. Wien: A. Holzhausen.

Grossmann, Hermann. 1918. "Herverzekering." *Jaarboekje van de Vereeniging voor Levensverzekering*, 230–239.

Haensel, Carl. 1965. *Revolutions Versicherung. Bekenntnisse aus rechtsverjährter Zeit. Eine Frankfurter Satire*. Frankfurt am Main: Verlag Frankfurter Bücher.

Haueter, Niels V., and Geoffrey Jones. 2017. "Risk and Reinsurance." In *Managing Risk in Reinsurance. From City Fires to Global Warming*, ed. Niels V. Haueter and Geoffrey Jones, 1–46. New York, Oxford: Oxford University Press.

Heemskerk Az., Jan. 1854. "De ontwikkeling van het contract van verzekering." *De Volksvlijt. Tijdschrift voor Nijverheid, Landbouw, Handel en Scheepvaart* 135–149: 192–207.

Hollitscher, Carl H. von. 1931. *Internationale Rückversicherung*. Berlin: E.S. Mittler & Sohn.
Holwerda, Allard O. 1924. "Management Problems of European Insurance Companies Since the Armistice." *Harvard Business Review* 2: 398–408.
Holwerda, Allard O. 1930. "De ontwikkeling van het technisch apparaat der levensverzekering." In *De ontwikkeling van de levensverzekering in Nederland gedurende de laatste 25 jaar 1905 1 januari 1930*, ed. H.T. Hoven, 115–126. Rotterdam: M. Wyt & Zonen.
Horlings, Edwin. 1995. *The Economic Development of the Dutch Service Sector 1800–1850. Trade and Transport in a Premodern Economy*. Amsterdam: NEHA.
Horstman, Klasien. 1996. *Verzekerd Leven. Artsen en levensverzekerings-maatschappijen 1880–1920*. Amsterdam: Babylon-De Geus.
Kader, Hale A., Michael Adams, Lars F. Andersson, and Magnus Lindmark. 2010. "The Determinants of Reinsurance in the Swedish Property Fire Insurance Market During the Interwar Years, 1919–39." *Business History* 52: 268–284.
Kiesselbach, Georg A. 1901. *Die wirtschafts- und rechtsgeschichtliche Entwicklung der Seeversicherung in Hamburg*. Hamburg: L. Gräfe & Sillem.
Kißkalt, Wilhelm. 1924. "Privatversicherung und deutsche Zahlungsbilanz." In *Probleme der deutschen Zahlungsbilanz*, ed. Rudolf Meerwarth, Wilhelm Kißkalt and Bernhard Karlsberg, 33–46. München, Leipzig: Duncker & Humblot.
Koch, Peter. 1978. *Bilder zur Versicherungsgeschichte herausgegeben von der Aachener Rückversicherungs-Gesellschaft anläßlich ihres 125jährigen Bestehens*. Karlsruhe: Verlag Versicherungswirtschaft.
Koch, Peter. 2012. *Geschichte der Versicherungswirtschaft in Deutschland*. Karlsruhe: Verlag Versicherungswirtschaft.
Kopf, Edwin W. 1929. "The Origin and Development of Reinsurance." In *Proceedings of the Casualty Actuarial Society xvi. number 33*, ed. Casualty Actuarial Society, 22–91. New York: s.n.
Kracht, Fritz. 1922. *Die Rotterdamer Seeversicherungs-Börse. Ihre Entwicklung, Bedeutung und Bedingungen*. Weimar: Straubing & Müller.
Kyrtsis, Alexandros-Andreas. 2006. "The Rise and Decline of Treaty Reinsurance: Changing Roles of Reinsurers as Financial Service Providers." In *Managing Risk in Reinsurance. From City Fires to Global Warming*, ed. Niels V. Haueter and Geoffrey Jones, 144–181. New York, Oxford: Oxford University Press.
Laar, Paul Th. van de, and Hubert H. Vleesenbeek. 1990. *Van Oude naar Nieuwe Hoofdpoort. De geschiedenis van het Assurantieconcern Stad Rotterdam Anno 1720 N.V., 1720–1990*. Rotterdam: Stad Rotterdam Verzekeringen.
Le Moine de l'Espine, J. 1753. *De Koophandel van Amsterdam, naar alle Gewesten des Werelds. Bestaande, In Een Verhandeling, van de Waaren en*

Koopmanschappen, die men daarheenen sendt en wederom ontfangt: Benevens vergelykingen der Munten, Maaten en Gewigten, en op wat wyse men over en weêr wisselt. Als mede: Een Verhandeling over de Wisselbank, Beurs en Koorenbeurs, Koorenboekje, Loon der Maakelaars, Convooylyst, Waagboekje, Nieuwe Bank- Rabat- Tarra- Reductie- en Agio-Tafels, en veele andere weetenswaardige saaken den Koophandel betreffende. Rotterdam: Ph. Losel, J.D. Beman, H. Kentlink, J. Bosch, N. Smithof, J. Losel en J. Burgvliet.

Lelyveld, Iman van, Franka Liedorp, and Manuel Kampman. 2011. "An Empirical Assessment of Reinsurance Risk." *Journal of Financial Stability* 7: 191–203.

Mailluchet, Félix. 1917. La réassurance en Europe en fin de l'année 1915. *Le Moniteur des Assurances sur La Vie* 50: 93–94.

Manes, A. 1931. *Versicherungswesen, System der Versicherungswirtschaft, Zweiter Band, Güterversicherung*. Leipzig, Berlin: B.G. Teubner.

Masius, Ernst A. 1846. *Lehre der Versicherung und statistische Nachweisung aller Versicherungs-Anstalten in Deutschland nebst Hinweisung auf den hohen Einfluß dieser Institute auf Nationalwohlstand, und die Gesetze darüber in den verschiedenen Staaten*. Leipzig: Fest'sche Verlagsbuchhandlung.

Mees, Marten. 1871. *Over de slechte uitkomsten in het assurantievak en de middelen tot verbetering*. Rotterdam: H.A. Kramer en Zoon.

Meidell, Birger. 1912. "Zur Theorie des Maximums." In *Septième Congrès International d'Actuaires. Amsterdam 2 au 7 Septembre 1912. Rapports, Mémoires et Procès Verbaux*. Tome Premier: Thèmes à Discuter, 85–99. Amsterdam: s.n.

Meyer, Hans. 1936. *Die Autarkiebestrebungen im Versicherungswesen in der Nachkriegszeit*. Walther: Oldenburg.

Ministerie van Financiën. 1861–1914. *Statistiek van het Konikrijk der Nederlanden. Bescheiden betreffende de geldmiddelen*. 's-Gravenhage.

Moll, Daniel P. 1912. "Die Rückversicherung in der Lebensversicherung." In *Septième Congrès International d'Actuaires. Amsterdam 2 au 7 Septembre 1912. Rapports, Mémoires et Procès Verbaux*. Tome Premier: Thèmes à Discuter, 101–114. Amsterdam: s.n.

Mossner, Bernd. 2012. *Die Entwicklung der Rückversicherung bis zur Gründung selbständiger Rückversicherungsgesellschaften*. Berlin: Duncker & Humblot.

"Naamlooze Vennootschappen." 1840. *Nederlandsche Staatscourant*: May 12 bijvoegsel.

"Niederländische Versicherungsgesellschaft in Tiel." 1854. In *Fortgesetzte Sammlung der im Gebiete der inneren Staats-Verwaltung des Königreichs Bayern bestehenden Verordnungen von 1835 bis 1852, aus amtlichen Quellen bearbeitet, Achter Band der neuen Folge*, ed. Fr. von Strauß, 1101–1102. München: s.n.

Niemeijer, Meindert. 1926. "Beschouwingen over herverzekering in het algemeen en levensherverzekering in het bijzonder." PhD diss., Rijksuniversiteit te Leiden.

Nierstrasz, Johannus L. 1924. "Een en ander over de werkwijze en de ervaringen van de levensverzekering-maatschappij 'De Hoop'." *Het Verzekerings-Archief* 5: 1–10.
Nolen, Willem, Albert A. Hijmans van den Bergh, and Jan Siegenbeek van Heukelom. 1925. *Lebensversicherungs-Medizin: Eine Anleitung für Ärzte und Studierende der Medizin.* Berlin: Julius Springer.
De Onderlinge Brandwaarborg-Maatschappij thans onder directie der firma De Jong & Co. gevestigd te Amsterdam ter gelegenheid van haar eeuwfeest beschouwd in het licht van hare geschiedenis en haar reglement. 1909. Amsterdam: s.n.
Organization for Economic Co-operation and Development. 2005. *Terrorism Risk Insurance in OECD Countries: Policy Issues in Insurance.* No. 9. Paris: OECD Publishing.
Otterloo, Anthony van, and Pieter Crans. 1873. *Officiëele gids van de Stoomvaart-Maatschappij Nederland.* Amsterdam: C.L. Brinkman and Scheltema & Holkema.
Overbeeke, J. van. 1970. "Medisch-statistische onderzoekingen voor het levensverzekeringbedrijf." *Het Verzekerings-Archief* 47: 190–210.
Overloop, J.F. Van., and J.H. Bastiné. 1857. "Cour d'Appel de Bruxelles. Troisième Chambre. Sentence du 28 février 1850". *La Belgique judiciaire. Gazette des Tribunaux Belges et Étrangers* 15: 1415–1417.
Pearson, Robin. 1995. "The Development of Reinsurance Markets in Europe During the Nineteenth Century." *The Journal of European Economic History* 24: 557–571.
Pot, W.H. 1984. *Korte historie van Molest-Risico 1917–1983. Vijf-en-zestig plus, maar niet in ruste.* S.l.: Centraal Beheer.
Radtke, Paul. 1903. *Die Stabilität der Lebensversicherings-Anstalten.* Berlin: E.S. Mittler und Sohn.
Roloff, Marita. 1988. "Die Entwicklung der Lebensversicherung in Österreich zwischen 1873 und 1936." In *Versicherungsgeschichte Österreichs. Band 2 Die Ära des klassischen Versicherungswesens*, ed. Wolfgang Rohrbach, 283–608. Wien: A. Holzhausen.
S. 1904. "De vakbeweging in het assurantie-bedrijf." *Algemeen Handelsblad, January 18.*
Schawacht, Jürgen H. 1973. *Schiffahrt und Güterverkehr zwischen den Häfen des Deutschen Niederrheins (insbesondere Köln) und Rotterdam vom Ende des 18. bis zur Mitte des 19. Jahrhunderts (1794–1850/51).* Köln: Rheinisch-Westfälisches Wirtschaftsarchiv.
Schevichaven, Samuel R.J. van. 1893. "Inleiding gehouden in de Vergadering van 3 September 1888, ter behandeling van het onderwerp: het contract van Herverzekering en zijne toepassing." In *Bijdragen over levensverzekering. Bundel van Voordrachten en andere Geschriften uit de jaren 1887–1891*, ed.

Vereeniging voor Levensverzekering, 93–121. Amsterdam: P.N. van Kampen & Zoon.

Schuddebeurs, Hendrik G. 1928. "Het Nederlandsche Verzekeringsbedrijf gedurende de laatste eeuwen, voor zoover dit werd uitgeoefend door Naamlooze Vennootschappen." *Economisch-Historisch Jaarboek* 14: 1–178.

Sleutelaar, Frederik. 1922. *Verslag van den Rechter-Commissaris in de zaken der Algemeene Maatschappij van Levensverzekering en Lijfrente*. Amsterdam: s.n.

Smits, Jan-Pieter, Edwin Horlings, and Jan Luiten van Zanden. 2000. *Dutch GNP and Its Components, 1800–1913*. Groningen: Groningen Growth and Development Centre.

Staatscommissie, benoemd krachtens de Wet van 19 Januari 1890 (Staatsblad no. 1). 1892. *Verslag van de Afdeeling der Staats- Commissie van Arbeids-Enquête aangaande "de verzekering of andere voorzorgen bij ongeval, ziekte, overlijden of ouderdom van werklieden, voor zoover die maatregelen niet in verband staan met eenige bepaalde inrichting van Nijverheid"* (Fondsen-Enquête). 's-Gravenhage: Van Weelden & Mingelen.

Teding van Berkhout, Hieronimus N. 1866. *De reassurantie*. Amsterdam: C. van Helden.

Tilly, Richard H. 1966. *Financial Institutions and Industrialization in the Rhineland 1815–1870. Madison (MIL)*. London: The University of Wisconsin Press.

Tilly, Richard H. 1980. *Kapital, Staat und sozialer Protest in der deutschen Industrialisierung. Gesammelte Aufsätze*. Göttingen: Vandenhoeck & Ruprecht.

Umbach, Kai. 2006. "Die Position deutscher Transportversicherer auf dem Weltmarkt 1880–1914." *Vierteljahrschrift für Sozial und Wirtschaftsgeschichte* 93: 413–437.

Umbach, Kai. 2008. *Das grenzüberschreitende Geschäft in der See- und Transportversicherung von Ende des 19. Jahrhunderts bis in die 1990er Jahre: Ein internationaler Gewerbezweig auf dem Weg hin zu "globalisierten" Verhältnissen?* PhD diss.: Philipps-Universität Marburg.

Verbaan, Joke. 2012. "De Hoop: Een unieke Nederlandse herverzekeraar." *De actuaris*, September, 16–7.

Vereeniging voor de Statistiek in Nederland. 1882. *Overzigt der naamlooze vennootschappen volgens de patentregisters over de jaren 1861/62–1880/81*. 's-Gravenhage: Smits.

Vereeniging voor Levensverzekering. 1890–1921. *Jaarboekje voor [1890–1921] uitgegeven door de Vereeniging voor Levensverzekering*. Amsterdam: Vereeniging voor Levensverzekering.

Vereeniging voor Levensverzekering. 1893. "Reglement van herverzekering en Algemeene Verzekerings-Voorwaarden. Beraadslagingen over die onderwerpen." In *Bijdragen over levensverzekering. Bundel van Voordrachten*

en andere Geschriften uit de jaren 1887–1891, ed. Vereeniging voor Levensverzekering, 345–410. Amsterdam: P.N. van Kampen & Zoon.
"Vereinigung Rhein. Versicherungsgesellschaften." 1843. *Allgemeines Organ für Handel und Gewerbe*, May 9.
"Versicherungen gegen Gefahr zur See und auf Strömen." 1853. In *Tabellen und amtliche Nachrichten über den Preussischen Staat für das Jahr 1849, IV. Die Resultate der Verwaltung enthaltend*, ed. Statistisches Bureau zu Berlin, 539–540. Berlin: A.W. Hayn.
Verzekeringskamer. 1924–1950. *Verslag der Verzekeringskamer over het jaar [1923–1949]*. Amsterdam: Verzekeringskamer.
Visser, Jacob. 1953. *Beoordeling van het weerstandsvermogen van levensverzekeringmaatschappijen*. Amsterdam: Noord-Hollandsche uitgevers maatschappij.
Winkelman, Petrus H. 1983. *Bronnen voor de geschiedenis van de Nederlandse Oostzeehandel in de zeventiende eeuw. Deel IV. Amsterdamse bevrachtingscontracten, wisselprotesten en bodemerijen van de notarissen Jan Franssen Bruyningh, Jacob Meerhout e.a., 1601–1608*. Rijks Geschiedkundige Publicatiën, Grote Serie, Deel 184. 's-Gravenhage: Nijhoff.

CHAPTER 5

The Rise and Fall of Swedish Non-Life Reinsurance

Mikael Lönnborg

5.1 Introduction

This chapter discusses the emergence and development of the Swedish reinsurance industry in the non-life sector. In particular, the focus is on major events that changed the circumstances and conditions for conducting reinsurance and how the business was organized. In Sweden, the reinsurance in the non-life sector was closely connected to direct insurance and almost every larger (and to some extent in medium-sized) insurance group, created an 'independent' reinsurance company (in practice totally dependent on the mother company). However, this changed considerably during the nineteenth and twentieth century, in particular after heavy losses. In addition, the reinsurance business became an important part for direct insurers in expanding on foreign markets.

M. Lönnborg (✉)
Department of Business Studies, School of Social Sciences, Södertörn University, Stockholm, Sweden
e-mail: Mikael.lonnborg@sh.se

© The Author(s), under exclusive license to Springer Nature Switzerland AG 2021
L. Caruana de las Cagigas and A. Straus (eds.), *Role of Reinsurance in the World*, Palgrave Studies in Economic History, https://doi.org/10.1007/978-3-030-74002-3_5

The discussion will revolve around the issue of how the non-life reinsurance business shaped the setting of the Swedish insurance industry and in particular highlight the part reinsurance played for the international business of Swedish insurers.

The purpose of the reinsurance industry is to provide insurance for primary insurers. Primary insurers have fairly standardized policies, whereas those of reinsurers are often less so, more internationally oriented and likely to cover very large risks. There is little doubt that primary insurance policies, as well as an insurance market based on fixed premiums, would be difficult to sustain over the long run without reinsurance. Reinsurance enables portfolio diversification by the primary insurer in order to avoid the kinds of devastating losses that could threaten its survival (Kopf 1929; Golding 1931; Pearson 1995, 1997; Doherty and Smetters 2005; James et al. 2014).

The innovation of reinsurance was introduced by joint-stock insurers in Great Britain in the late eighteenth century (Pearson 2020; Caruana and Straus 2017; Haueter and Jones 2016; Borsheid and Haueter 2012; Trebilcock 1985, 1998). Reinsurance made it possible to cover large risks without incurring too much exposure. Reinsurance stabilized the insurance industry and became mandatory globally among new-founded insurance companies. The definition and content of reinsurance have changed and evolved over time, but the basics remain the same, and this quotation covers the meaning of the concept:

> Taking over very large risks that would expose the insurer to the danger that a single policy could pay very high claims. Reimbursements could be so high for some years that the business would suffer major losses, and even find its survival in danger. To protect itself, the company reinsures the portion of any policy above its risk limit with one or more other insurers, which take over the corresponding risk. The amount that the company can keep without exceeding its risk limit depends on its size, solvency, average amounts insured, etc. The reinsurance company passes on (retrocedes) to other reinsurers the portion of the acquired policy that exceeds its risk limit. This guarantees that large insurance risks are diversified among many domestic and international companies. The company that accepts reinsurance obtains a re-insurance premium. In case of a loss event, the reinsurance company pays the agreed portion of total damages.

> From the policyholder's point of view, there is no risk associated with insuring large amounts with the same company. Reinsurance guarantees that the risk is no greater than if the policyholder allocated her/his personal risk among various companies (Durling 1937, pp. 63–64. Translation by the author).

In the Swedish case, the international business was closely connected to reinsurance and was to some extent the same story, but the intention of the chapter is to focus more extensively on reinsurance and how it was organized, and what kind of impact the reinsurance had on the setting of the insurance market. In addition, the chapter will focus on different periods in time when the reinsurance market did change substantially. The periods are the early setting of reinsurance in the mid-eighteenth century, the San Francisco earthquake in 1906 and World War I, the renewal of the reinsurance market after World War II, the 1970s and 1980s when almost every Swedish insurer started or heavily expanded their reinsurance portfolio and finally the 1990s and 2000s when reinsurance as a mode of internationalization was dismantled entirely.

The chapter will not engage in any discussion about different forms of reinsurance, that in fact was quite advanced already during the nineteenth century and would be even more sophisticated during the twentieth century. Another limitation is that the chapter will focus mainly on the larger players, but with some examples from other companies. The reinsurance business proceeded from the primary activities of the various insurance companies, as well as their need to minimize the associated risks. Thus, reinsurance allowed a company to accept extensive risks without jeopardizing its survival through outgoing reinsurance. Later on, several of these contracts became reciprocal (including both ingoing and outgoing reinsurance) as a measure to minimize moral hazard and compensation for premiums transferred to other companies. The ingoing reinsurance also became a measure to internationalize the business without investing in expensive offices abroad (Caruana and Straus 2017).

This chapter will focus only on the non-life insurance sector (which in itself was very extensive) because the life insurance reinsurance was arranged completely different in the Swedish context. Until 1914, joint-stocks and mutual life insurers used different modes of reinsurance but in particular smaller mutual insurers had signed treaties with foreign insurers that created heavy losses. The trust of the life insurers was damaged, and it could in the end have a major impact on the reputation of the entire industry. The solution was to create a common owned—by both joint-stock and mutual insurers—company, Sweden Re, that became responsible for dealing with life reinsurance for the entire Swedish market. This monopoly situation disappeared in the late 1980s when the financial market was deregulated, and today Sweden Re is a branch of the French company *SCOR* (see further in the Chapter by André Straus in current volume). In addition, the use of reinsurance as a way of diversifying risks or expand business abroad, is no longer used among Swedish life insurers (Larsson and Lönnborg 2014a).

5.2 The Early Reinsurance Business

The modern Swedish insurance market emerged during the 1850s. The first company, *Skandia*, was founded in 1855 in Stockholm with a mixed portfolio, selling both life and non-life insurance. Additional 'mixed' insurers followed in Gothenburg in 1866, *Svea*, and Malmö in 1884, *Skåne*. These were joint-stocks corporations but, after 1884, no other corporation received concessions from the government for combined business operations of this type. After 1884, only 'pure' life or non-life insurance companies were accepted. The advocates of separation claimed that a natural division existed between fire and life insurance and argued that the share capital should be limited because this benefited the customers (Hägg 1998; Bergander 1967; Bucht 1936).

The first company *Skandia* introduced a reinsurance programme that was more or less copied from British insurers. Reinsurance provided benefits to both insurers and policyholders. The latter could insure property, as for instance factories, which facilitated investments in capital-intensive assets. The insurance companies, on the other hand, could accept these risks, without endangering the survival of the companies. It can be pointed out that *Skandia's* reinsurance treaties were extensive and characterized by great turmoil during the first decades of business. Therefore, it has not been possible in this section to fully describe *Skandia's* indirect activities. A relationship that should be noted, which concerns all three mixed insurance companies, was that in the respective market, the general agent often handled his own risk allocation and the head office took care of reinsurance of the domestic business (and also the ingoing reinsurance). This meant that the different groups' risk allocation consisted of myriads of contracts and treaties, which further complicated a comprehensive analysis of all partners. However, the main partners were large insurers from countries like in particular Great Britain, Germany, France, Switzerland, Austria and the Netherlands.

In general, the management regarded reinsurance as a convenient way to avoid bad risks, without collecting a lot of information about potential policyholders, the partners had already conducted this. In particular, this concerned foreign risks, and foreign general agencies were instructed only to write reinsurance and avoid direct insurance. This became the general view among the management of Swedish insurance companies, with some exceptions.

As noted, *Skandia* was the first firm that used reinsurance and that was even defined in Skandia's statutes. The company's statutes from 1855 explicitly stated a maximum on every risk accepted. This limitation led to the initial establishment of reinsurance contracts with German, Austrian, Italian and in particular British companies. During the following years new contracts were established with companies in France, Belgium, Switzerland, Finland and Norway. Initially, relations with foreign companies were established, for which *Skandia's* first CEO, von Koch, previously had acted as general agent in Sweden. However, at this early stage, *Skandia's* international reinsurance contracts were not characterized by any significant stability. Collaborations were established and cancelled at a relatively high rate but over time the relationship became more stable and the treaties often became reciprocal, both leaving and receiving reinsurance from the same partner as a way of mitigating moral hazard (Lönnborg 2002).

However, due to heavy losses, some of the general agencies were closed down in the 1860s and *Skandia* kept the reinsurance on a very low level for about four decades. A very important contract was established in 1900 when *Skandia* received reinsurance from the British company *Royal Insurance Company* from Liverpool. As early as 1897, Skandia began to receive reinsurance from Royal's British risks, but the contract expanded in 1900 to include risks in Europe and the United States, but also spread to Asia, Australia, South America and Africa. As for the indirect activity, Skandia mainly used its contacts to distribute its portfolio, that is to say, outbound reinsurance, but foreign risks were also taken to increase premium income. Skandia's strategic alliances were mainly German, French and British insurance companies, and particularly the treaties with the company *Royal* became crucial until the early 1930s (Leffler 1905; Grenholm 1955).

In addition to these contacts, companies in the home market were also established that supported Skandia's risk allocation. Reinsurance AB *Freja*, formed in 1870 by Skandia-related persons, helped the company to internally spread some of its own risks, but after profitability problems, Freja was dissolved in 1882. In a shorter period (1873–1878) another related reinsurance company, *Widar*, was connected to Skandia. Following the San Francisco disaster in 1906, a new subsidiary, *Freja*, was formed, aimed at distributing part of Skandia's fire reinsurance. In this way, Skandia was relieved of part of its foreign business, and distribution the risk to a seemingly independent subsidiary. However, as noted, these subsidiaries, never gained true independence and never acted as freestanding companies, and the operations of reinsurance were organized by top management of the direct insurers.

Svea, the second company to sell both fire and life insurance, was founded in 1866 in Gothenburg. Several of *Svea's* founders had served as general agents for foreign insurers, and the CEO, Edouard Boye (born in Prussia), had acted as general agent for several German companies and was the Prussian consul in Gothenburg. The board also contacted representatives of Skandia to obtain company-specific knowledge about premiums and other details. This was a quick way to benefit from Skandia's experience while coordinating premium levels and other policy terms, including the use of reinsurance. However, due to Boyes connection to Germany, contrary to *Skandia*, *Svea* focused most of the reinsurance with companies from that country. *Svea* early on opened up general agency in the Nordic countries and would expand heavily on the international market. In 1866, two general agents were launched in Norway (Oslo, at the time called Kristiania, and Trondheim), and later on general agents were appointed in the following cities, Copenhagen (1867) and 1869 in Hamburg, Bremen and Amsterdam, St. Petersburg (1872), San Francisco (1874), Helsinki (1875), Mulhouse (Elsass-Lothringen, part of Germany 1871–1918, and thereafter French Alsace–Lorraine, 1879), London (1880), New York (1882), Vienna (1883) and finally in Valparaiso (Chile) (1885) (Bring 1918).

Several companies that sold either fire or life insurance were founded after 1866, but *Skåne*, established in 1884 in Malmö, was the last to be licensed by the government to sell both. Skåne had established agencies by 1884 in Denmark, Norway and Germany and a year later in

Russia, an establishment pattern with strong similarities with Skandia. The most important reinsurance partner was the Dutch *Nederlanden*, and Skåne received worldwide risks from them. In 1888, Skåne and Nederland opened up a common agency in San Francisco, but it was closed down due to heavy losses after only 4 years. However, *Skåne* continued to accept reinsurance from the Dutch company from all states within the United States. The entire international portfolio consisted of reinsurance, except in 1905 when *Skåne* together with a German insurer, established a common agency in Valparaiso, Chile, mainly accepting direct insurance (Bolin 1934).

In the early twentieth century, the Swedish insurers, the larger mixed companies, but also pure fire insurance and minor branch insurers were well integrated into the international insurance market. Reinsurance was a natural part of the international portfolios but was used differently by different companies. The international business of *Skandia* and *Skåne* consisted almost entirely of reinsurance, even risks written by their foreign general agents. The only exceptions were the general agents in the Scandinavian countries, where some direct insurance contracts were signed. This was also the case of the pure fire insurers and companies within the minor branches, with some Scandinavian direct insurance contracts but everything outside the Nordic area was reinsurance. The only exception was *Svea* from Gothenburg that accepts both direct and indirect insurance through the main office and the great number of general agencies around the globe. Over time, direct insurance became more important, mainly because the management realized that the profit level was higher for direct insurance than for reinsurance. In addition, in opposition with the rest of insurers in Sweden, the management of *Svea* also regarded direct insurance as a better way to avoid moral hazard in selecting risks (Lönnborg 1999; Elliot et al. 1995; Garethewohl 1980, 1982).

5.3 San Francisco and World War I

With the type of risks in the US market, especially the San Francisco earthquake of 1906 deeply affected the Swedish insurers. Immense losses in the wake of the disaster led them to question the entire foundation on which the foreign business was based. Skandia had a reinsurance agreement with *Royal*; *Svea* had a general agency on site (however with large bits of reinsurance), and *Skåne* had two reinsurance agreements. After careful reconsideration—in particular considering the pros and cons of doing business in the United States, *Skandia* and *Svea* remained in the market while *Skåne* phased out its operations. *Skandia* and *Svea* were primarily motivated by the fact that almost half of their net fire premium income was generated in the United States. *Skandia* even expanded its business on the West Coast when *Royal* took advantage of the withdrawal of its competitors, in particular from Germany, left the market after the disaster (Pearson and Lönnborg 2007, 2008).

Another consequence of the earthquake was that *Skandia* founded *Freja*, a new reinsurance company, as a means of diversifying the international portfolio. *Svea* initially limited its exposure in risky areas but had to revise its strategy in response to renewed competition. Their reinsurance company, *Astrea*, in practice went bankrupt and was totally reorganized and recapitalized. *Skåne*, which suffered major losses from San Francisco as well from an earthquake in Valparaiso latter in the year, left North and South America entirely and focused on the Russian market instead, a decision that turned out to be unwise. The nationalization of the Russian financial sector a decade later after the revolution meant that *Skåne* lost even greater sums on the extensive reinsurance portfolio governed from the office in Saint Petersburg (at the time named Petrograd) (Pearson and Lönnborg 2007).

In short, the consequences after earthquake in San Francisco were that *Skandia* and *Svea* expanded their reinsurance (and *Svea* also the direct insurance) business in the United States, while Skåne instead focused on the Russian market. In all, the heavy losses demonstrated that reinsurance was risky, and losses should be expected on a regular basis but still reinsurance was so profitable and had reached such volumes that it was not possible to close down. It became more important to diversify risks and generate hidden reserves to be able to continue with this lucrative business. After the earthquake many companies introduced different earthquake clauses (which had been the case before the disaster but not possible to exercise fully because of massive criticism from the public and the press) as a way to prevent disaster risks but the enhanced competition made it necessary to relax these clauses. The Swedish insurers tried to avoid too great exposure in the most dangerous areas, but due to collaboration with other companies, it was difficult to put this policy into practice. In sum, the San Francisco earthquake did not really change the practice of reinsurance for the Swedish insurers, although they activated their reinsurance companies as a way to limit the impact of disasters in the balance sheets of the mother companies.

During World War I the reinsurance business continued but on a much lower scale than previously. The international business suffered greatly from World War I; *Svea* and *Skandia* lost 10% of its overseas operations and *Skåne* lost almost 40%. Skåne and Svea temporarily closed their German agencies, which were owned by the general agents until the end of the war; nonetheless, economic turmoil held underwriting down. The Bolshevik Revolution, particularly the confiscation of foreign assets in 1918 resulted in severe losses, especially as noted for *Skåne* (Bring 1917; Bolin 1934; Grenholm 1955; Kader et al. 2010).

During the 1920s and 1930s, the reinsurance business was restored for all three Swedish insurers through new contracts or renewal of older ones and in the 1930s international business was on the same level as before the war. New ways of collaboration were tried as well, for instance *Skandia* and *Svea* started cooperation with a jointly owned corporation in the United States, *Hudson Insurance Company*—that had a smaller share of direct insurance, but the majority of the portfolio consisted of reinsurance agreements. Due to Great Depression and in particular due to heavy losses on so-called farm risks, the entire portfolio was set in run-off in 1933. However, *Hudson* would become the foundation for Skandia's expansion in the United States after World War II. In short, the economic crisis of the 1930s haltered the reinsurance business and that continued through World War II, however few new treaties were signed, but through general agreements older contracts were prolonged.

5.4 Reorganizing Reinsurance After World War II and the Merger Waves

After World War II every Swedish insurer restructured their reinsurance portfolios and all treaties with companies from Germany, Austria, Italy, Hungary and Japan were terminated. There was a shift to sign treaties with companies from Western Europe and the United States, and in particular with insurers from the Nordic region; Norway, Denmark and Finland. One of the reasons for focusing on Nordic countries was that Swedish insurers, during the occupation of Norway and Denmark, and while Finland participated in the war, had acted as reinsurers for companies from these countries. This created a close relationship among the insurers in the Nordic region and that continued after the war through intensive reciprocal reinsurance (Larsson and Lönnborg 2014a; Espeli and Bergh 2016; Ekberg and Myrvang 2017).

In the late 1940s and 1950s, reinsurance was a natural part of the companies' business, in particular of their international business, however the reinsurance business shrank in importance. Nevertheless, in the 1960s the situation changed considerably, mainly through changes in the market structure in Sweden. Two large companies were created through mergers. One of them was *Skandia*, which subsumed almost every joint-stock company in the 1960s. *Skandia* and *Svea* merged in 1960, followed by the *Skåne Group* and *Öresund Group* (mainly maritime insurance) in 1961 and the *Thule Group* in 1963. Twenty of the 23 insurers were eliminated through internal mergers over the next five years, leaving one life, one non-life and one reinsurance company (Lönnborg et al. 2020).

In the end of the 1960s *Skandia* had reorganized the domestic business into geographical zones and started to restructure the international business into zones as well, Europe, North America, South America and Far East (with the exception of the aviation insurance unit that was active worldwide) (Sjögren 2019). In 1968, when the merged new Skandia Group had integrated all of different business into a single corporation group, the management of *Skandia* made a crucial decision. *Skandia* controlled about one third of the entire insurance market in Sweden (in all different sub-branches), and the possibility to expand domestically, due to the legislation, was regarded as more or less impossible. The new strategy was to expand abroad, in particular in the United States, but also in Europe and South America, and in the Nordic countries, where *Skandia* previously had general agents or subsidiaries. Reinsurance became crucial in the foreign portfolio, mainly within non-life insurance, and in particular the US market was in the centre of the company's attention (Englund 1982).

Trygg-Hansa was also created through a series of mergers among mutual insurers (40 companies in 4 groups), the most important concluded in 1970/1971. The mergers were particularly important in creating cost synergies and making it possible to compete with Skandia particularly in economies of scale. In addition, international reinsurance became more important, but *Trygg-Hansa* initially focused on the Nordic and European market in contrary to *Skandia* where, as noted, the United States was most important (Fredrikson et al. 1972).

Mergers were not the only option available to improve efficiency and expand swiftly. *Folksam* (connected to the cooperative movement) grew dramatically in terms of premium income while avoiding extensive mergers. The strategy was to streamline the organization and increase collaboration with trade unions, but also offer low premiums. In 1949, *Folksam* commenced with international reinsurance (previously it only had treaties of outgoing reinsurance but now started to focus on ingoing business as well), however as we will see, it expanded that engagement more heavily in the 1970s (Grip 2009; Larsson et al. 2005).

In the 1970s, a new player surfaced and challenged the industry. After heavy losses due to increasing claims and high inflation, *Skandia*, *Trygg-Hansa* and *Folksam* were forced to raise their premiums. *Länsförsäkringar* (County Insurances) filled the gap. The group is today the largest Swedish provider of non-life insurance in the country. Explaining how it got there requires a little background. *Länsförsäkringar* is an alliance of 24 (today 23) independent provincial companies. They started in the early nineteenth century, the first in 1801, as mutual county insurers and concentrated on rural risks. They founded a joint organization to facilitate cooperation during World War I and established a common reinsurance organization in 1937. The latter organization became a joint-stock company in 1944 and operated on a nationwide basis by providing various types of insurance for the regional companies (these kept the mutual ownership form). The increased rate of urbanization—the rural population moved into cities—hampered their market share in the late 1960s. In response, they launched a new collaborative effort, including a common brand and intensified sales efforts in large and medium-sized cities. The principle of need (part of the new insurance legislation in 1948 that stated that any new company had to demonstrate for the Insurance Inspectorate that there was a need for their products on the market to receive a licence) made it impossible for individual regional companies to obtain concessions for some types of insurance, but the nationwide structure circumvented the obstacle when it came to third-party liability, motor vehicle and certain other policies (Svenberg 1997; Larsson and Lönnborg 2009).

In the 1970s, while the rest of the insurance industry was encountering difficulties and raising premiums, the wealthy regional companies established themselves in the big cities and were able to retain low premiums. The strategy was highly successful for *Länsförsäkringar*, enabling it to expand into life insurance (1985) and banking (1996) once the regulations were relaxed. In the 1980s the group started focusing more intensively on international expansion through reinsurance because it was regarded this as the only way to reach higher premium income (Hjärtström 2005). Another reason was of course, that all of Länsförsäkringar's competitors were active in the international reinsurance market.

The mergers in the 1960s and 1970s turned the Swedish insurance industry into an oligopoly with 4 major players and enhanced the domestic competition—and together with the regulation that all profits within life insurance should be returned to policyholders—pushed the actors to engage in international business in the non-life sector, and particular through reinsurance, that was regarded to be the less expensive and less risky way of expanding abroad. About 60% of *Skandia's* premium income was from international reinsurance and divided between half from the United States and half from Europe. In the case of *Trygg-Hansa* about one third of the premiums came from reinsurance in the Nordics and Europe. While *Folksam* and *Länsförsäkringar*, until the early 1970s only had about 10% of their portfolios in international reinsurance, mainly from Europe (Lönnborg 2002).

5.5 Expansion of Reinsurance in 1970s and 1980s

Inflation, oil crises and economic decline marked the development of Sweden's economy in the late 1970s. The Keynesian economic policy—with low-interest rates and unbalanced state budgets to stimulate the economy—could no longer solve the problem; instead the deficits in the state budget were a steadily increasing problem. A 16% devaluation of the Swedish krona in 1982 successfully stimulated growth and reduced unemployment. But these benefits put a brake on the kinds of institutional and structural changes that the Swedish economy so badly needed. Both the financial and the insurance markets underwent extensive regulatory changes in 1980–1994. Much of the previous regulation had become obsolete and needed to be modernized, particularly in view of globalization and European integration. Liberalization led to a sharp increase in lending, largely financed by capital raised on the international market, and would end up in a severe financial crisis in 1991–1993 (Larsson and Lönnborg 2014b).

As noted, *Skandia* increasingly expanded its operations abroad. Like the Swedish business, the international operation was organized in four geographical zones with offices in Stockholm, New York, Mexico City and Sydney. In Stockholm, the business in Europe, Africa and the Middle East was administrated. The Europe zone was the most important and accounted for almost 50% of the foreign operations. Direct insurance came from subsidiaries in Europe, Belgium, Denmark and Norway, as well as branch offices in West Germany and general agencies in France and the Netherlands. From New York, the United States and Canada operations were conducted, which accounted for two fifths of Skandia's international portfolio. In the United States, only reinsurance was carried out, but in Canada, both direct and indirect business was combined. However, in the latter market, low profitability meant that the operations were kept at a very low level.

Mexico City was the nod of the business in Latin American and South American, and offices established 1971 in Caracas (Venezuela) and Panama City, as well as a department of non-life insurance and a life insurance subsidiary in Colombia. In the latter case, the establishment was an example of where *Skandia* followed Swedish industry abroad. In addition, the fourth head office in Sydney was installed which managed the business in Australia and Southeast Asia. Unlike the other zones, most of the operations in the Far East consisted of direct insurance. In addition, international aviation insurance was operated from Stockholm, but the policies were from the entire world. Another business operated from the headquarters was a unit that catered to the Swedish industry's needs for insurance abroad (Skandia Annual Report 1971 and 1974).

In 1978 new shares were issued with the intention of strengthening Skandia's financial strength ahead of an intensified international expansion. The increased capital base also meant that the company could retain significant insurance amounts on its own account, which was supposed to strengthen its competitiveness both nationally and internationally. In 1979, the *Skandia Group* comprised of *Skandia*, *Skandia Re.*, 10 insurance companies abroad, and minority interests in the life insurance company *Hamburg-Mannheimer*, *Hanse-Merkur* (Hamburg) and *Skandia-Boavista* (Rio de Janeiro). The US operations were reorganized in 1977 to facilitate the expansion of the US market. Then the wholly owned holding company, *Skandia Corporation*, was formed and a subsidiary, *Skandia America Reinsurance Corporation*. In 1979, two companies in Bermuda were launched, owned by Skandia's subsidiaries in United States, Hudson Underwriting and Hudson Reinsurance. In addition, operations were expanded on the US mainland, when branch offices were established in Houston and San Francisco.

One important event happened in 1979 when *Skandia Life UK* started up in Southampton selling unit-linked products (policyholders could decide where the saved capital would be invested). This was the first step towards activating the Group's international life movement and was of major importance for the company's business focus in the mid-1990s. This line of business would become the dominant business for *Skandia* in the 1990s, and the UK branch and US branch would account for 80% of the entire company's premium income (Kallafatides et al. 2010). This business contained no reinsurance and the customers were from the United Kingdom and Swedish citizens that wanted to avoid taxation in Sweden.

The increased internationalization of the business in the 1980s led to the desire to separate the international and national operations. One important reason was that the international business suffered from severe losses, primarily from liability (long-tail) insurance in the United States. In order to avoid the results of the foreign operation also affecting the domestic market, the international operations were transferred to a subsidiary, *Skandia International* (SI), which was listed on the Stockholm Stock Exchange in 1985. Skandia's shareholding amounted to approximately 45%. This resulted in a geographical breakdown of operations; SI would do business abroad while *Skandia* concentrated on Swedish insurance and insurance of Swedish risks abroad. SI had offices in some twenty countries and was indirectly active in more than 100 countries (Kuuse and Olsson 2000, p. 231f; Edvardsson et al. 1992).

Skandia also launched a new business strategy and started to define the Nordic market as the company's home market. In 1987, SI acquired the majority stake in the Danish company Kgl. Fire and a minor post in Finnish Pohjola, which was an expression of closer cooperation between the companies. The new home market was further expanded in 1989 through the purchase of the Norwegian *Vesta* group and 10% of the Norwegian life company *David*. In short, the consequence of the increased presence in the Nordic countries was lower rate of reinsurance and higher amount of direct insurance in the respective country.

However, the initial launch of *Skandia International* was only a three-year parenthesis and in 1989 the outstanding shares were repurchased. The main reasons for integration were both internal and external factors. First, the two companies approached each other's areas and it became more efficient to coordinate the business. With regard to exogenous factors, major changes had occurred, such as international deregulation, elimination of trade barriers, deepening the European cooperation, the banking and insurance gap and changing conditions for reinsurance. All in all, capitalist organizations were required to compete in the international market, and through the merger between *Skandia* and *Skandia International*, one could take advantage of both economies of scale and scope and coordinating the entire group (Larsson and Lönnborg 2018).

Folksam had started international reinsurance in 1949 under the company name Leire, that changed its name in 1963 to *Folksam International* but all business was governed and supervised from Stockholm. In the 1970s the strategy changed, and in 1977 the company *Folksam International UK* was founded in collaboration with several Scandinavian mutual insurers connected to the labour movement. The same kind of construction with Nordic collaboration partners was used in 1979 when *Folksamerica Reinsurance Company* was created with office in New York. Another office was opened in Singapore in 1990 and all the three daughter companies were conducting only reinsurance (Grip 2009, p. 357).

The new market situation with major deregulation in the 1980s made insurers more interested in obtaining capital for gaining additional competition advantages. When *Trygg-Hansa* was demutualized and became a joint-stock company in 1989, its shares were distributed to policyholders and quoted on the Stockholm Stock Exchange. As a joint-stock company, *Trygg-Hansa* could pay for acquisitions with newly issued shares. However, the company also experienced the new structure as a reason to seek greater profitability and capacity to pay dividends. According to the management, a more efficient organization and expansion abroad would benefit both owners and policyholders.

As it turned out, the conversion fell short of management's expectations. Several expensive and ill-considered investments were made for expansion purposes. Two of them were particularly costly. The insurer *Home of New York*, which was twice the size of *Trygg-Hansa*, turned out to be an unwieldy acquisition and was sold a few years later at a considerable loss, around One Billion US dollars in current value. *Gota Bank*, a Swedish acquisition in the bank sector, suffered major credit losses after the financial crisis and was finally taken over by partly state-owned *Nordbanken* (today Nordea, no longer state-own and controlled by the Finnish insurer Sampo, Gratzer et al. 2021).

As noted, greater competition in the domestic market made it more tempting to launch or expand foreign operations. Internationalization generally increased in the late 1960s and 1970s when the Swedish central bank became more lenient in approving foreign investment. The newly merged *Skandia Group* consolidated its foreign agencies to improve efficiency and identify growth opportunities. *Skandia* became more involved in the US and European markets, but also through acquiring a series of Scandinavian companies. *Trygg-Hansa* and *Folksam* were also active in foreign markets, setting up in the United Kingdom and United States in the 1970s, albeit on a much smaller scale than Skandia. In sum, the 1980s was a period of powerful international expansion, which occurred first of all through an expanded commitment to the international reinsurance market.

5.6 Closing Down the Reinsurance Business

The last thirty-fourty years contain almost revolutionary changes in the Swedish insurance market. Deregulation started in the 1980s and continued until 1995 (when Sweden entered the European Union) was characterized by continued deregulation, mainly due to Sweden's entrance into the European Union during which most of the regulated system in Sweden was dismantled. Some of the regulations, however, did not disappear at once, for instance, prohibition for life insurers granting dividends to owners and the principle of equity (fairness). These were not ended until 2000.

The insurance market indeed changed considerably due to these deregulations, but even more changes would be caused by individual strategies of Swedish insurance companies. These strategies caused severe problems and the solutions had a deep impact on the market structure and the ownership of several insurers. One of these changes was the entry of large foreign insurance companies buying domestic insurers.

In the early 1990s, the view about reinsurance changed considerably. It became less profitable and associated with higher risks, in particular because of natural disasters. In addition, the Swedish insurers had less use for any kind of outgoing reinsurance because all of the companies had reached considerable size and it was no longer necessary to distribute their own risks. In addition, large industrial firms created their own captive insurance firms—for instance Atlas Copco, Electrolux, ABB and Volvo—and reinsured their larger risks with traditional insurers. These further reduced the need of using reinsurance.

In explaining the profound changes in the Swedish insurance market during the last 20 years, the development of the largest insurer *Skandia* is an illustrative example. Due to slow growth and low profitability in the domestic market, *Skandia* turned to the international market. This strategy was initially successful for the expansion of business, as noted since in the 1960s and the beginning of the 1990s *Skandia* was the tenth largest reinsurance company in the world, with its main focus on non-life insurance. In 1995, about 85% of the total premium income in non-life insurance stemmed from international reinsurance but was associated with immense losses and high costs in reserve capital. Deregulation and in particular the launching of unit-linked insurance in the United Kingdom, however, opened the life insurance market as a means of increasing profitability (Edvardsson et al. 1992; Kuuse and Olsson 2000; Lönnborg 2002).

In 1996, a new management (the previous CEO was in charge of the business for 17 years) totally altered the business strategy of the company and regarded non-life insurance as an outdated product with limited growth opportunities and weak profitability. As a consequence, the international non-life business was incrementally closed down while the business of unit-linked insurance—initially launched in the United Kingdom in 1979 as a means of circumventing Swedish legislation—showed rapid growth in Sweden as well as internationally. Thus, the company was completely reorganized, and the non-life Scandinavian portfolio was transferred to a new company. In collaboration with Norwegian *Storebrand* and Finnish Sampo, Skandia started a company called If, and transferred all their non-life insurance risks to this jointly owned corporation. Simultaneously, the business of selling variable annuities became the core industry for Skandia, in particular in the United States and the United Kingdom. In short, the insurance group was transformed into a life insurance and savings company and the entire international non-life reinsurance portfolio was acquired by *Hannover Re* in 1998—which marked the end for Skandia in this line of business after 143 years (Larsson and Lönnborg 2019a).

The initial phase of the new strategy and expansion of *Skandia* was more than successful; the business, particularly in the United States and the United Kingdom, grew substantially, and the share price skyrocketed on the Stockholm Stock Exchange. In the wake of the dot-com crash and 9/11, prices on stock exchanges started to drop and that started to call the strategy of *Skandia* into question. However, the main problem was that Skandia's reputation was severely hurt by a series of scandals, for instance illegal internal affairs with its subsidiary *Skandia*

Life (owned by the policyholders), providing executives (and their families) with subsidized apartments and finally by generous bonus schemes. Top management was fired and in three cases these issues ended up in court. The scandals of Skandia and the rapid downturn in the equity market made the company vulnerable, and in 2002—as a means of recapitalizing and surviving as an independent company, *American Skandia* was sold to *Prudential Financial* and the large business in Japan was sold or put into run-off. In 2005, South African *Old Mutual* made a bid on what was left of the company, which was met with resistance from management and domestic shareholders. The new management desperately tried to consolidate the company and among other things sold its shares in *If* to its Finnish partner *Sampo* (today the sole owner of *If*). But in February 2006 (after 151 years of business), the hostile takeover was completed, and Skandia was subsequently delisted in Stockholm and London. *Skandia* was the only stock that was still traded since the Stockholm Stock Exchange was founded in 1863 (Kallifatides et al. 2010; Larsson and Lönnborg 2009, 2019a).

Several mutual companies such as *Länsförsäkringar*, *Wasa* and *Folksam* closed down their portfolios abroad—including reinsurance treaties, agencies and subsidiaries—entirely during the 1990s. These portfolios consisted mainly of reinsurance contracts and losses were so extensive that it started to affect the domestic business and as mutual companies (owned by their customers), it became harder to justify the international engagements. The strategy of expanding through international reinsurance was also associated with a large need to reserve capital abroad, which was problematic for these mutual insurers and even caused problems on the domestic market (Larsson and Lönnborg 2018).

The mutual company *Folksam* was severely affected by the financial crisis in the 1990s and in particular by its international business. The international reinsurance venture turned out to be very costly for *Folksam*. It was initially run entirely from Stockholm, and the first foreign subsidiary was not formed until 1977. In Britain, the business was developed together with the Finnish company Kansa and the Norwegian company *Samvirke*. In 1979, a New York subsidiary was added—also in cooperation with other cooperative companies. In 1990, a branch was established in Singapore. At the beginning of the 1990s, the profitability in international reinsurance was low and as noted several Swedish companies left the market. *Folksam*, however, continued its international business but was hit by considerable losses and was forced to sell its parts (the business in Britain went bankrupt). At the beginning of the 2000s, *Folksam* once again operates only on the domestic market and still has considerable market shares. The ingoing reinsurance is entirely dismantled, and outgoing reinsurance is only randomly used (Grip 2009; Kennedy 1999; Larsson et al. 2005).

For *Trygg-Hansa* the problems, ironically enough, started after demutualization in 1989 when the group got access to new channels of capital and bought the American insurance company *Home of New York* and the Swedish '*Gota Bank*', and both transactions ended up in heavy losses and the end of *Trygg-Hansa* as an independent company. The economic problems of Trygg-Hansa contributed to the creation of a new financial constellation, when the SEB bank acquired the insurance company in 1997. Soon after this purchase, SEB sold the non-life operations (and the reinsurance business) of the company and rented out the brand name of *Trygg-Hansa* to the Danish 'Codan' (owned by British Royal & Sun Alliance, today RSA) and the entire portfolio of international reinsurance business was terminated.

In short, the reinsurance in the non-life sector in Sweden was in practice closed down when *Skandia* sold *Skandia International* in 1998 to *Hannover Re*, and Skandia was transformed into a life insurance and saving company. The remaining non-life portfolio—which contained risks from Scandinavia and bits and pieces of reinsurance—was transferred to a new company, *If*, owned by *Skandia*, Norwegian *Storebrand* and Finnish *Sampo* in 1999. In 2003, *Skandia* and *Storebrand* sold the shares in *If* to Finnish Sampo, and since then the company has not written any business within the field of non-life insurance, direct nor reinsurance.

5.7 Conclusion

Reinsurance—directly copied from in particular British insurers—was crucial for creating the modern Swedish insurance industry. First, it was a mean to distribute large risks without jeopardizing survival and offering fixed premiums for customers without possibility to claim additional premiums in wake of heavy disbursement. Second, it was a way to increase premium income and create portfolios with risks from a wide array of countries, which also was a method to secure long-term survival. Many of the contracts with foreign insurers would become reciprocal, admitting risk and receiving risks from the same partner, and thereby avoiding moral hazard issues. Over time, reinsurance would become the means of expanding the business abroad, and in particular before and during the deregulation of the financial market in 1980s and 1990s. This was a common feature among a large number of Swedish insurers.

When the Swedish direct insurers in the non-life sector were founded in the middle of the nineteenth century, reinsurance was thus a strategy to both distribute large risk to secure longevity and to compensate the reduction of premium income with risk from abroad. Many of the companies' CEOs had previously experience from acting as general agents for foreign insurers and many of these contacts were used to sign reinsurance treaties. The Swedish insurers in particular used insurance companies from United Kingdom and Germany but also insurers from countries such as Switzerland, Netherlands and France.

The large companies created their own reinsurance companies as a way to mitigate their risks and to separate the domestic portfolio from their international risks. Nevertheless, these reinsurance companies were closely connected to the mother companies and never had the possibility to enhance their business independently. This was the most important reason that the Swedish reinsurance companies never became larger corporations specialized in worldwide operations. The reinsurance companies only acted as a supplementary service to the direct insurers. In addition, this makes it difficult to separate the reinsurance business from the direct insurance business, in reality the businesses were closely interconnected.

The development of the insurance sector with higher concentration ratio, mainly through mergers, and increased competition that made it difficult to expand on the domestic market was an important driver behind a larger use of reinsurance. In addition, the stricter regulation—for instance governing the market structure, difficulties to found new companies, duty to invest in governmental bonds, and that all profits in life insurance should be returned to policyholders—made the international market even more crucial for the Swedish insurers. The way of expanding—even if subsidiaries were established abroad—was normally through reinsurance, because it was cheaper than building up an organization that should assess every individual risk. Reinsurance was to some extent a case of 'free-riding' where the direct insurer had the responsibility to evaluate risks and secure safe risk management.

In the 1990s the reinsurance business was seriously questioned because of extensive losses on foreign risk, in particular hurricane Andrew in 1989 caused heavy disbursement, but also because the financial crisis in Sweden in 1991–1993 created problems that questioned reinsurance. Several insurers—in particular the mutual ones—quite rapidly winded down their reinsurance portfolio because of the high risk and to continue with reinsurance would have required a lot of more capital than assumed to be reasonable.

The first joint-stock insurer in Sweden, Skandia, was taken over in 2006 by Old Mutual from South Africa. However, one company within the group, Skandia Life, could not—because of the legislation—be controlled by Old Mutual. Skandia Life was a joint-stock company but operated as a mutual and was controlled by its policyholders. In 2011, Skandia Life made an offer for the parent company Skandia (including its insurance and bank operations within Sweden), and the company was transformed into a mutual company (after a three year transition period). The previous international portfolio (only containing life insurance products) of Skandia is now under the trademark of Old Mutual, and the mutual Skandia only conduct business in Sweden (Larsson and Lönnborg 2019a).

The strategy of expanding business abroad among Swedish insurers was not by any measure successful, even though the preconditions were favourable in the 1990s. The deregulation of the financial market repealed almost every institutional obstacle for doing business abroad. However, in spite of Sweden's membership in the EU, the fall of the Communist regimes in Central and Eastern Europe, and the deregulation of markets in South America, Japan and China, the majority of Sweden's insurance companies decided to withdraw from foreign markets. Despite improved international circumstances during the 1990s and the beginning of the 2000s, the domestic market became increasingly important for almost every Swedish insurer. This seemingly illogical development was first and foremost explained by a lack of venture capital to compete in the international market. But fierce competition and severe losses also occurred in several foreign markets and made the wisdom of retaining worldwide operations doubtful. In addition, the deregulated Swedish financial market made it more urgent than ever to consolidate the insurers' positions in the domestic market.

This partly suggests that the strongly regulated environment did not hamper the insurers from doing business abroad; it even seems likely that the 'stable' domestic market was a vital precondition for international business, which is a surprising conclusion. In sum, in the 1990s, almost every Swedish insurance company withdrew from the international insurance market in the non-life sector and all reinsurance treaties were repelled.

In Sweden, the mutual insurers have prevailed in the market and when *Skandia* was turned into a mutual company in 2014 (three years after the subsidiary *Skandia Life* acquired the mother company from *Old Mutual*) it meant that the insurance market is now totally dominated by mutual insurers. Through mutual ownership, Swedish insurers are now protected from foreign hostile takeovers, but at the same time, the ownership form is associated with capital constraints. This makes it difficult to conduct business on the international market, however, the conclusion among Swedish insurers after being involved in international direct insurance and reinsurance for one and half century, it is not worth the risk.

Reinsurance was instrumental for building a solid insurance industry in Sweden. Firstly, it was a way to secure long-term survival and keep the ability to accept larger or dangerous risks and thereby fulfilling their responsibility to financial markets. Secondly, it was a measure for expanding the insurers business on the international market, both as a way to diversify their risk portfolio and as a means to increase premium income. Over time, the ingoing reinsurance (and to some extent direct insurance) became crucial for all insurers making growth of premium incomes possible. Mainly due to fierce domestic competition and strict regulations, it was necessary to expand into foreign markets from the 1970s. Ironically, the deregulation of the financial sector—that withdrew all obstacles for conducting business abroad—instead revealed that Swedish insurers did not possess enough capital to continue their foreign business. The heavy losses particularly in reinsurance made it clear the international business was not sustainable in the long run. In the last twenty years, reinsurance has entirely disappeared in the portfolios of Swedish insurers, the heavy losses and the greater risk of expensive reimbursement in the future and demand on capital reserves, made reinsurance an obsolete branch of business (Larsson and Lönnborg 2019a). The insurers in Sweden—both joint-stocks and mutual, the latter form of ownership dominating the market—are today only writing domestic risks and this seems to be a new feature among insurers from smaller countries, the risk for accepting ingoing reinsurance seems to be unacceptable for them.

REFERENCES

Bergander, Bengt. 1967. *Försäkringsväsendet i Sverige 1814–1914* [The Insurance Industry in Sweden 1814–1914]. Lund.

Bolin, Sture. 1934. *Skåne. Brand- och lifförsäkringsbolaget. Minnesskrift 1884–1934* [Skåne. Fire- and Life Insurance Company. Memories] Malmö: Skåne.

Borsheid, Peter, and Robin Pearson. (eds.). 2007. *Internationalisation and Globalisation of Insurance in the 19th and 20th Century*. Marburg: Philipps-University.

Borsheid, Peter, and Niels Viggo Haueter (eds.). 2012. *World Insurance: The Evolution of a Global Risk Network*. Oxford: Oxford University Press.

Bring, Ernst. 1917. "'Historik *[The History]*'". In *Brand- och lifförsäkringsaktiebolaget Svea. Minnesskrift 1866–1916* [The Fire and Life Insurance Company Svea. Memories 1866–1916]. Gothenburg.

Bucht, Otto. 1936. *Försäkringsväsendets företagsformer från antiken till våra dagar* [Business Forms in the Insurance Industry from the Roman Empire Until Today]. Stockholm: KF.

Caruana de las Cagigas, Leonardo, and Andre Straus. (ed.). 2017. *Highlights on Reinsurance History*. New York and Bruxuelles: Peter Lang.

Doherty, Neil, and Kent Smetters. 2005. "Moral Hazard in Reinsurance Markets." *Journal of Risk and Insurance* 3: 375–391.

Durling, Helge. 1937. *Kort handbok i allmän försäkringslära* [Short Handbook in General Insurance Theory]. Stockholm: Svenska Försäkringsföreningens publikationsserie No 9.

Edvardsson, Bo, Leif Edvinsson, and Harry Nyström. 1992. *Internationalisering i tjänsteföretag* [The Internationalization of Service Firms]. Lund: Studentlitteratur.

Ekberg, Espen, and Christine Myrvang. 2017. *Ulykkens frukter: Storebrand og forsikringsbransjen, bind 1: 1767–1945* [The Fruits of Accidents. Storebrand and the Insurance Industry, vol. 1: 1767–1945]. Oslo: Universitetsforlaget.

Ekwall, Johan, and Raoul Grünthal. 1990. "The Internationalization of the Swedish Insurance Industry." *Scandinavian Insurance Quarterly* 3: 165–197.

Elliot, Michael W., Bernard L. Webb, Howard N. Anderson, and Peter R. Kensicki. 1995. *Principles of Reinsurance*, vol 1. Malvern: American Insitute for Chartered Property Causulty Underwriters Insurance Institute of America.

Englund, Karl. 1982. *Insurance Companies on the Move: From Skandia to the Skandia Group, 1855–1980*. Stockholm: Skandia.

Espeli, Harald, and Trond Bergh. 2016. *Tiden går. Gjensidige 250 år* [As Times Goes by. Gjensidige 250 Years]. Bergen: Universitetsforlaget.

Fredrikson, Verner, Karl Hildebrand, Filip Lundberg and Waldemar Odhnoff. 1972. *Framtiden Livförsäkringsaktiebolag: De Förenade, Framtiden, Victoria. Minnesskrift* [Framtiden Life Insurance Company: De Förenade, Framtiden, Victoria. Memories]. Stockholm: Trygg-Hansa.

Garethewohl, Klaus. 1980 [1982]. *Reinsurance. Principles and Practice*, vols. 1 and 2. Karlsruhe: Verlag Versicherungswirtschaft.
Golding, Charles E. 1931. *A History of Reinsurance with Sidelights on Insurance*. Offered as a Memento of Fifty Years' Service in the Reinsurance World by Sterling Offices Limited. London: Sterling.
Gratzer, Karl, Mikael Lönnborg, and Mikael Olsson. 2021. "Collective Ownership in Sweden. The State, Privatization and Entrepreneurship." In *Beyond Borders: Essays on Entrepreneurship, Co-operatives and Education in Sweden and Tanzania*, ed. Mikael Lönnborg, Benson Otieno Ndiege, and Besrat Tesfaye, 175–198. Stockholm: Södertörn Academic Studies 85.
Grenholm, Åke. 1955. *Försäkringsaktiebolaget Skandia 100 år. 1855–1955* [The Insurance Company Skandia 100 Years, 1855–1955]. Stockholm: Skandia.
Grip, Gunvall. 2009. *Folksam 1908–2008. Folksams försäkringsrörelse* [Folksam 1908–2008. The Insurance Business of Folksam]. vol. 1. Stockholm: Informationsförlaget.
Hägg, Göran P. T. 1998. *An Institutional Analysis of Insurance Regulation—The Case of Sweden*. PhD diss., Lund Economic Studies 75. Lund.
Haueter, Niels Viggo, and Geoffrey Jones. (ed.) 2016. *Managing Risk in Reinsurance: From City Fires to Global Warming*. Oxford: Oxford University Press.
Hjärtström, Pär. (ed.). 2005. *Idéerna bakom länsförsäkringsgruppen: Från brandstodsbolag till finansiella varuhus* [The Ideas Behind Länsförsäkringar Group. From Brandstuth to Financial Retailers]. Stockholm: Länsförsäkringar.
James, Harold, Peter Borscheid, David Gugerli, and Tobias Straumann (eds.). 2014. *The Value of Risk. Swiss Re and the History of Reinsurance*. Oxford: Oxford University Press.
Kader, Hale A., Michael Adams, Lars Fredrik Andersson, and Magnus Lindmark. 2010. "The Determinants of Reinsurance in the Swedish Property Fire Insurance Market During the Interwar Years, 1919–1939." *Business History* 2: 268–284.
Kallifatiders, Markus, Sophie Nachemson-Ekwall, and Sven-Erik Sjöstrand. 2010. *Corporate Governance in Modern Financial Capitalism: Old Mutual's Hostile Takeover of Skandia*. Cheltenham: Edward Elgar.
Kennedy, Jim. 1999. *Not by Chance: A History of the International Cooperative and Mutual Insurance Federation*. Manchester: Holyoake Books.
Kopf, Edwin W. 1929. "The Origin and Development of Reinsurance." *Proceedings of the Casualty Actuarial Society* (Casualty Actuarial Society). xvi.
Kuuse, Jan, and Kent Olsson. 2000. *Ett sekel med Skandia* [A Century with Skandia]. Stockholm: Skandia.
Larsson, Mats, Mikael Lönnborg, and Sven-Erik Svärd. 2005. *Den svenska försäkringsmodellens uppgång och fall* [The Rise and Fall of the Swedish Insurance Model]. Stockholm Svenska Försäkringsföreningens Förlag.

Larsson, Mats, and Mikael Lönnborg. 2009. "Den svenska finansmarknaden i ett långsiktigt perspektiv [The Swedish Financial Market in a Long-Term Perspective]." In *Folksam 1908–2008. Mer än endast försäkring [Folksam 1908–2008. More Than Only Insurance]*, ed. Gunvall Grip, 210–255. Stockholm: Informationsförlaget.

Larsson, Mats, and Mikael Lönnborg. 2010. "The History of Insurance Companies in Sweden." In *Encuentro Internacional sobre la Historia del Seguro*, ed. Leonardo Caruana de las Cagigas, 197–237. Madrid: Fundacio Mapfre.

Larsson, Mats, Mikael Lönnborg, and Sven-Erik Svärd. 2011. "The Rise and Decline of the Swedish Insurance Model." In *Business History in Sweden*, ed. Mikael Lönnborg and Paulina Rytkönen, 405–434. Möklinta: Gidlunds.

Larsson, Mats, and Mikael Lönnborg. 2014a. *Scor Sweden Re. 100 Years of Swedish (Re)Insurance History*. Stockholm: Dialogos.

Larsson, Mats, and Mikael Lönnborg. 2014b. *Finanskriser i Sverige* [Financial Crises in Sweden]. Lund: Studentlitteratur.

Larsson, Mats, and Mikael Lönnborg. 2015. "Survival and Success of Swedish Mutual Insurers." In *Corporate Forms and Organizational Choice in International Insurance*, ed. Robin Pearson, and Takau Yoneyama, 93–113. Oxford: Oxford University Press.

Larsson, Mats, and Mikael Lönnborg. 2016. "Regulating Competition of the Swedish Insurance Business: The Role of the Insurance Cartel Registry." In *Regulation Competition. Cartel Registers in the Twentieth-Century World*, ed. Susanna Fellman, and Martin Shanahan, 248–267. Abidgon and New York: Routledge.

Larsson, Mats, and Mikael Lönnborg. 2017. "Swedish Life Reinsurance and Risk Management." In *Highlights on Reinsurance History*, ed. Leonardo Caruana de las Cagigas, and Andre Straus, 93–112. Bruxelles and New York: Peter Lang.

Larsson, Mats, and Mikael Lönnborg. 2018. *Ömsesidig försäkring. Bolag, kunder och marknad* [Mutual Insurance. Firms, Customer and Market]. Stockholm: Dialogos.

Larsson, Mats, and Mikael Lönnborg. 2019a. *Omvandlingar. Försäkringsbolaget Skandia 1990–2016* [Transitions. The Insurance Company Skandia 1990–2016]. Stockholm: Förlaget Näringslivshistoria.

Larsson, Mats, and Mikael Lönnborg. 2019b. "'Same But Different': Trust, Confidence and Governance Among Swedish Mutual Insurers." In *Managing Hybrid Organizations. Governance, Professionalism and Regulation*, ed. Susanna Alexius, and Staffan Furusten, 49–72. Cham: Palgrave Macmillan.

Leffler, Johan. 1905. "Historik". In *Försäkringsaktiebolaget Skandia 1855–1905* [The Insurance Company Skandia 1855–1905]. Stockholm: Norstedt.

Lönnborg, Mikael. 1999. *Internationalisering av svenska försäkringsbolag. Drivkrafter, organisering och utveckling 1855–1913* [The Internationalization of Swedish Insurers. Driving Forces, Organization and Development 1855–1913]. Uppsala Studies in Economic History 46. Uppsala: Department of Economic History.

Lönnborg, Mikael. 2002. "Skandiakoncernens internationella verksamhet 1887–1995" [The International Business of Skandia Insurance Company]. *Scandinavian Insurance Quarterly* 3: 237–256.

Lönnborg, Mikael, Peter Hedberg, and Lars Karlsson. 2020. "Swedish Insurance Institutions and Efficiency 1920–1980." In *Risk and the Insurance Business in History*, ed. Jerònia Pons, and Robin Pearson, 157–177. Madrid: Fundación Mapfre.

Pearson, Robin. 1995. "The Development of Reinsurance in Europe During the Nineteenth Century." *Journal of European Economic History* 3: 557–572.

Pearson, Robin. 1997. "British and European Enterprise in American Markets 1850–1914." *Business and Economic History* 2: 438–451.

Pearson, Robin, and Mikael Lönnborg. 2007. "Swedish Insurance Companies and the San Francisco Earthquake of 1906." In *Internationalisation and Globalisation of Insurance in the 19th and 20th Century*, ed. Peter Borscheid, and Robin Pearson, 27–40. Marburg: Philipps-University.

Pearson, Robin, and Mikael Lönnborg. 2008. "Regulatory Regime and Multinational Insurers Before 1914." *Business History Review* 1: 59–86.

Robin, Pearson. 2020. "Normative Practices, Narrative Fallacies? International Reinsurance and Its history." *Business History*. https://doi.org/10.1080/00076791.2020.1808885.

Sjögren, Hans. 2019. *Smorgasbord. Varumärke och flygförsäkring. När det skandinaviska flög ut över världen* [Smorgasbord. Brand and Aviation Insurance. When the Scandinavian Flew Around the World]. Linköping: Linköping University.

Skandia. 1971 and 1974. *Annual Report*. Stockholm: Skandia.

Svenberg, Staffan (ed.). 1997. *Den lokala historien: 80 år av framgångsrikt samarbete* [The Local History: 80 Years of Successful Cooperation]. Stockholm: Länsförsäkringar.

Sverige Reinsurance, 1965. *Sverige Reinsurance Company 1914–1964*. Stockholm.

Trebilcock, Clive. 1985 [1998]. *Phoenix Assurance and the Devolopment of British Insurance*, vol 2 . Cambridge: Cambridge University Press.

CHAPTER 6

The Ups and Downs of French Reinsurance in the Twentieth Century

André Straus

In France, as in England, before the First World War, reinsurance was the almost exclusive monopoly of reinsurance companies with headquarters in the central empires, Switzerland and Russia. A few French companies worked in the industry, but they had not acquired the know-how of their foreign competitors.

The first company established in France had been incorporated in 1884 (*Société anonyme de réassurances*) and in 1914 there were still only 5 with a subscribed capital of 31,000,000 francs and released 15,000,000. They were not able to compete with the German, Austrian, or Swiss companies that were preferred by the French ceding companies.

Some parts of this chapter are part of a book Forthcoming of the history of SCOR.

A. Straus (✉)
CNRS-Université Paris1 Panthéon-Sorbonne, Paris, France

© The Author(s), under exclusive license to Springer Nature Switzerland AG 2021
L. Caruana de las Cagigas and A. Straus (eds.), *Role of Reinsurance in the World*, Palgrave Studies in Economic History,
https://doi.org/10.1007/978-3-030-74002-3_6

The situation of French professional reinsurers was not bad as they were not in sufficient numbers to compete with each other, and they were therefore able to dictate their conditions to insurers who were not dreaming at that time of "reciprocity" and saw in reinsurance only a way to cover part of their commitments and did not imagine they could benefit from their relations with their reinsurers. Nevertheless, until the First World War, reinsurance was most often considered in France as a branch of insurance of secondary interest.

6.1 THE REINSURANCE MARKET BETWEEN TWO WORLDS WARS

The war changed this situation. The central empires put aside, the insurers were forced to turn to other centers to yield their overflow. Russia first, and after it the neutral countries, notably Sweden, Switzerland and Norway were very happy to receive this activity which had proved so profitable. Russia was best placed as an ally of France and seized French affairs as much as she could. But the Russian revolution brought new troubles to the French underwriters who began to realize the many disadvantages resulting from the reassurance of French business abroad and in particular with the companies of the neutral countries. These companies had continued to deal with the German companies to which they surrendered French affairs thus procuring, certainly without hostile intentions, what constituted in time of hostilities valuable indications on the industry and the trade, or on the maritime routes. To remedy this situation the French government took a little late, February 15, 1917, a law prohibiting reinsurance from companies belonging to hostile countries risks subscribed in France or Algeria, as well as some companies belonging to countries Neutral suspected of having too close ties with the reinsurers of the Central Empires. The Ministry of Labor established a "blacklist" of undesirable companies. Some companies had been forbidden to trade from the beginning of the hostilities, but their number was considerably enlarged in 1917.

This change in the reinsurance centers also caused the creation in 1915 of two new companies. Two others followed in 1917 (*Vulcan*), then two again in 1920 (*Les réassurances, Compagnie générale de réassurances*), one in 1921 (*France-Réassurances*) and two others in 1924 (*La Nationale, compagnie d'assurance Crédit et de Réassurances*, one of which dealt with life reinsurance). Other professional reinsurers dealt with all branches of insurance. They could be divided into two groups: the first group included the companies receiving their business from the companies to which they belonged (they would now be called "captives"); the second group included reinsurers who took their acceptances on the market.

In the 1920s, the movement of concentration that affected all branches of commerce and industry also extended to the French reinsurance. At the end of 1926 there were 14 companies in France whose main activity was reinsurance. They represented a subscribed capital of 87,000,000 francs, of which 46,000,000 had been released. During the financial year 1926, the premiums collected amounted to 790,000,000 francs, of which the retrocessions accounted for just over 44%. This figure was far from measuring the total amount of guarantees given in France, but the establishment of precise data is practically impossible to make, given the inaccuracy of statistics.

It should be particularly noted that many direct insurance companies had an ancillary branch that was reinsurance. At the end of 1926, reinsurers' reserves totaled 352 million and their investment in both movable and immovable property approached 400 million francs. During the year, the reinsurers had paid for 278 million claims (62%) and set aside 150 million for risks incurred and 121 million for exceptional losses. The commissions paid amounted to 15 million francs. Their investments had attracted interest of 18 million francs and the operating account for the year had a profit of nearly 6 million francs, of which a third had been distributed to the shareholders.

Given the general situation of the country in 1926, these results were satisfactory. The devaluation of the franc followed by its stabilization had had a serious impact on the affairs of several companies. The value of the franc had fallen gradually since the war and reached its lowest point in July 1926. At that date the pound sterling was worth 250 francs against 130 francs six months before. It is useless to insist on the profound difficulties caused by this situation to the French economy, and particularly to reinsurance: commitments initially carefully measured became disproportionate to the resources of the company after a further fall in the currency. The management of the foreign exchange reserves became a real headache and for the reinsurer, if he did not want to be brutally ruined, was forced to transform himself into a real expert on the foreign exchange market.

The business offered by the French companies to foreign companies did not naturally attract them, and the reinsurers of the hard currency countries watched the fall of the franc with anxiety and worry. The word "inflation" was on everyone's lips and one inevitably thought of the fate of the German mark and the Austrian crown. The franc seemed so ill that it was waiting for his death. French reinsurers offering or seeking business in the London or Stockholm markets were received freshly. The loss of confidence that prevailed inside the country had gained foreign markets. To complete the picture, it is necessary to consider the increase in corporate expenses following the rise in the cost of living as well as the instability of governments, which was not less than the instability of exchange. It would have been logical in this context that the results of the reinsurance companies suffer seriously. And in fact, after the stabilization, the first results of the reinsurers were mediocre insofar as the stabilization impacts on exports slowed down and put in difficulty trade and industry creating panic at the expense of insurers and reinsurers, especially in the fire division. The situation, however, recovered. The stabilization, although not officialized by the devaluation of June 1928, resulted in a return of confidence not only in France but also abroad and the year ended in a profit for the reinsurers whereas we could have expected a déficit (Table 6.1).

For several years, reinsurers and direct insurers had been divided into two opposing camps, and both were always keen to make their reciprocal complaints heard violently. The former criticized the ceding companies for abnormal tariff reductions. Rightly criticizing the fierce competition between the direct insurance companies. They complained of the increase in certain commission and acquisition rates, and for some companies, of a sort of clandestine selection of risks with, sometimes, certain administrative irregularities which would have been very harmful to them. Finally, the reinsurers denounced as abnormal the improvement noticed in the statistics of certain risks. An improvement which in their eyes, would only have been caused by the slowdown of the general activity with the crisis and which would thus have been only momentary. This cyclical improvement had served to direct companies to reshuffle their rates, a dangerous attitude, because a recovery of business could lead to a recovery of claims. The current would be difficult to recover, and it would take several years to bring the cost of insurance to its fair value.

On the other hand, insurers did not fail to point out the reasons for dissatisfaction with the uncompromising attitude of reinsurers. They complained of the often excessive and sometimes unjustified severity that they brought in the review of assignments, the auditing of accounting records and the strict application of treaty clauses. They complained of a sort of standardization of methods, reproaching their reinsurers for

Table 6.1 French reinsurance companies in 1927

Date of creation	Companies	Paid-up capital	Reserves Générales	Premiums IARD	Premiums Life Insurance	Interest received	Dividends paid Somme	Dividends paid Rate
1913	Cie européenne de réassurances	1,000,000	3,032,937	16,952,861	33,219,756	1,104,835	937,258	180,000	18
1916	Française de Réassurances générales	6,000,000	3,275,899	66,442,002	126,069,076	2,509,886			
1920	Cie Générale de Réassurances	3,750,000		7,428,169	15,394,992	469,976	417,399		
1905	Havraise de Réassurances	2,500,000	6,048,256	13,837,651	30,442,268		2,779,829	500,000	20
1916	Parisienne de Réassurances	250,000	722,270	2,830,036	4,933,008		198,030	62,500	25
1921	La France Réassurances	1,500,000	1,630,852	3,454,645	5,979,064	541,225	389,026	120,000	8
1904	La Réassurance nouvelle	2,000,000	9,985,975	31,595,096	42,775,838	2,241,678	2,256,609	500,000	25
1919	Les Réassurances	2,500,000	2,056,814	16,700,957	32,525,514	1,304,252	500,374	300,000	12
1884	Soc. An. De Réassurances	8,000,000	24,345,364	56,769,572	62,472,169	5,250,834	5,168,779	1,000,000	25

(continued)

Table 6.1 (continued)

Date of creation	Companies	Paid-up capital	Reserves		Premiums		Interest received	Dividends paid	
			Générales		*IARD*	*Life Insurance*		*Somme*	*Rate*
Total		27,500,000	51,098,367	216,010,979	353,799,685	10,912,800	15,157,190	2,662,500	9.7

The Review, London, November 16, 1928

ignoring the differences both commercially and administratively from one market to another, or even on the same spot, from one company to another. In short, cedants generally blamed their reinsurers for no longer participating equitably in all the costs they had to pay.

The tension between reinsurers and direct insurers had resulted in a fairly large number of amicable arbitrations and some lawsuits. On the other hand, reinsurers no longer hesitated in the early 1930s to denounce the deficit treaties and to put the companies in default to clean up their portfolios. This resulted in a sort of cleaning of the market that helped to improve the relationship between insurers and reinsurers without really talking about a return to the "gentlemen's agreement" that existed before the war. Nevertheless, in 1932 and 1933, the reinsurance companies noted a noticeable progress in their industrial results. It was the Fire Division that was the most profitable, while the "Accidents" business and in particular those of "Automobile Liability" were still sources of losses and the reinsurance companies had been led to reduce their commitments in this sector and to denounce treaties whose conditions could not be changed and whose economy no longer allowed for better results.

Overall the policy of reduction of the commitments joined to the consequences of the devaluation of certain foreign currencies led to a marked decline in the amount of the premium revenues. Between 1930 and 1933 the amount of premiums was reduced by 44%. In addition, because of declining foreign currency holdings and portfolio values, the companies were forced to make heavy depreciations, reinforce their technical reserves, and build up increasingly large deposits with the ceding companies. This situation was not peculiar to French reinsurance. *Münchener Rückversicherung* bore the same assessment.

Most reinsurers also pointed to a dangerous development (Table 6.2). Both as a result of the measures taken by the powerful reinsurance companies with regard to direct insurance, and because of the political and financial events that occurred in certain States. National companies, particularly in France, were reducing their business with the foreign reinsurance companies. Developed the exchange of premiums between them, yielded and retroceded, accepted and participated in the portfolios of their sisters, or simply carried their business to reinsurance companies of their country. This initiated a sort of "nationalization" of reinsurance, both from an economic and a technical point of view. Locking up reinsurance within the economic and political boundaries of a nation led to the

Table 6.2 Premium collected between 1930 and 1937

Premium collected	
1930	539,316,000
1931	461,781,000
1932	414,034,000
1933	374,277,000
1934	343,111,000
1935	332,589,000
1936	349,666,000
1937	480,612,000

Source Marché de l'assurance, Annuaires rouges, various years

destruction of the hedge essentially indispensable to the good guarantee of operations in international and global reinsurance.

The second half of the 1930s saw an improvement in the results of French reinsurance. Present mainly in the Fire Division which made most of its turnover in the elementary branches, it continued to suffer losses in business "Accidents" including the risk "Automobile." This situation due to the inadequacy of the tariff improvement was also noted for the "German, Italian and Polish" business. Regarding the "Life" business, the *Suisse de Ré* observed: "Our Life business, both production and the current portfolio, was affected by the depreciation of the French currency. On the other hand, (…), the cancelations continued their regression. The mortality rate has remained low and the final result is satisfactory. They added, "Few countries have so far achieved the necessary adjustment of their tariffs to the situation created by the fall in the rate of interest."

On the eve of the Second World War, foreign reinsurers dominated the French market. In fact, in 1939 there were hardly more than 10 French reinsurance companies in France. All were modest in size with no significant expansion beyond national borders. Few direct insurance companies had a department that did reinsurance like professional reinsurers, with the difference that they were primarily responsible for reciprocity.

6.2 French Reinsurance from the Second World War

The occupation of France accentuated the influence of foreign companies. The Swiss Reinsurance Company was in the first place. It had a large share of the disposals of French public limited companies, sometimes the largest, but it had also developed very close relations with mutual insurance companies. These relations were maintained by a remarkable policy of commercial and technical support that *Swiss Re* led with all its ceding companies. Confidence inspired by the Swiss franc strengthened its influence. And the Swiss company was a major shareholder of the *Compagnie française d'assurances générales*. Germany's leading reinsurer *Münchener Rück*, closely linked to Germany's largest insurer *Allianz*, was very active in the French market and had taken full control of the French company *Les Réassurances*, founded in 1919.

One major event in the recent history of French insurance and reinsurance was the nationalization in 1946 of 34 insurance companies and the establishment of the National Insurance Council, included in the program of the *Conseil national de la résistance*. The law of 25 April 1948 also created the *Caisse Centrale de Réassurances* (CCR), a "public establishment of a commercial character, endowed with financial autonomy." His role was double. It received on the gross receipts of all non-nationalized enterprises operating in France, French or foreign, a percentage initially fixed at 4%. The purpose of these "compulsory divestitures" was primarily to provide the administration with a statistical table of the activity of the sector to promote control of the insurance industry. Secondly, the *Caisse Centrale de Réassurances* had to carry out conventional operations. In practice, it might be thought that the most far-sighted and professional were aimed at providing the French market with a reinsurance company similar to those known in Germany, Switzerland or London. The war and its aftermath after 1944 had revealed this need with even greater clarity. Was not this the best approach and the best time to correct this situation specific to the French market? Since its creation in 1947, the CCR had not limited itself to cash in compulsory assignments. First, to manage its commitments, it must retrocede on foreign markets and accept reciprocities. And indeed, from the outset it has mainly set itself the goal of developing a portfolio of "conventional business," as authorized by the law of April 1946. It had to be known for foreign markets and recruit qualified staff. The comparison of the turnover with the balance sheets of 1947 and 1968 demonstrates this: 1947 turnover 1,482 MF including 37.8 MF (2%) of conventional business and 1967 turnover 590 MF including 230 MF (39%) of conventional business. The CCR was not the only French reinsurer on the French market but it had a special situation (Table 6.3).

Table 6.3 French reinsurance companies premiums between 1948 till 1954

French reinsurance companies (millions Fr)

	1948	1950	1951	1952	1953	1954
Premium in France	10,443	15,473	16,512	19,834	23,076	23,014
Premium in foreign markets	4,431	6,057	7,748	9,813	12,561	14,245
Total gross premiums	14,864	21,530	24,260	29,647	35,637	37,259
Retrocession with French companies	1,846	2,781	3,129	4,222	5,170	5,274
Retrocessions with foreign companies	2,508	3,309	4,326	5,460	7,117	7,912
Total retrocession	4,354	6,090	7,455	9,682	12,287	13,186
Net Premiums	10,510	15,440	16,805	19,965	23,350	24,073

Source For coming the book about SCOR of André Straus

These figures do not represent all the French reinsurance business since they do not include the business carried out by the direct companies. In 1954 the French companies had received a total of 86,534 million francs in reinsurance and retrocessions, compared to 80,389 a year earlier and 65,524 million in 1952, and had paid a total of 10,1703 million in 1954 as against 92,573 million in 1953 and 82,190 million in 1952. On a base of 100 in 1938, the index of premiums for acceptances amounted to 3,505 in 1954 against 2,653 in 1952. The excess of the premiums ceded on the accepted premiums amounted in 1954 to 15,169 as against 12,184 in 1953 and 1,6676 in 1952, thus representing a surplus in favor of foreign reinsurers. CCR also had to develop certain categories of risk in the social and economic interest of the country and to arouse and encourage the coverage of certain special risks. Thus in 1964 was created the National Fund for Agricultural Calamities (FNGCA) whose accounting and financial management was entrusted to CCR. Its object was the compensation for uninsurable material damage of exceptional importance affecting agricultural holdings and due to abnormal variations in the intensity of a natural agent.

The Treaty of Rome in 1957 and its progressive implementation constituted the main obstacle to the practice of legal cession. In 1964, the first Community directive on insurance was aimed at removing restrictions on the freedom of establishment and the provision of services in the field of reinsurance and retrocession. The incompatibility became clear. In addition, the evolution of the French insurance market was accelerating, and legal divestments were less and less well supported. The reflections then initiated in 1964 at the professional and political levels led to a first reform applied on January 1, 1967, which imposed the legal cessions to all companies in the market, public, and private, but reduced the transfer rate of 4–2% and 1.50% for the "life" business. In 1968, the CCR acquired the portfolio of *Compagnie Havraise de Réassurances*, a private reinsurance company. This is the first phase of a consolidation of reinsurance activities to create a large French reinsurance company. The evolution started in 1967 was then completed on January 1, 1970, with the elimination of the compulsory assignments which still accounted for 59% of the turnover of the CCR and a reinsurance company, an offshoot of the CCR and the French insurance market, was substituted for them: SCOR was the new framework that would allow to break the impasse of legal disposals and provide the French market with a reinsurance body deemed more appropriate than was the CCR public institution.

By the mid-1960s, however, the situation of French reinsurance was less serious than its many critics said. It was even astonishingly good compared to other countries in view of the difficulties it had had to overcome and which is still encountered. Regardless of the developing countries, the countries could be grouped into three groups about reinsurance. No developed country could clearly claim to outclass France under this area. At worst we could put France in a group that counted alongside its partners in the Common Market including Italy and the Benelux countries and the Scandinavian countries. Contrary to what was still sometimes asserted, the development of reinsurance did not invariably follow that of insurance and, all things considered, in some of the most important countries like the United Kingdom and the United States it had not developed in the form of specialized companies.

French reinsurance has never been protected from international competition, nor has it ever asked for it, but after the war it found itself in a bad position to fight against competition. Financial problems have been a decisive factor here. The devaluations of the franc led reinsurers operating abroad either directly or through their subsidiaries to limit their expansion to limit their commitments in relation to their perceived resources in France. Foreign exchange risk put France not only in an unfavorable position vis-à-vis Switzerland, which is obvious but also with Germany. This apparent paradox can be explained by the example of life insurance. In this branch, everything happened as if the two disappearances of the German currency had been less costly for life insurance and the confidence of investors less affected than by the slow erosion of the value of the franc during the half century that had preceded. This factor has also played an essential role to the detriment of French reinsurers. Financial uncertainty has long been linked to political uncertainty. From this point of view, the threat of nationalization, its extension, and then the existence of a public sector, in a field that seems to be one of those where the laws of the market must be exercised undoubtedly constituted a handicap.

To these political and economic factors must be added other explanations of more cultural order. For many years the French, unlike the Swiss or Germans, to say nothing of the British were not attracted by an activity whose character was essentially international. This did not prevent them from being more willing than many other countries to welcome foreign reinsurers on their territory and in their business. Finally, foreign reinsurers were able to receive directly subscriptions in France to an extent far from negligible and in any case much larger than in other countries and these accounts whose reinsurance was integrated with that of the central office were not covered by reinsurers.

Some French companies breaking their reinsurance were able to avoid having to deal with a total number of insurers considered too small. Which would have been the case if by choice or by obligation they had only resorted to French reinsurers. In the mid-1960s the persistence of such a mental reserve can be found in the discussion of many issues affecting insurance. French and British companies, especially after the war, tended to emphasize reciprocity, i.e., the acceptance of reinsurance premiums as consideration for those ceded to reinsurers. Direct insurance companies traded their business among themselves or asked reinsurers for unacceptable premium rebates for a professional reinsurer. The Germans, on the other hand instead of treating the reinsurance of each branch separately, willingly offered a "bouquet" to the reinsurers, the acceptance by them of cases on conditions for them less favorable then falling to a certain extent Reciprocity.

Motor insurance was an essential part of the "bouquet." On the other hand, the German companies re-insure their automobile business which form the biggest part of the premiums much more than the French. Therefore, auto premiums account for more than 40% of net reinsurance premiums accepted in Germany, with the largest share going to professional reinsurers. The proportion was much lower in France. Finally, in many countries, reinsurance was much more closely linked to insurance than it was in France. This is the reason why 7 German companies appeared among the top 10 reinsurers of the Common Market, all closely related to groups of direct insurers. The German reinsurers thus benefited from a surplus of premiums which would otherwise have been retained by the direct insurers or bartered. In 1968, the main nationalize companies were grouped into three super insurers: *Union des Assurances de Paris* (*Union, Sequanaise and Urbaine*), *Assurances Générales de France* (*General Insurance, Phénix*), and *Groupe des Assurances nationales* (*Nationale, Aigle-Soleil and Caisse Fraternelle de Capitalisation*). This operation stems from a general weakening of their performance, their market share having risen from an impressive 66% in 1946 to only 38% in 1968. This decrease can be explained by the large turnover of the managerial staff, which is composed of senior officials with no market experience, only by the arrival of more dynamic mutuals, who are beginning to gain market share.

The different national reinsurance markets were far from being developed as well. The ranking of the largest international reinsurers at the end of 1967 was as follows, in descending order of net retained premiums (in millions of US $). The Swiss (with the *Swiss Reinsurance Company*) and the Germans (with *Munich Re*) were by far the best in continental Europe. As for the English, if they did not have pure reinsurers the size of the *Swiss Re* or *Munich Re*, they had the Lloyds whose enormous subscription possibilities had made London one of the first places in the world (Table 6.4).

The figures available indicate that the overall needs of French life reinsurance can be evaluated by an amount of sales of around CHF 300 million. Assignments in damage reinsurance placed in France could be valued at between 2,600 and 2,700 million francs. For the property and casualty branches alone, total direct insurance acceptances amounted to approximately 1,488 million francs and reinsurance acceptances of Vie companies would have been reaching about 342 million. Apart from the three supplying institutions (CCR, CHR, *National Reinsurance*), a dozen companies specializing in reinsurance (SAFR, *Transcontinental Reinsurance Company, Reinsurance, Corena*, etc.) completed the French specialized reinsurance market; their aggregate receipts for 1967 had reached about 623 million. The total acceptances of the French market reinsurance market amounted to 1,106 million francs. The CCR, the *Compagnie*

Table 6.4 Largest reinsurance companies in the world

1	Compagnie Suisse de Réassurances (Suisse)	485,7
2	Münchener Rückversicherung (Allemagne)	407,0
3	General Reinsurance (USA)	136,9
4	American Reinsurance (USA)	123,7
5	American International Re (AIRCO) (Bermudes)	94,3
6	Caisse Centrale de Réassurance (France)	89,4
7	Gerling Reinsurance Group (Allemagne)	80,2
8	Mercantile and General Group (Angleterre)	75,4
9	Employers reinsurance (USA)	67,9
10	Kölnische Rückversicherung (Allemagne)	67,8
11	Frankona Rückversicherung (Allemagne)	57,9
12	Bayerische Rückversicherung (Allemagne)	46,8
13	Instituto Nacional de Reaseguros (Argentine)	42,8

Source Archives of SCOR

Havraise de Reinsurance and *National Reinsurance* accounted for 44% of the French reinsurance market. In 1968 the incomes of the three establishments accounted for 42.5% of the total. It is interesting to look at the distribution of these receipts by large monetary areas (Table 6.5).

There was some complementarity in the business coming from both the CCR Group and *Compagnie Havraise de Reinsurance* and the National Reinsurance Company. The first two increase their share in Italy, Germany, London, the Netherlands, the United States, and Sweden. The *Nationale Ré* increase their share in Canada, Belgium, Spain and

Table 6.5 Distribution of the different currencies in France

	In per cent
French Francs	55.1
Italian lire	9.3
German D	8.2
English books	6.1
Canadian Dollars	4
Belgian Francs	3.7
United States Dollars	3.3
Swiss francs	1.7
Spanish pesetas	1.3
Miscellaneous	7.3

Source SCOR Archives

Portugal, Switzerland, and Norway. The broad-based breakdown of the risks of acceptances by the CCR, *Nationale Ré* and the *Havre Reinsurance Company* for 1968 was as follows, which can be compared with the respective figures for the *Munich Reinsurance Company*, the *Swiss Reinsurance Company* and *Gerling* (Table 6.6).

Net acceptances, excluding retrocessions, of the CCR, *National Reinsurance* and *Le Havre Reinsurance Company* totaled 354 million for 1968, with a retrocession rate of around 36% broken down as follows: CCR 33%, National Re 44.3% and CHR 40.8%. Acceptances in "excess" appear to have been at that date of the order of thirty million.

The Insurance Department played a decisive role in the creation of SCOR in 1970. This creation marked the end of the legal disposals and the rapprochement with the direct insurance. SCOR would soon play a leading role in the French reinsurance market and its development would make it the world's fourth largest reinsurer in 2017, even as French reinsurance and the Paris marketplace as an international reinsurance market began disaffection and relative decline in the 2000s. In an article published in *The Review* on December 3, 1976, it reads: "The state-controlled company SCOR must now be considered as belonging to the professional market of international reinsurance … although it has not yet the size of the "majors" established for a long time." Moreover, for the author of the article, and although they forbid it, private French reinsurance companies (SAFR, COREFI-ex CORENA and *La Réassurance*) had

Table 6.6 Comparing the French companies with the Germanic companies

	CCR + Nationale Ré + Compagnie Havraise de Réassurance	Münchener	Swiss Re group	Gerling
Life	13	12.6	17.3	11.7
Fire	39.7	22	31	21.8
Auto, R.C., Accident	35.3	38.6	31.7	49.1
Transportation Aviation	8	9.4	6.7	8.6
Hail	4	0.6	0.7	?
Miscellaneous		16.8	12.6	8.8
	100	100	100	100

Source SCOR Archives

no doubt benefited from the creation of SCOR and recognition abroad that France was now able to offer a reinsurance market. The company's turnover rose from 525 million francs in 1970 to 2,740 million francs in 1979, representing growth at an average annual rate of 20% over the whole period. Taking into account the activity of the subsidiaries created by SCOR abroad, the consolidated turnover of the group amounted to FRF 3,141 million in 1979. The number of reinsurance treaties managed in Paris rose from 2970 to 5288 in 1979. The credit/surety sector had seen its inflow rise from 5 million in 1970 to 78 million in 1979. The geographical breakdown of the company's turnover in the property and casualty branches had changed as follows (in percentage terms) (Table 6.7).

The 1981 Corporate Plan outlined the strengths and weaknesses of the company after the first ten years of its existence. The launch of SCOR in the global reinsurance market was favored by technical and commercial acts. Among the favorable elements was the active international team presence of technically qualified underwriters, especially in major industrial risks, and the creation of a network of offices and subsidiaries abroad. This had allowed SCOR to quickly acquire a good brand image on a global scale, as well as a capacity for appetizing on a certain number of products and markets. Secondly, the company gained a reputation for financial soundness as a result of a rigorous policy on the valuation of technical liabilities and the measures taken to maintain its solvency margin at a satisfactory level. The ratio of equity to net premiums, which stood at 19.80% in 1980, had never fallen below 14%, even in years when the pace of growth had been high; it had always been higher on average than the 16% standard adopted by the Community directives for direct companies.

Table 6.7 Distribution of the premiums of SCOR in the world

	1970	*1979*
France	45.6	26.1
Other European countries	41.4	43.5
America	8	16.9
Asia and Australasia	4.2	8.2
Africa	08	5.3
	100	100

Source SCOR Archives

A last favorable external element had come to support the development of society: the stability of the French franc over the period considered.

But the corporate plan also highlighted a number of weaknesses that were rooted in the very speed of the company's growth. Coupled with external factors such as the strong competition in the global marketplace, reinsurance, and the instability of the financial markets in the past decade. In the technical and commercial field, the problems encountered were mainly the consequence of a lack of control and the profitability of underwriting in rapid growth as well as the volume of certain categories of business. This situation resulted in an excessively large share of the Transport Aviation business portfolio. The plan also reported negative profitability in some markets due to an overhead ratio that was too high and insufficient rigor in the selection of cases. Finally, with regard to the composition of its assets, the company's policy did not sufficiently emphasize the assets likely to retain their real value and taking into account the commercial constraints, had made an excessive share of the assets low yield (cash deposit, claims on ceding companies). It should be noted, however, that from 1980 the company had satisfactorily balanced its assets and liabilities in foreign currencies.

The technological management in accounting and IT systems and the control of the activity, had not been sufficiently adapted to the rapid development of the company. Return on equity had not been sufficient, especially in recent years (the year 1980 had been in deficit), to allow full self-financing of the solvency margin. Satisfactory in the early years of the company, when it was close to 20% reaching even 24% in 1974, the rate of return on equity after taxes and before dividend then deteriorated. On average, from 1973 to 1980, it stood at 11.4%. This rate, given a dividend distribution equal to 20% of the profit, would have made it possible to increase the self-financing but the growth having reached 16,2 the rate of self-financing did not exceed 60% and the financing of the margin had to be supplemented by capital increase.

The international economic environment in which reinsurers were operating was marked in 1978 by an increase in the difficulties encountered by most countries in preventing a fall in the pace of activity while keeping within acceptable limits their rate of return. Inflation problems arising from general economic and monetary conditions were compounded in 1978 by the symptoms of a typical reinsurance cycle, particularly in the North American markets, by excess capacity and increased competition leading to abnormal rate cuts as well as significant losses in certain industries such as marine and aviation risks. The reinsurance crisis since the late 1970s has been characterized by massive losses in US civil liability cases and some challenges to Lloyds operations.

Difficulties continued until the early 1980s, particularly as a result of rising oil prices. The general pace of activity had slowed further, inflation had increased in most regions, and foreign trade was deteriorating in all non-oil producing countries. This resulted in a multiplication of disorderly movements in exchange rates, while the level of interest rates, through sometimes abrupt variations, marked a general upward trend. In this unfavorable international context, the decline in insurance needs resulting from the decline in production, especially in the capital goods sector, could only contribute to greater competition between insurance providers and a deterioration in results of their technical operations.

Despite this environment, global reinsurance capacity has increased as a result of the continued attraction of high-interest rates to newly entered operators. Instead of exerting the normal regulatory influence on the direct insurance markets, reinsurance intervention had the effect of delaying the recovery of the imbalanced branches of insurance by allowing a large number of insurers to offload reinsurers from the losses generated by their activity. Thus, international reinsurers have seen the continuation of the deficit phases of insurance throughout the world, without being able to take advantage, according to the mechanisms that traditionally control the equilibrium of their operations, of compensation for the losses of certain markets by the profits of the other. In the period 1978–1983, the large reinsurance companies had a defensive strategy, adapted to the wealth and quality of their portfolios but maintained their strong technical influence, continuing for at least two of them (*Munich Re* and *Swiss Re*) to expand their network.

French reinsurers suffered less than others the difficulties of the market. First of all, the underwriters of the new reinsurance companies created in France in the 1970s were not made without experience; many of them had been trained in the reinsurance departments of the major French insurers who had brought their portfolio to these new "Ré." The capacities offered by their subscribers were thus more sophisticated than those sometimes very naive entrusted to the operators of the London market. This may explain in part that the damage done by some Anglo-Saxon underwriting agencies has on the whole. Less affected the French market than other foreign markets thanks to a better discernment as to the powers granted and a tendency of French professionals to select the proposals themselves. Secondly, with the exception of SCOR, the French market had fewer locations and commitments in the United States than the English, German or Dutch markets. Finally, the fact that most of the French "approved" belong to insurance groups explains the behavior of these companies. If they followed the guidelines of expansion on the international market given by their shareholders, their subscribers, contrary to those of the London market, largely interested in the turnover, operated in France in the strict framework of companies often administered by the services of parent companies. The nasty surprises, unlike the English market, brought to their managers only career problems.

It must also be said that this belonging to "institutional" entailed a certain discretion in the balance sheets of the French "Ré" on the extent and duration of their problems, probably variable from one society to another. The bottom line is that the structures have survived and that the French reinsurance market after the end of the crisis has been able to take stronger positions in the international market, as the creation of SCOR had allowed to do in the 1970s. It is true that when it was created in 1970, the portfolio that had been brought to it by these founding companies included relatively few foreign affairs (less than 50%); there were therefore more opportunities for development abroad than in France. SCOR was founded in 1970, after the severe crisis of 1965–1966, when a number of European reinsurers, including the London market, undertook a recovery. For five to six years, SCOR has therefore developed in a context of reassured reinsurance conditions. In the early 1980s, SCOR began a diversification program that expanded its reinsurance offering. From the early 1980s to the early 1990s, SCOR became the sixth largest insurer in the world. Several decisive stages brought him there. The commercially dangerous and financially heavy policy pursued by SCOR in the United States was redefined in 1983 and resulted in severe choices. SCOR will tighten and reorient its underwriting policy: installation in New York, recruitment of a new team, limited subscriptions with a strengthened surplus ($30 million), treaty subscriptions by brokers, specialization in facultative. These efforts focused mainly on the Transport and Aviation branches and the disposals of the American subsidiary. The company made many terminations in the Transport branch, whose subscriptions were reduced from 400 million in 1980 to 170 million in 1985. On the other hand, it decided to stop the Aviation branch and, above all, the selective but important reduction of fire deals to offset the impact of tariff cuts in Europe. SCOR US, like the SCOR group, was therefore abandoning almost Transport ("Hull") and Aviation risks, as well as its commitments in professional civil liability; however, it retained the Cargo ("Cargo" and "Trucking") business.

Conversely, the group significantly increased its position in General Liability, branch where the risks are in no way comparable. The company continued the development of its portfolio of facultative large industrial risks which had been continuously profitable: his risk added to an open policy passed from CHF 435 million in 1980 to CHF 600 million in 1984. This policy was intended to enable SCOR's US subsidiary to have a specific and recognized place in the US market and to contribute to the recovery of the US market. Implemented from 1981 to 1982, this strategy resulted in a record of discontinuous and segmented subscriptions on a case-by-case basis (under "optional" and "non-proportional" contracts) and in the so call subscription low tranches which are the first exposed to claims but have the advantage of offering good visibility on future risks. Experience showed that a truly international reinsurance company should in particular have sufficient capital. This is the reason that led to the capital increase of 310 million francs. In addition, many examples in both the domestic and international markets showed that a reinsurance company had the best chance of succeeding in its international development if it had strong links with its domestic market and had good credibility, especially at the technical level. The priority of the French market from 1984 was twofold. On the one hand, increase its share of the French reinsurance market in the medium term to improve the company's results and, on the other hand, develop cooperation with French insurance companies by associating them with some of the SCOR on the markets abroad. Thus, it opened the capital of its Hong Kong subsidiary for business underwriting in the Far East at the same time as it was considering a similar cooperation with other French groups in Great Britain and in United States. On the other hand, the company sought to involve French companies more closely in high-risk subscriptions where it had recognized expertise. From 1985, it created new optional business underwriting centers, one for offshore risks and the other for "space" risks. French companies participated in the first for 52% and the second for 63% of the total.

Until the late 1980s ceding companies did not want and could not encumber their proportional treaties with peaks of risk and were therefore moving toward facultative reinsurance. Reinsurers, however, who occasionally subscribed to facultative reinsurance, feared them. Behavior changed dramatically with the increasing openness of the international market and imbalances in national markets. From 1973, the Saltiel group, experienced in the underwriting of industrial risks, was inspired by this situation. This is hardly surprising since facultative reinsurance is closer to direct insurance than treaty underwriting. Farex was created in 1973, bringing together some of the largest direct companies in the private sector. This first step opened the way for other important groups, whether public or private. In the 1990s there was a well-organized facultative reinsurance market in Paris. The overall capacity had increased so much that a petrochemical risk could be placed, exclusively on an optional basis, only on the French market for a loss of up to $100 million. The main companies practicing facultative reinsurance were then SCOR, Abeille Paix Re, Sorema, Farex.

The competence of French reinsurers became widely recognized at the end of the 1980s, they were now quite frequently leader on large international risks. In 1992, the Corporate and Technical Risks Department of SCOR *Réassurances*, responsible for the optional business, had 70 employees, including 35 engineers, lawyers, and actuaries; it covered all aspects of the files, from the visit of the risks to the management of the claims.

French companies that used to depend almost exclusively on brokers, especially British for large international risks, changed the origin of their business. Since the end of 1982, French facultative reinsurers have forged closer ties with the direct companies. This redistribution took place at a time of diminishing global capabilities and was further strengthened by the development of these direct relationships rather than by weakening ties with the broker sector. Some international brokers, at the time of this drastic reduction in capacity, realizing the importance of the financial stability of reinsurers, discovered the existence of a well-established and high-quality facultative reinsurance market in continental Europe, particularly in Europe particularly in France.

The growth of the French facultative reinsurance market can also be attributed to three other causes. First of all, to the computer development that each facultative reinsurer has made, resulting in a better and faster knowledge of their portfolio. They were therefore able to react more accurately and quickly to any request. Secondly, the proliferation of telecommunications methods enabled the parties to reinsurance contracts to save time and increase the quality of their information. It had become possible to receive blanks, fonts, visit reports, which allowed for a more in-depth study of risk and speeded up the decision-making process. At the end of the 1980s, the delays of continental reinsurers were lower than those of a City broker. This speed was an attractive element for customers, selling as brokers. Finally, French subscribers were always willing to travel around the world to establish the closest possible contacts with their ceding companies and their brokers. This mobility contributed to the international recognition of the French market. The trip from Paris to London was still frequent but was no more than one of the international journeys among others. In fifteen years, the French market seemed to have reached maturity. Nevertheless, in the difficult economic environment of the end of 70s and the beginning of the 80s the French market suffered its share of Transport and Aviation underwriting losses, reinsurance from Lloyds, the London market and US business, which generally amounted to significant sums in absolute value. However, compared to other acceptance centers, various factors helped to moderate its losses of French reinsurers.

For several years, reinsurance had been engaged in a price war waged by the insurers who had sent him bad files. Between 1987 and 1990, tariffs had dropped from 20 to 25%. Premiums no longer made it possible to cover risks that were notoriously undervalued, particularly in the context of proportional treaties (60% of SCOR's turnover in 1992). Reinsurers were fiercely competing with each other. SCOR, which generated 70% of its turnover abroad, is suffering the effects of the rigors of the global market.

The early 1990s saw society face threats of another nature. In 1991 and most of 1992, the insurance industry was hit by a series of catastrophic claims, including Hurricane Andrew, which alone cost insurers $16.5 billion. SCOR's share in this incident amounted to 300 million French francs. However, the company was still much more affected by several industrial claims, which contributed for 1992 to a loss of 858 million francs on its technical results, and to a negative net profit of 135 million for a turnover of 8.4 billion francs. SCOR, however, maintained a solid foundation, with a capitalization of around CHF 5 billion and a cash flow of more than CHF 800 million. Despite the absence of significant natural events, all of the Group's property and casualty subsidiaries operating in Europe were in a loss. During the 1992 renewal, SCOR implemented a portfolio remediation and reinsurance improvement policy. As a result, the net cost of disasters in excess of CHF 300 million was partly offset by a strong improvement in optional business results in all Group companies and improved earnings from Life business.

The industry as a whole was not in the same state. This year of disasters was disastrous for many major reinsurers, leading to the disappearance of reinsurance companies such as English and American, NRG, the largest Dutch reinsurer, NW Re and Royal Re, which were among the top four London reinsurance companies. Even the Lloyds were eventually forced to cut their reinsurance business and their capacity was reduced by £3 billion.

The bottom line is that the structures have survived and that the French reinsurance market after the end of the crisis has been able to take stronger positions in the international market, as the creation of SCOR had allowed to do in the 1970s.

Reinsurance capacity, although having started to grow again in 1994, had been weak for several years. Insurers and reinsurers had slowly begun to recover. But it is clear that for the reinsurers any noticeable improvement was related to the behavior of the national direct companies. And indeed, the largest French insurers had obtained results for 1993 higher than those of 1992, even if their optimism had been undermined in April 1994 by the degradation of the rating of three of the main of them, the UAP, AGF, and AXA. In fact, Standard & Poor's point of view was only to take into account the damage that the French market had suffered.

The 1996 concentration of the reinsurance market, spectacular in its magnitude, was only the continuation of a movement that had begun ten years earlier. At the beginning of the 1980s, the number of active reinsurers in the world was about 500. After the great difficulties of the late 80s and early 90s, caused by the conjunction of multiple disasters—earthquakes, cyclones, storms—, the catastrophic development of old guarantees—asbestos and pollution in the United States in particular—and insufficient tariff conditions for reinsurance, the number was reduced to less than 200.

This decrease in the number of players resulted from the cessation of activity due to financial difficulties, but also from buy-outs and the fact that many direct insurance companies, such as ING in the Netherlands, had abandoned this activity. This is also the case for *Skandia* and *Unistorebrand* in Scandinavia and Royal in the United Kingdom. German reinsurance, first in the world by its importance, did not escape this movement of concentration, with the successive purchases in 1994 of the *Kölnische Rück* by the American General Re, and of *Frankona* and *Aachener Re* by Employer's Re.

The emergence, in the early 1990s, of a few new Bermuda companies, which were mostly specialized in disaster reinsurance at a time when the market was particularly attractive, did not change this trend. This movement of concentration was reflected in 1996 by a restructuring of the market. In 1996, Munich Re, the world's largest reinsurer, bought the American American Re, and the Swiss Reinsurance Company, the second reinsurer, took over the British Mercantile and General and the Italian *Unione italiana di riassicurazione*.

French reinsurance did not stay out of this movement. SCOR bought Allstate's US reinsurance business. The transcontinental Reinsurance Company (CTR), a subsidiary of Gan, was acquired by the Canadian financial group Fairfax, and Safr, a subsidiary of AGF. Nearly 50% was taken over in early 1997 by the Bermudan company Partner Re, close to the Swiss group Re. This disengagement of French direct companies from reinsurance was general in 1996. After having split from *Kölnische Rück* of the Colonia group in 1994, the UAP, which held nearly 40% of the SCOR, withdrew completely of its capital. Only now remained linked to direct insurance groups Sorema (Groupama) and AXA Ré (AXA group).

In 1995, the French reinsurance market (direct insurance companies and specialized companies) continued its development, with a turnover of 82.2 billion francs, an increase of 9.9%. Most of the transactions were in the property and casualty insurance sector (around 85%, of which 44% was fire, 15% in various types of risk and 12% in the automotive sector) and, to a lesser extent, the life insurance sector (15%). Optional reinsurance operations (which mainly concern large risks and specialized technical risks) were fairly developed in French reinsurance companies: they accounted for 15% of non-life insurance contributions in 1995. Consolidated turnover for the first 10 years French reinsurers had increased by 68% between 1990 and 1994, from 26.7 billion francs to 44.9 billion (gross premiums), but it had not exceeded 45.2 billion in 1995.

In 1996, French reinsurers made strong gains and strengthened their balance sheets. They practiced prudent and selective underwriting in the face of fierce global competition. Reinsurance operations by direct insurers amounted to 50 billion francs, down 7.6% from 1995. French reinsurers were mainly active in Europe (70% of acceptances, half of them in France). The remainder was essentially divided between the American continent (just under 20%) and Asia (nearly 10%).

These results are also the result of the recovery measures taken in previous years, both in direct insurance (tariff and protection measures) and in reinsurance (deductibles, lower intermediation costs). For all nine major French reinsurers, the results in 1996 amounted to 2.4 billion francs, a 57% increase compared to the previous year. These results are accompanied by significant growth in equity and technical provisions, contributing to the strength and credibility of French reinsurance. In 1996, French reinsurance (professional reinsurers and direct insurance companies carrying on this activity) saw its turnover fall by 10.3%.

Different factors, with sometimes opposite effects, explain this pace of growth. Some helped to anchor the activity of French specialized reinsurers: the good performance of the franc against foreign currencies; the Lloyd's crisis, far from being resolved, had nevertheless faded; the disappearance and cessation of activity of reinsurers had largely decreased, resulting in a reduction in available capacity; at the same time, demand had increased. But other factors slowed down the growth of French reinsurance. New contributors appeared, particularly in Bermuda, after hurricane Andrew, specialized in the field of disasters, attracted by reinsurance conditions. In addition, US reinsurance was strengthened on the European markets by the buyout of German companies. Thus, the intensification of competition, without weighing heavily on tariff conditions, was holding back the expansion of French reinsurance. In addition, the amendment of certain life insurance tax provisions in the United Kingdom had resulted in the non-renewal of important reinsurance business (Fig. 6.1).

In the second half of the 1990s, SCOR continued its expansion into new regions of the world by settling in Rio de Janeiro, Beijing, Labuan, Moscow, and Seoul. Long before its competitors SCOR had perceived the economic future of the Asia-Pacific. The first establishment of the company outside France had been opened in Hong Kong in 1972; it was followed by the 1976 establishment of an office in Melbourne, Australia. It moved to Sydney when the city became an insurance center. In 1978, SCOR opened an office in Singapore, which in 1996 became the regional center of the company at the same time as a new SCOR Reinsurance Asia-Pacific company was created.

In 1983 another SCOR office was opened in Tokyo. In the late 1990s another office was established in Seoul (1997). SCOR's presence in Asia

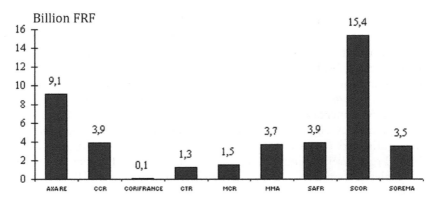

Fig. 6.1 1997 premiums (billion of francs) (*Source* Association des Réassureurs Français)

was already 25 years old. Premiums collected in Asia by SCOR in 96 amounted to 5% of the total turnover.

The development of the company in Asia was to some extent the result of an almost visionary perspective. The future of reinsurance—like countless other industries—resided in Asia. Over time, SCOR was able to develop a strategic advantage by forging close relationships with its customers in most Asian markets where there were only three or four major reinsurers who had settled before it. The company played there a leading role in the facultative reinsurance of some of the major construction projects like the new Hong Kong airport. This rapid penetration policy was helped by Singapore's role in serving South-East Asia, with the Hong Kong office still responsible for business development in China, Japan, South Korea and Taiwan. In 1997, the largest volume market for premiums collected in Asia was Japan, followed by Korea, Australia, Thailand, and Indonesia.

This Asian policy of SCOR had been facilitated by the wide experience in these markets of several Parisian executives. In order to better meet the needs of its customers, SCOR had developed a new approach by partnering with local companies. In Thailand, for example, a collaboration agreement was signed in Bangkok on August 15, 1996, between the reinsurer Thaï Reinsurance Company and SCOR *Vie*, which had a permanent representative there. Thai Re could benefit from the technical support of the entire SCOR Group. This approach was also developing in the emerging markets of North Asia. The society was also successful in Indonesia and the Philippines in association with local insurance companies.

The future stages of SCOR's development in Asia were indisputably the two largest potential insurance markets in the world, China and India. When the currency was fully convertible, the demand for reinsurance in both markets could be expected to grow rapidly. As the middle class grew, life insurance would drive market growth. Apart from some momentary difficulties, the Indian market where the opening to the outside was facilitated by the British tradition appeared in a favorable way.

The greatest challenge presented by the Asian market was its extreme diversity, which encouraged continuing to build long-term relationships with customers in the region.

The Group also took the opportunity to consolidate its presence in the US market by setting up in Miami. Between 2000 and 2001, SCOR expanded its life and non-life activities in the United States through the acquisition of Partner Re Life in 2000, and in 2001 from SOREMA SA and SOREMA North America, two subsidiaries of Groupama.

SCOR was one of the first reinsurers to realize the need for drastic measures to stop the deterioration of subscriptions since the mid-1990s. Subscription results were particularly bad in Western Europe and North America, accounting for nearly 80% total premiums from the company. The company deliberately decreased its acceptances in the regions where it considered that the underwriting conditions were not acceptable. At the same time, it refocused on the segments of the market that showed the first signs of recovery. SCOR was also one of the leaders of the French market in favor of stricter regulation of the domestic reinsurance market. French reinsurers thought that new regulations were essential if they could allow them to take a larger share of national business in the global market.

French reinsurers hoped to strengthen their international position thanks to the renewal of the market. The January 2001 renewals had shown the first signs that rates were becoming firmer. The importance of the turnaround was partly due to a significant expansion of the market as well as the efforts made by leading players such as SCOR or AXA re to refocus their activities. By emerging from unprofitable or low-margin activity in favor, also supported by the disappearance of a few small operators, French reinsurers had reduced their capacity to a level that allowed them to offer more acceptable rates for them. In some cases, in contrast, reinsurers had invested outside reinsurance, which found more value in other investments, particularly when securities markets were on the rise. France continued to benefit from an increase of nearly 20% of its activity in the United States, which was of vital importance for the European market.

However, the depth of the global economic crisis was a very negative factor. The decline in corporate revenues was detrimental to companies' risk appetite and lowered the level of insurable risk. As business activity declines, companies reduce their revenue forecasts and produce less. As a result, in many industries, inventory levels are declining. Companies have less exposure to risk on their inventories and are less inhibited by a possible business interruption than during boom periods.

The storms in northern Europe at the end of 1999 and many other events weighed heavily on the market in 2000 and weighed on French reinsurers, which did not stop their efforts to strengthen and consolidate. With a small share of their operations in the domestic market, companies like SCOR or AXA Re continued to expand geographically and strategically.

The good results achieved by global reinsurance had led to the emergence of a few new players, particularly in disaster coverage, and increased competition. French reinsurers have, on the whole, been led to limit and even reduce their commitments in this area and that of proportional treaties. In addition, the concentrations observed in both direct companies and reinsurance companies led to reductions in the sales of insurers and losses in sales during reinsurance portfolio mergers.

In the absence of catastrophic losses (cyclone, storm, or earthquake), the results of specialized French reinsurers had remained excellent despite certain negative factors: greater competition, manifested not only in terms of reinsurance rates, but also by the development or emergence of new techniques (captives, financial reinsurance ...), a loss of industrial risks which increased again in some European markets, the occurrence of major fire claims such as those of *Credit Lyonnais* or *Eurotunnel*.

While maintaining its active local presence policy in the main markets and new locations in fast-growing emerging countries, the Company continued its efforts in the following years to simplify its structures and streamline its organization. In 1997, SCOR absorbed its two French reinsurance subsidiaries (SCOR *Reinsurance* and SCOR *Vie*). In June of the same year, it regrouped all of its Italian reinsurance operations in

SCOR Italia. In 1999, it bought the 35% held by *Western General Insurance* in *Commercial Risk Partners*, becoming a 100% shareholder of this subsidiary, and in 2000, acquired Partner Re Life in the United States, thereby increasing its activity in the United States, notably in people reinsurance.

At the end of the 1990s, SCOR had thus benefited from a period of extreme tariff competition in the reinsurance sector to continue its growth. Gross written premiums jumped from 2,106 billion euros in 1998 to 4,890 billion euros in 2001. On the other hand, equity increased less rapidly, amounting to only 1,318 billion euros in 2001, compared with €1,231 billion in 1998. This period saw the gross provisions/premiums ratio reduced from 236 to 224%, while the proportion of long-term portfolios continued to rise. Although the French reinsurance companies did not really belong to the group of the most influential operators, their relatively narrow market had to be managed and developed in this period of continuous consolidation on a worldwide scale. The most recent deal was the acquisition by SCOR of *Sorema* of *Groupama's* reinsurance subsidiary for €344 million.

The year 2002 was a dark year for SCOR. The events of 2001—and especially the terrorist attacks of 11 September—had degraded the accounts of all reinsurers directly or indirectly affected by these acts of barbarism. The SCOR group was directly concerned because it partially reinsured the properties destroyed by the terrorist groups. It had begun well: the beginning of the year foreshadowed an upturn with the start of the rate adjustment. The tariff increases were at the rendezvous as evidenced by the figures for renewals published in the first quarter of 2002. They were absolutely necessary because the equilibrium prices corresponding to the true risk prices had been dangerously removed. But the improvement was short-lived because with the financial crisis that began in the spring of 2001 and amplified after the attacks, the downward trend took over and many values collapsed.

The stock market downturn resulted in both unrealized capital losses on the equity portfolio that had to be heavily funded and realized capital losses when reinsurers had to sell securities at a price lower than the purchase price. Lastly, developments in the loss experience in 2002 in respect of portfolio transactions written in previous years led many companies to make restocking arrangements which accentuated the deterioration of results. This is a direct record of subscriptions made in the lower phase of the cycle in the late 1990s. The scissors effect between the contraction of assets (financial investments) and the dilation of liabilities (reloading of provisions) was significant and the rate increases that occurred in early 2001 had only limited effects on the accounts. The bad news followed one another at a steady pace in 2002. SCOR gradually became aware of the deterioration of its situation and the deterioration of the economic and financial environment in which it was evolving. In 2002, however, it pursued the study of external growth issues, considering that the period was conducive to consolidation. But the room for maneuver to make such acquisitions was gone. The Group needed to be recapitalized, not to allow new developments, but to restore a level of solvency achieved by changes in assets and provisions. As the capital increase required seemed difficult for the management of the group that initially presented it as the counterpart of an external growth operation, the company appointed a new team.

At the end of 2002, under the direction of its new CEO, Denis Kessler, SCOR revised its strategy and launched the "Back on Track" strategic plan. This plan consisted in adopting the accounts for the third quarter of 2002, introducing for the technical provisions all available valuations, known as "best estimates," prepared by independent actuaries. He also stopped a new underwriting policy to rebalance the SCOR portfolio. Thus, it was decided to give priority to short tail branches to steer the new subscription policy more firmly toward non-proportional activities, less sensitive to the effects that may result from the ceding companies' clients, to develop the Guarantee of Large Business Risks rather than the Credit Guarantee or Alternative Risk Transfer operations as well as to increase the relative share of Life reinsurance.

Geographically, it was decided to refocus on Europe and Asia-Pacific compared to the United States. A capital increase of €381 million, made necessary to restore the adequate level of solvency corresponding to the subscription plan defined by the "Back on Track" recovery plan, was successfully completed in November–December 2002. The first fifteen years of the twenty-first century were SCOR's recovery and its rise to the world's fourth-largest reinsurer through a cautious and balanced policy that led the still generalist group to have more than half of its turnover in Life, to have developed remarkably particularly in Asia. In 2017, approximately 37% of the gross premiums issued by the Group were generated in Europe, Middle East and Africa (EMEA) (2016: 39%), with significant positions in France, Germany, Spain and Italy; 46% were generated in the Americas (2016: 46%); and 17% was generated in Asia (2016: 15%).

This growth has been achieved through strategic mergers and acquisitions such as with *Revios* or *Converium* and more recently with *Sorema*. What illustrates its transformation into an international player is its decentralized management structure in regional hubs. In this sense we can take some distance from the national market even if it remains the main player. SCOR's competitors have independent reinsurers or of States, subsidiaries or affiliated companies world-class insurance companies, and reinsurance of some leading insurance companies. Its main competitors include European reinsurers (for example, *Swiss Re*, *Munich Re* and Hannover Re) and Americans and Bermudians (for example, *PartnerRe*, RGA, *Chubb*, *Axis Capital*, *TransRe*, *Odyssey Re*, *GenRe*, and *Everest Re*). The Englishman Lloyd's is also recognized as a major competitor. SCOR SE and its consolidated subsidiaries form the 4th bigger reinsurer in the world in 2016 and 2015, with more than 4,000 customers.

In contrast, the place of Paris as a place of reinsurance is down on the main indicators (dedicated equity, net premiums accepted) and is outpaced by new places. The decrease in reinsurance activities carried out from France is primarily due to the gradual disappearance of traditional French reinsurers following the sale by French insurers of their reinsurance subsidiaries and the concentration of the reinsurance market (mergers and disappearances). Secondly, it is worth mentioning the relocation of French reinsurance activities to foreign markets that are more attractive than the Paris financial, tax, regulatory, and social centers. Indeed, in the last two decades new reinsurance positions have emerged such as Dublin, especially for securitization vehicles, Luxembourg for "captive" insurance and reinsurance clients, or Bermuda. In addition, foreign reinsurance groups have converted their French subsidiaries into branches with repatriation of the central functions and geographic specialization of their French subsidiaries to the foreign head office. In addition, many captives of French industrial groups have settled abroad mainly because of the lack of an appropriate regime for captives. Lastly, we should mention the near-disappearance of French reinsurance brokers who had an international activity, with a specialization of large international reinsurance brokerage by local markets and a sharp decline in international business placed in Paris (like foreign reinsurers).

References

Archives: SCOR Archives.

Interviews FFSA. I Also Used the Oral Archives of the Insurance That I Constituted on Behalf of the FFSA (French Federation of Insurance Compagnie), and Notably the Interviews of Claude Bébéar, Jacques-Henri Gougenheim and Mikael Hagopian.

Gerathewohl, K., et al. 1982. *Reinsurance, Principles and Practice*. Karlsruhe: Versicherungswirtschafts e. V.

Golding, C.E. 1927. "A Reinsurance Survey". *Journal of the Chartered Insurance Institute*.

Golding, C.E. 1927. *A History of Reinsurance with a Sidelight on Insurance*. London: Waterloo and Sons.

Golding, C.E. 1954. *The Law and Practice of Reinsurance*. London: Buckley Press.

Hagopian, M., and M. Lappara. 1991. *Aspect théorique et pratique de la réassurance*. Paris: L'Argus de l'assurance.

Kopf, E.W. 1929. *Notes on the Origin and Development of Reinsurance*. New York: Globe Prining Company.

L'Argus de l'assurance. 2002–2019.

La Réassurance. 1917–1977.

Le Blanc, H. 1948. *La réassurance au point de vue économique*, 2e ed. Paris: LGDJ.

The Post Magazine and Insurance Monitor. 1910–1920.

The Review. Reinsurance Numbers every year.

Richard, P.-J. 1956. *Histoire des institutions d'assurance en France*. Paris: Editions de L'Argus.

Risques, dec 2009 n° 80; juin 2005 n° 62 ; dec 2001 n°48 ; juin 1998, n° 34 ; mars 1996, n°25.

Straus, A. Forthcoming. History of SCOR.

Sumien, P. 1927. *Traité théorique de pratique des assurances terrestres et de la réassurance*, 2e ed. Paris.

Thorin, P. 1929. *La réassurance contre l'incendie, son organisation technique et économique*. Orleans: Imprimiere Orleanaise.

CHAPTER 7

Currency Constraints, Risk Spreading Regulation, and the Corporate Demand for Reinsurance: A National Reinsurance Market in the Spanish Autarky (1940–1959)

Pablo Gutiérrez González and Jerònia Pons Pons

The reinsurance industry is extremely sensible to the changes on the regulatory framework. While soft regulations during the nineteenth century allowed for the spreading of reinsurance, increasing restrictions posed during the twentieth century deeply affected the development of the industry. In the Spanish case, the international isolation of Franco dictatorship from 1940 and the implementation of an autarkic economic policy transformed the structure of the reinsurance business. Certainly,

---

P. Gutiérrez González (✉) · J. Pons Pons
Department of Economics and Economic History,
University of Seville, Seville, Spain
e-mail: pgutierrez1@us.es

J. Pons Pons
e-mail: jpons@us.es

© The Author(s), under exclusive license to Springer Nature Switzerland AG 2021
L. Caruana de las Cagigas and A. Straus (eds.), *Role of Reinsurance in the World*, Palgrave Studies in Economic History,
https://doi.org/10.1007/978-3-030-74002-3_7

the obstacles to the access to international risk exchange networks forced Spanish insurers to seek alternate mechanisms as the creation of dependent reinsurers within the main insurance groups. The aim of this paper is to examine the nature and structure of these corporate groups and their effects on the Post-War Spanish insurance market.

7.1 Introduction

From the last third of the nineteenth century, the Spanish economy began a steady trend of growth in capital stock and international trade (Prados de la Escosura 2009; Prados de la Escosura and Rosés 2010). Indeed, the development of the Spanish economy triggered the need for risk management services, which resulted in the progress and growth of the insurance industry (Pons Pons 2003, 2005). Foreign insurers coming from advanced markets such as the United Kingdom, France and the United States established branches in the country, while domestic offices expanded by adopting modern management techniques and actuarial tools (Pons Pons 2007; Pons Pons and Gutiérrez González 2016).

Thus, reinsurance became a widely used device in order to deal with one of the main shortcomings of the Spanish insurance market: the limitations of the financial system. Despite the trend of modernization experienced by the Spanish economy from 1880, the financial system suffered from several imbalances at the beginning of the twentieth century. As noted by Martín Aceña (1987, 1993), Comín Comín (2013) and Martínez Ruiz (2013), non-adhesion to the Gold Standard complicated the internationalization of Spanish finance, while the excessive weight of the Bank of Spain in the whole banking system and its subordination to fiscal needs hindered the development of a sound domestic capital market. Consequently, Spanish insurers faced chronic difficulties to access financial resources within a trend of expansion. Moreover, the new Insurance Law passed in 1908 boosted the withdrawal of foreign offices from Spain, which left the market free for domestic insurers (Pons Pons 2012). In this context, although insurance business grew steadily despite the extended lack of capital funding over the next four decades, this development suffered from deep financial imbalances. Indeed, as noted by Gutiérrez González and Andersson (2018), the Spanish insurance industry had to face high levels of leverage due to their chronic undercapitalization, what made domestic offices heavily dependent on foreign reinsurance. Therefore, following the terms defined by Mayers and Smith (1982), Powell and Somner (2007) and Deelstra and Plantin (2014) within the ruin theory framework, foreign reinsurance became an imperfect substitute of capital funding for Spanish insurers during the first third of the century.

Beyond this structural trend, major changes on the evolution of international risk exchange networks arose from the regulatory changes implemented during the First World War. In fact, the redistribution of freight and insurance services toward neutral countries during the conflict boosted the demand of reinsurance, especially in those peripheral countries affected by financial shortcomings as Spain. As a result, new regulations were passed to limit the purchases of foreign reinsurance in order to avoid currency and capital outflows, as argued by Gutiérrez González and Pons Pons (2017). Furthermore, James et al. (2013: pp. 175–178) examined how the trends of economic nationalism and the attempt to control the reinsurance business were generalized during the decades following the conflict.

While these dynamics converged with monetary and financial disturbances affecting international markets during the 1920s and 1930s, additional difficulties arose in the Spanish case: in a context of disintegration of the global economy, social and political instability and the outbreak of Civil War in 1936 increased the isolation of the Spanish economy. Moreover, the victory of general Franco with the support of the Axis powers posed additional obstacles to access an almost blocked international financial market, while the insurance industry had to face the consequences of the war, namely: the effects of three years of monetary dualism; the massive claims due to the war destructions; and the changes on the international with the outbreak of the Second World War. The aim of this paper is to examine the regulatory changes arising from this environment and the strategies performed by domestic insurers to face the increasing isolation of the Spanish economy during the 1940s.

The remainder of this paper is organized as follows. Second section features the situation of Spanish insurance in 1940 and the regulatory changes introduced by the francoist dictatorship. Third section analyzes the changes on risk management strategies of domestic offices, that is: the creation of corporate networks in Spanish insurance through the mechanism of interlocking directorates. Fourth section examines the impact of corporate networks on the performance of Spanish insurers. Fifth section explores the partial deregulation initiated in 1951 and its effects on the reinsurance market. Finally, we conclude the paper.

7.2 The Spanish Insurance Market in 1940 and the New Regulatory Framework for the Reinsurance Business

Immediately after the end of the Civil War in 1939, the francoist government had to deal with the economic disturbances provoked by the war. The destruction of capital equipment and infrastructures converged with the financial imbalances resulting from three years of monetary dualism. In the case of the insurance industry, the handling of war claims became a major challenge for domestic offices: the heterogeneity among the policies issued in Spain resulted on wide divergences on the management of the claims. Moreover, the payment of the premiums on Republican pesetas during the war years introduced additional problems to set compensations for the policyholders. In parallel to these problems, the attitude of the new government posed additional obstacles to the normalization of the insurance industry. Indeed, the autarkic ideas within the new government sought to organize the economic activity and exacerbated inflationary trends, while the international economy remained almost blocked after ten years of deglobalization and, especially, after the outbreak of the Second World War.

In this scene, financial shortcomings and undercapitalization issues that traditionally had affected the insurance industry were exacerbated. Besides the obstacles to get capital funding from a distressed financial system, those companies operating in marine insurance had to face a huge increase in the demand in the international market. In a similar way as explained by Gutiérrez González and Pons Pons (2017) for the WWI, the outbreak of the war in 1939 placed neutral countries as Spain among the main providers of freight and insurance services (Martínez Ruiz 2003a). The rise of loss ratios due to the riskiness of marine traffic and the increase on the underwriting of new policies affected the financial balance of Spanish insurers: since they had to face new liabilities, companies had to increase their reserves through new capital funding or to purchase reinsurance. As noted by Gutiérrez González (2014), the rigidities of the Spanish financial system led companies to massively resort to foreign reinsurance, which in turn resulted on increasing outflows of currencies in the form of reinsurance premiums.

This dynamic, along with the ideas and trends on autarky within the new government, led public authorities to build a new regulatory framework for the reinsurance business (García Ruiz and Caruana 2009).

Indeed, the monetary authority devoted to the control of flows of foreign currency, the *Instituto Español de Moneda Extranjera* (IEME) attempted to identify the cessions of premiums abroad.[1] To do that, an Official Committee on Marine Insurance was created in 1942 and a new regulation was passed, by mean of which insurers had to get an administrative authorization to sign new reinsurance treaties abroad.[2] Moreover, Spanish offices had to give major details on the features of the risk, the amount reinsured and the conditions of the treaty, which broke the basic principle of confidentiality in the reinsurance treaty.[3]

Furthermore, two additional obligations were introduced in the new regulations: first, a compulsory cession to the Committee on Marine Insurance of a share of all marine insurance policies written in Spain was introduced; and second, Spanish companies aiming to purchase foreign reinsurance had to seek for foreign risks in such a way that premiums reinsured abroad, and currency outflows, should be compensated by risks ceded by foreign companies to domestic ones, namely: currency inflows. This new directive introduced an anomalous element into corporate risk management strategies: companies seeking for foreign reinsurance had to share the information of individual policies and contracts with the regulatory agency.

These changes generated sound protests by Spanish offices: the conditions to cede premiums to foreign reinsurers were so difficult that they could not cover the demand of the market. After long negotiations, an agreement was reached between private companies and public authorities: the Committee on Marine Insurance would retrocede to domestic offices those risks accepted from the market that did not generate currency outflows, which was a major share of the business initially affected by the

---

[1] As the new monetary authority, the IEME centralized the access to foreign currencies and fixed the rates of exchange of the peseta. However, the deviation of official rates from those in the international market and the arbitrary criteria to approve foreign currency purchases almost blocked this market. For a detailed description of these mechanisms of control, see Martinez Ruiz (2003b).

[2] Decree of 13 March 1942, in *Boletín Oficial del Estado (BOE)* no. 87, 27 March 1942.

[3] As noted by Gerathewohl (1993) and Pearson (1995), reciprocal trust between the reinsurer and the reinsured about the protection of the financial information included in the reinsurance treaty is a key element of the business, since it reflects vital market information as the soundness of the portfolio, the claim experience or the commissions applied.

regulation. Moreover, as noted by Gutiérrez González (2014, pp. 34–35), this capture and reallocation of marine insurance was implemented with a clear inclination toward domestic marine insurers. Indeed, while foreign companies had to cede a share of their policies to the Committee, the retrocession strategies implemented by the latter only took domestic companies into consideration, in such a way that their market share rose from 69 in 1942 to 83% in 1945 (Gutiérrez González 2017, p. 181). In line with the trend of economic nationalism initiated three decades before, these measures forced a shift of market share from foreign offices to Spanish insurers.

While this framework worked during the war years, the end of the conflict in Europe led Spanish authorities began to design the adaptation to the postwar era: the links of the dictatorship with the Axis powers would increase the isolation of the country, while the weakness of the peseta could deeply affect the international relations of the Spanish economy. In the field of reinsurance, the Committee on Marine Insurance was renamed as an Official Committee on Reinsurance, with the power to supervise not only the marine business, but reinsurance in all lines.[4] The new agency kept a minor role reinsuring marine risks and covering the policies of public enterprises.

However, its main goal was to identify and supervise all reinsurance operations involving both Spanish companies and Spanish risks in all branches of the market.

To do that, the Committee would take a 1% share of every policy underwritten in Spain by domestic or foreign companies and reinsured abroad.[5] As for the marine branch during the war, companies purchasing foreign reinsurance were required to send the authorities all the information of the reinsurance treaty. As noted by private companies as *La Unión y el Fénix*, this mechanism posed severe difficulties to access international risk exchange networks, since it would give public officers a wide knowledge on the risk portfolio of both insurers and reinsurers.[6] In addition,

---

[4] Decree of 8 July 1945, in *BOE* no. 197, 16 July 1945.

[5] The compulsory cession of 1% of all risks reinsured abroad was actually introduced by a previous regulation passed in September 1944 but, as explained by officers of the Committee, it was not fully implemented until the transformation of the institution. See Decree of 29 September 1944, in *BOE* no. 293, 19 October 1944.

[6] Historical Archives of the Bank of Spain (ABE), Departamento Extranjero, IEME, Comité Oficial de Reaseguros, Correspondencia y Actas del Comité, c.85, f. 6.

the criteria applied by the Committee to grant permission to purchase foreign reinsurance were quite restrictive, and they do not rely on actuarial or financial elements, but on political decisions related to monetary policy of the IEME. This regulatory environment, along with the international isolation and the shortcomings of the financial system, would lead Spanish insurers to seek for new risk management strategies to keep pace with insurance demand.

7.3 Corporate Networks and Risk Management Strategies: A National Reinsurance Market in Spain?

Regulatory obstacles and international isolation were not the only problems affecting Spanish insurance during the 1940s. Indeed, direct insurance remained stagnated during the period before 1952. The drop on private savings burdened the growth of the Life branch, while the difficulties arising from the lack of financial resources for the reconstruction of industrial equipment and dwellings hampered the demand of property insurance (Pons Pons 2010, pp. 64–65; Prados de la Escosura and Rosés 2010, Appendix 6A). In parallel, the lowering of capital requirements for new companies introduced in 1944 contributed to the proliferation of small local companies and mutual societies featured by high levels of financial leverage. As a result, and despite the stagnation of the market, the demand of reinsurance services by domestic insurers maintained its trend of growth, while the access to international reinsurance networks remained almost blocked by public controls.[7] In this scene, Spanish insurers implemented a new risk management strategy that would avoid the collapse and that redefined the performance of the insurance industry in Spain: the consolidation of corporate groups through interlocking directorates.[8]

---

[7] For instance, the presence of the international reinsurance leader *Swiss Re* dropped to a minimum since 1942, along with the introduction of the first regulation on reinsurance. In 1943, the market share of the company barely reached a 0.32% of the total (Gutiérrez González 2017, p. 236).

[8] The theoretical framework of interlocking directorates was firstly posed by Mizruchi (1996) and has been widely used to analyse links among companies. For its applications in business and financial history, see Rubio and Garrués (2016) or Lilljegren (2019).

Indeed, the functional division inside insurance companies by creating specialized companies was not entirely new. In 1928, one of the biggest Life insurers in Spain, *La Equitativa—Fundación Rosillo*, created two separated companies: *La Equitativa Riesgos Diversos*, devoted to sell property insurance policies; and *La Equitativa Reaseguros*, which would be the reinsurer of the portfolios of the other two companies. As noted by Pons Pons (2018), the company managers, the Rosillo brothers, tried to avoid the high commissions charged by international reinsurers to Spanish companies. While this was an isolated practice before 1940, the outbreak of the Second World War and the regulatory changes led to its proliferation during our period of study. Consequently, the difficulties to access international reinsurance services led the main Spanish insurers to create their own dependent reinsurers to manage their risk portfolios.[9]

Table 7.1 shows the first twenty companies accepting reinsurance premiums in Spain from 1943 to 1951, in life, fire, and marine branches. As noted in the table, three types of company appeared in the market: first, primary insurers acting as the head of corporate groups, whose business is the results of risk allocation with the other firms of the group, more than actual reinsurance; second, primary insurers whose main business is to offer reinsurance services to other companies, instead of underwrite new policies with individuals; and third, pure reinsurers. Within the last group, all companies were constituted after 1939, with the sole exception of the *La Equitativa Reaseguros*.[10] In addition, there was only one foreign company, *Asicurazioni Generali*, within the group of the top-twenty reinsurers.

While it seems clear that the Spanish market was dominated by domestic companies, the role of the main insurance leaders requires a deeper analysis. Indeed, by examining the boards of administration of the companies, we identify the presence of common counselors, which is the main foundation of the interlocking directorate: following Mizruchi (1996), if the same person serves as a counselor for the firm A and for the firm B, there is a link between the two entities that could result in market coordination or cooperation.

---

[9] For a detailed narrative of the process of constitution and the links of the core of this group, see Caruana (2017, pp. 138–141).

[10] Out of this ranking, Caruana (2017) notes also the existence of the company *La Garantía*, founded in 1918.

Table 7.1 Ranking of companies reinsuring Spanish risks, in Life, Fire, and Marine branches (1943–1951)

	Company[a]	Year of constitution	HQ location	Suscribed capital[b]	Paid capital
1	Mediterránea de Reaseguros	1942	Barcelona	2.000	2.000
2	Compañía General de Reaseguros	1942	Barcelona	5.000	1.938
3	La Equitativa Hispano Americana	1944	Madrid	5.000	2.608
4	*La Unión y el Fénix Español*	1864	Madrid	18.000	16.091
5	Cía. Española de Reaseguros	1941	Madrid	12.000	6.000
6	La Equitativa Reaseguros	1928	Madrid	10.000	5.000
7	Nacional de Reaseguros	1939	Madrid	6.000	4.500
8	Reaseguradora Española	1940	Bilbao	10.000	4.000
9	*Compañía Hispano Americana*	1924	Madrid	5.000	5.000
10	Continental	1943	Madrid	10.000	8.000
11	Assicurazioni Generali	1831	Trieste	No capital declared in Spain	
12	*Covadonga*	1924	Madrid	5.000	2.250
13	*Minerva*	1932	Madrid	10.000	5.157
14	*Plus Ultra*	1887	Madrid	5.000	5.000
15	*Cervantes*	1930	Madrid	9.000	3.500
16	*Banco Vitalicio de España*	1880	Barcelona	15.000	7.500
17	Consorcio Español de Reaseguros	1939	Sevilla	10.000	3.000
18	*La Vasco Navarra*	1900	Pamplona	8.000	6.000
19	*La Catalana*	1864	Barcelona	5.000	5.000
20	Mare Nostrum	1942	Baleares	5.000	3.351

[a]In italics, direct insurance companies whose reinsurance portfolio is over 50% of total underwritings
[b]Subscribed and paid capital in million pesetas
Source Anuario Financiero y de Sociedades Anónimas, 1941–1952 y Revista del Sindicato Vertical del Seguro, Años 1943–1953, Relaciones de primas aceptadas en reaseguro por entidades autorizadas en España, cited in Gutiérrez González (2017, p. 246)

By utilizing the data compiled in the *Anuario Financiero y de Sociedades Anónimas*, we have analyzed a sample of 76 companies including pure reinsurers, direct insurers operating as reinsurers and direct insurers leading the branches of life, fire and marine during the period 1941–1952.[11] As a result, we find that 126 of a total of 601 seats at the board of administration of these companies are occupied by common counselors. Moreover, within these 126, at least 38 involve main positions as general directors, chief executive officers, and executive presidents. Consequently, half of the sample shows connections with other companies at the highest executive level. Furthermore, when looking at the map of relations of the companies analyzed, we find four corporate groups, headed by direct insurance leaders and with a clear coordination and functional separation to allocate risks in different portfolios. The first group was formed around the fire and life company *La Unión y el FénixEspañol* (see Fig. 7.1). As the leader of the market in property insurance, the executive board decided to constitute a pure reinsurer at the end of 1940, with the goal of channeling the reinsurance necessities of the marine and fire branches of the company. In fact, while this role had been traditionally assumed by the office of the firm in Paris, the war and the rumors about a change on the regulation of reinsurance led the executive director, Ernesto Atanasio, to seek for an alternative. Finally, it was the constitution of *Compañía Española de Reaseguros (CERSA)*, a pure reinsurer dependent of *La Unión y el Fénix*.[12] In the case of the life business, the expansion of the group was not planned with a newly created company, but with an already existing firm. Concretely, it was *Minerva*, a life insurer constituted in 1932 which was close to bankruptcy in 1940. In 1941, *La Unión y el FénixEspañol* took over the company, modified its statutes and registered the company to reinsure life risks.[13] Under the same director as *CERSA* and *La Unión y el Fénix*, the group set a comprehensive risk management strategy, in which the latter would focus on direct insurance operations, while *Minerva* would manage the reinsurance of Spanish risks in all branches and *CERSA* would be in charge of the reinsurance of fire and marine risks through international operations. As a result, during the

---

[11] See Gutiérrez González (2017) for a detailed description of the source.

[12] As noted by Caruana (2017, p. 139), the acronym *CERSA* was also used by the firm *Consorcio Español de Reaseguradores*.

[13] Archivo General de la Administración (AGA) (1) 26—Caja I-74, Top. 13/31.

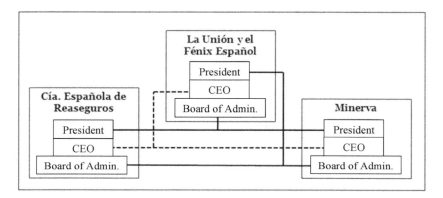

Fig. 7.1 The corporate group of *La Unión y el Fénix Español* (*Source* Anuario Financiero y de Sociedades Anónimas de España, 1942–1952)

period 1942–1952 the group kept its financial solvency while increasing its market share in the reinsurance market: a 16.8% of the life branch; a 13.8% in fire and a 14.1% in marine.[14]

In contrast to the case of *La Unión y el Fénix*, the strategy of internal specialization had worked within the group *La Equitativa* for the last decade, with the companies *La Equitativa Reaseguros* and *La Equitativa—Riesgos Diversos*. In addition to these companies, during the 1930s the group took over minor firms with financial problems, as *Atlántida* or *El Fénix Austríaco*. However, when the group was intended to be the national champion of the insurance business, family problems between the Rosillo brothers led to the division of the group in 1944: Miguel and Fernando kept control over the original life company and the property insurance company, while Fermín retained the command over the reinsurer: *La Equitativa Reaseguros* (see Fig. 7.2).[15]

After the separation, two independent groups were formed. In the first case, the necessity of reinsurance services and the obstacles to access international risk exchange networks led in 1944 to the constitution of a new

---

[14] Revista del Sindicato Vertical del Seguro, Años 1943–1953, Relaciones de primas aceptadas en reaseguro por entidades autorizadas en España.

[15] Pons Pons (2018) notes the disagreement between the Rosillo brothers around the management of the group, but also underlines the conflict around the marriage and following divorce of Fermín Rosillo.

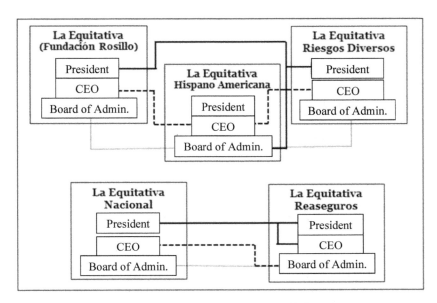

Fig. 7.2 The Rosillo brothers and the Split of '*La Equitativa*' (*Source* Anuario Financiero y de Sociedades Anónimas de España, 1942–1952)

dependent reinsurer, *La Equitativa Hispano Americana*, which served to the group headed by the original *La Equitativa Fundación Rosillo*. Thus, the group composed by these two companies and *La Equitativa Riesgos Diversos* kept its position among the main actors in the Spanish insurance industry. In the same year, Fermín Rosillo, who kept control over *La Equitativa Reaseguros*, tried to make the inverse way, that was: to associate a direct insurer capable of providing reinsurance premiums to his reinsurance company. In this way, Fermín bought a small and stagnated company specialized on sickness insurance, *La Equitativa Nacional*. After changing the statutes and renewing its registration as a life insurer, he began to announce these companies as the actual heirs of the group, what generated legal conflicts because of the use of the commercial brand *La Equitativa*.

At the end of the decade of 1940, the competition between the two groups showed a clear winner: despite the inclusion of high officers of the new government in the board of administrators, as Nicolás Franco, brother of the dictator, the group directed by Fermín Rosillo lost a wide share of the market share of *La Equitativa Reaseguros* since the separation from his brothers: from a total 8% of all the reinsurance market in 1945, its business dropped to the 2.1% in 1952. In the case of the other *Equitativas*, the evolution was the opposite: supported by the direct business underwritten by *La Equitativa Fundación Rosillo* and *La Equitativa Riesgos Diversos*, *La Equitativa Hispano Americana* reached the leading position in life reinsurance in 1952 with an 18.2% of the market, while it consolidated its place among the five top property reinsurers at the end of the 1940s and for the next decade.

Without reaching the levels of corporate integration of the previous cases, the insurance companies based in Catalonia formed cooperation networks including both primary insurers and pure reinsurers created during the 1940s (see Fig. 7.3). Thus main providers of life insurance (*Banco Vitalicio de España*), marine insurance (*Compañía Hispano Americana de Seguros o Reaseguros*, hereinafter *CHASYR*), work-accident insurance (*Mutua General de Seguros*) and fire insurance (*La Catalana*) got directly involved in the management of pure reinsurers as *Mediterránea* or *Compañía General de Reaseguros*, as well as direct insurance companies devoted to the business of reinsurance, as *Covadonga*. Indeed, by mean of common counselors and shared executive officers, these companies coordinated their action by focusing in one branch of business, in such a way that they did not compete among themselves and share the costs of maintaining dependent reinsurance providers.

CHASYR shapes a very special case since it was not only linked to other consolidated companies but formed its own corporate group around the businesses of the Millet family (see Fig. 7.4). As noted by Tortella, Ortiz-Villajos, and García Ruiz (2011, pp. 94–97), *CHASYR* was under the control of Felix and Salvador Millet, who were also the owners of the insurance company *Castellón Vital*. In 1941, after changing the statutes of *CHASYR*, moving its headquarters to Madrid and registering the company in the marine branch, it began to operate by taking the risks retroceded by the Committee of Marine Insurance. Political influence and contacts at the Ministry of Industry made of *CHASYR* one of the main clients of the Committee. Moreover, the insurance coverage of the main public firms turned the company on the first provider of risk

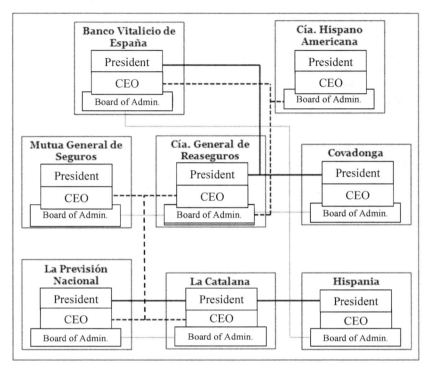

Fig. 7.3 Catalonian insurance and the new reinsurers (*Source* Anuario Financiero y de Sociedades Anónimas de España, 1942–1952)

management services for the Spanish government.[16] Despite the political boost, *CHASYR* had to face the same problems in the access to foreign reinsurance. Consequently, by using resources from *CHASYR* and from another life insurer of the family, *El Porvenir de los Hijos*, the Millet brothers constituted in Barcelona in 1942 the pure reinsurer *Mediterránea*. Always close to the operations of *CHASYR*, *Mediterránea* also performed a strong trend of growth during the 1940s: in 1946, the firm reached the 15% of the marine reinsurance market; from 1948, it was well

---

[16] Tortella et al. (2014, p. 518) notes the size of the portfolio of the company in 1943 and its fast growth: with 60.5 million pesetas, it was only exceeded by *Banco Vitalicio de España* and *La Unión y el Fénix Español*.

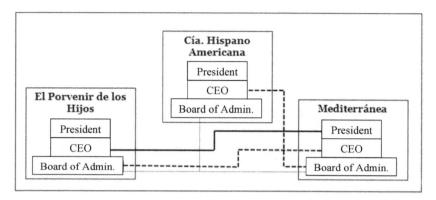

Fig. 7.4 The network around *Compañía Hispano Americana (CHASYR)* (*Fuente* Anuario Financiero y de Sociedades Anónimas de España, 1942–1952)

over the 20%, until 1951, when changes on the regulation forced the slow decline of the company.[17]

Beyond these coordinated groups, the practice of seeking for subsidiary companies devoted to serve as dependent reinsurers was well extended among smaller offices. Thus, Caruana (2017, p. 140) examined how basque marine insurance companies as *Bilbao* and *Vizcaya* shared the control of a pure reinsurer, *Reaseguradora Española*, by mean of common counselors. Similar cases can be found at *Nervión Reaseguros*, controlled by *La Polar*; *Centro Levantino de Seguros* and *La Unión Levantina*; or *Guipúzcoa Reaseguros* and *Compañía Vascongada de Seguros*.

7.4 An Empirical Approach to the Actual Effect of Corporate Networks on the Performance of Insurance Firms

Once identified the existence of dense corporate networks linked by mean of common counsellors, we seek to test their actual impact on the performance of the involved companies. Following Mizruchi (1996) and,

---

[17] Moreover, along with *CHASYR*, the group dominated the branch of marine reinsurance with more than the 30% of the total business (Gutiérrez González 2017, p. 260).

especially for the case of the insurance industry, Bartolomeo and Canofari (2015) and Liljegren (2019), the belonging to these networks should have a positive impact on the results of the company when controlling for firm-specific financial factors. Moreover, we aim to examine the effect of these networks on risk perception (and aversion) and, definitely, on reinsurance practices.

To do that, we have built a novel dataset from annual statistics included in the *Revista del Sindicato Vertical del Seguro*, in the period 1943–1952. From these figures, we have built our variable QUOTA, that is, the share of the market in the branch of fire, marine, life, and work-accident insurance. In addition, we get the financial indicators of direct insurers and pure reinsurers from the balance sheets published in the *Boletín Oficial de Seguros y Ahorro*. Due to the lack of information for several years and companies, we have limited the sample from the initial set of 205 companies to a reduced group of 44 firms, which involves no less than 76.4% of the market in each branch and year. Table 7.2 shows the main characteristics of the sample, including the typology of the firms included, the kind of links between them and the roles identified. Therefore, we have nine companies acting as head of networks and 24 subsidiaries.

With all this information we have built the variables REINSURANCE, expressed as reinsured premiums over gross premiums underwritten; GROSSLOSS, expressed as paid claims over premiums underwritten; NETLOSS, expressed as paid claims less claims paid by reinsurers over premiums underwritten less premiums reinsured; LIQUIDITY, expressed as cash and bank account resources over ongoing-risks reserves; RETURN, expressed as the annual result over equity; and LEVERAGE,

Table 7.2 Typology of the sample: Reinsurers and direct insurers authorized to reinsure in Spain (1943–1952)

Type of company		Type of link		Head of Group (HQ)	Dependent Firm (SUBSIDIARY)
Affiliated companies	33	Strongly linked (NETWORK1)	12	3	9
		Weakly linked (NETWORK2)	21	6	15
Non-affiliated	11	–	–	–	–

Source *Revista del Sindicato Vertical del Seguro*, 1943–1952, and *Anuario Financiero y de Sociedades Anónimas de España*, 1943–1953

expressed as total premiums underwritten over paid capital plus technical reserves. In order to introduce the information regarding the role of the firm within a corporate group, we have built three dummy variables: REINSURER, that identifies if the company is a pure reinsurer or a direct insurer; NETWORK1, that features those firms strongly connected to a corporate network, that is: to share more than 50% of their counsellors with other firms, or if the shared counsellor acts as chief executive officer; NETWORK2, that identifies weaker links to a network: to share less than 50% of the counsellors with other firms, and always without affecting executive positions. Finally, we have introduced the variable NETWORKPOL to identify those companies inserted in the dense network around the public administration and the government. Indeed, as noted by Sánchez Recio et al. (2003, pp. 50–53), this net of interests played a major role in the performance of Spanish companies during the first decade of the dictatorship (Gutiérrez González 2017, pp. 271–272). In addition to these firm-specific variables, we introduce the following set of country-level indicators: GDP growth in real terms (GRTH), the official exchange rate the peseta with the French franc (EXCH_FF) and with the Sterling pound (EXCH_UK). As a result, we have built an unbalanced panel with 484 complete observations involving 44 firms (one of them is a mutual society, *Mutua General de Seguros*) during the period 1943–1952.

To empirically examine the effect of belonging to a network on the performance of the firms, we employ a panel data analysis. Since all our network variables are time-invariant, we have run a Hausmann test to use the most accurate method. As a result, we see that difference between random-effect and fixed-effect estimators were not systematic, so we can use a standard random-effect model following the next equation:

$$QUOTA_{it} = \alpha + \sum \beta X_{it} + \beta U_t + \beta V_{it} + \varepsilon_{it} \qquad (7.1)$$

Where $QUOTA_{it}$ displays the share of the market of the company i in the year t; X_{it} is the vector of dummy variables identifying the belonging of the firm to a network; U_t is the vector of macroeconomic indicators that serve as control variables; and V_{it} is the vector of firm-specific financial variables.

Table 7.3 shows the results of the analysis including the set of estimators obtained for each variable. In the first model, we include only

Table 7.3 Corporate networks and their effect on the reinsurance market (1943–1952). Random-effect regression models

	(1)	(2)
NETWORK1	1.709[a]	0.945[a]
	(0.193)	(0.328)
NETWORK2	0.481[a]	0.608[c]
	(0.130)	(0.421)
NETWORKPOL	2.756[a]	2.957[a]
	(0.256)	(0.717)
LEV	–	0.060
		(0.057)
GRLOSS	–	0.001
		(0.001)
LIQ	–	−0.001
		(0.004)
RENTAB	–	0.037
		(0.049)
Const.	(0.142)[a]	0.587[c]
	(0.045)	(0.097)
R^2		
Within	0.041	0.034
Between	0.421	0.231
Overall	0.153	0.098

[a, b, c] Statistically significant at the 1, 5, and 10%

Source Revista del Sindicato Vertical del Seguro, Years 1943–1953, Relaciones de primas aceptadas en reaseguro por entidades autorizadas en España, Anuario Financiero y de Sociedades Anónimas de España (1943–1950)

the set of network variables, while in the second equation we include also the set of firm-specific variables. In both cases we have set country-level indicators as control variables, though they are not included in the table. As shown in the table, network variables hold a strong, positive, and statistically significant impact on the market share of the company, that is: the belonging of the company to a corporate network affects positively to its performance in the reinsurance market. Indeed, the links between firms, especially those of a more intense character (NETWORK1), would have contributed to coordinate more efficient risk management strategies: concretely, the capacity to retain risks would be wider, while possibilities of risk allocation and portfolio design would be multiplied. With lower intensity, indirect links and relations between companies (NETWORK2) would also enhance the position of the firm, since it could access market information and additional risk exchange opportunities. Beyond the links between companies, the presence of political and public officers in the boards of administration showed a wide and intense effect on the performance of insurance firms (NETWORKPOL). However, we need to be cautious with this indicator: the inclusion of political officers within these companies could be a powerful instrument to enhance the market position of new companies as *CHASYR*, but also as a way of preserving a consolidated status for companies with an extended trajectory.

In summary, we could affirm that, beyond the role of firm-specific financial indicators, the inclusion of a company within corporate networks had a strong and positive impact on its market position. While the data used do not allow to examine the concrete effect of these networks on reinsurance practices, we can thus underline their substantive role in the shaping of the insurance market under a strict regulatory framework.

7.5 The First Steps Toward the Liberalization and the Re-opening to the International Reinsurance Market

As noted in previous sections, the evolution of the reinsurance industry in Spain was deeply affected by public regulations and economic nationalism. The efforts to control capital flows and to enlarge foreign currency reserves led to the rupture of one of the main foundations of the reinsurance business: the confidentiality of the treaty. This change, along with difficulties for domestic companies to overcome the isolation of the Spanish economy, contributed to reduce the traditionally dense relations between the industry and the international risk exchange networks.

Indeed, Fig. 7.5 shows the transformations described from 1940, when national reinsurance was almost residual, to 1951, when reinsurers constituted inside corporate networks reached around 75% of the demand for reinsurance coverage in Spain in all branches, while in marine and fire the figure increased to 90%. Except for *Assicurazioni Generali*, none of the big international insurers or reinsurers were present in this business. Quite the opposite, it was absorbed by newly created, dependent, and subsidiary domestic companies. In contrast to this flourishing market, which would grow to almost 1,100 million pesetas in 1951, reinsurance abroad barely reached 300 million pesetas in the same year.

Nevertheless, while this performance was the direct result of the regulatory changes introduced between 1942 and 1945, the first steps toward

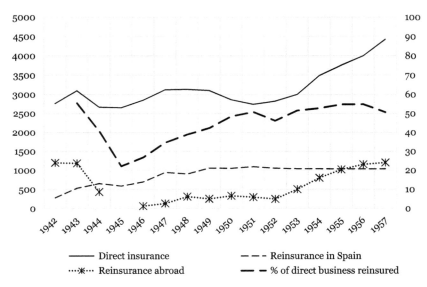

Fig. 7.5 Direct insurance premiums over Spanish risks, reinsurance in Spain and reinsurance abroad, in all branches (million pesetas, 1951 price-level) (left axis) and total percentage of reinsurance over premiums underwritten (right axis) (1942–1957) (*Source* Memoria de la Dirección General de Banca e Inversiones, 1953; Revista del Sindicato Nacional del Seguro, 1943–1958; AGA (12) 1.14 Libro 473 Top. 65/79101; ABE, Departamento Extranjero, IEME, Comité Oficial de Reaseguros, Caja 85, Estadísticas y Memorias Anuales del Comité Oficial de Reaseguros, años 1946–1955 y libros 113–115, Libro de Registro del Impuesto del 1% [Caballero Sánchez1960])

the softening of the supervisory role of the IEME and the slow opening to the international economy would abort this expansion. In fact, the limits of the autarkic model began to appear when the pressure of the financial system led to the restoring of a regulated foreign exchange market in 1950. As noted by Cavalieri (2014, pp. 62–69), changes within the economic ministries of the government in 1951 and, especially, the international talks to the rapprochement of Spain to the International Monetary Fund contributed to the softening of the requirements to access to the international financial system. In this trend, which would culminate with the end of isolation in 1953 through the signing of *Madrid Agreements* with the American government, the reinsurance business gradually recovered its traditional freedom. The monopoly of the IEME in the foreign exchange market ended in December 1951, while the compulsory cession of risks to be reinsured abroad to the Official Committee on Reinsurance was retired in April 1952.[18] Furthermore, the process to get the mandatory authorization of reinsurance operations by the committee was removed, in such a way that companies had only to report aggregate figures on their annual operations (Gutiérrez González 2017, pp. 282–286).

The convergence of these changes served to overcome the two main obstacles for Spanish companies to purchase foreign reinsurance: the difficulties to access foreign currencies and, especially, the obligation to share information of the operations with the regulatory agency. The removal of the first problem allowed domestic insurers to avoid additional costs when reinsuring risks in pesetas. Therefore, firms could agree both risk cession and the payment of losses in other currencies and in this way to dodge the effects of the unsteady evolution of the price of the peseta. Regarding the second obstacle, the restoration of the principle of confidentiality served to attract international reinsurers to the Spanish market. Finally, the process of partial liberalization of the reinsurance business culminated with its fiscal standardization. Indeed, the legislation passed in July 1952 removed the special tax system coordinated by the *Official Committee on Reinsurance* and inserted the reinsurance business in the same legal framework as direct insurance.

Returning to Fig. 7.5, the effects of the changes on the regulation and the liberalization of reinsurance appear clearly sketched. From its peak in 1951, national reinsurers became to a standstill during the next years, while direct insurance underwritings began a steady trend of growth: between 1951 and 1957, the size of the industry rose from 2,700 to 4,400 million pesetas (in constant prices). In fact, if Spanish companies reinsured almost 40% of the direct premiums underwritten in the country in 1951, this percentage drop to less than 23% in 1957. Far from a parallel behavior, the increase on the demand for reinsurance and risk management services by primary insurers was not covered by Spanish reinsurers, but by international firms. While these domestic companies have flourished during the years of isolation of the market, their unstable financial

---

[18] Decree of 21 of March 1952, in *BOE* no. 119, 28 April 1952.

performance and their dependence from big insurance groups made them highly vulnerable when the barriers to foreign reinsurers were retired.

7.6 Conclusions

Reinsurance became a widely used device in the Spanish insurance industry since the turn of the twentieth century. Moreover, internal imbalances within insurers and the limitations of the Spanish financial system made domestic firms heavily rely on the capital funding provided by foreign reinsurance. Indeed, within the framework of ruin theory, international risk exchange networks became vital sources of capitalization for the Spanish insurance industry.

This dependence worsened during the economic turmoil in the 1930s and especially, in 1940. The convergence of the effects of three years of civil war in Spain, the outbreak of the Second World War and the unsteady position of the Francoist government triggered the financial imbalances of Spanish insurers and boosted the demand of foreign reinsurance what, in turn, drove reforms in the regulation of the industry. Indeed, in a scene of increasing scarcity of foreign currencies, the autarkic and nationalist ideas of the new government led to a restrictive regulation of the purchases of foreign reinsurance. This new legal framework, enhanced in 1945 with the increasing isolation of the Spanish economy, broke the principle of confidentiality of the reinsurance treaty and forced the participation of the Spanish regulators in transnational risk cessions, in order to avoid the outflows of foreign currencies provoked by the demand of reinsurance.

The increase in the costs to find reinsurance services abroad moved main Spanish insurers to build up their own risk management facilities through subsidiary companies. Thus, by means of interlocking directorates and the construction of corporate networks, direct insurers enhanced their capacity to design sound portfolios by means of internal risk exchanges. This practice, extended over the whole industry, resulted on the creation of a national reinsurance market led by the main direct insurers, as *La Unión y el FénixEspañol*, *La Equitativa—Fundación Rosillo*, *Mututa General de Seguros* and *La Catalana*, and pure reinsurers directly dependent of them.

Moreover, we have empirically confirmed the relevance of these networks by analyzing the effects of the inclusion of a firm. In fact, we see that, controlling for country-level variables and beyond the firm-specific financial conditions of the companies, the belonging to one of these corporate networks had a strong, significant, and positive impact on the market performance of the firm, that is: far from a competitive performance, the reinsurance industry formed from the regulatory changes implemented in 1942 resulted in a restricted market in which the key was the figure of captive reinsurers and the barriers to international risk exchange networks were fundamental.

Therefore, the changes on the regulation at the beginning of the 1950s and the progressive opening of the Spanish economy to the international financial system wiped this national industry out. The withdrawal of the regulatory agency from the participation and tight supervision of the reinsurance treaties resulted in the restoration of the principle of confidentiality, which de facto opened the Spanish market to international reinsurers. Once subjected to foreign competition, domestic reinsurers began a trend of decline extended to the next decades.

References

Bartolomeo, Giovanni, and Paolo Canofari. 2015. "Interlocking Directorates and Concentration in the Italian Insurance Market". *Journal of Industry, Competition and Trade* 15 (4): 351–362.

Caballero Sánchez, Ernesto. 1960. *Inversiones extranjeras en materia de seguros y reaseguros*. Madrid: Centro de Estudios Tributarios.

Caruana de las Cagigas, Leonardo. 2017. "The Development of Spanish Reinsurance from 1940 to the Present Day". In *Highlights on Reinsurance History.*, ed. André Straus and Leonardo Caruana de las Cagigas, 135–152. Bruxelles: Peter Lang.

Cavalieri, Elena. 2014. *España y el FMI: la integración de la economía española en el Sistema Monetario Internacional, 1943–1959*. Serie Estudios de Historia Económica, 64. Madrid: Banco de España.

Comín Comín, Francisco. 2013. "Las crisis de la deuda: el largo camino recorrido desde los impagos a la gestión responsable". In *Las crisis financieras en la España contemporánea, 1850–2012*, coords, Pablo Martín-Aceña, Elena Martínez Ruiz and María Ángeles Pons Brías, 197–240. Barcelona: Crítica.

Deelstra, Griselda, and Guillaume Plantin. 2014. *Risk theory and reinsurance*. Londres: Routledge.

García Ruiz, José Luis, and Leonardo Caruana. 2009. "La internacionalización del seguro español en el siglo XX". *Revista de Historia Industrial*, 41 (3): 17-48.

Gerathewohl, Klaus. 1993. *Reaseguro: Teoría y Práctica*. Madrid: Reaseguros Gil y Carvajal.

Gutiérrez González, Pablo. 2014. *El control de divisas durante el primer franquismo. La intervención del reaseguro (1940–1952)*. Serie Estudios de Historia Económica, 68. Madrid: Banco de España.

Gutiérrez González, Pablo, and Jerònia Pons Pons. 2017. "Risk Management and Reinsurance Strategies in the Spanish Insurance Market (1880–1940). *Business History* 59 (2): 292–310.

Gutiérrez González, Pablo. 2017. "El mercado reasegurador en España (1870–1952). Estrategias empresariales, prácticas financieras e iniciativas de control público". PhD Dissertation, University of Seville.

James, Harold, Peter Borscheid, David Gugerli, and Tobias Straumann. 2013. *The Value of risk*. Oxford: Oxford University Press.

Liljegren, J. 2019. "Networks That Organised Competition. Corporate Resource Sharing Between Swedish Property Underwriters 1875–1950". PhD Dissertation, University of Seville.

Martín-Aceña, Pablo. 1987. "Desarrollo y modernización del sistema financiero, 1844–1935". In *La modernización económica de España*, ed. Nicolas Sánchez Albornoz, 121–46. Madrid: Alianza Editorial.

Martín-Aceña, Pablo. 1993. "Spain During the Classical Gold Standard Years, 1880–1914. In *Monetary Regimes in Transition*, ed. Mike Bordo and Forest Capie, 135–172 Cambridge: Cambridge University Press.

Martínez Ruiz, Elena. 2003a. *El sector exterior durante la autarquía. Una reconstrucción de las balanzas de pagos de España (1940–1958)*. Serie Estudios de Historia Económica, 43. Madrid: Banco de España.

Martínez Ruiz, Elena. 2003. La distribución de divisas en el sector industrial: poder público y poder privado en lucha por las divisas. *Historia y Política: Ideas, Procesos y Movimientos Sociales* 9: 95–122.

Martínez Ruiz, Elena. 2013. "Papel mojado. Crisis inflacionarias". In *Crisis económicas en España. 1300–2012: lecciones de la historia*, coords. Francisco Comín Comín and Mauro Hernández Benítez, 203–226. Madrid: Alianza Editorial.

Mayers, David, and Clifford W. Smith. 1982. "On the Corporate Demand for Insurance". *Journal of Business* 55: 281–296.

Mizruchi, Mark S. 1996. "What Do Interlocks Do? An Analysis, Critique and Assessment of Research on Interlocking Directorates. *Annual Review of Sociology* 22: 271–298.

Pearson, Robin. 1995. "The Development of Reinsurance Markets in Europe During the Nineteenth Century". *Journal of European Economic History* 24 (3): 557–572.

Pons Pons, Jerònia. 2003. "Diversificación y Cartelización en el seguro español 1914–1935". *Revista De Historia Económica* 21 (3): 567–592.

Pons Pons, Jerònia. 2005. "Large American corporations in the Spanish life insurance market 1880-1922". *The Journal of European Economic History* 34 (2): 467–481.
Pons Pons, Jerònia. 2007. "The Influence of Foreign Companies in the Organization of the Spanish Insurance Market: Diversification and Cartelisation 1880–1939". In , *Internationalisation and Globalisation of the Insurance Industry in the 19th and 20th Centuries*, ed. Peter Borscheid and Robin Pearson, 49–65. Zurich: Philipps-University, Marburg and Swiss Re Corporate History.
Pons Pons, Jerònia. 2010. "The Difficulties of Spanish Insurance Companies to Modernise During the Franco Years. The Mechanisation of Administrative Tasks (1950–1970). In *The Development of International Insurance*, ed. Robin Pearson, 63–101. Pickering and Chatto, Londres.
Pons Pons, Jerònia. 2012. "Spain: International Influence on the Domestic Insurance Market". In *World Insurance*, ed. Peter Borscheid and Niels V. Haueter, 189–212. Oxford: Oxford University Press.
Pons Pons, and Jerònia Gutiérrez González, Pablo. 2016. "The Actuarial Practices of British Life Insurance Companies in Peripheral Countries: The Case of Spain (1890–1936)". *Enterprise and Society* 17 (2): 237–264.
Pons Pons, Jerònia. 2018. "Los Hermanos Rosillo". In *Empresarios madrileños*, coord. Eugenio Torres, 100. Madrid: LID Editorial.
Powell, Lawrence S., and David W. Somner. 2007. "Internal Versus External Capital Markets in the Insurance Industry: The Role of Insurance". *Journal of Financial Services Research* 31 (3): 173–188.
Prados de la Escosura, Leandro. 2009. "Spain's International Position, 1850–1913". *Revista De Historia Económica* 28: 173–215.
Prados de la Escosura, Leandro, and Joan Rosés. 2010. "Capital Accumulation in the Long-Run: The Case of Spain, 1850–2000". *Research in Economic History* 27: 93–152.
Rubio, Juan Antonio, and Josean Garrués. 2016. "Economic and Social Power in Spain: Corporate Networks of Banks, Utilities and Other Large Companies (1917–2009). *Business History* 58 (6): 858–879.
Sánchez Recio, Glicerio, and Tascón Fernández, Julio 2003. *Los empresarios de Franco: política y economía en España (1936–1957)*. Madrid: Crítica.
Tortella, Gabriel, Ortiz-Villajos, José María, and García Ruiz, José Luis. 2011. *Historia del Banco Popular. La lucha por la independencia*. Madrid: Marcial Pons.
Tortella, Gabriel, Leonardo Caruana, García Ruiz, José Luis, Alberto Manzano, Pons Pons, and Jerònia. 2014. *Historia del seguro en España*. Madrid: Fundación MAPFRE.

CHAPTER 8

The Role of Foreign Reinsurance in the Setting of Insurance in Spain (1960–2000)

Leonardo Caruana de las Cagigas

8.1 Introduction

The reinsurance industry will be mainly in hands of foreign companies or explained in another way, they are the leaders in the process in Spain. In all moment they will sustain the risk of the insurance industry. This chapter will concentrate in the second half of the twentieth century, from 1960 to 2000, and explain how the international reinsurance companies diminish the risk and reinforce the insurance business in a useful way to make it possible that Spain joins the developed countries in this matter. In many ways, this is a general process in many countries, because reinsurance is mainly a business that is concentrated in few countries that expand in the entire world, and in fact we should mainly refer to few companies that control or support the reinsurance development in the world and naturally the main purpose, the insurance industry.

Spain has been described in Europe as a peripheral country, which showed evidence of backwardness over the past century, despite its earlier

L. Caruana de las Cagigas (✉)
Faculty of Economics and Business, University of Granada, Granada, Spain

© The Author(s), under exclusive license to Springer Nature Switzerland AG 2021
L. Caruana de las Cagigas and A. Straus (eds.), *Role of Reinsurance in the World*, Palgrave Studies in Economic History,
https://doi.org/10.1007/978-3-030-74002-3_8

political predominance in Europe and its great empire: "the empire on which the sun never sets." The thought of peripherally has been a clear explanation about Spanish economic and political history after the beginning of the industrial revolution in Britain. Spain did not complete the industrial revolution in the nineteenth century, which meant, that the gap with France or Great Britain was greater. Spain's dependency started with the lack of human capital, technology and financial capability (Nadal 1989). Comparing with other European countries we can analyze with the GDP per capita that Spain between 1870 and 1913 could count a mere 60% of the GDP per capita of the average of Great Britain, Germany, France and Italy. The gap is still with us today, but far less, and Spain is considered already between the developed countries.

Undeniably, if we rank Spain with Wallerstein's world system theory, Spain has a semi-peripheral position in the world, and a peripheral position in European scale. Anyway, what is crucial to take in, the enormous progress that Europe and Spain had achieved and more specifically in this historical moment. Which include a crucial political change from a dictatorship to democracy, that was helpful because it was close geographically to more developed countries, but another concept that must be taken into consideration is globalization, that is one of the explanations that succeeded to reduce the gap between Spain and the most developed country that we will see in reinsurance. As Kenneth Arrow said, globalization: "permits real economic growth, and stimulates economic development abroad" (Arrow 2000). To make it more understandable, the economic growth in the 60s was outstanding in Spain with growth in some years over 10% and with an average growth in 15 yearss of 8.3% (Carreras and Tafunell 2010, p. 338). The famous caching up of Walt Whitman Rostow was on its move.

As Acemoglu said Economic growth is one of the fields that economic theory is really concern about and even "exciting." Naturally the development of the countries and the change from an agrarian economy to a developed country—industrialize country was also said—is a key question in economic history that happen in Spain during this period 1960–2000. The changes that produce were immense and growing more and more. In a great way the catching up was in its way. Indeed, we can refer to Adam Smith the father of modern economy that searches in the economy of his time and considered that the differences were not so great between the countries in general in Western Europe. In many ways that again happen in the year 2000. Anyway, as Acemoglu explains, the gaps did grow, increase, extended, and are far greater between the rich and poor. Again, this was not so great in the eighteenth and nineteenth century and did grow more in the twentieth century. That is one of the reasons for the great disparity around the world today. Finally, he said "western Europe and western European offshoots around the world, have grown rapidly during the 19th and early twentieth centuries, while many others have stagnated. This differential growth led to a huge gap in income per capita and living standards that continues to this day" (Acemoglu 2012).

Another aspect about economic development was explained in this case by Kuznets that emphasized to understand economic growth is important to highlight that is multifaceted, not only a simple aggregation of output and essentially it must include a broader concept of transformation that contains sectorial structure and social and institutional change. This means that it does require a full study of many aspects that take account of political, social and demographic issues. In the Spanish case the change between 1960 and 2000 is from dictatorship to democracy and joining the Common Market and from a country developing to a developed country and finally from high birth rates to one of the lowest birth rates in the world.

As is well known, economic growth needs both micro and macro analysis. Lastly, is essential the empirical field that opens new questions and answered some others. In this case reinsurance probably opens more questions than answered because it is practically a new field in economic history. The relevance of reinsurance in each moment of the insurance industry in the case of Spain, must be analyzed, to answered the role that it did had and how. What is empirically clear the fast growth during these 40 years, but why, how and who? Undeniable, the relation so special between reinsurance companies and insurance companies is complex by definition and probably the key question is how do they manage the risk with all the elements of prevention and so on. All this analysis in economic history is far better understood with the analysis of growth and development. Obviously, many economists search the complex relation between firms but this case is less a study about reinsurance and insurance companies. The field of economic growth includes technology diffusion and structural change, especially in the Spanish case of this chapter, the technologic diffusion was extremely relevant because was introduce the computer in all the companies. The insurance companies in Spain invested in the latest technology, that close the gap with other countries. This was in many ways push by foreign competitors—reinsurance companies and insurance companies that is explained by Daron Acemoglu, Gino Gancia and Fabrizio Zilibotti "Competing engines of growth: innovation and standardization" (Acemoglu et al. 2012).

As a slow technology diffusion, that does include skill-intensive innovation and the process of standardization. The aim as usual with standardizing is to achieve cheaper costs. But also, can be a barrier to growth if you do not do it. For example, practically all the insurance companies had IBM as the central computer in the 70s in Spain, if you did not you would have a serious loss. And the other aspect that they argue is that with standardizing technology it opens the option to use workers with less skill that was really abundant in Spain in that period. Eventually this will increase the use of technology that will increase productivity and the employees of the company do increase their income. Definitely with standardizing you manage to reduce complex management, you simplify the different process that can reduce time and also cost and you can have less qualified people that are paid less in the company. This will also arrive in Spain, coming from the most advanced countries, especially from other European and from USA. This was one of the paths for growth. On the other hand, as Robert Solow points out it is always difficult to know exactly how much that can be: "you can see the computer age every-where but in the productivity statistics" (Solow 1987, p. 36). For the insurance companies, directed or oriented or forced by foreign reinsurance companies, for example in prevention, they had a great relevance because obviously they were deeply concern to reduce risk in the big Spanish industry: refineries, nuclear plants, electric plants, dams, etc.

This chapter scrutinizes the issue of reinsurance industry in Spain from 1960 to 2000. Spain marks up a noticeable delay in building up reinsurance in many ways because the insurance industry develops slowly, also the financial market and because on the other hand the general economy also did develop insufficiently for the demand of the Spanish companies and that includes the insurance companies. The chapter suggests that this backwardness was also applicable to the management of the insurance business, which began to take on a better shape only in the late 1980s. The investigation confirms, ad abundantiam, the fact that Spain was behind developing modernity and however becoming part of the European core in 2000. Precisely in 1986, in official international statistics Spain join the "club" of the developed countries and also join the Common Market.

From 1966 until 2000 the Spanish economy grew in a substantial way, multiplied by 385%, but is far more impressive the growth in premiums, multiplied by 1,262% and it started to be a product of mass consumption in the country. One of the explanation of this process was exports (goods and services, adding with imports jumping from 27% of GDP in 1970 to 62% in 2000).

In all this fast change, what was the role of reinsurance? Here we must explain the difficulties of the Spanish financial situation that made it more difficult to develop credit because Spain was not in the World Bank until September 1958. That same year and in the same month also Spain joined the IMF. The next year was the start of the *"plan de estabilización"* in 1959 that aimed for liberalization of the exchange rate but in a very limited way and abolished the multiple currency practices. The peseta became convertible with major European currencies and integrated into the Bretton Woods System in July 1959. The international institution gave in exchange: "$25 million and the equivalent of $12.5 million each in sterling and in French francs, and entered into a stand-by arrangement for a further $25 million" (Annual IMF Report 1960, p. 17). That was not the only credit given, also there was a credit of $100 million given to Spain by the European Fund and another $200 million from other sources, between them $70 million from commercial banks. Another positive aspect was more control of prices and less inflation. Exports began to increase; important debts were repaid, and by the end of 1959 exchange reserves had increased by $120 million. Clearly, they were indications that Spain was going in the right path in monetary policy and in general it was the beginning of the Spanish economic miracle (Sardá 1970; Varela Parache 2004; Fuentes Quintana 1984; González 1979). Nevertheless, all was not positive, because people lost their jobs and there was less growth at the start of the *Plan de Estabilización*. However, the fact is that Spain integrated into the international market at last.

On the other side, the change from autarky to the open market was not complete, and internally the government still had strict control in many ways that did not change so fast. Anyway, things were going in the correct direction because the economy started growing more and they could cancel the credit of $71 million with commercial banks related to the stabilization program, in addition was repaid $24 million of the European Fund. On February 24, 1961, Spain canceled $75 million, of the credit from the OEEC, and several other payments were done in advance of the scheduled dates with IMF (Annual IMF Report 1961, p. 32).

Another big change was the reform law: *La Ley de Bases de Ordenación del Crédito y la Banca de 14 de abril de 1962.* That will allow the government to change all the financial systems in the country. The Bank of Spain was nationalized in June 1962, the Institute of Credit, the Institute of the Saving Banks and also official banks such as the Bank of Industrial Credit, *Banco Hipotecario de España* (mortgage Bank), *Banco de Crédito Local* (Local Banking), *Banco de Crédito Agrícola* (Agriculture Bank) and several others. They develop the effort to distinguish commercial banks and industrial banks and business banks. They impose harder regulations on this last one, oblige a minimum capital and prohibition of other banks to participate more than 50% (Pablo Martín Aceña 2005, pp. 8–9). And harder requirements to create a new bank. Even if the norms of 1962 did manage some golds, Pablo Martín Aceña considered that the modernization of the Spanish financial system will not happen till the summer of 1974. In that moment they did introduce a more homogenous legal system for all types of financial institutions. Another crucial process in Spain was the investment in public education that will make it possible that the great majority of people will be able to study and also started in the 60s.

8.2 The Relevance of Foreign Reinsurance Companies in the Development of Spanish Insurance Companies

Reinsurance considers that the best solution to reduce risk from a financial point of view is to spread it across different regions in the world and with all types of insurance: life, goods, etc. Despite its importance the business of reinsurance has been ignored, despite its great impact on the economy and society. A fine example of this important impact on the economy is major catastrophes that have a great cost that is an important part are covered by reinsurance companies and naturally have a very important social impact for all the people that suffer the consequence of the catastrophe (Haueter and Jones 2017). What is coming to be essential is to manage all these difficult moments and for the reinsurance world to prepare the insurance companies for the next one, if possible, the latest possible but they always do appear again. Naturally the financial capability is crucial and if you do have more financial resources far better. In that sense Munich Re or Swiss Re are fine examples of having extremely large financial capability. So, if the disaster appears, they are prepared to cover a large part of the cost.

Here we must point out three crucial aspects about reinsurance, first, the limited number of reinsurance companies with large financial capability, second, the important number of countries that do develop insurance, practically all the countries in the world with very few exceptions that do not do it with private insurance or private reinsurance. And third and last, clearly a more developed country has more insurance business and naturally more reinsurance so it needs more financial capabilities in both. Consequently, even if it is obvious, in the world are many countries but few reinsurance companies with large financial capability. In that sense Spain is not different and is like many others or said in another way is really a normal pattern of the development of the reinsurance business, that is mainly with foreign companies. We can even go in more detail, mainly four in Europe: German (Munich Re), Swiss (Swiss Re), French (since recent years SCOR) and British, always different because it is not primarily a reinsurance company and is the famous and important company name "Lloyds."

In the Spanish case the development of national reinsurance was a big effort with practically no achievement because the insurance industry was small and the financial capability of the country also since 1940 till 1960. Nevertheless, this did change in a substantial way in the last 40 years of the twentieth century. It did change in such a way because it did develop the Spanish insurance companies in a highly successful way. Naturally in the process they were companies that disappear because assume too much risk or bad management, etc., and even big reinsurance companies in the world market suffer the same consequence. This emphasizes the true difficulty to manage risk, with the last responsible for the reinsurance market.

One of the explanations for this important development so successful in Spain was the increase of reinsurance because it solves the poor financial capability in the country. In the early 60s we can say clearly, they were not much financial capacity, few banks or saving banks with sufficient economic capability. The important economic growth of the country during 40 years made an important growth of the banks and also of the insurance companies. Therefore, the situation did change in a substantial way. In fact, Spain joined the Euro and in the year 2000 had a robust financial system and one of the most important banks in the world: Banco Santander. The growth of the insurance industry also was very successful

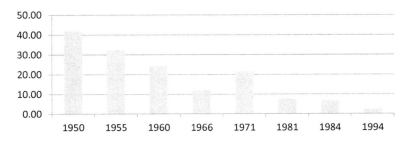

Fig. 8.1 Percentage of direct insurance related to reinsurance (*Source* Anuario Español de Seguros 1951–1995)

and the percentage of premiums related to reinsurance drop substantially (Fig. 8.1).

At international level we can also see the change, Spain grew even more than Italy; in the year 2000, it reaches 6.7% of premiums relative to GDP, when Italy was 5.8%. Spain was between France 9.4% and Italy ($23,318 per capita in the year 2000, France; $20,117 per capita in the year 2000, Italy; $14,725 per capita in Spain and United Kingdom $27,828, estimation of the IMF). What was outstanding was the growth in relation with the GDP, since 1964 and the year 2000, it practically triple, exactly 2.91, it did grow even more than France that is was 2.61, also excellent. Even though the leader country was clearly Britain, there was a caching up of the other countries, in the case of Spain was from 3.74 times greater in Britain than in Spain in 1964 to 2.36 times greater in 2000. In the case of France, it also drops from 2.4 to 1.7. In the case of the year 1980 was general the drop of all the countries, mainly because the oil crisis in the 70s.

To understand the process of reinsurance in Spain, one way is to see the evolution in one holding that is a fine example and will explain in a large way the general process in the country and also the process "learning by doing."

8.3 The Instituto Nacional de Industria

The company that we focus on is the INI (Instituto Nacional de Industria) the State Holding Company that managed over 150 companies in the 1970s. This company was established in 1941, in the autarchy period and during the Second World War with a starting capital of fifty million pesetas and with a major problem, the strong control that the allies had on trade because Spain politically was friendlier with the Axis (Caruana and Rockoff 2007). This situation triggered the purpose of producing all types of goods in Spain and reducing trade abroad. The political aim was to be self-sufficient. The model followed in many ways was that of the Italian State Holding Company *Istituto per la Ricostruzione Industriale* (IRI), established in 1933.

INI was at the start very inefficient, but later, was an important part of the Spanish economic miracle. In the 60s and 70s it was the most important industrial conglomerate in the country. Naturally it signed important insurance contracts and those companies had a great part of the risk distributed with reinsurance contracts. Unquestionable it was one of the best clients in the country and all the insurance companies were willing to have a contract with them. It also had another advantage, this company had the guaranty of the State, in a country that was already financially solid and reliable.

The story of the INI had developed quickly. At the beginning it followed the autarchy concept of being the main developer of Spanish industrialization because the government believed that private initiative had failed. Naturally this ambitious target was also too much for INI and clearly it failed. However, in short time was one of the biggest developers of Spanish industrialization and it shared with the private sector a major change in the industry of the country with an important part in several industrial sectors where the private sector was not so capable and it even served as the rescuer of private companies. Undeniably, it was a very confused holding with too many objectives that changed rapidly over time. What we can say is that the purpose and aims were so many that it was impossible. One of the goals that it had to develop was absolutely out of the capability of the country, private or public and that was to produce a local technology—made in Spain—for all industry, for a "late comer" that was simply a dream and not realistic, because of the lack of capability of the country in that period. First it was necessary to learn from the leader countries and in a second stage innovate and produce new technology and only in some industrial sectors in a global world. Nevertheless, in the end INI was a major player in the fascinating change of the country in a highly successful way.

One of the strong capabilities of the INI from the beginning was its financial strength because the State was supporting it with the taxpayers' money. In the long run it was a great success in some industrial sectors. To be more precise, it was successful in major industrial sectors, that is in energy: electricity, oil refined and coal or improving all type of transport and in heavy industry to produce steal. All this was essential for any country, that in the Spanish story these sectors had the advantage of practically unlimited financial support. Another idea that is crucial, that all are industries that need long periods to develop in an efficient way, so with the support of the State in the long run they did manage to be successful as happened in the 60s.

To understand better how important this was, we can mention the most important companies: for example, SEAT (Sociedad Española de Automóviles de Turismo) produced and sold all the cars in the 60s; they even had a waiting list because the demand was greater than the production. And it was a great percentage of the cars that were on the roads of Spain, in addition they did produce an outstanding car, the Seat 600, that for many people is the symbol of Spanish industrial revolution. Today, this company is part of the German group Volkswagen. For the production of buses and trucks INI had ENASA with the commercial name Pegaso. Another well-known company is Iberia, the national air company was the main air business in the country and today forms part of the air group: International Consolidated Airlines Group, S.A. an Anglo-Spanish holding company with British Airways. CASA the airplane manufacturer, today forms part of Airbus Group, the second or first largest company in the world in producing airplanes. All these companies had a very important part of their development during the period when they formed part of the INI. In shipbuilding Spain became one of the world largest producers in the 60s and 70s and mainly thanks to the State Holding Company INI, with the company E.N. Bazán–ASTANO.

Oil production was one of the main aims of INI because during World War II, Spain suffered two oil embargoes and severe oil restriction because it was pro-Axis (Caruana and Rockoff 2007). That made it absolutely necessary to produce oil if possible in Spain, that is why it started in the early 40s, with ENCASO to produce petrol with bituminous slate, and another company for refining oil, REPESA. The first was a big disaster because production was terribly costly, but the second was a great success because instead of the Americans or British refining the oil for Spain, the Spanish industry was starting to do so. The investment was enormous in the 40s for these two projects, reaching 40% of all the investment of INI in 1949 (Aceña and Comín 1991). Nevertheless, these projects followed the autarky ideas even if the cost was enormous. Following the success of the second company, they increased the refining production with American technology. In addition, they invested in more companies that refined oil, and they searched for oil in Spain with practically no success. Eventually these companies merged to form the well-known company REPSOL in 1987, one of the biggest companies in the world. For electricity, INI, develop another big company ENDESA in 1944. Finally, with coal the INI had a company HUNOSA with over 20.000 workers in 1967. In the north of Spain in Asturias, they were producing steel, ENSIDESA (Empresa Nacional Siderurgica). For fertilizers ENFERSA and for weapons E.N. Santa Bárbara. This holding was enormous and specially for Spain, with a huge number of workers, in 1970 this was 199,339 and will increase up to 254,941 in 1980 and drop to 146.625 in 1990 (Aceña and Comín 1991).

As in the rest of the world the ideas of Milton Friedman arrived in Spain and with the socialist government and with large debt that the country had, in certain percent was reduced by selling excellent public companies that were part of the INI, for example REPSOL and ENDESA. As in other European countries the government reinforced several other public companies that also were important, for example CAMPSA established in 1927 (oil), RENFE, established in 1941 (railways), Tabacalera, one of the very old state companies that began in 1636 and produced tobacco, and Telefónica with state control since 1945 (telecommunications).

8.4 The Insurance Company of INI: MUSINI

This part is written with the internal documents of the insurance company MUSINI that was given to me thanks to the Fundación MAPFRE. The INI holding company developed a strategic change related to insurance when it created the *Mutualidad de Seguros del Instituto Nacional de Industria* (MUSINI) in 1966. The purpose was to ensure all the companies in INI with their own insurance company. Because the board of directors of the company considered that if they created their own insurance company, in the estimation of the experts they could reduce the cost by 20%. The reason was that the private companies charged too much when they insured INI, probably because it was state run.

This insurance company encountered several problems. First, MUSINI was a mutual. In some situations this option was excellent because all the companies held by INI were from the start mutual, so all the companies from the beginning where on the Board of Administration. However, it was not as positive from the point of view of the reinsurance business because regulation was more restrictive for mutual companies than for stock companies in Spain (Gabriel et al., 2013). On the other hand, these companies with big industrial buildings with sophisticated machinery meant that they had enormous risk that had to be insured. This means that a great proportion of the risk had to be distributed with other insurance companies, because if not, the capital of this new insurance company had to be enormous, and that obviously was not possible at its start. Nevertheless, the company was prudent and reinsured or coinsured.

The board of directors of MUSINI considered the solution at the beginning was to cede a large part of the risk assumed by the mutual. The Managing Director, Ernesto Caballero Sánchez, expressed his desire to reduce the percentage of assignment to the company. To do this, there was the possibility to develop coinsurance but that had three drawbacks. First, lower return than that of reinsurance. Second, excessive concentration: only 14 insurance companies channel 74% of the cessions. And third, the dissatisfaction of the reinsurance companies that do not receive enough business to be able to give better conditions to the Spanish mutual. Hence, the board of directors of the firm aimed to reduce coinsurance to give a greater part to the reinsurance companies.

In addition, the development in MUSINI is a fine example of the process of learning by doing. Already in 1969, instead of a few companies for coinsurance they increased to 107 companies and only represented 39% of the total ceded. So, they worked successfully in the direction of diversifying risk. Coinsurance was different in each branch of insurance, fire was 69%, construction was 24%, ship insurance 60%, air planes 7% and freight 51%. In transport there is an interesting case that points out the process that in general is pushing the market: 80% more or less of aviation transport was done with reinsurance mainly foreign companies and payments in hard currency.

Another important introduction to improve the management of risk will be the establishment of a full department on prevention in 1970. It works on technical issues; the reason or explanation will come from abroad as it was said by the board of directors. The international reinsurance companies demanded a more rigorous effort to reduce industrial risk that needed highly qualified experts, that in that moment they did not have and so they needed the know-how of foreign experts. The board of directors had a clear conclusion that they learned. The premiums related to industry increasingly hardened because the dimensions reached by each industrial facility, was more complex, costlier and probably riskier. The new processes presented greater risks and major economic value in each case, reasons why insurers gave great importance to knowing if those facilities that are the subject of the insurance, are in conditions of greater or lesser security against the risk of a possible accident. This also makes it possible to obtain greater coverage and to distinguish what is essential. This is important because thanks to the commitment that the Institute is proposing in the revaluations of insured capital, these are increasing by tens of thousands of millions of pesetas and you have to seek the economic support of foreign reinsurance companies. There was a lot of talk and discussion in the company meetings about maximizing the prevention of accidents and that MUSINI must contribute. Constant reports are required on security in all companies of the group, because that meant millions of pesetas and even lives are saved because accidents are reduced each year in each company.

Prevention and protection that is enforced to build up since the late 60s. They emphasized that protection must be introduced because they must also take into account that the insurance does not end in the insurance company of INI, but in the second step, in the reinsurance, and international reinsurance on industrial risks increasingly required better information and greater security measures. The reason is clear: the industrial technique has advanced enormously, the dimensions of the plants, the dangerousness of the processes. It is not a thing that affects only INI, not only Spain, it is worldwide and therefore reinsurance, which ultimately assumes the greatest economic risk, increasingly calls for greater guarantees in the world, and in this case for a big holding company in Spain. In the case of MUSINI, 1971 was a terrible year, since the accident rate in the patrimonial branch was 202%. And to reach this percent, it had been necessary to have a retail accident rate that must be avoidable. That is why the story that comes now is really important. For prevention they referred to the mobile laboratory that had been developed by Munich Re. This truck went to all the companies that were assure by MUSINI to spot potential risks and put the techniques in place to reduce them. All the instruments or devices were used to analyze the risk, this was a turning point. Prevention was more professional, more sophisticated and more highly qualified people were working on it. Or put in another way, the professionalization was improving. The work spread extensively from the Prevention Service that verified protection measures in ENCASO, Repesa, Intelhorce, ENSIDESA, ENDESA, Frigsa, Invecosa, Fegasa, Igfisa, Celulosas, Iberia, etc.

The foreign reinsurance company was leading the process of prevention and this was in many ways the common way, because the know-how came from abroad and was developed by foreign reinsurance companies. The Managing Director, Ernesto Caballero, highlights two parts of the company: first, managing risk with the Insurance Company MUSINI that would pay any accident and second, building up Industrial Prevention Service, which also develops research and professional training and technical advising to set up new industries about the possible risk and how to minimize. They specified the necessity of industrial engineers and prevention service that visited factories and industrial facilities of their companies, as well as supervising projects of new installations. This was so important and was needed for the Spanish companies that MUSINI organized conferences on industrial protection and prevention for the holding group already in the 1970s which focused mainly on implementation with the National Symposiums on Prevention and Industrial Protection. The idea was to instill the habit and the know-how about prevention in all the people of the company or to put it in another way, increase this concept in the people that were working in the companies of the group. In addition, in the research service was include five higher industrial insurance technicians that were trained in the First Higher Course that MUSINI organized in collaboration with the E.O.I. (*Escuela de Organización Industrial*).

This institution is very important for Spain, E.O.I. also comes from the general trend of the more developed countries. Because since the industrial revolution the relevance of the engineer did increase in a substantial way, mainly because they are the managers of processes, we can go back to H. R. Towne in 1886 who wrote in the *American Society of Mechanical Engineers* "The engineer as an economist" (Towne 1886). Sure, they are many others in the nineteenth century that assure the same, and that is why a plant management is important work for an engineer. From an institutional point of view will be in the twentieth century with probably the first Industrial Engineering studies created at Penn State University in 1908, following the theories of Frederick W. Taylor the so called "Scientific Labor Organization" and "Scientific Directorate of Production" as the central and differentiating factor. Even though it may not be as important as in other fields the first doctorate in Industrial Engineering was started in 1933 at Cornell University. Another step in its development was the creation of the American Institute of Industrial Engineering in 1948. Industrial Engineering thrived in the USA as can be seen from the number of universities that teach it and for the demand of this type of professional. However, these studies do not have the same development in Spain till the 1950s. Spain was a latecomer. It is not until 1955 that the Industrial Organization School (E.O.I.) under the Ministry of Industry was created, teaching postgraduate courses. And it is in 1964 when engineering in Industrial Organization is created as a specialty of Industrial engineering studies together with the classics of Mechanical Engineering, Electrical-Electronics, Chemistry, Textile and other newer ones such as Metallurgy and Energy Techniques. All was summarized by UNESCO in its 1979 document, *"Formation des Ingenieurs et environment: Tendences et perspectives"* which defined the types of engineers by the function they perform: Project Engineer, Manufacturing Engineer, Management Engineer, Research Engineer and Engineer dedicated to education.

The Management Engineers had a broad area to understand and manage. Because in their duties they had commercial, economic, financial, statistical aspect, but also human aspects like know about psychology, etc. He participates in the scientific management of business, carries out market studies and can access the high levels of management of the company. In addition, they had the technical background, with high level of administration training. In summary, there are two degrees one with a long tradition in Spain such as the degree of Industrial Engineering (since 1857) and the new degree of Industrial Organization Engineering (since 1964). The objective of both has traditionally been the training of professionals in the management of industrial companies or processes of technological content with more emphasis on scientific and technological training in Industrial engineers and with more emphasis on management training in organization for all the Industrial plants. In addition, specifically in insurance development, they introduce new policies and formulas for coverage in life insurance and retirement pensions, but also for covering the risk in oil business or the new energy, nuclear energy or insurance related to communication that grow so fast in those year, etc. (see appendix).

In INI, in relation to vocational training, a Special Commission for Vocational Training was created, presided over by the Head of the Studies Service whose Executive Secretary was one of the graduates trained in the company as a Scholar and as "Superior Industrial Insurance Technicians." That included Internal training courses in all of its branches. For external people they organized the Second Higher Course of Industrial Insurance under the sponsorship of the INI Foundation. All this investment in education was introduced by companies like Munich Re. In this specific case, the ultimate source of the advance was foreign reinsurance companies even though it was a state company under a dictatorship that was very nationalist. When the Board of Managers looked for Spanish reinsurance companies that could handle this form of training, they found there were none. The only real solution was Munich Re.

MUSINI had a long and beneficial financial relationship with Munich Re that might have been expected. But what is less known is its contribution that are related to calculation of risk. After1960 the company introduced more powerful computers, that provided more exact calculations of mortality statistics. They introduced the calculation of the increases in life expectancy that meant the reduction of premiums. It was beneficial for both sides, insurance company and reinsurance company, through the development of stochastic calculations. All these calculations improved in a substantial way until the year 2000. The experts in the company did not have university degrees, but did have an excellent capacity to work out the calculations (Bähr and Kopper 2017). Information from Munich Re also made in non-life fields by actuaries also complete for better premium and reserve calculations. They track the history of damage and to understand the cost of future premiums and the reserve needed. In addition, each year was revised in case of underrated. In addition, the commissions were flexible.

This had an important consequence for MUSINI or any other company that signed for reinsurance with Munich Re. The premium of this company was supervised by the reinsurance company with a high guaranty of a closer calculation of the risk. And probably they had to change many things to avoid being considered an unacceptable risk. To manage risk in the industry, for example a large refinery, complex and full of risk or danger, some of the main questions are technical, to point out the potential engineering aspects that can create a great catastrophe. The German reinsurance company will have experts that explain what type of risk is considered unacceptable, so must be changed or improved before signing the reinsurance contract. In addition, experts from Germany will come to Spain to give many seminars to introduce know-how about managing risk in industry and all types of risk related to buildings. Much of this is explained by Bähr and Kopper (2017). The pricing, the cession, etc., was calculated in a more consistent way with the help of Munich Re that made them more competitive for MUSINI. There was a borderline between good and bad risk within the Spanish companies. Spain was obviously not Germany and the Munich Re criteria had to be adapted for the Spanish market, to reflect the legislation and the more severe regulation.

At the beginning MUSINI lacked knowledge and had to rely on improvisation. In order to resolve the risk of industrial losses, coinsurance was initially the solution. However, reinsurance companies were also used for their knowledge, clear specialization or expertise. On the other hand, from a financial consideration they had to admit the reality of Spain in the mid-sixties. They signed contracts with a well-known pool of Spanish companies specialized in reinsurance, named Pool AGARA. The surprise for the board of directors of MUSINI was the scarce resources of this pool. For example, in a policy as important as that of Iberia, MUSINI found that the Pool had only retained 1.13% of the total, with the rest going to foreign reinsurance companies. The counselor Fernández-Vegué Gómez affirmed that this demonstrated the scarce effort that Spanish insurance companies were developing in reinsurance. It was simply losing a business of millions of pesetas. A solution as poor as the one offered by the Pool inevitably led to a question: would it not be better for MUSINI itself to contract reinsurance directly with foreign reinsurers? Eventually this was done. Another question here is whether this pool, AGARA, was really capable in the two areas, qualifying risk and financial capability, especially calculating the price. The answer was no. Reinsurance in the sixties developed an enormous financial capability, but also an enormous knowledge in the calculation of risk and the last part, maybe the most important, prevention.

Eventually MUSINI signed with foreign reinsurance companies. This decision was going against the policy of the Spanish government which was to strengthen what was Spanish and to prevent national resources from leaving the country. As a nationalist government these remained as an important objective. For this reason, the company continued to try to contract reinsurance with Spanish companies, although it finally had to accept the reality that only foreign companies could cover reinsurance; large companies for example Royal Insurance, Munich Re and Swiss Re. This weakness of the sector could explain why Carlos Sunyer Aldomá, on behalf of the reinsurance union, tried to make MUSINI part of it, which was not possible because its statutes did not permit it. The truth is that in those years, the company had neither knowledge nor sufficient assets to participate in the insurance market as a reinsurer. It had enough to fulfill its obligations with all the INI companies.

In the long run the coinsurance in MUSINI was reduced substantially. In ten years, it was 26% of the total. As is the normal policy of any mutuality they were very prudent. Thus, in 1969, the first full year for the company, compensation for the losses had a cost to the company of 570 million pesetas, of which 338 were paid for with coinsurance and 232 million pesetas by MUSINI itself; but of this amount, most corresponded to reinsurance. Thus, the net loss ratio, that is, what MUSINI actually paid, was a small amount (Board of Directors of January 20, 1970). The following year, at the General Assembly on May 19, 1971, the Technical Group for Protection and Prevention was created. President Manuel Sainz highlighted "The seriousness and the attention that is being paid to these technical works that have an effective impact on the international reinsurance, which is increasingly hardening because the dimensions reached by each industrial installation and the new processes, present risk (…) of greater economic importance, is why insurers give great importance to know if those facilities that are the object of the insurance, are or not in conditions of greater or lesser security against the risk, compared to losses. This also makes it possible to obtain greater coverage facilities, which is essential and substantial; because it should be taken into account that thanks to the efforts that the Institute is making in the revaluations of insured capital, these are increasing by tens of thousands of millions of pesetas and we must seek the economic support of reinsurance for all that."

8.5 Conclusion

The reinsurance business in Spain was strongly influenced by foreign reinsurance companies. The general situation of the economy in the country will have its relevance starting with the strong economic growth in the 60s, the integration of the peseta into the Bretton Wood system, the strengthening of the financial system in Spain and the better education of the Spanish people. When we refer specifically to the foreign reinsurance companies, we must understand that back in the 60s or 70s they covered a great part of the risk. In a great measure they sorted out an important part of the financial problems of the entire insurance market.

So, the role of foreign reinsurance companies was crucial for the development of Spanish insurance industry which reached over a 6% of GDP in the year 2000.

In addition, and as important as the financial part although less known, is the technical knowledge brought by the reinsurance companies. Industrialization was bringing sophisticated equipment to Spain that required workers who had been taught how to prevent any type of accident. The number of dangerous possibilities grew in an incredible way and the skill that had to be learned required far more engineers and experts in prevention and even departments specializing in accident prevention in factories that introduced this new stage of the industrial revolution in the 60s. The method to achieve this was by training the workers, by the thousands to minimize risk on the job. All the electric installations had to be checked and double checked; probably with a greater concern if it was industries related to oil, air traffic, etc.

Munich Re is one of the great international reinsurance companies. It and Swiss Re are the two major reinsurance companies in the world. The business that Munich Re developed with the Spanish holding company INI (by far the biggest holding company in Spain) and in the case of its mutual, MUSINI, played an important role in their ability to manage risk. In addition, we can see the process of learning by doing in the development of all reinsurance in Spain and eventually the achievement of advanced business know-how. Finally, the case of the reinsurance company AGARA is a perfect example of how incapable the Spanish reinsurance companies were in the late 60s. This eventually will change at the end of the century with important Spanish reinsurance companies related to the big Spanish insurance companies.

Appendix

Key elements to manage risk in the industry

Issue area	Key element (contributor)
1:	Site issues
	1.1 Wharves, loading areas, pipelines
	1.2 Hydrocarbon processing areas
	1.3 Hydrocarbon storage, tanks and bullets

(continued)

(continued)

Issue area	Key element (contributor)
	1.4 Fire protection and emergency response 1.5 Non-processing buildings 1.6 Neighbors
2:	Other issues 2.1 Technical processes and standards: operations, maintenance, inspection, engineering 2.2 People processes, training and culture 2.3 Environment, community, licensing and compliance 2.4 Other matters: strategic matters, company business issues, market changes

Rating	Description	Detailed description
A	Frequent	High likelihood in the next 10 years; has occurred in the last 2 years in the company
B	Reasonably probable	Could occur at least once in the next 10 years; expected frequency once per 1–10 years
C	Occasional	Has occurred in the industry worldwide; expected frequency once per 10–100 years
D	Remote	Low probability the situation will occur; expected frequency once per 100–1,000 years
E	Very unlikely	Possible but very unlikely; less than once per 1,000 years

Priority risk groups

Source	Discussion
Major catastrophes (fires and explosions in the refinery area)	Major catastrophes are rare events, with potentially catastrophic consequences for all the criteria. They included fires, explosions, toxic releases, BLEVEs (boiling liquid expanding vapor explosions), lightning and major operational errors leading to fires, explosions or unplanned releases
Risks associated with the fire protection system	Fire protection risks are relevant primarily if there is a major incident such as a fire and the system is not capable of responding as required to protect people and assets. They included loss of the water supply, failure of the fire water system due to pump failure or pipe rupture, inadequate capacity in the system and failure of the fire fighting vehicles that provide mobile protection and response
Wharves, shipping, loading and unloading	Risks associated with the movement of raw materials and product into and out of the plant included spills and major leaks, pipeline rupture and ship collisions or breakaways. An assessment of the risks associated with the crude oil pipeline from the wharf to the refinery was conducted separately
Site security	Risks associated with access to the wharves and the refinery site by people with potentially malicious intent included security breaches, vandalism and sabotage
Local community	Several strategic risks were noted, including competitive pressures associated with imported refined products and changes in product quality specifications associated with changed environmental standards for vehicle fuels and emissions
Other risks	Several other important risks were identified, including matters associated with the company's ability to change to meet new market requirements and some specific safety matters

References

Archive Musini

Acemoglu, Daron. 2012. "Introduction to Economic Growth". *Economic Theory* 147 (2012) 545–550.

Acemoglu, Daron, Gino Gancia, and Fabrizio Zilibotti. 2012. "Competing engines of growth: Innovation and standardization". *Journal of Economic Theory*, 147(2): 570–601.

Arrow, Kennet J. 2000 "Globalization and Its Implications for International Security". ECAAR seminar Kenneth J. Arrow.

Bähr, Johannes, and Kopper Christopher. 2017. *Munich Re, the Company History 1880–1980*. München: C.H. Beck.

Carreras, Albert and Tafunell, Xavier. 2010. *Historia Económica de la España Contemporánea*. Barcelona: Critica.

Caruana, Leonardo, and Hugh Rockoff. 2007. "An Elephant in the Garden: The Allies, Spain, and Oil in World War II". *European Review of Economic History* 11 (2): 159–187.

Fuentes Quintana, Enrique. 1984. "El Plan de Estabilización Económica de 1959: veinticinco años después". *Información Comercial Española* (612–613): 25–40.

González, Manuel Jesús. 1979. *La economía política del franquismo (1940–1970): dirigismo, mercado y planificación*. Madrid: Tecnos.

Haueter, Niels H., and Geoffrey Jones. 2017. *Managing risk in Reinsurance*. Oxford: Oxford University Press.

International Monetary Fund. 1960. *Annual IMF Report 1960*. Washington, D.C.

International Monetary Fund. 1961. *Annual IMF Report 1961*. Washington, D.C.

Martín Aceña, Pablo. 2005. "La conformación histórica de la industria bancaria española". *Los restos de la industria bancaria en España*. Coord. Francisco de la Oña Navarro. Mediterráneo Económico, nº 8.

Martín Aceña, Pablo, and Francisco Comín. 1991. *INI. 50 años de industrialización en España*. Madrid: Espasa Calpe.

Nadal, Jordi. 1989. *El fracaso de la Revolución Industrial en España*. Barcelona: Ariel.

Sardà, Joan. 1970. El Banco de España, 1931-1962. In *El Banco de España: una historia económica*, 419–479. Madrid: Banco de España.

Solow, Robert M. 1987. "We'd Better Watch Out". *New York Times Book Review*, July 12.

Tortella, Gabriel et al. 2013. *Historia del Seguro en España*. Madrid: Fundación Mapfre.

Towne, Henry R. 1886. "Engineer as an Economist". *Transactions of the American Society of Mechanical Engineers*, 7: 428–432.

Varela Parache, Manuel. 2004. "El Plan de Estabilización: elaboración, contenido y efectos". In *Economía y economistas españoles*, ed. E. Fuentes Quintana, vol. VIII, pp. 129–162. Barcelona: Galaxia Gutenberg.

CHAPTER 9

Few and Small: The Reinsurance Industry in Italy in the Twentieth Century

Giorgio Cingolani and Giandomenico Piluso

9.1 Introduction

Since the political unification in 1861, the Italian insurance sector has long been characterised by a certain degree of backwardness, quite consistently with the related macroeconomic and institutional features. Particularly, as a long-term characteristic of this industry in Italy, the relatively lower income per capita levels, compared with the core of Europe's, at the time of her political unification affected the relative low propensity to insure in the very long run, typically in the life insurance segment,

G. Cingolani
Università Politecnica Delle Marche, Ancona, Italy

G. Piluso (✉)
University of Turin, Turin, Italy
e-mail: giandomenico.piluso@unito.it

© The Author(s), under exclusive license to Springer Nature Switzerland AG 2021
L. Caruana de las Cagigas and A. Straus (eds.), *Role of Reinsurance in the World*, Palgrave Studies in Economic History,
https://doi.org/10.1007/978-3-030-74002-3_9

as recent data suggest (De Simone 2007).[1] Actually, the Italian insurance market shows a very long-term tendency to be an underinsured market, even when incomes per capita began to grow steadily from the early twentieth century, probably associated to relatively modest levels of schooling, influencing social capabilities, and competing state-backed assistance schemes emerging with the first experiences of welfare state (Piluso 2012, pp. 167–188; Cingolani 2018, pp. 309–350).

In such an overall framework, the reinsurance segment was doomed to remain marginal, although there are also different reasons explaining its small size and functional underdevelopment. The first reason why reinsurance stayed marginal in Italy was the general development trajectories that reinsurance had in Europe throughout the nineteenth century, particularly from the mid-1850s, making Italy a marginal actor within the emerging international market structure. The early prominence of German professional reinsurance companies—followed by British, French and Swiss reinsurance companies—acted as a powerful catalyst reducing opportunities amongst less specialised companies, particularly for those operating in peripheral countries like Italy (Pearson 2017, pp. 71–78). The second reason was the dualistic nature of the Italian insurance sector, deeply divided between, on the one hand, a number of small- to medium-sized companies and, on the other hand, the two large transnational companies dominating the market, *Assicurazioni Generali* and *Riunione Adriatica di Sicurtà* (RAS), which, prior to 1918, were actually Austrian companies, although with an Italian double legal seat, respectively in Milan and Venice, and affiliated networks. The two Austrian-based companies had combined market shares well above 50% and adopted co-insurance practices in order to hedge their risks and spread their insurance liabilities (Golding 1931; Favaretto 2011, pp. 111–113; Millo 2019, pp. 104–106). This is a rough measure of how weak were the incentives

---

[1] See In the last twenty years insurance spending on GDP has been almost constantly lower in Italy compared both to the average of the OECD countries (by one to three percentage points) and of the European Union state members. Cf. OECD, OECD data, Insurance Spending, Chart on Insurance spending by selected indicators (i.e., OECD, European Union country members, Eurozone country members) at https://data.oecd.org/insurance/insurance-spending.htm#indicator-chart. Accessed on 27 September 2020). See, for instance, cross-countries data on natural catastrophe protection for the 1975–2014 period and insurance penetration as of 2014 in Swiss Re 2015, respectively, p. 6, Fig, 7.4 and p. 6, Table 7.1.

to build up a reinsurance segment within the Italian domestic market (*The Review* 1901, p. 415; Piluso 2012, p. 173).

In effect, reinsurance appeared as an out-of-reach objective for a slowly catching-up domestic industry, on the one side, and a sort of duplicate for the two largest companies which were consistently engaging themselves along alternative strategies, on the other side. In a way, *Assicurazioni Generali* and RAS developed a sort of internal mechanism of risk hedging through co-insurance practices and their own multinational networks which, at least partially, reduced the costs related to monitoring and agency problems (Pearson 2017, pp. 75–78). These essentially endogenous factors determining the insurance sector trajectories coupled with the even stronger exogenous factor represented by the international specialization which saw Germany and Switzerland being emerging as the main reinsurance centers in Europe (Pearson 2017, p. 302, Table A.2; Hasler 1963; Gugerli 2013, pp. 154–183).

This chapter presents, in its first section, some data on the insurance sector as a whole in the twentieth century, by looking at insurance indicators since the early 1920s and at individual balance sheet data for the entire insurance sector for a string of benchmark years covering the whole century, from 1903 to 2000. Relying upon such balance sheet data, this section provides top 20 insurance companies ranking by total assets, characterised by a remarkable concentration level (the five largest firms over the overall population), evaluating the relative weight of reinsurance companies and their ability to remain within this sub-sample over time as a proxy indicator of their market performance. This section presents some explanations as to the underdevelopment of reinsurance in Italy during the whole twentieth century. The second section deals with the evolution of the insurance industry in Italy since the late 1820s to understand why reinsurance was a marginal branch, although a demand for related services emerged as an obvious result of sectoral growth, up to the Second World War. The third section highlights the main factor explaining its underdevelopment after the Second World War in relation with dynamics typically pertaining to the emergence and partial retrenchment of the welfare state. Finally, the chapter provides some conclusions on the reinsurance branch in the Italian case in the long term.

9.2 Few, Small and Subsidiary

As observed, the Italian insurance market has been characterised by a very long-term tendency towards underinsurance, consistent with relatively low incomes per capita. Such a tendency is equally true for the two main branches, life and non-life. As shown in the chart plotting data on life and non-life premiums on the gross domestic product (cf. Figure 9.1), underinsurance is plainly apparent almost for the entire period considered, that is the last century. Even in presence of a steep growth in premiums on the aggregate income, as registered since the early 1990s, the Italian market still appears relatively underinsured compared to economies with similar levels of income per capita (Sacerdoti 1966, pp. 263–269; Swiss Re 2015, p. 6, Table 7.1). Data show a relative increase in premiums relative to aggregate output in the interwar period and a modest recovery in the two post-war decades. Yet, the relative increase of premiums in the 1930s is misleading due to the lack of data for the 1920s for the non-life branch premiums, since life premiums tend to be rather constant over the whole decade. As expected, life premiums fell during the Second World War, together with incomes, and slowly recovered in the following decades getting back to the highest war or pre-war point (1942) only in 1991. If the life and non-life premiums appear closely associated throughout the

Fig. 9.1 The size of the Italian market: life and non-life premiums as a share of GDP, 1921–2014 (*Source* Istat, *Serie storiche*, Life premiums and non-life premiums, Tab. 19.4, 1921–2014; GDP estimates provided by Banca d'Italia 2017)

1930s, their ensuing dynamic is clearly divergent in the post-war era up to the late 1980s, when life premiums robustly recovered converging in a few years (see Fig. 9.1) (Agliardi 2011, pp. 175–178). After the Second World War, the dynamic of the branch seems to be rather dependent on the dominant role played by the State, particularly in the public assistance and social security areas (Bico 2011, pp. 67–92; Lindert 2004; Nullmeier and Kaufmann 2010, pp. 81–84).

Major changes are concentrated in the last few decades, after privatisation processes and reforms of the state-backed pension schemes. In fact, all of the most relevant changes in the size of the Italian insurance market seem to be positively related to a series of regulatory interventions aimed to reduce the state's presence in the economy through privatisations and to introduce substantial reforms in the pension system after the severe fiscal and currency crises experienced in 1992 (Ciocca 2007, pp. 307–315; Ferrera 2010, pp. 625–627). These changes fostered a relative shift from the public to the private sector for assistance and pension plans which provoked a dramatic growth in premiums relative to the aggregate income, although it was so only in relative terms and susceptible to fluctuations in phases of acute recession, as occurred in 2007–2008 and 2011–2012 when incomes per capita fell dramatically.[2] On the contrary, in the last two decades the non-life premiums tend to stagnate substantially, mirroring the overall long-term gloomy trend that the Italian economy has been experiencing since the early 1990s. An important trait characterising the insurance ratio of Italy in the last decades is its greatly increased volatility depending upon the higher volatility of the life insurance premiums component, which in turn is related to variations in income per capita. Such a difference in the dynamic of the two components is noticeably depicted in the chart, which is split in two sub-periods, after the Second World War years. Thus, liberalisation in the early 1990s has paved the way for a relative reduction in the degree of underinsurance, by scaling up the overall size of the entire sector, but at a price, that is it has increased volatility, if not even instability, in the varying propensity of the public to get access to insurance services. This partial convergence process towards higher insurance levels has been supported, since the early 1980s, also by central monetary authority, the Bank of Italy, by actively

---

[2] According to estimates by the World Bank income per capita in Italy fell, at constant prices, from about 30,700 euros in 2007 to circa 27,000 euros in 2014 and it is still, as of 2018, well below the level attained in 2007.

promoting bancassurance (sale of insurance to bank customers) as a new channel of distribution of financial products conceived to integrate bank services and insurance services (Ciocca 2000, pp. 14–25; Falautano and Santucci 2011, pp. 235–271).

Macroeconomic data on the sector should be a natural backdrop on which to assess the scope for growth and diversification of any sector, particularly when a sector is rather sensitive to variations in such variables as income per capita, as is the insurance industry. In this aspect, the insurance to GDP ratio represents a sort of playing field for each firm operating within the sector and defines the actual market size and the very existence of scope for developing forms of business specialisation between enterprises. Under these circumstances, the relevant degree of underinsurance of the Italian market constituted a serious constraint to growth and specialisation for any firm, regardless of its nationality, size, strategy and standing. The structure of the Italian insurance market was also characterised by a stark dualism in terms of firms' size, between a few large companies (namely, *Assicurazioni Generali*, RAS and the state-owned INA), flanked by a small group of medium-sized companies (like *Alleanza, Fondiaria*, SAI and *Toro*), and a great constellation of minor companies.

In the twentieth century, in such a context, reinsurance companies in Italy were relatively few and small, particularly compared with Germany and Switzerland or the United States. In fact, there are no Italian companies amongst the top 15 reinsurance firms ranked by Robin Pearson, for benchmark years, from 1929 to 2014 (Pearson 2017, pp. 303–307, Tables A.3.1–A.3.10). Their relative weight has been equally modest and decreasing in the last decades up to the disappearance of the component today.[3] To assess the weight of the reinsurance sub-sector in the insurance industry as a whole, individual balance sheet data can be collected and compared from two different statistical sources, complementary as to their respective ability to cover the entire period here considered. The first source is represented by *Notizie statistiche*, published every two years initially by *Credito Italiano*, from 1908 to the mid-1920s, and, until the mid-1980s, by *Assonime-Associazione fra le società italiane per azioni* (Coltorti 2011). The second source is the yearly sectoral *Annuario* published by *Ania-Associazione nazionale fra le imprese assicuratrici* since

---

[3] The absolute absence of reinsurance companies is referred to firms operating exclusively in the reinsurance branch (Cf. Ania 2014, part V, Tab. 3).

Table 9.1 Insurance companies, insurance and reinsurance companies, purely reinsurance companies in Italy, 1903–2000

	1903	1913	1919	1927	1938	1950	1960	1970	1980	1990	2000
insurance companies	12	20	55	76	61	63	76	110	127	150	184
insurance and reinsurance companies	1	2	13	15	9	12	17	24	5	4	14
purely reinsurance companies	1	1	3	5	3	7	5	4	3	3	2

Sources Assonime, *ad annos* (1903–1960); Ania, *ad annos* (1970–2000) (our calculations)

the 1950s. Both sources provide essential balance sheet data for a large number of firms instituted as joint-stock companies, with a relatively low threshold although it varied over time, in the first source and for all the insurance companies operating in Italy in the second one. Data from the first source cover the period from 1903 to 1970, whilst data from the second source provide information for the period from 1970 to 2000. The balance sheet data collected allow one to rank the top 20 insurance companies by total assets and calculate the number of reinsurance companies for benchmark years for almost the entire twentieth century (1903, 1913, 1919, 1927, 1938, 1950, 1960, 1970, 1980, 1990 and 2000).[4]

As to the demography of the reinsurance branch in Italy it is worth observing its lasting modest size throughout the twentieth century, particularly when purely reinsurance companies are taken into account. As Table 9.1 shows, purely reinsurance companies constituted a tiny fraction within the sector as specialised firms, whilst more robust in numerical terms is the sub-sample represented by insurance companies operating a reinsurance branch as well (see Table 9.1).

As a whole, the insurance sector experienced a surge in the number of firms from the early twentieth century onwards. Although the total number of insurance companies actually established and operating in Italy

---

[4] Hence, here are used two different data sets. The first one is based on information from *Notizie statistiche* and covers the period from 1903 to 1960. The second one is based on the *Annuario* published by Ania and covers the period from 1970 to 2000.

might be underestimated by the source (*Notizie statistiche*) for the two early benchmark years, their overall number grew during the first three decades of century, significantly decreased in the interwar period and started to grow again after the post-war recovery almost tripling since 1950. The initial underestimation should be attributed to the specific threshold, as defined in terms of equity capital, which typically excluded the smallest companies, such as those established as cooperative firms. The two major trends observable in the twentieth century, upwards and downwards, could be ascribed to the relative openness of the Italian market to foreign companies. The steady growth of insurance firms in the first three decades was fostered by the lack of significant entry barriers and, secondarily, by increasing incomes per capita. The growing public presence in life insurance and accident insurance from the early 1910s was not, per se, a factor hampering the sectoral dynamic, whilst new restrictive policies and the related reduction of the degree of openness of the Italian economy gravely affected such a dynamic during the 1930s pushing the number of firms down, regardless of their specialisation.

At the end of the Great War, an important variable was represented by the annexation of Trieste which transformed both *Generali* and RAS into Italian multinational companies from their former peculiar status of transnational companies based within the Austro-Hungarian Empire (Stefani 1931; Riunione Adriatica di Sicurtà 1939; Sapelli 1990, pp. 138–142; Baglioni 1997; Mellinato 2019). A true reversal in the negative trend experienced in the 1930s occurred only from the early 1980s onwards, coincident with liberalisation processes and privatisations launched in the early 1990s, with which the large state-backed company, INA, entered the private companies ranking. A less rigidly regulated sector—more open to foreign companies and direct investments—made reinsurance companies, particularly purely reinsurance firms more scarce, as shown in Table 9.1. In effect, reinsurance companies and mixed companies appear to be a feature related to higher regulation and less foreign competition, as occurred in the 1930s and during the first post-war decades. On the other hand, the remarkable upsurge in mixed companies operating both branches in the 1960s, coupled with a falling number of purely reinsurance companies, would suggest that companies decided to pursue a fundamentally adaptive strategy in an uncertain context. Thus, the very few surviving reinsurance firms progressively climbed down along the ranking and, eventually, disappeared in the new century. In 1990 the largest Italian reinsurance company, *La Vittoria*, was 34th in the ranking with total assets equal to less than 0.5% of the whole sample, whilst in 2000 the largest one, SCOR Italia (the subsidiary of a French-based group), was just 86th with total assets equal to a mere 0.077% of the entire sample.[5]

As to the relative weight of different size classes within the insurance sector it is quite apparent that the largest companies had an overwhelming position throughout the whole century, even though a certain reduction in concentration levels shows up in the last decades. In fact, the top 20 insurance companies by total assets account for more than 80% of the entire sector for all the benchmark years, although the first two are biased by the very nature of our source, except the two final ones (76.36% in 1990 and 73.13% in 2000). It is even more apparent how much the Italian insurance industry was concentrated by looking at the relative weight of the two largest companies by total assets. Prior to the First World War the two greatest companies, *La Fondiaria* and *Milano Assicurazioni*, totalled about 40 in 1913 and 47 in 1910 in per cent of the sector; in 1919 Assicurazioni Generali and RAS had total assets equal to more than 63% of the entire industry. Although both *Generali* and RAS had established their registered head office in Italy, respectively in Venice (1875) and Milan (1908), before the Great War they could not be registered as Italian companies and, therefore, were omitted from *Notizie statistiche*, albeit the largest insurance firms operating in Italy from their start.[6] A rough measure of the pre-war combined relative weight of *Generali* and RAS could be obtained by observing how *La Fondiaria* and *Milano Assicurazioni* performed in terms of total assets' joint share just after the end of the conflict. In 1919 *Milano Assicurazioni*, in third position in the ranking, scored a 8% of the whole sector's total assets, whilst *La Fondiaria*, regressed to the fifth place, counted for a mere 2.6% (and the fourth in the ranking, *L'Anonima Infortuni*, less than 4.4%). Moreover, in the interwar period the sector concentration level in terms of total assets, a rough proxy of market shares, peaked to a bit less than 70% for *Generali* and RAS in 1938. After the second world war their total assets'

---

[5] Our calculations on data yearly published by Ania in its *Annuario*, respectively, for 1990 and 2000.

[6] Of course, pre-1919 *Generali* and RAS as Austro-Hungarian companies had total assets largely located in the Empire, not in Italy, and it is thus rather hard to estimate their total assets as Italian ones. On this topic see Ministero dell'Industria, del Commercio e dell'Artigianato (1967).

share on the entire industry slowly decreased, from 61.3% in 1950 to 43.3 in 1960, and from 34.5% in 1970 to 33.7 in 1980. Such a high level of concentration within the insurance sector amplifies the concentration level measured as a share of total assets of the top 20 companies leaving to reinsurance companies a minor share within the industry. As Fig. 9.2 shows the combined total assets of reinsurance companies amongst the top 20 was always below 10% of the overall sector's total assets, except in 1950 (12.5%). The purely reinsurance companies had combined total assets comprised between 1.15% in 1919 and 5.97% in 1927 (relatively good levels were reached in 1950 and 1960, around 5.5%).

Remarkably enough, since 1980 reinsurance companies have completely disappeared from the top 20 ranking, when the largest firm, *La Vittoria*, was 26th in the ranking. A detailed map of the top 20 insurance and reinsurance companies, whether specialised or not, is provided in Tables 9.2 and 9.3. These tables offer a clear insight into the specific structure of the Italian insurance sector for benchmark years since 1903. Some key features are: (i) the notable concentration level of the sector in terms of total assets, as explained above; (ii) the dualism observable even within the top 20 sample, regardless of specialisation;

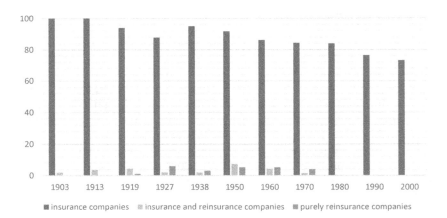

Fig. 9.2 Top 20 insurance companies, insurance and reinsurance companies, purely reinsurance companies in Italy, by total assets, 1903–2000 (*Source* Assonime, *ad annos* [1903–1960]; Ania, *ad annos* [1970–2000] [our calculations])

(iii) the substantially marginal role of reinsurance companies, with a rather modest increase in 1938, 1950 and 1960.

Besides, only one reinsurance company was able to stay in such a ranking for more than three benchmark years continually (*Unione Italiana di Riassicurazione-Uniorias*, from 1903 to 1970). Two of them remained within the top 20 ranking for three benchmark years—*Levante* (1927, 1950 and 1960) and *La Consorziale* (1927, 1938 and 1950), whilst four companies stayed within the same sample for two years: *La Riassicuratrice* (1919 and 1927), *Società Anonima Italiana di Assicurazioni* contro la *Grandine e Riassicurazione* (1919 and 1927), *Pravidentia* (1938 and 1950), *Compagnia di Roma Riassicurazioni* (1950 and 1960), *Fiumeter* (1950 and 1960) and *Reale di Riassicurazioni* (1950 and 1960). The rest of them, five companies, have just one entry within the top 20 ranking (cf. Tables 9.2, 9.3, 9.4).

The high turbulence within the top 20 reinsurance companies by total assets is quite consistent with the general tendency observed for the sample represented by the 200 largest Italian firms by total assets (Vasta 2006, pp. 99–104). In fact, apart a few large insurance companies, such as *Assicurazioni Generali*, RAS, *La Fondiaria*, *Toro*, *Reale* and *Cattolica*, also the vast majority of the top 20 firms of this industry tended to stay for a limited number of benchmark years, possibly reflecting a certain widespread turbulence, rather common to the rest of the Italian sectors, services as well (Giannetti and Vasta 2012, pp. 96–101).

An explanation of such turbulence can be found in the persistent low insurance spending, on the one hand, and in the market structure, on the other hand. Actually, if relatively low incomes per capita could at least partially justify the modest insurance penetration which afflicted the Italian market, this enduring characteristic defined the actual size of the market, largely determining the dualism of the insurance sector. Thus, on the one side, there were a few efficient large companies—*Generali* and RAS, above all—that had multinational structure and international projection, whilst, on the other side, a great number of companies had to compete to get clients and premiums having to manage risks in suboptimal conditions. The dualistic sectoral structure could shed some light on the derived turbulence: a very few insurance companies were able to reach adequate size and profitability, having access to a lesser risky clientele, whilst, on the other end, many firms had to strive to maintain size and profitability, quite often climbing up and down the ranking. Besides, *Generali* and RAS, as multinationals, could manage and distribute risks

Table 9.2 Top 20 insurance companies and reinsurance companies in Italy, by total assets, 1903–1927

1903		1913		1919		1927	
LA FONDIARIA VITA COMPAGNIA ITALIANA DI ASSICURAZIONI A PREMIO FISSO SULLA VITA	30.630	COMPAGNIA DI ASSICURAZIONE DI MILANO	28.055	ASSICURAZIONI GENERALI	46.169	ASSICURAZIONI GENERALI	38.251
COMPAGNIA DI ASSICURAZIONE DI MILANO	17.160	LA FONDIARIA VITA COMPAGNIA ITALIANA DI ASSICURAZIONI A PREMIO FISSO SULLA VITA	12.515	RAS RIUNIONE ADRIATICA DI SICURTA'	17.458	RAS RIUNIONE ADRIATICA DI SICURTA'	20.895
REALE COMPAGNIA ITALIANA DI ASSICURAZIONI GENERALI SULLA VITA DELL'UOMO	16.900	SOCIETA' ANONIMA ITALIANA DI ASSICURAZIONE CONTRO GLI INFORTUNI	11.366	COMPAGNIA DI ASSICURAZIONE DI MILANO	8.011	L'ANONIMA INFORTUNI	4.811
LA FONDIARIA INCENDIO COMPAGNIA ITALIANA DI ASSICURAZIONE A PREMIO FISSO CONTRO L'INCENDIO	8.456	LA FONDIARIA INCENDIO COMPAGNIA ITALIANA DI ASSICURAZIONE A PREMIO FISSO CONTRO L'INCENDIO	8.058	SOCIETA' ANONIMA ITALIANA DI ASSICURAZIONE CONTRO GLI INFORTUNI	4.370	UNIONE ITALIANA DI RIASSICURAZIONE	3.420

1903		1913		1919		1927	
SOCIETA' ANONIMA ITALIANA DI ASSICURAZIONE CONTRO GLI INFORTUNI	5.377	REALE COMPAGNIA ITALIANA DI ASSICURAZIONI GENERALI SULLA VITA DELL'UOMO	7.257	LA FONDIARIA INCENDIO COMPAGNIA ITALIANA DI ASSICURAZIONE A PREMIO FISSO CONTRO L'INCENDIO	2.603	COMPAGNIA DI ASSICURAZIONE DI MILANO	2.562
ALLEANZA ASSICURAZIONI	4.743	L'ASSICURATRICE ITALIANA	5.369	L'ASSICURATRICE ITALIANA	2.175	LA FONDIARIA INCENDIO COMPAGNIA ITALIANA DI ASSICURAZIONI	2.219
ITALIA SOCIETA' DI ASSICURAZIONI MARITTIME FLUVIALI E TERRESTRI	4.619	ALLEANZA ASSICURAZIONI	4.073	LLOYD ITALICO COMPAGNIA DI ASSICURAZIONE E RIASSICURAZIONE	1.579	L'ASSICURATRICE ITALIANA	2.120
SOCIETA' ANONIMA DI ASSICURAZIONI A PREMIO FISSO CONTRO LA GRANDINE	3.998	ITALIA SOCIETA' DI ASSICURAZIONI MARITTIME FLUVIALI E TERRESTRI	3.471	REALE COMPAGNIA ITALIANA DI ASSICURAZIONI GENERALI SULLA VITA DELL'UOMO	1.235	LA RIASSICURATRICE	1.853
COMPAGNIA ANONIMA D'ASSICURAZIONE DI TORINO	2.066	UNIONE CONTINENTALE SOCIETA' ITALIANA DI ASSICURAZIONI E RIASSICURAZIONI GENERALI	3.113	ITALIA SOCIETA' DI ASSICURAZIONI MARITTIME FLUVIALI E TERRESTRI	1.197	SOCIETA' DI ASSICURAZIONI GIA' MUTUA MARITTIMA NAZIONALE	1.414

(continued)

Table 9.2 (continued)

1903		1913		1919		1927	
UNIONE CONTINENTALE SOCIETA' ITALIANA DI ASSICURAZIONI E RIASSICURAZIONI GENERALI	1.948	SOCIETA' ANONIMA DI ASSICURAZIONI A PREMIO FISSO CONTRO LA GRANDINE	3.091	CASSA NAVALE E D'ASSICURAZIONI	1.176	LEVANTE SOCIETA' ITALIANA DI ASSICURAZIONI E RIASSICURAZIONI	1.230
L'ASSICURATRICE ITALIANA	1.945	COMPAGNIA ANONIMA D'ASSICURAZIONE DI TORINO	2.378	LA RIASSICURATRICE	1.154	ITALIANA PER L'ASSICURAZIONE CONTRO L'INCENDIO	1.217
LIGURIA SOCIETA' DI ASSICURAZIONI	1.261	ITALIANA PER L'ASSICURAZIONE CONTRO L'INCENDIO	2.334	ITALIANA PER L'ASSICURAZIONE CONTRO L'INCENDIO	1.067	LE ASSICURAZIONI D'ITALIA	1.153
SAVOIA SOCIETA' ITALIANA DI ASSICURAZIONI	0.896	SAVOIA SOCIETA' ITALIANA DI ASSICURAZIONI	1.773	UNIONE CONTINENTALE SOCIETA' ITALIANA DI ASSICURAZIONI E RIASSICURAZIONI GENERALI	0.910	SASA SICURTA' FRA ARMATORI	1.078
	100.000	LIGURIA SOCIETA' DI ASSICURAZIONI	1.548	MERIDIONALE COMPAGNIA DI ASSICURAZIONI GRANDINE E DI RIASSICURAZIONI	0.835	SOCIETA' ITALIANA PER L'ASSICURAZIONE SULLA VITA	0.947
		LA REALE GRANDINE	1.491	SOCIETA' ANONIMA ITALIANA DI ASSICURAZIONI CONTRO LA GRANDINE E RIASSICURAZIONI	0.726	ALLEANZA E UNIONE MEDITERRANEA	0.933

1903	1913		1919		1927	
	CATTOLICA DI ASSICURAZIONE CONTRO I DANNI DELLA GRANDINE DELL'INCENDIO DEI FURTI E SULLA VITA DELL'UOMO	1.415	CATTOLICA DI ASSICURAZIONE CONTRO I DANNI DELLA GRANDINE DELL'INCENDIO DEI FURTI E SULLA VITA DELL'UOMO	0.704	COMPAGNIA ANONIMA D'ASSICURAZIONE DI TORINO	0.778
	LA FONDIARIA INFORTUNI COMPAGNIA ITALIANA DI ASSICURAZIONI	1.055	COMPAGNIA ANONIMA D'ASSICURAZIONE DI TORINO	0.690	CATTOLICA DI ASSICURAZIONE CONTRO I DANNI DELLA GRANDINE DELL'INCENDIO DEI FURTI E SULLA VITA DELL'UOMO	0.759
	PROVVIDENZA	0.943	SAVOIA SOCIETA' ITALIANA DI ASSICURAZIONI	0.622	**SOCIETA' ANONIMA ITALIANA DI ASSICURAZIONE CONTRO LA GRANDINE E RIASSICURAZIONI**	0.754
	L'ITALICA SOCIETA' DI ASSICURAZIONI E RIASSICURAZIONI	0.528	LA FONDIARIA INFORTUNI COMPAGNIA ITALIANA DI ASSICURAZIONI	0.570	**SOCIETA' ITALIANA DI RIASSICURAZIONE CONSORZIALE**	0.700
	COOPERATIVA ITALIANA PER L'ASSICURAZIONE SULLA VITA	0.169	OCEANUS	0.532	COMPAGNIE RIUNITE DI SICURTA	0.652

Source Assonime, *ad annos* (1903–1960); Ania, *ad annos* (1970–2000) (our calculations)

Table 9.3 Top 20 insurance companies and reinsurance companies in Italy, by total assets, 1938–1950

1938		1950	
ASSICURAZIONI GENERALI	45.433	ASSICURAZIONI GENERALI	40.057
RAS RIUNIONE ADRIATICA DI SICURTA'	24.456	RAS RIUNIONE ADRIATICA DI SICURTA'	21.283
L'ANONIMA INFORTUNI	3.254	**UNIONE ITALIANA DI RIASSICURAZIONE**	4.394
UNIONE ITALIANA DI RIASSICURAZIONE	2.758	COMPAGNIA ANONIMA D'ASSICURAZIONE DI TORINO	3.806
COMPAGNIA DI ASSICURAZIONE DI MILANO	2.586	**LEVANTE SOCIETA' ITALIANA DI ASSICURAZIONI E RIASSICURAZIONI**	2.516
COMPAGNIA ANONIMA D'ASSICURAZIONE DI TORINO	2.585	COMPAGNIA DI ASSICURAZIONE DI MILANO	2.454
L'ASSICURATRICE ITALIANA	2.146	L'ASSICURATRICE ITALIANA	2.351
LA FONDIARIA VITA COMPAGNIA ITALIANA DI ASSICURAZIONI SULLA VITA DELL'UOMO	2.049	SOCIETA' ASSICURATRICE INDUSTRIALE	1.989
PRAEVIDENTIA ASSICURAZIONI RIASSICURAZIONI E CAPITALIZZAZIONI	1.915	**COMPAGNIA DI ROMA RIASSICURAZIONI E PARTECIPAZIONI ASSICURATIVE**	1.766
LA FONDIARIA INCENDIO COMPAGNIA ITALIANA DI ASSICURAZIONI	1.335	LE ASSICURAZIONI D'ITALIA	1.701
CATTOLICA DI ASSICURAZIONE CONTRO I DANNI DELLA GRANDINE DELL'INCENDIO DEI FURTI E SULLA VITA DELL'UOMO	1.040	**PRAEVIDENTIA ASSICURAZIONI RIASSICURAZIONI E CAPITALIZZAZIONI**	1.482
LE ASSICURAZIONI D'ITALIA	0.885	LA FONDIARIA VITA COMPAGNIA ITALIANA DI ASSICURAZIONI SULLA VITA DELL'UOMO	1.478

(continued)

Table 9.3 (continued)

1938		1950	
SOCIETA' ITALIANA PER L'ASSICURAZIONE SULLA VITA	0.793	ALLEANZA ASSICURAZIONI	0.963
SOCIETA' ITALIANA DI ASSICURAZIONE PER I DANNI DI INCENDIO E PER I RISCHI DIVERSI	0.732	**FIUMETER ASSICURAZIONI E RIASSICURAZIONI**	0.908
SOCIETA' ASSICURATRICE INDUSTRIALE	0.674	**REALE RIASSICURAZIONI**	0.892
L'ANONIMA GRANDINE	0.490	**LA CONSORZIALE SOCIETA' ITALIANA DI RIASSICURAZIONI**	0.880
SASA SICURTA' FRA ARMATORI	0.486	LA FONDIARIA INCENDIO COMPAGNIA ITALIANA DI ASSICURAZIONI	0.865
SOCIETA' ITALIANA DI RIASSICURAZIONE CONSORZIALE	0.484	ISTITUTO ITALIANO DI PREVIDENZA	0.661
LA VITTORIA COMPAGNIA DI ASSICURAZIONI GENERALI	0.412	LA FONDIARIA INFORTUNI COMPAGNIA ITALIANA DI ASSICURAZIONI	0.606
SOCIETA' DI ASSICURAZIONI GIA' MUTUA MARITTIMA NAZIONALE	0.376	**EUROPA SOCIETA' ITALIANA DI ASSICURAZIONI E RIASSICURAZIONI MARITTIME**	0.568

more effectively either through their own networks or by getting direct access to reinsurance circuits in the most advanced European markets.[7] The ability of the largest companies to get access directly to the great Swiss or German reinsurance companies should help explain why the Italian reinsurance firms were few, small and relatively unstable, lacking of serious and continuous commitment to develop this branch in the domestic market.

In fact, at least since the late 1870s, prompted by its Director General Marco Besso (1843-1920), *Assicurazioni Generali* constantly pursued a multinational strategy implying the international risk diversification on a

---

[7] The dominant position assumed by *Generali* and RAS depended upon their efficient organisations, size and quality of their management (cf. Millo 2004, pp. 163–180).

Table 9.4 Top 20 insurance companies and reinsurance companies in Italy, by total assets. 1950-1990

1960		1970		1980		1990	
ASSICURAZIONI GENERALI	29.954	ASSICURAZIONI GENERALI	25.390	ASSICURAZIONI GENERALI	22.753	ASSICURAZIONI GENERALI	20.062
RAS RIUNIONE ADRIATICA DI SICURTA'	13.323	RAS RIUNIONE ADRIATICA DI SICURTA'	9.137	RIUNIONE ADRIATICA DI SICURTA'	10.947	RIUNIONE ADRIATICA DI SICURTA'	9.310
COMPAGNIA ANONIMA D'ASSICURAZIONE DI TORINO	6.168	SOCIETA' ASSICURATRICE INDUSTRIALE SAI	7.250	INA - ISTITUTO NAZIONALE DELLE ASSICURAZIONI	9.325	ALLEANZA ASSICURAZIONI	6.218
SOCIETA' ASSICURATRICE INDUSTRIALE	5.276	ALLEANZA ASSICURAZIONI	5.989	ALLEANZA ASSICURAZIONI	7.579	SAI - ASSICURATRICE INDUSTRIALE	6.107
UNIONE ITALIANA DI RIASSICURAZIONE	4.121	TORO ASSICURAZIONI COMPAGNIA ANONIMA D'ASSICURAZIONI DI TORINO	5.105	SAI - ASSICURATRICE INDUSTRIALE	5.771	LA FONDIARIA ASSICURAZIONI	4.560
L'ASSICURATRICE ITALIANA	4.057	L'ASSICURATRICE ITALIANA	5.076	LE ASSICURAZIONI D'ITALIA	4.301	TORO ASSICURAZIONI	3.578
ALLEANZA ASSICURAZIONI	3.778	LE ASSICURAZIONI D'ITALIA	4.310	TORO ASSICURAZIONI	3.531	ASSITALIA - LE ASSICURAZIONI D'ITALIA	3.574
COMPAGNIA DI ASSICURAZIONE DI MILANO	3.031	UNIONE ITALIANA DI RIASSICURAZIONE	4.004	LA FONDIARIA	3.142	FONDIARIA	3.356
LA FONDIARIA VITA COMPAGNIA ITALIANA DI ASSICURAZIONI SULLA VITA DELL'UOMO	2.715	COMPAGNIA DI ASSICURAZIONE DI MILANO	3.659	REALE MUTUA DI ASSICURAZIONI	2.959	REALE MUTUA DI ASSICURAZIONI	2.986
COMPAGNIA DI ROMA RIASSICURAZIONI E PARTECIPAZIONI ASSICURATIVE	1.923	COMPAGNIA TIRRENA DI CAPITALIZZAZIONI E ASSICURAZIONI	1.984	COMPAGNIA DI ASSICURAZIONE DI MILANO	2.026	COMPAGNIA ASSICURATRICE UNIPOL	2.793

9　FEW AND SMALL: THE REINSURANCE INDUSTRY　215

1960	1970	1980	1990
LE ASSICURAZIONI D'ITALIA	1.856 S.A.R.A. SOCIETA' ASSICURAZIONI RISCHI AUTOMOBILISTICI	1.948 LLOYD ADRIATICO	1.790 LLOYD ADRIATICO 2.485
COMPAGNIA TIRRENA DI CAPITALIZZAZIONI E ASSICURAZIONI	1.368 LA FONDIARIA VITA COMPAGNIA ITALIANA DI ASSICURAZIONI SULLA VITA DELL'UOMO	1.937 COMPAGNIA TIRRENA	1.461 MILANO ASSICURAZIONI 2.140
S.A.R.A. SOCIETA' ASSICURAZIONI RISCHI AUTOMOBILISTICI	1.279 **LLOYD ADRIATICO DI ASSICURAZIONI E RIASSICURAZIONI**	1.394 COMPAGNIA ASSICURATRICE UNIPOL	1.339 FIDEURAM VITA 1.779
COMPAGNIA MEDITERRANEA DI ASSICURAZIONI	1.210 LA FONDIARIA INFORTUNI COMPAGNIA ITALIANA DI ASSICURAZIONI	1.263 ITALIA ASSICURAZIONI	1.295 COMPAGNIA TIRRENA 1.329
REALE RIASSICURAZIONI	1.099 LA PREVIDENTE COMPAGNIA ITALIANA DI ASSICURAZIONI	1.104 SARA ASSICURAZIONI	1.151 CATTOLICA DI ASSICURAZIONE 1.165
FIUMETER **ASSICURAZIONI E RIASSICURAZIONI**	1.049 F.A.T.A. FONDO ASSICURATIVO TRA AGRICOLTORI	1.029 CATTOLICA DI ASSICURAZIONE	1.139 MEDIOLANUM VITA 1.099
LA FONDIARIA INCENDIO COMPAGNIA ITALIANA DI ASSICURAZIONI	1.037 INTERCONTINENTALE ASSICURAZIONI	1.005 LA PREVIDENTE	0.972 LA PREVIDENTE 1.036

(continued)

Table 9.4 (continued)

1960	1970	1980	1990
LEVANTE SOCIETA' ITALIANA DI ASSICURAZIONI E RIASSICURAZIONI	1.006 LA FONDIARIA INCENDIO COMPAGNIA ITALIANA DI ASSICURAZIONI	0.993 LLOYD ITALICO & L'ANCORA	0.945 AUSONIA ASSICURAZIONI 0.977
L'ABEILLE COMPAGNIA ITALIANA DI ASSICURAZIONI	0.979 L'ABEILLE COMPAGNIA ITALIANA DI ASSICURAZIONI	0.909 F.A.T.A. - FONDO ASSICURATIVO TRA AGRICOLTORI	0.741 SARA ASSICURAZIONI 0.974
LA FONDIARIA INFORTUNI COMPAGNIA ITALIANA DI ASSICURAZIONI	0.955 COMPAGNIE RIUNITE DI ASSICURAZIONE C.R.A	0.805 LLOYD INTERNAZIONALE	0.724 UAP ITALIANA 0.834

Sources: Assonime, *ad annos* (1903-1960); Ania, *ad annos* (1970-2000) (our calculations)

large basis.[8] Moreover, Marco Bresso and his brother Giuseppe (1839–1901) crucially concurred to develop internationally Swiss Re, Giuseppe being Director General between 1865 and 1879 before joining *Generali* (Millo 2016, pp. 190–194; Straumann 2013, pp. 250–251). Furthermore, *Generali* and RAS, as multinationals, developed a widespread network of relations through which they were able to extend co-insurance and reinsurance relations and contracts. Along these same lines, for instance, from the early 1930s and still in early 1940s both *Generali* and RAS attempted to create an alliance with Munich Re on the ground of political alliance between Germany and Italy (Feldman 2004, pp. 41–61). The same deep conviction that internationalisation would be the natural and proper dimension of the insurance industry in the 1980s was reaffirmed by Fabio Padoa, a former chief executive officer at *Generali* (Padoa 1983; Piluso 2019, pp. 160–188).

A closer look at the insurance industry throughout its modern history should provide basis to better understand why there coexisted a long-term low insurance penetration, a deep sectoral turbulence and an underdeveloped reinsurance subsector.

9.3 A Neglected Branch Within the National Insurance Industry

In the first half of the nineteenth century, the demand for insurance in the Italian peninsula was still rather weak, but some circumstances, negative in themselves, such as the severe fire in Saronno in 1827, which destroyed most of the city, favoured the practice of fire insurance amongst property owners. The *Compagnia di assicurazioni di Milano* (called *Milano*, 1825), the *Compagnia anonima d'assicurazione di Torino* (called *Toro*, 1833) and the *Società Reale di assicurazione generale e mutua contro gli incendi*, (called *Reale mutua*, 1829) were not the first insurance companies to establish themselves on the Italian peninsula, but they were certainly the most solid companies with adequate financial resources and thanks to this they were able to expand their activity in the pre-unification

---

[8] *Generali* and RAS massively recurred to co-insurance contracts and relationships as a way to spread and hedge risks, as documented in Sanzin (1942). On this practice referred to *Generali* see, for instance, Sterling Offices Limited 1931, «Appendix F», [pp. 1–2] and p. 45.

states and then, after the Unification of Italy, to establish themselves with a dense network of agencies in almost all regions of the Kingdom.

In the peninsula two Austro-Hungarian companies also operated, born in the cosmopolitan and rich environment of entrepreneurial projects of Trieste; in the second half of the nineteenth century, the *Imperialregia privilegiata compagnia nominata Assicurazioni generali austro-italiche* (1831), which from 1848 simply assumed the name of *Assicurazioni Generali* and the *Riunione Adriatica di Sicurtà* (1838) emerged out of the Julian context and established themselves in Italy, in the rest of Europe and even beyond its borders. From their beginnings, *Generali* and Ras distinguished themselves from the other companies operating within the Empire's borders because they were the only ones to operate both in the non-life branches (fire, transport, hail) and in the life branch and to widen their range of action to many countries, becoming real multinationals.

The directors of these two Trieste companies had in fact realised that the main limitation of many insurance companies and the first cause of their financial instability was the lack of diversification of risks both on a geographical basis and by business sector, and therefore they had started to work in all branches and in many countries. The *Generali* and Ras therefore had a strategic advantage over their Italian competitors, which was already evident in the mid-fifties of the nineteenth century and which marked the evolution of the Italian insurance and reinsurance market in the years to come up to the following century: the two Trieste-based companies, strong in their international structure, divided into dozens of subsidiaries in different continents, had organic relationships, exchanges and collaboration with other insurance and reinsurance companies, with which the risks were divided so as to make the pool of risks covered extremely fragmented, heterogeneous and geographically very diversified. In the first half of the nineteenth century, reinsurance activities were carried out mainly in the form of co-insurance by the primary companies, rather than by actual reinsurance companies. In this way, the risks were transferred on an optional basis to other insurers, thus allowing a providential splitting of the guaranteed risks. However, this practice revealed the conditions applied in the contracts to the competitors in the primary market and to overcome this issue, the companies began to sell part of the risks subscribed to foreign insurers. This practice spread quickly and with it the international nature of modern insurance and the practice of reinsurance was consecrated (Holland 2009; Schwepcke and Arndt 2004).

In the last years of the nineteenth century, in a large part of Europe the rapid process of industrialisation and urbanisation further concentrated the risks, forcing insurers to diversify their exposures; in this scenario, the use of reinsurance became habitual, not only for the younger companies, which did not have substantial reserves, but also for the more solid and organised ones. Some companies, in addition to passive reinsurance, functioned as active reinsurers, acquiring shares of risks from other geographical areas and thus making the mass of risks guaranteed more heterogeneous (Porri 1928, p. 143).

A series of catastrophic events with considerable consequences for primary insurers contributed to the development of specialised reinsurance companies. In 1861, following a fire that had destroyed the Swiss town of Glarona, local insurers had been inundated with requests for compensation greater than five times their reserves and the unfortunate circumstances had revealed to the entire insurance world the threat posed by large-scale catastrophes (Swiss Re 2013, p. 24). Two years later, Swiss Re was founded, one of the first specialised reinsurance companies. Its founder was Ignaz Grossmann, former director of the Helvetia insurance company, and Giuseppe Besso from Trieste, who along with his brother Marco had worked at *Generali* for a long time (Swiss Re 2013, p. 17). The Italian origins of Giuseppe Besso and the blood bond with one of the most enduring and important managers of *Generali* allowed Swiss Re to become the most important reinsurer in Italy as early as the 1880's, a reliable interlocutor of primary importance which many companies operating in the Italian primary market turned to.

In the following decades, other epochal events, such as the San Francisco fire in 1906 and the Messina earthquake in 1908, where 86,000 people died, confirmed the operating limits of primary insurers and the need for recourse to reinsurance, especially for events with low frequency and unprecedented severity. In the last years of the nineteenth century, the use of a particular type of reinsurance became widespread: "excess of loss" contracts, with which only claims exceeding an agreed level were paid, rather than a percentage of all claims occurring in a particular field. This new approach marked the beginning of modern reinsurance practice and allowed reinsurers to approach catastrophic risks, which are by nature less frequent.

In the 1890s and in particular from the early years of the new century, the expansion of the Italian market required companies specialised in reinsurance capable of absorbing substantial shares of risks, and at the

Table 9.5.
Reinsurance in some European countries in 1927. (premiums in Italian lire)

Country	Number of active companies	Collected premiums
Great Britain	9	794.297.000
Germany	12	1.407.955.000
Switzerland	9	958.873.500
Italy	5	91.006.000

Source Author's re-elaboration of data from «L'Assicurazione», n° 2, January 1929.

same time foreign investors with considerable capital were looking for investment opportunities in the country's services. In response to this double demand, the first pure Italian reinsurers were born; the first, the *Ausonia*, was founded in Genoa in 1898, followed by the *Vittoria* in 1912. At the same time, the main companies active in the primary market such as *Generali*, Ras, *Milano*, *Fondiaria* also became involved in reinsurance. But the portfolios guaranteed by the pure Italian reinsurers were modest, there was a lack of professionalism and these companies failed to draw in customers and portfolios outside the narrow confines of the national insurance market. Within the framework of the European reinsurance market, Italian companies would never have been able to reach the dimensional and technical profile of the top Swiss and German firms, despite being able to cover an appreciable share of the Italian primary market (See Tables 9.5 and 9.6).[9]

The technical and retention limits of domestic reinsurance companies emerged in full force during the First World War, when the insurance and reinsurance market faced an unprecedented scenario: private companies rejected the risks associated with war, but such coverages were indispensable since otherwise trade by sea would have been impractical. Furthermore, financial relations with enemy countries such as Germany, where important reinsurers were based, were interrupted. In that climate, the intervention of the newly constituted INA was decisive, which, in August 1914, was authorised to assume the risks of war for goods and hulls of the merchant vessels on behalf of the State and also the reinsurance on behalf of foreign companies, since Italy was neutral. In 1917,

---

[9] A significant portion of Italian direct work went to French reinsurers as *Union, Royale, Paternelle, Métropole*, to Austrian *Donau* and to the already mentioned *Swiss-Re*.

Table 9.6 Reinsurance in Italy in 1927 (premiums in Italian lire)

Company	Foundation year	Collected premiums
Ausonia	1898	5.741.000
Generale di riassicurazioni	1923	4.267.000
Consorziale	1918	11.048.000
La Riassicuratrice	1918	34.108.000
Unione Italiana di Riassicurazione	1921	35.842.000
Total		91.006.000

N.B. Only the companies that exclusively carry out reinsurance are included in the table, whilst there are no four companies that mainly carry out insurance and only on a complementary and additional basis carry out reinsurance activity.
Source Author's re-elaboration of data from «L'Assicurazione», n° 2, January 1929.

with a new decree, INA's field of action was further extended, taking on the ordinary risks of navigation too. However, INA could only partially solve the problems associated with the outbreak of the conflict, which prevented the insurance industry from accessing international markets. The impossibility of reciprocal contractual relations between companies of countries that had become enemies provoked increasing difficulties up to the point of creating a situation of real "reinsurance shortage".

In the first post-war period, the Bonomi Government tried to find a solution to the Italian reinsurance weakness, with the birth of a state-owned reinsurance company, supported, however, by the entire national insurance market. At the end of 1921, the *Unione italiana di riassicurazione* (UIR or Uniorias) was born (RDL 1737 of 11/24/1921): an "anomalous" joint-stock company (as it was subject to derogations from the Civil Code) in which only insurance companies participated, alongside the INA, which was the largest shareholder, there were about 70 private insurance companies, practically most of the national insurance market.

The birth and consolidation of a solid national reinsurance company like Uniorias, which stands out, for its size and professional quality, compared to the other four or five small Italian reinsurance companies, proved to be decisive in the Fascist period. The protectionist policy of Fascism, followed by autarchy and international sanctions following the war in Africa (1935–1936), placed severe limitations on primary Italian insurance companies in the search for foreign insurance markets. From the early thirties, therefore, national insurance companies identified Uniorias as the privileged reinsurance partner, able to satisfy their needs regarding the placement of risks. Moreover, in this phase, also Ras and *Generali* experienced problems due to the restrictions in the transfer of capitals, which make the transfer of financial resources from and to Italy difficult. There were attempts, partly successful, by the Ministry of Finance and the Ministry of Foreign Affairs to include transfers of financial resources in the clearing agreements with the countries of Central-eastern Europe and the Balkans; however, the problem of remittances from abroad troubled the two Trieste companies until the threshold of the Second World War.

With the outbreak of the Second World War, new difficulties arose, largely linked to the Mussolini ambition of Italian supremacy in the Mediterranean countries and the Balkans (Turkey, North Africa, Yugoslavia, Greece), which clashed with German military dominance in the framework of the Axis alliance. In the insurance field, the expectations were considerable: in all, the Balkans Ras and *Generali* were present and, furthermore, the president of the *Generali*, Giuseppe Volpi was appointed as head of the Italian-Croatian Economic Commission, which aimed to promote economic integration between the two states, with a view to a future customs union. In June 1941, the Croatian government set up *Domovina*, with which it took over the insurance portfolios of the rival companies and decided to sell all the reinsurance to the *Münchener Ruckversicherungs-Gesellschaft*. After the immediate Italian reaction and a tiresome negotiation, a different breakdown of Croatian reinsurance was negotiated: 45% for the Italians and Germans and 10% for the Croats (Archivio storico del Ministero Affari Esteri 1941). The difficulties encountered in the economic penetration of the Balkans persuaded Volpi to co-opt ambassador Carlo Galli, who had been Italian ambassador in Belgrade (from 1928 to 1934) and who in the war years followed *Generali's* interests in Croatia and in Romania, into the *Generali* board of directors (Romano 1997, p. 225).

9.4 Why Did the Reinsurance Sector Not Develop in Italy?

The modest development of the reinsurance sector in Italy was, in part, a reflection of the modest diffusion of private and voluntary insurance.

All the statistics, whether comparing the per capita premiums (the so-called insurance density) or the ratio between premiums and GDP (the so-called insurance penetration), highlighted the difference between Italy and the main countries of Europe, in the life insurance branch, as well as in the non-life sector.[10] This has been a constant, from 1861 to the present day. In Italy the main guarantors, who offered a decisive defense in social security, health and coverage of catastrophe risks, were the state and the family, where the latter term means a combination of economic (for example, private savings), physical and moral resources. After the Second World War, the State dealt almost completely with social security, health care and illness, catastrophic risks, disability and, in part, unemployment and other minor risks. The family was responsible for the care of the elderly, of non-self-sufficient people, of youth unemployment, and of the risk linked to income (Saraceno 1994, 1998; Da Roit and Sabatinelli 2005). Some macroeconomic and sector variables have also influenced the development of private insurance in Italy, influencing demand: amongst the most important a higher average inflation rate and a lower national income than in the main European countries; secondly, the inadequate investment policy by the companies which has favoured real estate investments, drastically reducing the financial returns of the management, and the lack of competition that has caused high costs of the service and of research for consumers.

If all these reasons have affected the development and spread of voluntary primary insurance in Italy, similar problems have plagued the reinsurance industry. Moreover, the particular structure of the Italian market, polarised between two major companies, *Generali* and RAS, and a great number of medium and small companies, has accentuated the difficulties of the reinsurance industry and hindered its development.

Strengthened by its international structure, divided into dozens of subsidiaries and associates in different continents, *Generali* and RAS have consolidated relationships of exchange and collaboration with many insurance and reinsurance companies, in various parts of the world so as to

---

[10] Italy has the lowest insurance penetration in non-life branch compared to the main Western European countries. Amongst other things, Italy is the country with the highest incidence of the motor business (mandatory insurance) compared to GDP and the only one in which the percentage of the motor business is greater than non-motor in non-life. If you exclude the motor, Italy has a non-life insurance penetration which is half of that in France, just over half of that in Spain and 40% in Germany (Millo and Carmeci 2011, p. 276).

be autonomous and independent from the restricted domestic reinsurance market. In addition to engaging directly in reinsurance, the two Trieste companies had solid and very close strategic relationships with the largest European reinsurance companies: in the case of *Generali* with *Swiss Re*, in the case of Ras with the German *Munich Re (Münchener Rückversicherungs-Gesellschaft)*. The rest of the reinsurance demand in Italy came from small- or medium-sized companies, which turned to large European reinsurers or to Uniorias.

In the second post-war period, this scenario did not change substantially, even though the growth in size of the primary domestic market led to an unprecedented redefinition of roles and responsibilities. From the 1950s and particularly from the early 1960s, the importance of Uniorias in reinsurance in Italy has increased. This was to a large extent linked to the figure of Mario Luzzato, who lead Uniorias from 1962, until December 1992. A character of great charisma and authority, Mario Luzzatto also had a consolidated and recognised international standing, through the knowledge of the markets in which Uniorias conducted business was thanks to the presence of its offices in various countries of the world.

With its head office in Rome and a branch in Milan, Unioras established itself as a leading professional reinsurer on the Italian market, managing all the main insurance Consortiums (Pools), with a gross premium volume at the time of its privatisation, in 1995, was about 1504 billion lire, of which about 70% was collected in Italy. Uniorias conducted reinsurance activities in both the life business (22%) and the non-life (78%).

The presidents of Ras and *Generali* and the managing directors of other main Italian companies, took a seat on the Uniorias board of directors, so that the board of the reinsurance company outlined itself as the control room of the Italian market, which was characterised by coherent control strategies and strict weakening of the push towards competition. Moreover, the Italian insurance market was distinguished by a significant presence of industrial groups which were perceived by the main national companies as bearers of spurious interests compared to those of the insurers, intended as non-speculative management of private savings; for all this, Mario Luzzatto and the Uniorias board of directors played a leading and guiding role for most of the second post-war period. In this way, the functions of the Uniorias were original and crucial for the Italian market; on the one hand, it responded to the reinsurance demand of small- and medium-sized Italian companies, which had more difficulty accessing international markets and lacked the bargaining power to deal with large European and global reinsurance companies and, at the same time, absolved the function of guardian of the system, a role very dear to the great Italian companies who, through Uniorias, sealed pools and cartel agreements on industrial risks in the fire, hail and transport branches, thus exercising complete control of the market. The Italian pool for atomic risk insurance was also established under the aegis of Unorias. This body was set up amongst the main Italian insurers and had the purpose of studying the technical bases and distributing the catastrophic "atomic" risks amongst the insurance companies involved.

The privatisation process that flooded the Italian market from 1992 also involved Uniorias. In 1996 the company was sold to the Swiss Re group, which absorbed its insurance activities and the majority of employees, whilst the substantial real estate assets were liquidated. With the sale of the Uniorias, the only pure Italian reinsurer worthy of the name disappeared, the only one who by vocation and size had managed to stand out above the modest, or very modest, size of the other Italian reinsurers. However, Uniorias was not able to conquer other markets than the domestic one, a necessary goal and a categorical imperative for every reinsurer. The lack of competition and the limited penetration and insurance density of the Italian market were ultimately to be the major obstacles to the assertion of reinsurers of adequate size, able to compete with the major continental companies.

9.5 Conclusion

On the whole, reinsurance as a sectoral specialisation played a rather minor role and size in the insurance sector in Italy throughout the twentieth century. The Italian reinsurance companies were few and small, whilst their ability to remain within the 20 largest firms of the sector—as an indicator of their overall performance—was rather weak, being characterised by a high degree of turbulence. Such a finding is quite consistent with what we know about the relative stability of the sample constituted by the 200 largest firms in Italy during the twentieth century. As a matter of fact, the very few companies operating in the reinsurance branch show a certain discontinuity, but for one, Uniorias.

The reasons why reinsurance did not develop in Italy could be ascribed to a series of factors. The first factor affecting their development is represented by the long-term low insurance penetration, depending on the relatively modest per capita income levels in the first post-unification decades, on the one side, and on the ensuing emergence of public assistance and a welfare machinery backed by the State in the early 1910s, on the other side. Welfare state and public insurance agencies, such as INA, particularly influenced the life branch, but they defined more broadly the very specific market environment and regulatory context, in which insurance companies operated (Bico 2011; Lindert 2004). Other factors are more sector-specific and are related to the sectoral structure and to strategies pursued by the largest insurers, *Generali* and RAS. As seen, the sector structure has been strongly characterised by a marked dualism, that is by two great multinational companies, *Generali* and RAS, and many companies small- to medium-sized. This chapter assesses such a dualistic structure by ranking insurers by total assets, as data on their respective market shares are overall scarce. Within the sample represented by the top 20 insurers for benchmark years, reinsurance companies tend to disappear almost completely from the 1970s, when even Uniorias exited from the sample. The other relevant factor affecting reinsurance in Italy is constituted by the strategies pursued by the two largest companies, that is adopting reinsurance mechanisms throughout internationalisation. Since the late 1870s, in fact, the top management of both *Generali* and RAS conceived the insurance industry as an intrinsically international business, whose multinational dimension was required in order to effectively manage and hedge risks in markets larger than the domestic one. Their multinational networks and co-insurance contracts concretely epitomised the international nature of insurance. Along these enduring strategic lines, *Generali* and RAS created a large network of insurers throughout all of Europe and even outside Europe.

These endogenous factors reinforced the exogenous factor, that is the existence of a specific international structure of the sector in which reinsurers first developed in more advanced contexts, such as France, Germany, Switzerland and UK. The emerging sector specialisation at the close of the nineteenth century, to which *Generali*'s management, however, was not a stranger, suggested to strictly limit investment in the reinsurance branch in Italy to the minimum required. These tendencies have been reinforcing themselves over time declaring the reinsurance branch virtually inexistent at the end of the twentieth century.

References

Agliardi, Antonio. 2011. "Mercato assicurativo e dinamica degli investimenti tra le due guerre". In *Assicurare centocinquant'anni di Unità d'Italia*, ed. Garonna Paolo. Rome: ANIA.

ANIA-Associazione nazionale fra le imprese assicuratrici, *Annuario 1970–2000.* 664 Rome: ANIA.

Andreas, Schwepcke, and Dieter Arndt. 2004. *Reinsurance: Principles and State of the Art*. Karlsruhe: Verlag Versicherungswirtsch.

Archivio storico del Ministero Affari Esteri, Rome, *Affari generali*. b. 32, 1941, Accordo italo-croato per le assicurazioni.

Assonime-Associazione Italiana fra le società per azioni, *Notizie statistiche*. Rome: Assonime, 1903–1960.

Baglioni, Roberto. 1997. "L'affermazione delle società assicurative nel capitalismo italiano, 1919–1940". *Studi Storici* 38 (2): 431–468.

Bico, Elena. 2011. "Lo stato e le assicurazioni in Italia: lo sviluppo delle assicurazioni sociali e l'Istituto Nazionale delle Assicurazioni". In *Assicurare centocinquant'anni di Unità d'Italia*, ed. Garonna Paolo. Rome: ANIA.

Cingolani, Giorgio. 2018. *Le assicurazioni private in Italia. Gestione del rischio e sicurezza sociale dall'Unità a oggi*. Bologna: il Mulino.

Ciocca, Pierluigi. 2000. *La nuova finanza in Italia. Una difficile metamorfosi (1980-2000)*. Turin: Bollati Boringhieri.

Ciocca, Pierluigi. 2007. *Ricchi per sempre? Una storia economica italiana (1796-2006)*. Turin: Bollati Boringhieri.

Coltorti, Fulvio. 2011. *Grandi gruppi e informazione finanziaria nel Novecento*. Rome-Bari: Laterza.

Da Roit, Barbara, and Stefania Sabatinelli. 2005. "Il modello mediterraneo di welfare tra famiglia e mercato". *Stato e Mercato* 74 (2): 267–290.

De Simone, Ennio. 2007. *Breve storia delle assicurazioni*. Milan: Angeli.

Falautano, Isabella, and Guido Santucci. 2011. "La liberalizzazione del mercato delle assicurazioni nell'ultimo trentennio. in un'ottica europea: dall'internazionalizzazione alla bancassicurazione". In *Assicurare centocinquant'anni di Unità d'Italia*, ed. Paolo Garonna. Roma: ANIA.

Favaretto, Tito. 2011. "Lo sviluppo dell'attività internazionale delle Assicurazioni Generali tra il XIX e il XX secolo". In *Assicurare centocinquant'anni di Unità d'Italia. Il contributo delle assicurazioni allo sviluppo del paese*, ed. Paolo Garonna. Rome: ANIA.

Feldman, Gerald D., 2004. "Competition and Collaboration among the Axis Multinational Insurers: Munich Re, Generali, and Riunione Adriatica, 1933-1943". In *European Business, Dictatorship, and Political Risk, 1920-1945*, ed. Christopher Kobrak and Per Hansen Hansen. New York: Berghahn Books.

Ferrera, Maurizio. 2010. "The South European Countries". In *Oxford Handbook of the Welfare State*, ed. Francis A. Castles et al. Oxford: Oxford University Press.

Giannetti, Renato, and Michelangelo Vasta. 2012. *Storia dell'impresa italiana*. Bologna: il Mulino.

Golding, Charles E. 1931. *A History of Reinsurance with Sidelights on Insurance*. Offered as a memento of fifty years' service in the reinsurance world by Sterling offices limited. London: Sterling.

Gugerli, David. 2013. "Cooperation and Competition: Organizationa and Risks in the Reinsurance Business, 1860–2010". In *The Value of Risk. Swiss Re and the History of Reinsurance*, ed. Harold James. Oxford: Oxford University Press.

Hasler, Kurt. 1963. *Schweizerische Rückversicherungs-Gesellschaft Zürich. Rückblick 1863-1963*. Zürich: Schweizerische Rückversicherungs-Gesellschaft.

Holland, David M. 2009. "A Brief History of Reinsurance". *Reinsurance News* 65 (19): 4–29.

Istat, Istat, Serie storiche, *Life premiums and non-life premiums*, Tab. 19.4, 1921–2014. http://seriestoriche.istat.it/index.php?id=1&no_cache=1&tx_usercento_centofe%5Bcategoria%5D=19&tx_usercento_centofe%5Baction%5D=show&tx_usercento_centofe%5Bcontroller%5D=Categoria&cHash=f1be941b0834e73a479f10a3f0c4c394. Accessed on 27 September 2020.

Lindert, Peter H. 2004. *Growing Public. Social Spending and Economic Growth Since the Eighteenth Century*. Cambridge: Cambridge University Press.

Mellinato, Giulio. 2019. "La stabilizzazione sfuggente: Le Assicurazioni Generali tra le due guerre". *Italia Contemporanea* 70 (219): 123–159.

Millo, Anna, 2004. *Trieste, le assicurazioni, l'Europa*. Arnoldo Frigessi di Rattalma e la RAS, Milan: Angeli.

Millo, Anna, 2016. Marco Besso. In *Generali nella Storia*. Racconti d'Archivio, Venice: Marsilio.

Millo, Anna, 2019. "Tra libero scambio e prima globalizzazione. Le Assicurazioni Generali dal 1880 al 1914". *Italia contemporanea* 70(219), 102–122.

Millo, Giovanni, and Gaetano Carmeci. 2011. "Non-life Insurance Consumption in Italy: A Sub-regional Panel Data Analysis". *Journal of Geographical Systems* 13 (3): 1–26.

Ministero dell'Industria, del Commercio e dell'Artigianato, Ispettorato delle assicurazioni private. 1967. *Le assicurazioni private in Italia*. Rome: Istituto Poligrafico dello Stato.

Nullmeier, Frank, and Franz-Xaver Kaufmann. 2010. "Postwar Welfare State Development". In *Oxford Handbook of the Welfare State*, ed. Francis A. Castles et al. Oxford: Oxford University.

OECD. https://data.oecd.org/insurance/insurance-spending.htm#indicator-chart. (accessed on 27 September 2020).

Padoa, Fabio. 1983. *L'assicurazione internazionale*. Milan: Hoepli.
Pearson, Robin. 2017. "The Evolution of the Industry Structure". In *Managing Risk in Reinsurance. From City Fires to Global Warming*, ed. Niels Viggo Haueter and Geoffrey Jones. Oxford: Oxford University Press.
Piluso, Giandomenico. 2012. "Italy: Building on a Long Insurance Heritage". In *World Insurance. The Evolution of a Global Risk Network*, ed. Peter Borscheid and Niels Viggo Haueter. Oxford: Oxford University Press, 2012.
Piluso, Giandomenico. 2019. "Una multinazionale o una 'comunità internazionale'? La ricostruzione della rete estera delle Assicurazioni Generali, 1945–1971". *Italia Contemporanea* 70 (219): 160–188.
Porri, Vincenzo. 1928. "Lo sviluppo delle imprese assicuratrici in Italia nei rami elementari". In *Lo sviluppo e il regime delle assicurazioni in Italia*, ed. G. Prato, V. Porri e F. Carrara. Turin: S. Lattes & C.
Riunione Adriatica di Sicurtà. 1939. *Nel primo centenario della Riunione Adriatica di Sicurtà, 1838–1938*. Trieste: La Compagnia.
Romano, Sergio. 1997. *Giuseppe Volpi*. Venice: Marsilio.
Sacerdoti, Piero. 1966. "A Century of Insurance in Italy. Its Environment, Development and Future Prospects". *The Review*, March 21.
Sanzin, Luciano Giulio. 1942. *Cent'anni di accordi fra le Compagnie italiane nelle assicurazioni incendio*. Trieste: Editoriale Libraria.
Sapelli, Giulio. 1990. *Trieste italiana. Mito e destino economico*. Milan: Angeli.
Saraceno, Chiara. 1994. "The Ambivalent Familism of the Italian Welfare State". *Social Politics* 1 (1): 60–82.
Saraceno, Chiara, ed. 1998. *Mutamenti della famiglia e politiche sociali in Italia*. Bologna: il Mulino.
Stefani, Giuseppe. 1931. *Il centenario delle Assicurazioni Generali, 1831–1931*. Trieste: Editrice la Compagnia.
Straumann, Tobias. 2013. "The Invisible Giant: The Story of Swiss Re 1863-2013". In *The Value of Risk: Swiss Re and the History of Reinsurance*, ed. Harold James. Oxford: Oxford University Press.
Swiss RE, 2013. La storia delle assicurazioni in Italia. https://www.swissre.com/dam/jcr:1a10f44c-0996-4ba4-9cc5-42ba0df7de3a/150Y_Markt_Broschuere_Italy_webN.pdf.
Swiss Re, Sigma, Underinsurance of Property Risks: closing the gap". n. 5/2015. *The Review*, 3 July 1901.
Vasta, Michelangelo. 2006. "The Largest 200 Manufacturing Firms (1913–2001)". In *Evolution of Italian Enterprises in the 20th Century*, Renato Giannetti and Michelangelo Vasta. Heidelberg: Physica Verlag.

CHAPTER 10

Government Intervention in Rural Insurance and Reinsurance Markets in Mexico: 1940–2000

Gustavo A. Del Angel

10.1 Introduction

Since the first half of the twentieth century, the Mexican government has sought to stimulate, later intervene in, and eventually (up until 1990) monopolize insurance and reinsurance of agricultural activity. Given this is an activity characterized by correlated risks and high operating costs, its offering was lacking in a country with underdeveloped financial markets, like Mexico at that time. In most countries, the government usually intervenes in cases like these, either as offeror of insurance or by means of subsidies.

This paper explains how the Mexican government intervened in the insurance and reinsurance markets from the 1940s forward in order to

---

G. A. Del Angel (✉)
Department of Economics, Centro de Investigación y Docencia Económicas (CIDE), Mexico City, Mexico
e-mail: gustavo.delangel@cide.edu

© The Author(s), under exclusive license to Springer Nature Switzerland AG 2021
L. Caruana de las Cagigas and A. Straus (eds.), *Role of Reinsurance in the World*, Palgrave Studies in Economic History,
https://doi.org/10.1007/978-3-030-74002-3_10

provide that service to rural producers who were not covered by private insurance companies. It explains that the government's insurance offering was practically monopolized by Anagsa (*Aseguradora Nacional Agrícola y Ganadera*), a state-owned firm, from the late sixties. That prevented reinsurance, because insurance losses were absorbed by the government itself. Moreover, the government encouraged a perverse scheme whereby rural insurance was used to cover the risks of loans granted to farmers by the government's agricultural development banks. The scheme also fostered corruption between policy holders and the government's insurance company. That, combined with the indiscriminate expansion of insured crops, destroyed the possibility that insurance would be affected in a technical basis with actuarial criteria. In addition, it led to big losses in the national budget.

The government sought to resolve the problem in 1989 when it liquidated Anagsa and replaced it with another state-owned insurance company, Agroasemex. The new company would specialize in reinsurance. The adoption of a practice of agricultural reinsurance by the government was aimed at avoiding large fiscal losses and stimulating private insurance markets. By implementing reinsurance, fiscal losses were reduced. However, the government did not fully stimulate rural insurance markets, as it continued to intervene in crop insurance markets.

In Mexico's financial, agricultural, and rural history, agricultural insurance and reinsurance are relevant to understanding the relationship between the Mexican State and agricultural producers. Moreover, they also help to understand why it is so difficult to develop an insurance and reinsurance industry in a developing economy. Nevertheless, rural insurance and reinsurance has been "the elephant in the room." Notwithstanding its relevance, there is a lack of research into it, with the exception of the contributions by Reyes Altamirano (for instance, Altamirano 2001a, b). This paper aims to contribute to a better understanding of these issues in historical perspective. It also aims to provide insights that contribute to understand the influence of politics in rural insurance markets. For this purpose, this research is based on corporate reports, press files from the Archives of the Mexican Ministry of Finance (Archivos Económicos, Secretaría de Hacienda), and contemporary literature and reports.

The paper is organized as a chronological narrative. To provide a context of insurance in Mexico, the next section explains some of the general precedents of insurance industry in Mexico, in its origins and the twentieth century. Section 10.3 describes the early attempts to introduce rural insurance in the mid-twentieth century. Section 10.4 explains the works of Anagsa, from its beginnings to its liquidation. Section 10.5 is about the early years of Agroasemex and its challenges. Section 10.6 is the concluding remarks.

10.2 Precedents of the Insurance Industry in Mexico

Professional insurance in Mexico became established at the start of the nineteenth century. The two major developments during that century and the first quarter of the twentieth century were the establishment of diverse insurance companies and the design of a legal and regulatory framework. For the most part, Mexico's insurance industry owes its origins to a transfer of knowledge from British firms, although the high levels of political and economic instability that the country experienced provided few opportunities for growth,[1] at least until greater stability emerged during the last third of the nineteenth century. In about 1845, *Watson Phillips y Cía.* created an insurance office in Mexico in the city of Veracruz; this company was a Mexican incorporated firm started by British entrepreneurs, and it specialized in international trade. At the start of the twentieth century, twenty-two insurance companies were operating in Mexico. There were two national and five foreign life insurance companies. There was also one national fire company and fourteen foreign firms in this line of business. More companies began to operate, including both Mexican firms and foreign representative offices (Del Angel 2012).

By 1954, the direct insurance business had been transferred entirely from foreign companies to local firms. One exception was marine insurance, where the regulatory situation remained ambiguous. However, it is thought that there was proprietary participation by American, Italian, French, and Swiss insurers in insurance companies that were operating in the country, and which, in practice, functioned as subsidiaries, although the precise details are not known (Del Angel 2012).

As regards reinsurance activities, there was significant participation by multinational firms and this remained the last bastion where companies

---

[1] Between the start of the War of Independence in 1810 (it ended in 1821) and the consolidation of the republic in 1867, Mexico experienced a lengthy period of political and economic disruption.

that were not Mexican could operate in a relatively open manner. This was the case even though at this time Mexico had three major reinsurers: *Alianza*,[2] *Unión*, and *Patria*, the latter established in 1953. At the end of the 1940s and in the 1950s, conditions for reinsurance in the country were regarded as good, and to some extent this view was due to the performance of the local reinsurers. Nevertheless, from the end of the 1940s onwards, it was noted that reinsurance commissions were high. The problem of over-supply of reinsurance services prompted some companies to offer commissions and improved conditions to gain market share, eventually weakening the reinsurance providers. Furthermore, the local operators regarded the regulation of reinsurance as obsolete.[3] In addition to their reinsurance products, some European companies offered training and technology for the reinsurance operators, while in some cases it was necessary to invest capital. As regards cession of risks to reinsurance, this activity developed at its own pace, dictated by a combination of domestic events in the Mexican economy and conditions on global markets. Until the 1980s, the international reinsurance markets operated with Mexico according to the principle of good faith; this worked efficiently, given that the majority of treaties were for reinsurance on a pro rata basis (Del Angel 2012).

However, private insurance and reinsurance targeted the private sector (mainly medium size and large firms), high income households, and the government. Rural markets were uncovered, with the exception of large agroindustrial complex.

10.3 Early Attempts at Rural Insurance in the Twentieth Century

The majority of the agricultural industry operates under uncontrolled environmental conditions. It is subject to climate variations, which can produce excess moisture and dampness (tropical storms, cyclones, hurricanes, etc.) or drought. Extreme temperature conditions, such as frosts, delays or advances in the minimum chill hours, or even high temperatures, can seriously damage crops or cause damage that has direct repercussions

---

[2] Among other companies, *Swiss Re* and *Munich Re* were participants in *Alianza*, Del Angel (2012).

[3] For specific sources see Swiss Re *The Review*, 26 August 1955, 817; 10 December 1948, 912; and December 1956, 1290; all cited in Del Angel (2012).

for the level of production and product quality. Also, risks in rural areas are complex, which makes measuring them and evaluating their impact a difficult task. They usually exhibit correlated risks (e.g., plagues can be associated with weather events like drought). Furthermore, damage can occur across whole regions, which makes risk to production facilities in the same area correlated.

This risk profile makes insurance for agricultural activity a complicated business. Likewise, in countries with large swathes of land and rugged terrain, insurance operating costs in rural areas are increased or even unworkable in many cases. Over at least the last 70 years, governments in many countries around the world have intervened to deal with the absence of an insurance and reinsurance markets for agricultural activity.

In its early days, agricultural and farming insurance was linked to credit operations for these activities. The 1926, 1931, and 1934 *Leyes de Crédito Agrícola*, agricultural credit laws, stated that farming groups (cooperatives, for example) should create contingency funds that partially covered some of the risks to which production could be exposed. The aim was to protect production against natural risks, like hail, and thereby cover the risk of funding rural producers.

Toward the end of the 1930s, the government authorized the creation of insurance fund managers, which arose from rural production companies. However, the results were not as expected. For complex risks in underdeveloped markets, there were two important factors. On the one hand, those funds failed in part because of the country's lack of experience with agricultural insurance. On the other hand, the absence of a practice of reinsurance for this sector, as well as its small scale, did not allow those funds a satisfactory reinsurance market (Altamirano 2001a; Correu Toledo 1962).

In spite of the difficulties with rural insurance in Mexico, in 1942 a mutual, the *Mutualidad Comarcal de Seguros Agrícolas "La Laguna"* was created in the region of La Laguna, in the north of the country. This mutual benefit society sought to protect members against specific risks—hail and frost, to a large extent. Its activity was regulated by the insurance law, *Ley General de Instituciones de Seguros*. One of the main objectives when creating the mutual benefit society was to unite the agricultural producers in the region that received funding from the *Banco Nacional de Crédito Ejidal*, a government development bank that financed agricultural producers on "ejidos" (collectively owned land). In this way, recovery of loans was guaranteed through insurance. In 1945, the mutual benefit society expanded its protection to include fire risks (Altamirano 2001a; Escamilla and Quitzaman 1993; Correu Toledo 1962).

Subsequently, in 1953 the Mexican government created a guarantee fund for credits, the *Fondo Nacional de Garantía Agrícola* by presidential decree. The fund's main aim was to incentivize private banks to channel funding to the countryside via shared risk schemes, in which the government would guarantee loans in the event of damage due to natural phenomena usually covered by insurance. Again, despite this being a modern public policy for those times and diversifying the government's tools for promoting rural insurance, the results were not as planned.

Consequently, in 1954 the government decided to establish two offices to study rural insurance, the *Oficina de Estudios del Seguro Agrícola* and the *Comisión para el Estudio y Planeación del Seguro Agrícola Integral* (CEPSAI). As a result of the CEPSAI's work, agricultural insurance activity was included in the insurance regulation, the *Ley sobre el Contrato de Seguro* and the *Ley General de Instituciones de Seguros*. It contributed to the creation of mutual societies and a consortium of private insurance companies for agricultural insurance.[4]

In 1954, the Ministry of Finance authorized private mutual societies to issue agricultural insurance. Taking the mutual benefit society of La Laguna as a model, farming groups from the main agricultural regions in Mexico created their own mutual benefit societies, on the whole with the government's support, and formed a federation of mutual benefit societies, the *Federación de Sociedades Mutualistas de Seguro Agrícola y Ganadero*. The new mutual benefit societies—20 of them in 1955— directed their attention toward recipients of funding from the *Banco Nacional de Crédito Ejidal* and the *Banco Nacional de Crédito Agrícola*. The latter was another government development bank that focused on small- and medium-sized agricultural producers.[5] In so doing, the government encouraged these banks to include the cost of the insurance premium in their funding. The cost of the policy was estimated using

---

[4] In addition to Correu Toledo (1962), other contemporary studies shed light about the interest of this issue then, such as Martinez Moreno (1944), Ortega San Vicente (1958), Sandoval Cuellar (1961), Porte Petit Minivielle (1962), Portes Gil (1964), Pelayo Gómez Montiel (1968), and Velasco Oliva (1970).

[5] The most important ones were in the states of Chihuahua, Guanajuato, Jalisco, Nayarit, Tamaulipas, Puebla y Veracruz, see Escamilla and Quitzaman (1993) and Correu Toledo (1962).

Table 10.1 Operation of mutual benefit societies. Data in Hectares (Has) and millions of current pesos

Agricultural cycle	Land insured (Has)	Land damaged (Has)	Income (pesos)	Operational expenses (pesos)
1955/56	691,329	252,629	26	65
1956/56	468,189	160,611	16	29
1956/57	693,685	300,439	29	74
1957/57	424,681	153,429	16	36
1957/58	862,107	334,419	31	90
1958/58	511,071	162,128	18	53
1958/59	881,942	409,244	36	127
1959/59	512,054	179,290	20	56

Source Correu Toledo (1962) and Escamilla and Quitzaman (1993)

actuarial methods, but since they lacked statistical information, they used geographical characteristics of the regions, analysis of the soil, extension of the crops, past crop yields, climate and temperature variations, rainfall variations, among other data (Escamilla and Quitzaman 1993; Correu Toledo 1962).

In 1954, several private insurance companies created a syndicate for agricultural insurance, the *Consorcio Mexicano del Seguro Agrícola Integral y Ganadero*, a private organization that 11 private insurance companies began to participate in. The consortium's insurance coverage was for damage to crops by hail.[6]

Mutual benefit societies managed to cover a considerably bigger area—over a million hectares on average per year—as shown in Table 10.1. As in the previous case, the difference between the payouts and the various operating costs was considerable, which again reveals the use of government subsidies as a means of operating. It must be stressed, however, that the mutual benefit societies registered higher expenses per hectare and per policy holder than were reported by the consortium.

With regard to the period when the consortium of private insurance companies was in operation, it is worth noting from Table 10.2 that, first of all, the total insured area underwent substantial variations. Second, the

---

[6] These private companies were: América, El Mundo, Generales El Sol, La Atlántida, La Azteca, La Comercial, La Oceánica, La Provincial, Seguros y Reaseguros La Territorial,

Table 10.2 Operation of the private *Consorcio*. Spring–Summer and late summer agricultural cycles. Data in Hectares (Has) and millions of current pesos

Agricultural cycle	Land insured (Has)	Land damaged (Has)	Amount Insured (pesos)	Net policy (pesos)	Indemnity (pesos)	Operating expenses (pesos)	Risk Expenses (Gastos de Ajuste, pesos)
1955/56	85,857	27,819	71.58	3.38	9.23	0.18	0.21
1956/56	39,562	28,320	48.58	2.90	3.83	0.18	0.11
1956/57	119,399	11,942	113.10	5.73	5.50	0.36	0.19
1957/57	77,177	9,483	103.43	4.91	3.43	0.30	0.14
1957/58	52,838	1,519	60.69	3.07	0.42	0.21	0.14
1958/58	65,058	9,968	62.66	3.25	3.18	0.23	0.26
1958/59	67,901	14,985	65.87	3.51	4.49	0.25	0.33
1959/59	65,994	9,586	56.72	3.23	2.30	0.23	0.23
1959/60	69,630	21,516	82.32	3.93	6.61	0.28	0.21
1960/60	106,155	44,660	119.23	6.95	12.70	0.47	0.43

Source Correu Toledo (1962) and EscamillaQuitzaman (1993)

relatively low proportion of damaged areas stands out when compared with the total insured area, given that this was around 22.8% for the years under scrutiny. As shown below, this figure is in contrast with the state monopoly scheme that would operate in subsequent periods. As previously mentioned, this can be explained by the fact that the individual insurance companies worked mostly with commercial producers, with a low risk profile and irrigated land.

Conversely, despite the low loss occurrence, the amount of premiums was substantially less than payouts and operating expenses. This is shown in Table 10.2. Private activity was made sustainable only by government subsidies.

The government's participation did not stop at creation of the consortium and mutual societies. In fact, the government increased its participation in the incipient national rural insurance scheme by creating a new guarantee fund, the *Fondo de Garantía y Fomento a la Agricultura* (which absorbed the *Fondo Nacional de Garantía Agrícola*), with the

Aseguradora Reforma y Aseguradora Mexicana; see Escamilla and Quitzaman (1993); Correu Toledo (1962).

aim of continuing to promote private sector participation. In addition to fund guarantees, members of the consortium would benefit from subsidies when their results showed an operating deficit. With regard to mutual societies, a compensation fund was created and managed by the *Banco de México*, the central bank, which would absorb the differences observed between the premiums and the payouts issued to producers. In this way, a mixed public–private insurance system was formed in which both offerings ended up being semi-public, in light of the financial responsibilities assumed by the government over insurance activity. This led to cases of corruption within mutual benefit societies, which motivated the government to eventually take over the insurance sector in a monopolistic manner (Altamirano 2001a; Escamilla and Quitzaman 1993 and Correu Toledo 1962).

In 1956, an amendment to the agricultural credit law, the *Ley de Crédito Agrícola*,[7] provided that recipients of agricultural loans could apply for insurance with the support of the banks that financed them. However, market penetration remained low and there was no adequate reinsurance mechanism. In addition, the mutual benefit societies and the consortium had operational deficiencies that required larger subsidies (Altamirano 2001a; Escamilla and Quitzaman 1993; Correu Toledo 1962).

10.4 The *Aseguradora Nacional Agrícola y Ganadera* (Anagsa)

The government then sought a way of solving the rural insurance problem. It did so by establishing a virtual state monopoly. In 1961, a law for rural insurance, the *Ley del Seguro Agrícola Integral y Ganadero*, was enacted. One of the main features of that law was the creation of the state-owned company *Aseguradora Nacional Agrícola y Ganadera, S.A.* (Anagsa) in 1961. The company's main objective was to offer comprehensive agricultural insurance, because until that point the previous insurance schemes had only partially covered risks. Besides that, Anagsa offered reinsurance services to mutual societies (Altamirano 2001a; Escamilla and Quitzaman 1993; Correu Toledo 1962).

---

[7] Article 123 of the Ley de Crédito Agrícola.

With the new law and the creation of Anagsa in 1961, the government made the purchase of agricultural insurance a requirement to obtain funding from its agricultural development banks. It thereby created a link between insurance and agricultural credit. Years later, that would become the means of sustaining the agricultural development banks' non-performing loan portfolio. This feature was present for nearly 30 years in the form of the country's agricultural and rural insurance activity. Initially, the main objective of this practice was to avoid decapitalization of borrowers who suffered damage due to climate and other natural phenomena. However, as land selection criteria became laxer—particularly during the 1980s when the government launched measures geared toward food self-sufficiency—insurance became an instrument to support the state banks rather than the producers themselves.

The creation of Anagsa was a milestone in Mexico's history of agricultural insurance because it ended a more than 30-year cycle of attempts to define an insurance system that never became established. The CEPSAI's work had been fruitful in the sense that it had helped form a consortium of private insurance companies, as well as found a federation of mutual benefit societies arising from rural production organizations. However, its scope was limited. The required supply to address the rural sector's insurance problems in Mexico continued to be very limited. Both private and mutual companies operated with agricultural companies in agricultural areas that were developed in terms of infrastructure, yield, and market viability. This meant that a significant proportion of the cultivated area of the country was neglected. In other words, the most developed producers had access to agricultural insurance, while the majority of producers did not. On average, around 1.6 million hectares were insured during the 1950s. That is just 15% of the 11 million hectares of agricultural land available in Mexico at that time (Escamilla and Quitzaman 1993; Correu Toledo 1962).[8]

In addition to low coverage, the insured area was highly concentrated in certain regions. More than 40% of the insured land was concentrated

---

[8] At the start of the Anagsa operations, the study by Correu Toledo (1962), points out that this firm would allow a considerable increase in land covered, not only among the creditors of the government banks, but also between producers lacking a credit history. This because although the performance of previous years showed high operational costs, they expected that the learning and experience accumulated could lead to improvements in the operating insurance costs.

Table 10.3 Operation of ANAGSA. 1964–1969. Data in Hectares (Has)

	Land insured (Has)	Land damaged (Has)	Ratio
1964	1,502,000	481,000	0.320
1965	1,522,000	581,000	0.382
1966	1,484,000	568,000	0.383
1967	1,351,000	496,000	0.367
1968	1,600,000	656,000	0.410
1969	1,500,000	660,000	0.440

Source Escamilla and Quitzaman (1993), Pelayo Gómez Montiel (1968), and Herrera Vizcarra (1989)

in the states of Chiapas, Durango, Jalisco, Michoacán, and Sinaloa. The government believed that the only way of achieving significant coverage against the risks affecting the bulk of Mexican agricultural activity was through greater participation by the state, whether by complementing the existing support for private and mutual companies or by providing the service directly.[9]

With Anagsa, agricultural insurance in Mexico would go through a phase of government monopoly. In light of the high administrative costs that the mutual benefit societies registered from the offset, and that caused growing outlays for the treasury due to government subsidies issued to help them operate, Anagsa decided to liquidate them in 1976. The state-owned company opened regional offices to replace them, located in the country's main agricultural production regions.

We have not found evidence of Anagsa's reinsurance activity with mutual benefit societies. According to studies from the time, Anagsa followed technical actuarial criteria for direct provision of insurance during its early years—something that was lost in subsequent decades. Indeed, there were high expectations for its operations and performance.[10] Table 10.3 shows the company's activity during its early years.

Anagsa's activity led to a considerable increase in the insured area. As Table 10.4 shows, 5.3 million hectares were covered by agricultural insurance in 1980. That said, part of the increase in coverage can be explained

---

[9] *Ley del Seguro Agrícola Integral y Ganadero*, Law Proposal to the Mexican Congress, 1961.

[10] Files F04357 Archivos Económicos, Secretaría de Hacienda.

Table 10.4 Operation of ANAGSA. 1970–1989. Data in Hectares (Has) and millions of current pesos

	Land insured (Has)	Land damaged (Has)	Ratio	Net policy (pesos)	Indemnity (pesos)	Loss Ration (Índice de siniestralidad)
1970	1,778,724	714,772	0.402	240.21	274.63	114.33
1971	2,028,320	871,515	0.430	309.19	224.79	72.7
1972	1,917,339	982,581	0.512	327.22	350.7	107.18
1973	2,238,198	833,506	0.372	430.17	254.94	59.27
1974	2,514,189	1,094,884	0.435	783.13	562.9	71.88
1975	3,854,974	1,997,724	0.518	1,318.93	1,220.84	92.56
1976	3,450,164	1,915,692	0.555	1,421.26	1,368.50	96.29
1977	3,539,026	2,169,089	0.613	1,894.21	1,577.64	83.29
1978	3,203,054	1,714,014	0.535	1,992.96	1,351.48	67.81
1979	2,979,480	1,990,558	0.668	2,350.63	2,604.38	110.79
1980	5,263,325	3,464,491	0.658	6,715.66	5,404.37	80.47
1981	7,444,047	4,497,807	0.604	17,563.75	11,570.44	65.88
1982	8,197,720	5,873,102	0.716	28,677.94	20,820.21	72.6
1983	6,755,927	3,955,124	0.585	45,156.94	27,538.06	60.98
1984	6,135,974	3,625,698	0.591	77,884.48	56,151.14	72.1
1985	7,011,308	4,406,978	0.629	124,304.77	126,883.50	102.07
1986	7,063,717	5,373,885	0.761	227,886.93	275,297.74	120.8
1987	7,328,069	5,461,992	0.745	569,478.34	637,530.16	111.95
1988	6,584,686	4,989,405	0.758	1,105,791.44	1,346,371.65	121.76
1989	4,913,537	3,467,437	0.706	990,941.15	977,246.41	98.62

Source Escamilla and Quitzaman (1993), Gómez Montiel (1968), and Herrera Vizcarra (1989)

by the legal link between insurance and credit from the government development bank. Even though this legal framework was designed to shield funded producers financially in the face of potential damage, it included the implicit risk that insurance would be used for other purposes. Notably, incentives were geared toward insurance helping maintain "good" levels of recovery for funding bodies in the agricultural sector.

Anagsa's expansion in the 1970s and 1980s occurred in an environment where the state's participation in the economy was growing rapidly. The Mexican government increased its influence over economic activity through state-owned companies, subsidies, and other types of intervention (Del Angel and Perez 2014).

At the peak of this intervention process, a new piece of legislation (the *Ley del Seguro Agropecuario y de Vida Campesino*) was issued in 1981, bringing another change in rural insurance. From 1962 to 1981, Anagsa reinforced the state's role in the provision of rural insurance. In subsequent years, and particularly from 1981 to 1989, there was a gradual and severe deterioration in the state-owned company's operating results. The decline was firstly a consequence of the sustained increase in government financing for agricultural activity, and therefore an increasing demand for insurance coverage. That increase stemmed from a public policy of expansion of the agricultural frontier (which indeed was contained in the 1981 Law (Altamirano 2001a; Escamilla and Quitzaman 1993).

In this regard, the so-called *Sistema Alimentario Mexicano* (SAM)—a government program established in 1980 that targeted agricultural self-sufficiency for the country—strengthened the government's intervention in agricultural markets (Tellez 1994; Vélez 1995; Warman 2001). For Anagsa, the SAM was an additional factor for increasing coverage.[11]

In fact, the objective of food self-sufficiency would result in more government loans for agriculture as well as a vast, complex structure of government support instruments, including mainly subsidies on consumables and guarantee prices. That incentivized moral risk and adverse selection in insurance implementation. More plots of land entered into funding and insurance under that scheme, but those plots were less productive as many were seasonal. Credit and insurance risk was therefore ever increasing. This also made reinsurance impossible, at least actuarially.

The proportion of seasonal crop land insured by the company increased in the 1980s. This figure was 64% of the insured total in 1979, increasing to 75% by 1989. Insurance covered nearly 8 million hectares by 1982, which is the highest level of agricultural insurance in Mexico's history. During the 1980s, an average of 6.5 and 7 million hectares were insured (Altamirano 2001a; Escamilla and Quitzaman 1993).

It must be noted too that, in light of monitoring problems affecting a large part of the newly insured land, there were increasing information asymmetries between Anagsa and policy holders. This was mainly because this land was in areas where the terrain was inaccessible during certain seasons. This enabled an adverse selection problem, whereby insured projects had less productive value than the insured amount. It is estimated

---

[11] In 1981, the director of Anagsa declared in a press conference that, independently of the regular insurance by the company, the coverage of the crops contemplated in the *SAM* would be expanded to support this program. El Nacional, 4 July 1981, Files F04357 Archivos Económicos, Secretaría de Hacienda.

that 50% of Anagsa's operating deficit at the end of the 1980s was owed to the growing discrepancies between the real value of insured projects and the insured amount.[12]

In terms of crop type, the company's coverage was not very diverse. Corn represented more than 40% of the total insured area in 1983. Taken together, corn, sorghum, and beans made up around 70% of the total insured area, while all basic grains constituted almost 95%, all of them were products with decreasing market prices at that time.

Changes in operational guidelines for insurance offered by the company as a result of the 1981 Law would significantly increase its exposure to risk and, in the long run, its financial health. The 1981 Law changed the previous framework and allowed an increase in the limit applied to the insured amount: up to 100% of the cultivated area, where originally this limit was 70%. This meant that, at best, producers were indifferent to achieving a successful harvest during the farming cycle, because their whole yield was backed up by insurance (and therefore the value of the loan that financed the crops). In fact, the anticipated compensation was more attractive for producers, considering the discrepancies between the land's actual yield and the insured amount. Another relevant aspect is that the insurance term began at the point of application. There were even cases of insurance for nonexistent land, due to the monitoring problems implicit in insurance activity.[13]

The aforementioned aspects were the source of a corrupt scheme that came to be known as the "damage industry" in the 1980s. Under this scheme, both policy holders and employees of the company responsible for supervising the land saw opportunities to seek rents through collusion between producers and insurance adjusters. Likewise, employees of the government's agricultural development banks saw an opportunity to extend credit between farmers with guaranteed recovery of the loans, financed by Anagsa from the government's budget, ultimately coming from taxpayers.[14]

Consequently, the considerable growth of the damaged area as a percentage of the total insured area is not surprising. By the end of the

---

[12] Files F04357 Archivos Económicos, Secretaría de Hacienda: 21 mayo 1984, 22 noviembre 1984, 5 febrero 1985, 12 noviembre 1987, 18 noviembre 1987, 22 diciembre 1987.

[13] Ibid.

[14] Interview to Salvador Mayoral, September 1, 2007.

1980s, more than 75% of the insured area was declared damaged (see Table 10.4). By the end of the 1950s, before the creation of Anagsa, less than 40% of the total insured area was damaged.

The link established by the legal framework between development bank loans and agricultural insurance not only derives from the latter operating as collateral for funding more than as an instrument for risk coverage, but it condemned insurance and Anagsa's financial health to depend on government development banks' allocation criteria for rural credit. The political, rather than technical, nature of rural funding allocation led to many of the plots of land in Anagsa's portfolio lacking the minimum essential characteristics to be insured from a healthy risk perspective. In this sense, the evolution of rural credit recovery through insurance company payouts is surprising. Between 1983 and 1988, 32% of the bank's agricultural portfolio was recovered through Anagsa. In some farming cycles, such as Spring/Summer 1988, 51% of portfolio recovery came from insurance company payouts (Altamirano 2001a; Escamilla and Quitzaman 1993).[15]

By virtue of this, Anagsa suffered increasing losses caused by the rising disparity between the total received in premiums and the compensation paid. The latter was covered by the government, which made transfers to fund the state-owned company's operating costs.[16]

In 1989, complaining about Anagsa's 1.5 trillion peso deficit, the then Agriculture Secretary declared that rural insurance only served to "[...] encourage corruption, lose crops and discourage farmers."[17]

Table 10.5 shows the federal government's contributions to the financial bodies responsible for dealing with the countryside—government development banks that dealt with rural areas, government financial resources for agriculture and Anagsa. It shows an upward trend in the resources allotted to Anagsa. By 1989, government support allotted to Anagsa reached nearly 25% of the value of transfers to the government's rural financial bodies.

---

[15] See also Files F04357 Archivos Económicos, Secretaría de Hacienda: 21 mayo 1984, 22 noviembre 1984, 5 febrero 1985, 12 noviembre 1987, 18 noviembre 1987, 22 diciembre 1987.

[16] Interview to Salvador Mayoral, September 1, 2007.

[17] Files F04357 Archivos Económicos, Secretaría de Hacienda y Crédito Público, Excélsior, 15 July 1989.

Table 10.5 Transfers of the federal government to the state-owned rural financial institutions. Millions of pesos, inflation adjusted 1992=100

	1983	1984	1985	1986	1987	1988	1989
Banrural	5,454.00	3,920.00	3,989.00	4,275.00	1,429.00	4,502.00	3,251.00
(%)	43.8	41.8	33.1	31.3	14.1	46.9	44.4
FIRA	4,952.00	3,396.00	5,403.00	6,618.00	6,175.00	2,001.00	2,068.00
(%)	39.79	36.19	44.83	48.41	60.72	20.86	28.26
Anagsa	1,253.00	1,393.00	1,930.00	2,302.00	2,195.00	2,476.00	1,778.00
(%)	10.07	14.84	16.01	16.84	21.58	25.82	24.30
Otros	785.00	676.00	731.00	475.00	371.00	612.00	221.00
(%)	6.31	7.20	6.06	3.47	3.65	6.38	3.02
Total	12,444.00	9,385.00	12,053.00	13,670.00	10,170.00	9,591.00	7,318.00

Source Altamirano (2001a)

The government accepted this as a direct transfer of resources to poor farmers, but this income was captured by more organized stakeholders and those who formed part of corporativist groups that supported the government in return. Anagsa had managed to achieve the highest levels of agricultural insurance in the country's history, but it was clear that its subsidy basis had distanced it from its nature as a protective mechanism against risks. Rural insurance became a tool of political patronage in the rural setting and Anagsa the flagship of corruption in the sector. Reform became necessary to re-establish the country's agricultural insurance apparatus. Given the general context of state reform in Mexico by the end of the 1980s, this would need to be done in a way that allowed adjustment of insurance and its alignment with a more efficient operative structure.[18] In 1989, the government decided to liquidate Anagsa. A year later it was replaced by Agroasemex, a new state-owned company (Agroasemex 1991, 1992, 2000a, nd; Tellez 1994).

At the time of its liquidation, Anagsa not only faced a financial crisis but it also underwent a "moral crisis" that implicated both the insurance company and the policy holders and had become a reputation problem (Agroasemex 1991, 1992, 2000a, nd).[19] The company's problems had also permeated the culture of agricultural insurance. For

---

[18] Vélez (1995); Tellez (1994).

[19] Also interview with Salvador Mayoral, September 1, 2007.

example, Warman (2001, 160) points out that "it had got to the extreme of actuarially allocating claims before planting, without taking plagues or natural disasters into consideration. Many prospered, and corruption spread [...]."[20] But in addition to corruption, the mechanism had inhibited participation by the private sector, except in rare cases, and destroyed an insurance culture among Mexican farmers.[21]

The government began the liquidation on February 9, 1990. The technical reasons given for liquidation were having lost all capital, not having constituted technical reserves, and operating with a growing deficit, fundamentally due to a technical–economic imbalance that made it unsustainable as an insurance institution. Some of the grounds that were officially recognized in the documents were: a technical and operational structure of insurance coverage and benefits that resulted in adverse selection, overinsurance, and relaxing of standards; administrative and operational organization that was highly vulnerable to moral risk, with both Anagsa and adjusters showing signs of corruption; and excess staff, so that the organization had problems with bureaucracy and inefficiency while lacking an adequate system of supervision and control (Agroasemex 1991, 1992, 2000a, nd).

Tellez (1994, 164–165) summarizes some aspects of this transformation: "Anagsa was liquidated, which resulted in policy holders no longer reporting false damages to pay [Banrural debt payments] with the compensation, as well as ending a growing outlay of public financial resources to the government's insurance company. Agroasemex was created in its place under actuarial criteria, insuring investments made by the producer [...]. Agroasemex's services were realigned to cover the risks to which producers' people, property and activities were exposed [...]."[22]

10.5 Financial Reform, State Reform, and the Creation of Agroasemex

Agroasemex was formed on June 7, 1990. This state-owned firm would operate as an insurance and reinsurance company for the rural economy. In addition, it was intended to be a development agency to meet the

---

[20] Warman (2001), p. 160.

[21] Interview to Salvador Mayoral, September 1, 2007.

[22] Tellez was then Deputy Minister at the Ministry of Agriculture.

insurance needs of Mexican agriculture. Its creation was part of a series of reforms and it was called "the technical reform of agricultural insurance." Its aims were: to consolidate an agricultural insurance system with technical bases for its activity and the participation of private actors; to optimize the allocation of tax revenue to development of this activity; and to maintain an impactful development framework that caused the least market distortion possible. Agroasemex's reinsurance role was indispensable for this objective (Agroasemex 1991, 1992, 2000a, nd). This was a revolution compared to the previous rural insurance scheme in Mexico. However, less than ten years after its creation, Agroasemex would find itself with financial and operational problems, causing market distortion.

The liquidation of Anagsa and foundation of Agroasemex were part of a series of reforms carried out by the Mexican government at that time. Through the so-called "State Reform," which was a liberal reform, the government sought to reduce the size of the public sector, organize public finances, and control the national deficit. It also involved redesigning rural support programs. At the same time, the government carried out a financial liberalization process, which significantly affected the insurance industry. It was hoped that the above-mentioned reforms and financial liberalization would lead to greater private participation in the agricultural insurance sector.

In that context, the agreement that authorized the formation and organization of Agroasemex was published in the government gazette, *Diario Oficial de la Federación*, on June 7, 1990. The initial share capital would be 304 million pesos.[23] The company would be authorized to carry out duties relating to "life insurance operations and damages in the areas of civil liability and occupational, maritime and transportation risks, fire, earthquake and other catastrophic, agricultural, animal- and car-related and other risks."[24]

The government had an interest in organizing the administration of public funds and making it transparent but, at the same time, it knew it did not want to abolish subsidies nor instruments of development.

---

[23] At the time of the establishment, of the 304 million of capital, 204 would be paid, and 100 million would remain to be paid. Agroasemex (nd).

[24] The shareholders were financial organizations of the federal government: FIRA, Nafin, Banobras, Bancomext, and the federal government itself. At the beginning also a state-owned insurer, Asemex, was a shareholder, when Asemex was privatized in 1992, sold its stock to the federal government.

In the documents that gave rise to Agroasemex, insurance was intended to generate added value for producers and contribute to their competitiveness. The aims were to shape a competition-friendly market and continually attract capital to this activity. It was hoped that, with time, the market would be extensive in size, diverse in its product range and profitable, and would allow for a broad conglomerate of insurance companies that would compete among themselves.[25] While Anagsa was in operation, producers stayed away from sharing responsibility for risk. Insurance cover was set at a maximum of 90% with Agroasemex, and a policy of deductibles was launched that ranged from 5 to 30%. Both of these aspects meant producers had joint responsibility for risk.

The *Sistema Nacional de Aseguramiento al Medio Rural*, a national strategy to provide rural insurance, would be made up of Agroasemex, private insurance companies that participated in rural markets and rural insurance funds. The rural insurance funds were mutual benefit societies to which Agroasemex would offer reinsurance and technical advice. They were largely made up of producers with a high organizational capacity, a high yield, and a low loss occurrence (Agroasemex 2000b; Altamirano 2001b).

In light of the circumstances surrounding the agricultural market and the low participation by private insurance companies during the first half of the 1990s, Agroasemex focused its activity on the objective of developing markets. It did so by offering insurance directly, as well as promoting the rural insurance funds (via reinsurance and technical assistance). However, the company had created unrealistically high expectations given its actual potential. It had been expected to start with 2 million hectares insured, reaching at least 7 million—the amount that Anagsa had insured (Agroasemex 1991, 1992, 2000a, nd).[26] This would impose a very high-cost structure for the institution's activity.

In this sense, the company had been conceived with original sin. By designing it to insure between 4 and 7 million hectares, two errors had

---

[25] Interview to Salvador Mayoral, September 1, 2007.

[26] A relevant fact was that at the start of operations there was a problem of inertia: Banrural's portfolio was expected to be insured, as the old Anagsa used to do. This would have guaranteed the expansion of the land coverage as in other times. However, since the firm aimed to follow actuarial criteria for insurance, the technical filters only allowed insuring 400 thousand hectares in that first operation. Cleaning the Banrural portfolio for insurance led to both institutions ceasing operational relations, and hence breaking the old scheme in a definitive manner. Interview to Salvador Mayoral, September 1, 2007.

Table 10.6 Crop coverage Agroasemex, rural insurance funds and private insurance companies. 1990–2000. Data in millions pesos (current and inflation adjusted 1990 = 100)

	Total current pesos	Total1990 = 100	Agroasemex current pesos	Agroasemex 1990 = 100	Fondos current pesos	Fondos 1990 = 100	Private insurers current pesos s	Private insurers 1990 = 100
1990	871.68	871.68	762.92	762.92	108.76	108.76	–	
1991	1,035.87	856.71	468.11	387.15	567.76	469.56	–	
1992	2,000.69	1,412.08	899.66	634.97	1,101.04	777.10	–	
1993	2,064.07	1,327.37	951.39	611.82	1,112.68	715.55	–	
1994	2,493.55	1,499.13	1,212.76	729.12	1,270.88	764.06	9.91	5.96
1995	2,768.38	1,232.87	1,261.93	561.99	1,418.93	631.91	87.52	38.98
1996	5,260.39	1,743.33	2,316.11	767.57	2,602.68	862.55	341.60	113.21
1997	7,536.60	2,070.60	2,633.60	723.55	2,977.61	818.07	1,925.40	528.98
1998	8,526.67	2,020.74	2,675.60	634.09	3,078.00	729.46	2,773.07	657.19
1999	9,295.12	1,889.48	2,352.75	478.26	3,466.82	704.72	3,475.56	706.50
2000	8,841.77	1,641.52	2,762.36	512.84	3,107.31	576.89	2,972.11	551.79

Source Data from Agroasemex

been committed. The first was to consider penetration of insurance as a target for the company's direct operation, which would be detrimental to its viability. The second was to compare coverage levels with those of its predecessor Anagsa, when dealing with two different things: one had been a transfer arrangement framed as an insurance contract; the other was insurance with technical criteria and a development policy. The company's financial viability and ability to promote the market would be affected.[27]

The operations and financial situation of Agroasemex are shown in Tables 10.6, 10.7, and 10.8. As shown, it was able to activate the rural insurance funds, but at the same time it expanded its direct offering of insurance becoming a competitor to the private market. Table 10.7 also shows that it was far from financial sustainability.

By March 2000, the company had again registered shortfalls in its regulatory coverage of capital and was at the point of bankruptcy, even potentially losing its license to operate.[28] After a large injection of capital

[27] Interview to Salvador Mayoral, September 1, 2007.

[28] The financial situation was published in the government gazette, Diario Oficial, 17 August 1999.

Table 10.7 Cattle coverage Agroasemex, rural insurance funds and private insurance companies. 1990–2000. Data in millions pesos (current and inflation adjusted 1990 = 100)

	Total current pesos	Total 1990 = 100	Agroasemex current pesos	Agroasemex 1990 = 100	Fondos current pesos	Fondos 1990 = 100	Private insurers current pesos s	Private insurers 1990 = 100
1990								
1991	638.59	528.14	516.45	427.13	122.14	101.01		
1992	1,034.41	730.08	900.15	635.32	134.26	94.76		
1993	991.62	637.70	954.13	613.59	37.49	24.11		
1994	1,145.71	688.81	1,134.39	682.00	11.32	6.81		
1995	1,296.46	577.36	1,291.73	575.26	4.73	2.11		
1996	3,255.17	1,078.78	3,250.00	1,077.07	5.17	1.71		
1997	5,000.22	1,373.76	4,801.56	1,319.18	8.52	2.34	190.15	52.24
1998	6,879.84	1,630.46	6,485.50	1,537.00	8.86	2.10	385.47	91.35
1999	8,855.75	1,800.16	7,112.23	1,445.75	11.37	2.31	1,732.15	352.11
2000	18,195.44	3,378.07	10,024.66	1,861.12	1,255.43	233.08	6,915.34	1,283.87

Source Data from Agroasemex

Table 10.8 Profit and Losses of Agroasemex. 1990–2000. Millions of current pesos

1990	37.8
1991	1.8
1992	− 49.3
1993	1.1
1994	− 32.5
1995	− 0.8
1996	− 11.9
1997	− 29.4
1998	− 185.0
1999	− 106.3
2000	− 168.2

Source Data from Agroasemex

by the government, the *Agroasemex* Board held an extraordinary meeting at the offices of the Ministry of Finance on March 20, 2001. There it was decided that Agroasemex would suspend direct sales of agricultural, life, and damage insurance from April 1, 2001, and would later abandon its livestock insurance sales program. The body would be an agency specializing in reinsurance and development (Agroasemex 2005; 2000a, nd).

That specialization as a reinsurer and development agency never fully happened. Agroasemex supplied reinsurance and strengthened its capacity in that market, but it would also continue to operate as a subsidized direct insurer (competing against private insurance companies). However, in the subsequent years, the company developed an innovative catastrophic insurance scheme through indexed insurance methods. The company became an innovative as well as highly technically proficient insurer for the rural economy in Mexico. It was a technical role model for rural insurance.

However, Agroasemex faced pressure from the government to be financially sustainable, meaning that it had to diversify its supply on the market. Furthermore, it suffered the same burden as its predecessor Anagsa, albeit in a different way: it was an attractive political instrument to benefit agricultural and livestock producers (via subsidized insurance). Such contradictory demands from the government itself would mark its performance in the following years.

10.6 Concluding Remarks

Rural insurance and reinsurance, when provided by government insurers, might be an activity influenced by politics. Anagsa is a historical case that shows the distortions of the interweaving of political interests and financial activity that occurs in these cases. But the interaction between politics, risk, financial decisions, and public policy is still a contemporary problem. Duru (2016) shows how government incentives to provide farmers with disaster relief impedes insurance market formation. According to that author, farmers knowing they get relief from the government have no incentive to purchase an insurance product. Then, the government might target specific groups, allocating insurance according to political objectives. The problem is yet to be resolved for developing economies. This research aims to provide a story that helps to gain insights to this question.

References

Agroasemex. nd. *Las razones del gobierno federal para la redefinición de Agroasemex.* México: Mimeo.
Agroasemex. 1991. *Informe Anual 1991.* Santiago de Querétaro: Agroasemex.
Agroasemex. 1992. *Informe Anual 1992.* Santiago de Querétaro: Agroasemex.
Agroasemex. 2000a. Diez años de seguro agropecuario en México. Memoria 1990-2000. Santiago de Querétaro, QE: Agroasemex.
Agroasemex. 2000b. *Reglas generales para la constitución, operación y funcionamiento de los fondos de aseguramiento agropecuario, de vida campesino y conexos a la actividad agropecuaria y sus modificaciones.* Santiago de Querétaro: Agroasemex.
Altamirano, J. Reyes. 2001a. "El seguro en la administración de riesgos de la actividad agropecuaria". Tesis Doctor en Problemas Económico Agroindustriales. Universidad Autónoma de Chapingo, CIESTAAM.
Altamirano, J. Reyes. 2001b. "La Experiencia de los Fondos de Aseguramiento en México". Revista Teorema Ambiental. Núm. 30. Septiembre.
Agroasemex. 2005. *Administración de Riesgos Agropecuarios. Manuales para el Fortalecimiento de los Fondos de Aseguramiento Agropecuario.* México: AGROASEMEX.
Correu Toledo, Guillermo. 1962. *El seguro agrícola integral en México: Señalamiento de algunos problemas que se han presentado durante su operación.* México: Curso Internacional de Crédito Agrícola.
Del Angel, Gustavo. 2012. "A History of the Insurance Industry in Mexico". In *World Insurance: The Evolution of a Global Risk Network,* ed. Peter Borscheid and Niels Viggo Haueter. Oxford: Oxford University Press.
Del Angel, Gustavo, and Lorena Perez. 2014. *Palanca de la minería. 80 años del Fideicomiso de Fomento Minero.* México: Fifomi - Biblioteca Mexicana del Conocimiento.
Duru, Maya Joan. 2016. "The Politics of Economic Risk". Doctoral Dissertation in Political Science. San Diego: University of California.
Escamilla, Jesús, and P.J. Quitzaman. 1993. "Ensayo sobre el seguro agrícola en México". Revista Actualidad en Seguros y Fianzas. Vol. I, Núm. 9. Octubre-Diciembre. México: Comisión Nacional de Seguros y Fianzas (CNSF).
Herrera Vizcarra, José A. 1989. *Seguro Agrícola (Diagnóstico y Propuesta de Reestructuración).* México: Mimeo.
Ley del Seguro Agrícola Integral y Ganadero. 1961. México: Law Proposal to the Mexican Congress.
Martínez Moreno, Rita. 1944. "Comentarios sobre los seguros agrícolas en México". Tesis para obtener el título de Licenciado en Economía. México: Universidad Autónoma de México. Escuela Nacional de Economía.
Ortega San Vicente, Rene. 1958. "Funcionamiento y organización del seguro agrícola en México". Trabajo de tesis para obtener el título de Contador

Público y Auditor. México: Universidad Autónoma de México. Escuela Nacional de Comercio y Administración.

Pelayo Gómez Montiel, Matías. 1968. *El Seguro Agrícola Integral en México*. México: Universidad Autónoma de México. Escuela Nacional de Economía.

Porte Petit Minivielle, Jorge. 1962. *El Seguro Agrícola*. México: Editorial Libros de México.

Portes Gil, Emilio. 1964. *Las instituciones de seguros y el estado mexicano*. México: Sociedad Mexicana de Geografía y Estadística.

Sandoval Cuellar, A. 1961. "El seguro agrícola integral y ganadero mutualista mexicano". Tesis. México: Universidad Autónoma de Chapingo.

Secretaría de Hacienda. Archivos Económicos. Colección de la Biblioteca Miguel Lerdo de Tejada. México: SHCP.

Tellez, Luis. 1994. *La modernización del sector agropecuario y forestal*. México: Fondo de Cultura Económica.

Velasco Oliva, Jesús Cuauhtémoc. 1970. "La política agrícola y el seguro agrícola en México". Trabajo de tesis para obtener el Título de Licenciado en Economía. México: Universidad Autónoma de México. Escuela Nacional de Economía.

Vélez, Félix. 1995. "Los Desafíos que enfrenta el Campo en México". In *México a la hora del cambio*, ed. L. Rubio and A. Fernández. México: Cal y Arena.

Warman, Arturo. 2001. *El Campo Mexicano en el siglo XX*. México: Fondo de Cultura Económica.

CHAPTER 11

The Introduction of Life Reinsurance in Japan Before WWII

Takau Yoneyama

11.1 Background and Research Questions

Risks on lives have been globally growing since 2000. Although we believed that infectious diseases were stamped out by spread of medical knowledge in the twentieth century, some infections still threaten us.

This paper is written by a report at the 18th WEHC, Boston, 2018. The author has already published it in Japanese in a bulletin of Tokyo Keizai University. The permission has already been received by the editor. This paper is not a simple translation of the Japanese paper. After publishing, the author's interests are slightly changing, so both the papers are not all the same. Especially the author rewrote the part of conclusion. Cf. 'Role of Reinsurance in the Setting of Insurance in the World', World Economic History Congress, Session B 030,215, Room West: Samberg Conference Center, MIT, Boston, 3 August 2018.

T. Yoneyama (✉)
Hitotsubashi University, Kunitachi, Japan
e-mail: takau_yoneyama@ybb.ne.jp

© The Author(s), under exclusive license to Springer Nature Switzerland AG 2021
L. Caruana de las Cagigas and A. Straus (eds.), *Role of Reinsurance in the World*, Palgrave Studies in Economic History,
https://doi.org/10.1007/978-3-030-74002-3_11

Moreover, we should recognize the risks created by increased longevity especially in the advanced nations. When we combine an aged population with a low birth rate as is the case in many developed countries, the government should respond to serious problems including the worsening of the public pension system. We have just been confronted with longevity risk as well as infectious risk in the twenty-first century.

Although there seems to be no connection between longevity risk and infectious risk, both are the same in the sense of influencing negatively our lives and personal finances. Moreover, they are measurable by actuarial methods and modelling analysis. They can be insured by reinsurers. But the reinsurance market is often at the limit when catastrophic disaster occurred and new risks emerged. After the turn of the century the 'life markets' have been developed among the advanced countries as an alternative to reinsurance market.

The important difference is the players in the markets. For example, investors who buy insurance-linked securities underwrite risks instead of reinsurers in the life market. There are many devices for these investors, and new life products are still developed.

At first, the new life market drives out the traditional reinsurance market. However, we recognize that reinsurance market and life market are not mutually exclusive. Both markets have equal advantages and disadvantages. The traditional reinsurance market has still been important in the twenty-first century.

For the most part, the reinsurance business focused on non-life insurance. But we must not miss life reinsurance business. Life reinsurance became more important partly because of epidemic diseases such as SARS, and partly because of increased longevity risk in the advanced countries. Recently, life reinsurance has been a large percentage of total reinsurance business.

Even though life reinsurance is clearly important, Japanese life insurance companies were indifferent to the life reinsurance business. Japan has no reinsurance company specialized in the life business that is not foreign owned. There is no regulation against the life reinsurance. Why then do Japanese life insurers have no interest in doing life reinsurance? And how do they manage diversification of their risks?

Answers should be discovered in the history, so we go back to the period before WWII and recognize the introduction process of life reinsurance in Japan. The Japanese history of life reinsurance was started when a German insurance company proposed introducing life reinsurance on substandard lives (at first, we called 'weak-body lives' instead of substandard lives in Japan. In this chapter, we use substandard lives for unification of terminology). The proposal was not successful, and the discussion of the introduction of life reinsurance finally resulted in the establishment of an insurance company, the Kyoei Life, specialized in the life reinsurance business. It gave rise to a long and complicated history. There are lots of historical materials and company histories. And then, historians had already explained the process of introducing life reinsurance. However, one important research question remains. We could recognize characteristics among Japanese life insurance companies in the process of introducing life reinsurance into Japan. The characteristics may continue to influence the attitude against life reinsurance even after the WWII. The main purpose is to answer the above questions after making an explanation of historical characteristics among Japanese life insurance companies.

11.2 'Spanish Flu' and Promotion of Life Reinsurance Business

Influenza spread worldwide in 1918, and Japan was no exception. The peak was in 1919 and 1920 in Japan. Thousands of people died from influenza. They called it the 'Spanish flu' without good reasons (in records of the insurance company, they wrote simply about 'Influenza', but we use 'Spanish flu' because this has become the standard term). It hit the life insurance business in the short run. However, no life insurers received a mortal blow in financial conditions.

According to the annual reports of Nippon Life, the largest life insurance company, actual mortality did not surpass the expected mortality. The annual report says, 'Total death claims were 3,065,550 yen, and the actual mortality against expected mortality was 88 percent' in 1919 (Nippon Life Insurance Report 1919). The same percentage barely fell below 100%, 99% to be exact in the next year (Nippon Life Insurance Report 1920, p. 2). The other companies were not the same as the Nippon Life. The Dai-ichi Mutual Life, the second largest life insurance company in the late 1920s, had a slightly different story. For Dai-ichi Mutual Life, the actual mortality was larger than the expected mortality both in 1919 and 1920. Each percentage was 110.3 and 109.4 based on the sum of claims, and 109.9 and 109.5 based on the number of claims (Dai-ichi Mutual Life Report 1919 and 1920, pp. 19–20).

The Meiji Life Insurance, Ltd., the oldest life insurance company in Japan, did not report expected and actual mortalities, but the following mention were added in the annual report which said, 'the 870 policies and the amount of 635,900 yen were paid for deaths from influenza, and we recognize that they were special and temporary payments. Overall, 21% of total insurance policies and the 23% of total claims arose from the influenza (Meiji Life Insurance Report 1920, p. 2). The company recognized financially the negative impact on 'Spanish flu'.

The Nippon Life comparatively dominated the rural market and the Dai-ichi Mutual Life and the Meiji concentrated in urban areas. These three life insurers were the largest. What was the impact on medium and small life insurers? Table 11.1 shows the different impacts of 'Spanish flu' in whole life insurance industry.

Although the business year is different for life insurance companies, the percentages in Table 11.1 are generally reliable ones for 1919. As for all companies, the percentage on policies is 115.60% and 109.87% on claims. We understand that the results of Nippon Life is exceptionally better. Even among the largest seven companies including the Nippon Life, both percentages on policies and claims are more than 100%. The medium and small life insurers suffered from 'Spanish flu' more severe than the larger companies, because the medium and small companies underwrote more invalid lives than the larger companies.

Influenza was the most important cause of death in both 1919 and 1920 for the Dai-ichi Mutual Life. The annual report said, 'Although the most important cause of death had been lung tuberculosis, the influenza became the most important in the last year and had still been important this year. As for influenza, the 153 policies out of total death of 520

Table 11.1 Percentage of actual deaths compared with expected deaths in 1919

	Actual death/expected death (%) on policies	Actual death/expected death (%) on insurance money
All companies	115.60	109.87
Larger 7 Co	111.48	106.74
Medium and small Co	122.00	115.58

Source The Dai-ichi Mutual Life, The 18th Annual Report, 1919, pp. 19–20

meant 29% of all death, whilst deaths from tuberculosis were 89 policies and only 17%' (Daichi Report, 1919, p. 20).

For Meiji Life, influenza also became the most important cause of policyholders' death in 1919. The ranking of the cause of death is shown in Table 11.2. Although influenza was the most important cause, the other causes were important as well. It did not seem that the impact of influenza on the mortality was particularly important at Meiji Life (Meiji Life Report 1919, pp. 32–39).

The different picture between Dai-ichi and Meiji was caused by differences in the data. Meiji reported half-year than Dai-ichi because of its business year. It is unfortunate that Meiji Life did not give the same data in the next annual report. We can only imagine that the impact of the influenza became more severe than in the previous year.

Lastly, we recognize the impact of influenza in the long term using the data of Dai-ichi Mutual Life. Figure 11.1 shows, as a percentage, the actual mortality relative to expected mortality from its start-up to 1920.

Table 11.2 The cause of policyholders' death in 1919

Male	Cause of death	%	Female	Cause of death	%
1	Influenza	14.045	1	Influenza	13.846
2	Lung tuberculosis	13.968	2	Pneumonia	12.189
3	Cerebral apoplexy	12.279	3	Lung tuberculosis	11.479

Source Meiji Life, The 39th Annual Report, 1919, pp. 32–39

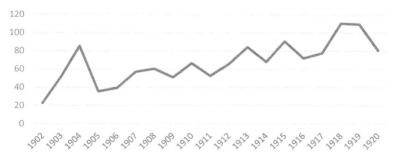

Fig. 11.1 Rate of actual death against expected death, 1902–1920 (Source The 19th Annual Report of the Dai-ichi Mutual Life 1920, pp. 19–20)

We can find that the percentage continued to be increasing in the long term. However, we can recognize that the years 1918 and 1919 are the only ones with more than 100%. As for the Dai-ichi Mutual Life, the business year 1918 means the period from 1 September 1918 to 1 August 1919. So, the impact of the Spanish flu on mortality is clear.

To summarize the impact of the 'Spanish flu' on life insurance companies in Japan: there were certain negative impacts due to the increase in mortality. However, the degree of the impact was different among life insurers. Even during the epidemic, actual mortality did not surpass expected mortality at Nippon Life. But Nippon Life was an exception. Most life insurers suffered from an excess of actual mortality over expected mortality.

On the other hand, the impact on the financial conditions of life insurers was limited. No life insurance company failed to meet insurance claims during the epidemic. This means that life insurers could manage to diversify epidemic risk and/or to have enough capital for unexpected events.

11.3 Reinsurance Plan of Munch Re and a Response of the Japanese Life Insurers

After the outbreak of 'Spanish flu', foreign insurance companies tried to enter the Japanese market. A newspaper reported that representatives of a foreign company visited some life insurers and offered reinsurance contracts on epidemic risks (Tokyo Asahi Newspaper 16 May 1926). The proposal comes to fruition that the 'Spanish flu' had not devastated the Japanese life insurers. So, they did not feel an immediate need for diversifying an epidemic risk.

Among the foreign reinsurers, a proposal from the Munch Re was impressive to Japanese life insurers. Dr. Emdem, a representative of the Munch Re, was dispatched to Japan in order to explain the proposal in detail (Yoneyama 2012, p. 508, and Osaka Jiji-Shinpo, 4 March 1927). The proposal was not a reinsurance contract on pandemic risks, but insurance on substandard risks in the form of reinsurance contracts. Although Japanese life insurers did not understand that they had serious problems on pandemic risks, they had interests in the rejection of high-risk policyholders.

An overview of the Munch Re proposal which was written by Dr. Miura is contained in the material held by the Association of Life

Insurance Companies (Historical Documents of Life Insurance in the Showa Period, Vol. 1, pp. 686–87). According to Dr. Miura, Dr. Emden proposed establishing a new company to insure high-risk policyholders in Japan. The new company would be a joint venture with Munch Re, and should make reinsurance contracts with the Munch Re. As for Japanese primary insurers, they would be permitted to make use of the rate table for high-risk policyholders made by the Munch Re, which would reinsure 80% of substandard contracts of the new company. If there would be excess of retention limit, 20% of the excess should be reinsured. The reinsurance contract was based on the primary insurance policy, and the primary insurers should pay premiums yearly and could pay back new business commission and collection fee.

Half of the contracts of the new joint corporation should be ceded to Munch Re. And then, the new company should pay a half of the premiums to Munch Re, as well as premiums for excess reinsurance. In return, Munch Re would have the responsibility to make claim payments to the new company, and also should make a payment of 5% of operating costs and commission for excess reinsurance.

All Japanese life insurance companies gathered in the Association of Life Insurance Companies and discussed the proposal. At last, they made a decision. They said that insurance for high-risk customers was necessary for all life insurance companies, but this is a matter which could wait. Furthermore, they concluded that it would be carried into effect by themselves, after studying it and accumulating their own data on substandard risks (Historical Documents of Life Insurance in the Showa Period, Vol. 1 p. 685).

The life insurers created a commission for research on substandard risks which started on July 1927. Mr. Masato Isono, a lecturer of Kyoto Imperial University, was appointed chief of the commission. He completed his mission for the commission in 6 years. A newspaper reported that the table was a perfect one for an insurance company because the data was limited to persons rejected by insurers, as well as based on our complete family register system (ibid.). Moreover, the article emphasized that the report had good effect to an assured who regarded it as a substandard risk. It said, 'Persons who regarded as an invalid or having anamnesis could not make life insurance contracts, but the table could make them insurable under new contract conditions' (Tokyo Asahi News, 1 December 1932). For example, person who had *Rasselgerausch* could be insured with extra premium if they were aged over 40 years).

The final report was completed in February 1933 and was published as a Report for Research on substandard risks by the Association of Life Insurance Companies. The Association asked special members to investigate the business practice on substandard risks. Lastly, 'a Guideline on the establishment of special life insurance company for substandard' was agreed by all members of the Association in November 1934 (Historical Documents of Life Insurance in the Showa Period, Vol. 1, p. 685). And then, Kyoei Life insurance company was established by joint capitals of all life insurance companies in December 1935. The company insured both primary insurance and reinsurance of substandard risks in Japan.

While the movement described above towards substandard insurance under leadership of the Association was completed, some life insurance companies had been looking for their own measures on substandard insurance. We will discuss this case in the next section.

11.4 Provisional Reinsurance Contract of a Japanese Life Insurance Company with a Foreign Insurer

After the indirect rejection from the Association of Life Insurance Companies, Munch Re did not give up its plan. When the commission had been investigating Japanese substandard risks, Munch Re tried to negotiate reinsurance contracts with individual life insurance companies. The Union Re, Switzerland, which was financially connected to Munch Re, provided an operation for promoting the use of reinsurance contracts for life insurance on substandard risks with individual companies (*Chugai Shogyo News*, 9 May 1931). Mr. Hans Grieshaber, a representative of Union Re, travelled to Japan and called on some companies in Osaka and Tokyo for encouraging reinsurance for life insurance on substandard risks. Osaka was the second largest commercial city, and a center of life insurance business. For example, the head office of the Nippon Life, the largest life insurer, was in Osaka. On behalf of the Association of Life Insurance Companies, Mr. Orido wrote in a business journal that in his judgment the introduction of reinsurance contracts for life insurance for substandard risks was premature (Diamond, Vol. 19, no. 15, 11 May 1931). Nevertheless, a Japanese life insurance company was prepared for making reinsurance contracts with the Union Re on policies issued on substandard risks. Toyo Life insurance company decided to make a provisional reinsurance contract with Union Re. The Toyo Life began to sell substandard life insurance. After reinsurance with Munch Re and Union Re had completed, the Government would permit to sell it (*Osaka Mainichi News*, 13 June 1931). But actually, the authority did not approve the Toyo Life's application. And then, Toyo Life applied for the authority to issue life insurance contracts on substandard risks.

As to application of substandard life insurance, Shigenao Kanai, a managing director, said, 'we made a provisional reinsurance contract on substandard risks with Munch Re. Just after the application was approved by the authority, we would like to make formal contract with Munch Re, and start in a life policy insuring substandard risks. We investigated substandard risks, but we can accomplish nothing without accumulating experience in the business. Although our experience was not enough, we agreed with the thinking of Dr. Grienhaber, and tried to follow his ways experimentally. I would like to emphasize the introduction was not for pursuing profits, but only for experiments. Consequently, the introduction of life insurance for substandard risks was not an eccentric decision but a trial for study and experience for all Japanese life insurers. Toyo Life was sure enough to apply the license of sub-standard life insurance. The company made a provisional contract with foreign reinsurer ahead of the other life insurers', *Ginko Hoken Jiho*, No. 1522, 20 May 1931). Toyo Life Insurance Company was established in October 1900 in the name of Kyokei Life. The company renamed Toyo Life in January 1905. In the early financial troubles, Jiro Odaka (1866–1920) made an effort for rebuilding its business. After his death in 1920, his son, Housaku Odaka (1894–1944), succeeded the business as a president. Keizo Shibusawa (1896–1963), a grandson of Eiichi Shibusawa (1840–1931), became a director in 1928. The Odaka family had intimate relation with Eiichi Shibusawa who was one of the most eminent business leaders in the Meiji Era. Although Sigenao Kanai (1887–1979) who was an excellent businessman and a son-in-law of Jiro Odaka became the managing director in 1931, the business performance had been still poor. Lastly, all life contracts of the company were transferred comprehensively in September 1936 to the Teikoku Life (Report Toyo Life several years).

Understanding the above, Toyo Life emphasized that Japanese life insurers should acquire considerable experience in the substandard life business, and its trial would contribute to Japanese business in the future. We cannot deny that there was a strategic viewpoint to get more new business in the severe competition period just after the Showa Financial

Collapse in 1928, but it was also true that the managing director believed that the insurance for substandard risks needed business experience before introducing the plan of the Association of Life Insurance Company.

Although Toyo Life believed optimistically that the company would get the license, the authority did not approve it. There is no evidence on why the license was denied. Although the Association of Life Insurance Companies did not like a trial by an individual company, we could not find any negative pressures on Toyo Life from the Association. At this time, it was decided that life insurance for substandard risks would be introduced by all life insurance companies. And then the private introduction of this sort of insurance by individual companies was clearly forbidden.

Before closing the section, it will be interesting to point out the difference in the organization of the insurance business before and after WWII. After the WWII, competition in the life insurance market was organized by the Ministry of Finance (MOF). The Association of Life Insurance Companies changed from the controlling agency to a trade association during the war. After the defeat, the Association was reorganized as a trade association and renamed the Life Insurance Association again. In the process of the reorganization, the MOF tried to rebuild the life business in collaboration with the life insurers. At this time, the regulatory framework was drastically changed. The life insurance companies became more cooperative with each other than in the old Association, and continued the trait of being cooperative with the MOF that began in the war economy. The MOF also made an effort to create a developing but stable market in life insurance under rate regulations and entrance restrictions (Yoneyama 1997). Compared to the postwar life insurance system, the action of the Toyo Life looked unusual. Under the Association of Life Insurance Companies, the system before the WWII, the member companies did not always have the same strategy and opinions. In fact, Toyo Life was a formal member of the Association, but it decided to follow its own strategy on insurance contracts for substandard risks. Under the postwar life insurance system, no company followed a strategy opposed to the one determined by the Life Insurance Association. A managing director said in a journal, 'Fortunately the investigation on Japanese sub-standard lives made advance by a committee of the Association, but it took a long time for introducing sub-standard life insurance in practice. Since our insurance would make lots of experience on sub-standard lives, it was sure that the experience would be use of introduction of the sub-standard insurance system by the Association'. 'It is happy if our advance trial would be use for introducing the sub-standard insurance system by the Association' (*Ginko Hoken Jiho*, No. 1522, 20 May 1931). It is clear that the managing director did not believe that his plan competed with the project of the Association, but such an action was not just a cooperative one after the WWII.

11.5 Introduction of Life Insurance for Substandard Risks

As we have shown, after the Association of Life Assurance Companies published the Report on Life Insurance for Substandard Risks in February 1933, the Association established a special committee for putting it into effect (*Showa Seimei Hoken Shioryo*, Vol. 1, p. 685). When a draft plan was completed, they began to make a final plan in June 1934 (Tokyo Asahi Newspaper, 29 May 1934). A board for the establishment of substandard life insurance company was started in November, finally 'by joining capitals from every life assurance company, Kyoei Life Reassurance company, Ltd., was established in December 1935' (Showa Seimei Hoken Shiryo, Vol. 1, p. 685).

We should recognize the characteristics of life insurance for substandard risks in Japan. The main points of the final plan for the launch of the business are the following. The members consisted of 16 persons, who were mainly representatives of life insurers, including 2 members from the Association of Life Assurance Companies. The name and company of members are as follows. Tsuneto Yamashita (Meiji Life), Takao Takada (Meiji Life), Natuji Natori (Teikoku Life), Giichiro Aso(Chiyoda Mutual Life), Otoine Tanaka (Nippon Life), Toshikazu Suzuki (Dai-Ichi Mutual Life), Makoto Hirasawa (Daido Life), Kiyomatsu Takeshita (Yasuda Life), Bungei Terumichi (Aikoku Life), Shigenao Kanai (Toyo Life), Chikutaro Nosaka (Sumitomo Life), Tatuji Noe (Mitsui Life), Yataro Takahashi (Nikka Life), Gido Maura (The Assosiation), and Tamesaburo Tamaki (The Association). First, a part of the insurance for substandard rising all primary life insurers should be reinsured by the new reinsurance company. Second, primary insurers reinsure only the difference between claims and reserve. They said the reinsurance method was so-called 'rest premium reinsurance'. Third, the primary life insurance companies should receive reinsurance promotion from the new company. Lastly, the new company would reinsure both substandard and large risks (Jiji Shinpo, 8 August 1934).

Just before the start of the new company, the descriptions of business were changed with some minor revisions. The capital was set at 2 million yen of which one quarter should be paid initially. The line of business was limited only to life insurance for substandard risks, and the introduction of reinsurance business for ordinary lives should be discussed further. Moreover, the limitation of insurance amount of substandard lives changed to 10 thousand yen from 20 thousand yen (Board for Substandard Life Assurance nominated, *Tokyo Asahi News*, 28 November 1934).

The capital was collected from all life insurers which were members of the Association of Life Insurance Companies. They had already experimented in forming the Life Insurance Securities Joint Stock Company, whose aim was to support securities by buying together. The joint provision of capital from all life insurers was not a matter of concern. This company was only an institution which supported the price of securities by life insurance assets. The result of the meeting between the Minister of Finance and life insurers at 27 June 1930 introduced the establishment (Showa Seimei Hoken Shiryo, Vol. 1, p. 70).Munich Re and Swiss Union Re dispatched Mr. Grieshaber hoping to invest in the new company. A newspaper reported that (on Japanese side) the joining with a foreign company was not absolutely unacceptable given the purpose of establishing a new company, but they would wait to give any answer on reassurance business, until they had checked the results of the new company (Tokyo Asahi Newspaper, 25 April 1935).

The new life reinsurance company, Kyoei Life Reinsurance Company, Ltd., received its license in January 1936, and prepared to open for business. At first the primary life insurers did not respond positively to the availability of reinsurance for life insurance for substandard risks. The initial plan provided that the businesses of the Kyoei were 'both reinsurance for the primary life insurers and direct underwriting of substandard risks without using a direct sales force'. However, many life insurers could not underwrite substandard risks because of no articles of incorporation were provided for insurance for substandard risks at that time. So, the new company lost hope growing its reinsurance business rapidly just after the opening (Chugai Shogyo Newspaper, 8 February 1936). Since the company wasted time changing its plans to concentrate on direct underwriting of life insurance for substandard risks, the opening of business was delayed. In the meantime, demands for reinsurance on substandard risks gradually expanded (*Hochi Newspaper*, 1 August 1936, *Chugai Syogyo Newspaper*, 22 August 1936). Finally, one of the most important life insurers, the Nippon Life decided to apply for a license to sell life insurance for substandard risks and others followed it (Tokyo Asahi Newspaper, 20, 9, 1936).

11.6 Historical Lessons from the Introduction of Life Reinsurance Before WWII

Reinsurance is not a wholly new idea, but it is an old and traditional technology for diversifying risks. Is this out of fashion? No, it is still important in global markets. Although the art of reinsurance has not changed, the important factors connected with reinsurance were changing dynamically especially after the turn of the century. For example, the development of ART, the evolution of ICT, and the environmental changes were deeply connected with the changes of the reinsurance market. We should recognize that the reinsurance business and market have been changing globally.

Before the WWII, Japanese life insurers had a chance for getting knowledge and experience in the reinsurance business from the European reinsurance companies. But they postponed the possibility of cooperation with European companies. Unfortunately, the Kyoei Life Reinsurance Company did not make any arrangements with European reinsurers. It mainly depended on the war economy and political factors. Nonetheless economic and business forces were also important.

First, the Japanese life insurers did not place so much merit on life reassurance. True, pandemic risks like the 'Spanish flu' could affect the life insurer's decisions, but almost all life insurers managed to pay their insurance claims. Consequently, they were confident that they could diversify pandemic risks.

Japanese life insurers were interested in the plan of Munch Re because it was not about pandemic risks but rather about substandard risks. Munch Re had considerable knowledge and information, as well as reinsurance technology. It may be interesting that Japanese life insurers were not necessary to have a device of diversifying substandard risks, but to use it for saving the sales costs. An Economic Journal said, 'From 10 to 20% of potential clients would be usually rejected by medical check. It ended up being to total waste of sales person's efforts. Life assurance for substandard lives is necessary for saving sales costs' (The Economist (Japan), 1 February, 1927).

Next, although the Japanese life insurers had an interest in life reassurance for saving sales costs, why did they reject the plan of the European reinsurers? The key to solve the question is in Mr. Kanai's remark. He told that 'the profit of life insurers deeply depended upon life assets. Policy dividend and shareholder dividend were paid mainly from profit by difference between expected interest rates and actual interest rates' (Hoken Ginko Johore, No. 1522, 20 May 1931). On the contrary, other profit were achieve because the actual death rate was lower than the estimated rate was not so much, as well as profit from managing costs.

The dependence on the profit from life asset was the most important factor that withdrew the introduction of life reassurance business. A newspaper reported that since a half of profits were earned by life assets in Japanese life insurers, they lost the profits by reassuring their business (Hoken Ginko Johore, No. 1522, 20 May 1931). In short, too much profits from life assets were features of life product in Japan, if they reassure their business, they lose its profit at the same time.

Under the plan of Dr. Emden, the primary life insurers should reassure 80% of the business to reassurance company, Japanese insurers were not willing to lose the possible profits. After all, the profit structure of Japanese life insurance market induced a decision to reject the Foreign reinsurance company's plan. They did not prefer the transfer of reserves even among Japanese companies (Tokyo Asahi Newspaper 29 May 1934). Although they recognized the importance of international networks, the characteristics in profit structure prevented Japanese life insurers from developing these connections globally. Mr. Kanai emphasized the importance of internationalization in an interview. 'I believe our life business should be more international. By the exchange of insurance technology and information, we should make more profits, and the sub-standard life assurance will be a typical case in Japan' (*Hoken Ginko Jiho*, No. 1522, 20 May 1931, p. 692).

After the WWII, life assurance market was well organized under the supervision of the Ministry of Finance. They could keep stable fair profits in exchange for competitions in price and products. The structure prevented them to develop their business in the form of reinsurance. The more stable their business became, the less interests in reassurance they had.

The situation has changed in Japan after 1996, when the insurance business act was revised largely. Recently, the strategies of the larger life insurers are diversifying. Some companies pursue to be more international, and the others concentration is in domestic markets. Anyway, international networks and global knowledge connected to insurance business became more important. Japanese life assurance companies have been still late comers in international business because of its historical reasons. At the same time, they abandoned to learn related knowledge to life reassurance, and the possibility to develop life reassurance business was lost in the future.

References

Bulletin of the Association of Life Assurance Companies, Vol. 16 and Vol. 25.
Historical Manuscripts. 1963. Vol. 1, Kyoei Life Assurance Company.
Showa Seimei Hoken Shiryo (Historical documents of Life Assurance in the Showa era). 1970. Vol. 1, Tokyo.
Takau Yoneyama, 1997. Transformation of the Post-war System of Japanese Insurance Business Dobunkan Publisher, Ltd. pp. 1–159.
Takau Yoneyama, 2012. "Ch.21 Japan: The Role of Insurance in the Rapid Modernization of Japan." In *World Insurance: The Evolution of a Global Risk Network*, ed. Peter Borscheid and Niels Viggo Hayeter. Oxford: Oxford University Press.
The Association of Life Assurance Companies, ed. 1933. Reports of Research on Sub-standard Lives in Japan. The Association.

Others

Annual Reports of Nippon Life, Dai-ichi Mutual Life, Meiji Life, Toyo Life, and So On in Each Year.
Newspapers and Journals: Tokyo Asahi, Hoken Ginko Jiho, Osaka Mainiti, Jiji Shinpo, Hochi.

CHAPTER 12

Conclusions: Reinsurance, Politics, and Missed Opportunities

Niels-Viggo Haueter

The chapters in this book, unsurprisingly, bring out a variety of factors that influenced differing paths in different markets. Ben P. A. Gales argues that alternative secondary risk markets reduced the need for a local reinsurance industry in the Netherlands. Robert Wright looks into regulation that turned out to be the main hindrance to the formation of professional reinsurers in the U.S. Inversely to Gales, he argues that it was the absence of a local reinsurance industry that fostered the development of alternative risk transfer mechanisms, rather than vice versa.

Giorgio Cingolani and Giandomenico Piluso show how, in Italy, the government directly intervened in the private markets with state-backed insurance and reinsurance, although with limited success in the long run. Pablo Gutiérrez and Jerònia Pons describe how Spain in the 1940s followed the Italian approach of state intervention and forced the direct industry to resort to corporate networks. While these functioned under

N.-V. Haueter (✉)
Swiss Re, Zürich, Switzerland
e-mail: NielsViggo_Haueter@swissre.com

© The Author(s), under exclusive license to Springer Nature Switzerland AG 2021
L. Caruana de las Cagigas and A. Straus (eds.), *Role of Reinsurance in the World*, Palgrave Studies in Economic History,
https://doi.org/10.1007/978-3-030-74002-3_12

an autarkic economy, the system collapsed when Spain rejoined the international economy. Spain's subsequent dependence on foreign risk capital and expertise is illustrated in Leonardo Caruana's description of the influence of foreign reinsurers on Spanish insurers from the 1960s on. Gustavo Del Angel's research on Mexico reveals the difficulties of dealing with the erratic risks affecting the agricultural sector and the government's limited success in steering the development of agricultural insurance and reinsurance.

Takau Yoneyama depicts a cautious Japanese life insurance market that kept the need for life reinsurance low but embraced an initiative led by a foreign reinsurer that promised to enhance the life market with formerly uninsurable lives. Sweden, unlike the other markets here, appears to have been much more growth driven, and more successful. Yet, according to Mikael Lönnborg, the national reinsurance market virtually vanished in the 1990s. It had been challenged by a combination of losses from natural catastrophes, deregulation and market consolidation, and radical changes in product focus of one of their dominating insurers. France, finally, as André Straus writes, was one of the few markets in this collection to bring about a top tier private reinsurer, albeit only rather late.

12.1 Path Dependency

The universal truth, that these markets acknowledged, was that they all needed their own reinsurance industry. Yet, aspirations mostly failed. As Ben P. A. Gales puts it in his research on the Netherlands, reinsurance was a "dream not achieved". Why did this dream come about? And why did most markets not succeed in creating a significant national industry?

It is tempting to assume that risk specifics determined the evolution of the industry in respective areas. Certainly, reinsurance markets were created by risks. And risk landscapes differed. Especially regions exposed to irregular and severe hazards such as natural catastrophes needed reinsurance and consequently developed larger markets. Yet Gales cautions that the characteristics of markets and path-dependent evolution had stronger impacts than national risk landscapes. This probably does not apply for the demand for reinsurance. The U.S. developed the largest reinsurance market in the world, not just because of the size of the country but because of its exposure to virtually all kinds of natural catastrophes and, in the nineteenth and twentieth centuries, the world's largest city conglomerations prone to fire hazards. Japan, similarly exposed to natural catastrophes, also created a huge demand for reinsurance. Yet, both countries only developed their reinsurance industry relatively late.

Gales point is, however, very valid when we look at the supply of reinsurance. Path dependency very much appears to have determined the global distribution of supply. Reinsurance companies thrived mostly on the European continent. Even in Europe, it was by no means a widespread phenomenon but, in the long run, mainly the privilege of two countries. Germany and Switzerland emerged as the most active players early on and have kept this position until today. Britain had chosen a different path from the start when it developed a range of alternative ways to cede excessive risks via coinsurance, pooling, and reciprocity. In addition, some of Britain's insurance companies were big enough to provide risk capital and reinsurance to the rest of the market, including foreign companies. Consequently, the Anglo-Saxon market-based economy did not produce any significant reinsurance companies but created the dominating global risk exchange, the so-called London market.

The British alternatives to reinsurance were at least partly adopted in most of the countries described in this book. They reduced the perceived need for professional or continental reinsurance as it eventually came to be called. In most world markets, hardly any significant new reinsurance companies came into existence before some decades into the post-World War II era. The reinsurance paths of Germany and Switzerland on the other hand were set early on when these markets brought about some of the first reinsurance companies. Their head-start made it difficult for competitors to catch up.

Several examples, however, show that path dependency did not last forever. In the post-World War II era, most of the countries described here did catch up, at least to some degree. Japan's *Toa Re* was already founded in 1940 as a response to the lack of foreign reinsurance. *Toa Re* started international business in 1952. The Netherlands saw the *Nederlandse Reassurantie Group (NRG)* being formed out of a merger in 1968. In France, *SCOR* emerged out of the state-backed *Caisse Centrale de Réassurance (CCR)* in 1970. Spanish insurer *Mapfre* created *Mapfre Re* in 1982 and immediately set out to expand globally. Growth was largely achieved through mergers and acquisitions. The two U.S. reinsurers, *General Re* and *Employers Re* both significantly increased their market shares after World War II, as Wright demonstrates. Even though neither achieved a size comparable to the market leaders, they, respectively, had risen to global positions four and three by 1990. Their speedy growth had also been fuelled by mergers and acquisitions. *General Re*, acquired *Cologne Re*, the first independent reinsurer founded in the 1840s. In 1998, *Berkshire Hathaway* in turn acquired *General Cologne Re* and managed to join the rank of first tier reinsurers. The global lead of just two companies, however, Munich Re and Swiss Re, has persisted until today.

12.2 Reinsurance Versus Alternative Risk Sharing

While the market leaders absorbed the lion share of professional reinsurance around the world, they could not absorb all excess risks in the industry. Alternative methods therefore grew along with the spread of reinsurance. Gales raises the question if, then, reinsurance was necessary at all. The rise of the several large companies mentioned above suggests that there was demand for reinsurance. Part of the reason for their growth after World War II lay in the more or less continuous upswing of the economy and with this the insurance industry. But reinsurance grew faster than direct insurance in the post-war era. Partly, reinsurance followed a general trend towards larger corporations and conglomerates. But the particular reason for the growth of the industry also had to do with a changing risk landscape. Risks grew exponentially in size and number with large airplanes, factories, tankers, and so on. Such risks were difficult to deal with through co-insurance and reciprocity. Also, large single risks required more engagement than just offering capacity. Risk management, as Caruana demonstrates, became an essential part of reinsurance services.

So, was reinsurance necessary before the war? Obviously, reinsurers argued in favour. Their clients clearly thought so too, as becomes apparent in several of the histories told here. One aspect not dealt with in these chapters helps understand why. Early proportional reinsurance had a different function from later products that capped the maximum exposure of insurers and protected against fluctuations of balance sheets. Traditional proportional business, apart from spreading risks, was basically a way to provide direct insurers with risk capital so that they could expand their business. For growing markets, reinsurance became essential.

Regulators, as well, generally highlighted the importance of reinsurance. Some explicitly tried to promote professional reinsurance over alternatives, as illustrated in Wright's chapter. William H. Hotchkiss, whom Wright quotes, offered detailed explanations why reinsurance companies were important for the U.S. when presenting to the insurance commissioners' 1914 National Convention in Chicago. Substitutes such as reinsurance bureaus and clearing houses, surplus line practices, pools, and the like, he argued, were not managed professionally and prone to excessive control exercised by large companies.[1] Reinsurance by direct companies also turned out to be an imperfect substitute, as it implied sharing market and business intelligence with competitors. To avoid this dilemma, insurers had to seek cover across national borders. Many insurance companies were thus in favour of creating an independent local reinsurance industry. The foundations of the first reinsurers such as *Cologne Re* and *Swiss Re* were indeed explained with the need to create national risk capacity to circumvent foreign providers.

12.3 Reinsurance and Autarky

As the examples of Italy and Spain here witness, the strongest voices for national reinsurance came from politicians. Mostly, they advocated some form of state-guided national institutions. What were the reasons for politicians' call for national reinsurance? Gales mentions political concern already in the mid-nineteenth century over a Dutch market that did not attract enough international business. A national reinsurance industry, it was believed, would attract foreign clients and boost Dutch insurance.

In the 1920s, the USSR, Italy, Chile, and Turkey led the way to state reinsurance. Business was usually enforced with restraints on foreign companies and compulsory cessions. This not only provoked criticism from the international reinsurance community. Insurers were also wary of the compulsory cession of risks to state-owned institutions. In some cases, they resorted to founding their own pools or reinsurance companies to prevent government reinsurance such as in Mexico where *Alianza* and *La Union Reaseguradora Mexicana* were founded in 1940 and 1946, respectively.

State reinsurance could, of course, have its advantages, if not for the markets, then at least for governments. Mainly, it allowed to easily collect market information to regulate insurers. Spain's *Official Committee on Reinsurance*, for example, only required one per cent cession of risks but used this to gain market intelligence. Similarly, the French state-backed

---

[1] Hotchkiss (1914: 4ff.).

Caisse Centrale de Réassurance (*CCF*), founded in 1948, required only a four per cent cession of risks from insurers but through these gained an excellent overview of the market. The same goal was partly behind the foundations of state-backed reinsurers in Italy, and Japan as well as in other markets not featuring in this book.

Several problems emerged with state reinsurance. Unless done out of economies with a strong currency, national reinsurance became closely tied to economic autarky. As the example of Spain described by Pons and Gutiérrez shows, this could go more than awry. Any connection with the world economy implied foreign exchange risks. These had to be reinsured internationally. One of the main problems, though, was that autarkic reinsurance was at odds with the need to spread risks internationally. Foreign reinsurance fulfilled an important function in spreading risks beyond political borders. For states with weak currencies, taking out foreign reinsurance could furthermore help avoid depreciation of risk reserves.

In many cases, therefore, the call for state reinsurance must have been based on other motives. It appears that politicians often judged reinsurance by the tenets of mercantilism. Their main argument was that the outflow of currencies in the form of reinsurance premiums would negatively impact current account balances, ignoring the fact that loss payments flowed back into the economy. Problems arose as state reinsurers were hardly able to absorb all the business that was directed in their way without state guarantees or subsidies. Especially since they were often forced to accept bad risks that were difficult to place on the private market. Also operating costs tended to be higher than in private companies. Self-sufficient reinsurance could, if at all, only function in conjunction with exporting reinsurance services to create a large enough pool to accommodate national risks.

But not all countries were able to export. Fewer still, achieved a positive net export balance. Countries needed economic and political stability, a strong currency, and market friendly regulation. Most state operations were then forced to reinsure their risks again on the international markets via so-called retrocession. One way around the dilemma of international risk spreading would have been to create cross-border networks or regional reinsurers. There were only few attempts, though. In the markets described here, only Spain, although in vain, tried to set up a Hispanic network of national reinsurers together with Chile and

Argentina in the 1930s. It fell victim to a lack of interest on the South American continent.[2]

The strongest government intervention in the cases described here happened in countries with totalitarian regimes and developing or struggling economies. The histories of Italy and Spain suggest that national pride played a significant role. In many ways, the conditions in the two countries resembled each other. Both felt the impact of nationalism turning into fascism. In both markets, insurers looked to reinsurance to provide risk capital to support the growth of their then underdeveloped markets. Italy, as described by Cingolani and Piluso, for some time remained trapped in the vicious circle of a sluggishly evolving direct market. The country was among the earliest to nationalise life insurance with the foundation of the *Istituto Nazionale delle Assicurazioni* (*INA*) in 1912. In 1923 the market was liberalised, but *INA* remained a state-supported competitor and furthermore mandated life insurers to reinsure forty per cent of their premiums. The non-life market, from 1921 on, was to be reinsured by the *Unione italiana di riassicurazione* (*Uniorias*) in which *INA* held a majority.

Its initial success was limited. A contemporary comparison of *Uniorias*' activities revealed that, in the 1920s, it was forced to recycle about eighty per cent of its non-life risks through retrocession. This compared to less than forty per cent retrocession of, for example, the *Compagnie Française de Réassurance Générales* (*C.F.R.G.*), a private company of the same size in France. *Uniorias* furthermore generated operating costs that were almost four times those of *C.F.R.G.* By the late 1920s, the company had to apply for government subsidies. Not all the misfortunes were though due to bad management. Severe problems were added as the government forced loss making marine business on *Uniorias*.[3]

The political approach in Italy is surprising since the market would have offered a more than viable alternative. The disintegration of Austria–Hungary turned *Generali* and *RAS* into Italian insurers in 1918. Both were significant global players and, albeit direct insurers, also very active in reinsurance. The addition of their Austria–Hungarian parts to Italy provided the country with even more surplus of reinsurance capital, mostly in fire business. In fact, it secured Italy the capacity to be a net

---

[2] Swiss Re Company Archives (SRCA) 10.169 265.10.
[3] SRCA 10.145 792.01.

provider of reinsurance. The limitations of the Italian reinsurance market, however, forced *Generali* and *RAS* to turn to the international markets, both to sell their products and to seek reinsurance cover for themselves. By the 1930s, they had become such important reinsurance players in the Spanish market that contemporaries attributed the severe anti-foreign measures adopted by the Spanish authorities to their presence.[4] More research is clearly needed to find out why the need for reinsurance in Italy could not be covered by these two direct companies and why professional, albeit state-backed reinsurance was preferred.

In Spain, reinsurance became even more of a political playground. This was certainly a reaction to the fact that Spain had one of the highest proportions of foreign insurers in Europe around 1930,[5] despite having implemented an insurance law in 1908 to curb the presence of foreigners. As for reinsurance, Spain was almost entirely dependent on imports. But nationalisation plans turned out to be ill conceived. Partly, this was due to a plethora of authorities responsible for insurance. But there was also a problem in pursuing nationalisation plans too conspicuously. Spain tried to make foreign reinsurers pay for civil war losses which in most contracts had been excluded. In order not to upset these companies, the government played down endeavours to nationalise reinsurance. Plans to create either a public–private or a fully state-owned reinsurance institute were officially abandoned after Swiss and British intervention, supported by the Spanish insurer *Fénix*.[6] Meanwhile, the director of *La Equitativa* with the backing of politicians tried to create a reinsurance monopoly for his company. The basic idea was to channel all Spanish reinsurance through this operation and secure international reinsurance capital through retrocession. The plan was heavily opposed by other Spanish insurers. A more secret plan to have *La Equitativa* act as a front for the Spanish government to set up a reinsurance operation in Switzerland to access hard currency was equally unsuccessful.[7] However, once a compromise on the civil war losses was in sight, plans for government steered reinsurance intensified.

---

[4] SRCA 10.169 265.09.
[5] *The Review*, March 13, 1931.
[6] SRCA 10.169 265.10.
[7] SRCA 10.169 265.02.

These plans, as described by Gutierrez and Pons, depended heavily on economic autarky and on the war in Europe. The decision to focus state intervention on hull reinsurance was short-sighted as marine business rates drastically declined after the war. The 1942 decree of the *Committee on Marine Insurance* to only reinsure with foreign reinsurers in exchange for reciprocal business was largely ignored by Spanish insurers.[8] Also, the temporary autonomy of Spanish insurance networks only worked within a closed economy and proved more than vulnerable in the end, as they made the country even more dependent on international reinsurance. While the direct sector managed the transition of Spain's integration into the world economy somewhat well, its national reinsurance industry almost entirely collapsed. As becomes evident in Leonardo Caruana's chapter, years of isolation exacerbated the dependency of the Spanish direct industry to training from foreign reinsurers.

12.4 Politics and Limits of Insurability

In some areas, however, state intervention was even welcomed by the reinsurance industry. Two types of risks were especially difficult to insure and reinsure—natural catastrophes and violence related risks such as war, civil commotion, and terrorism. Such risks have always been and continue to be a challenge for direct insurers as well as reinsurers and, ultimately, for governments. Since governments act as lenders of last resort, many started investigating state insurance and reinsurance to avoid fiscal impacts. Government backstops that functioned along reinsurance principles were adopted in many markets around the world. Government cover for terrorism, for example, was introduced after the impact of 9/11 in the U.S. Similarly, France created a public–private partnership *GAREAT* in 2002 to protect against terrorism. Government solutions for natural catastrophes were even more common. In the 1940s, Spain created a pool for uninsurable risk including natural catastrophes as well as war and civil commotion risks. France in 1960s set up state backstops for natural catastrophes and agricultural risks.

Mexico was thus no exception. The country had initiated several laws, credit institutions, and insurance services much earlier to support the agricultural sector but the market remained too small to be interesting for

---

[8] SRCA 10.169 265.09.

reinsurers, as Del Angel describes. The creation of *Anagsa* in 1961 was an attempt at finally creating a centrally responsible organisation that could also provide reinsurance. Government support at least managed to spread agricultural insurance so much that by the 1980s, it had reached the highest ever distribution. This came at a price, though, as moral hazard and corruption increased. When collecting state-guaranteed indemnities became more attractive than farming, agricultural productivity dropped.

The U.S. as well has a long history of failed attempts at controlling agricultural risks. The *Federal Crop Insurance Corporation (FCIC)*, for example, established in the wake of the Dust Bowl in the 1930s to promote economic stability for the agricultural sector triggered a record number of political debates. Attempts to stabilise it with reinsurance in the 1940s did not help. Future research into these debates might help explain some of the confusion over reinsurance regulation described in Wright's chapter. Looking at the numerous reinsurance bills that were proposed for flood, war, terrorism, health coverage, or private pension plans, it becomes clear that a wide range of U.S. politicians were more than aware of the importance of reinsurance, yet they tolerated or even promoted the regulatory hindrances for private reinsurance.

As Wright points out, reinsurance was on the agenda already in the 1920s, when a *Liberty Insurance League* that would have reinsured member organisations was proposed to Congress. Reinsurance very much appears as a magic trick that kept resurging on political agendas when insurance failed. Yet, overall the success of government reinsurance in the U.S. was limited, be it state reinsurance of private pension plans that was proposed to Congress in 1966[9] or President Johnson's *Urban Property Protection and Reinsurance Act* in 1968 to protect the fire insurance industry against losses from riots that was abandoned soon after (Haueter, 2021). Later initiatives such as President Bush's *Terrorism Risk Insurance Act (TRIA)* in 2002 were more successful, although it has been criticised for crowding out the private sector. More research is required to solve the conundrum why U.S. politicians accepted or even promoted policies that hindered the development of a sound national U.S. reinsurance

---

[9] "Federal Reinsurance of Private Pension Plans, Hearing Before the Committee on Finance, United States Senate", *Eighty-ninth Congress, Second Session on S. 1575, a Bill to Establish a Self-supporting Federal Reinsurance Program to Protect Employees in the Enjoyment of Certain Rights Under Private Pension Plans, August 15, 1966*.—United States. Congress. Senate. Committee on Finance.

industry. The numerous Senate debates point to an oddity. State reinsurance was often seen as interfering less with the private sector than direct state insurance. Dwight Eisenhower thus proposed "limited Government reinsurance service" in order to avoid difficulties with "socialized medicine" (quoted from Haueter, 2021).[10] Senator John F. Kennedy, when debating state reinsurance versus state insurance after the Great Kansas River Flooding in the 1950s argued that to "the extent that broad, economical and fair coverage could result, [state] reinsurance would be the ideal way to provide flood insurance with the greatest amount of private enterprise" (quoted from Haueter, 2021).[11]

Possibly, the virtual absence of American reinsurance companies made politicians feel that they did not invade private market territory. Also, the direct industry may have been more interested in indirect subsidies from government reinsurance than in doing business with professional reinsurers. The twisted journeys of the various U.S. state insurance and reinsurance schemes to control natural catastrophes did, however, rarely produce the desired results. The advent of innovative products for risk transfer thus provided attractive alternatives from the 1990s on.

12.5 Free Markets

So why did the markets with less government intervention not develop exporting reinsurance companies? Sweden, France, and the Netherlands all had thriving insurance markets and benefitted from a high degree of political and economic stability during peacetime. Overall, their national reinsurance sectors certainly were more successful than other markets featuring in this volume. Sweden was early in founding reinsurers, although mostly captive organisations that did not last long. The Netherlands saw a relative surge in reinsurance companies after World War I through the 1930s.[12] However, hardly any of the early Dutch reinsurers reached a significant size. France was even one of the earliest market leaders in reinsurance, albeit owing to its large and important direct insurers rather than professional reinsurance companies. But it was also

---

[10] "Annual Message to the Congress on the State of the Union," *Public Papers of the Presidents of the United States, 1954.*

[11] "Kennedy-Saltonstall Bill, *1955 Senate Banking and Currency Committee Hearings on Federal Disaster Insurance.*

[12] SRCA database of reinsurance foundations.

among the earliest countries to found reinsurers. Trade press lists several foundations of reinsurance companies already in the 1860s.[13] By 1900 a total of ten had come about. Overall, more than fifty reinsurers were founded in France (including subsidiaries of foreign companies).[14] Yet France had to wait until 1970 in order to produce a global player with *SCOR*. The company was created out of the state-backed *Caisse Centrale de Réassurance* (*CCF*).

As mentioned above, also other countries produced important reinsurers in the post-war era. Apart from Lloyd's, most important reinsurance players outside of Germany and Switzerland appear to have come about some decades after World War II. There may have been two partly opposing components that shaped supply and distribution in the post-war era. On the one hand, large risks and an overall upswing increased the demand for insurance and reinsurance. Reinsurance markets became much more interlinked as large risks had to be distributed more effectively. On the other hand, larger risks also created larger losses. The 1980s saw a series of catastrophes that continued into the 1990s such as U.S. liability crisis, Piper Alpha, Exxon Valdez, the Northridge earthquake and hurricanes Hugo and Andrew. This increased the need for well capitalised and thus large reinsurance companies while many smaller players exited the market. The M&A wave of the 1990s further consolidated the market. In this turbulent environment, *Skandia* ceased to do reinsurance but French *SCOR* grew to become the global number five reinsurer by 2014. The Swedish exit from reinsurance raises questions as to how sustainable this market-based approach was. While the case described here does not in itself provide sufficient indication that a dedicated reinsurer was more likely to succeed in a competitive environment, it would be interesting for future research to compare the two cases or other instances of large insurers' reinsurance engagement.

One more free market conundrum remains unsolved. If local reinsurance developed only sluggishly in the U.S., how was it possible for foreign reinsurers to grow their business? There were some instances when American companies could have seized the opportunity to create a national market. Yet this happened neither when German companies were banned in World War I nor when the significant Russian reinsurers were severed

---

[13] Assekuranz-Compass 1902, 1915, and 1923.

[14] SRCA database of reinsurance foundations.

from their parent companies with the 1918 revolution. The timing for an American reinsurance industry would have been ideal, not only because important foreign competitors disappeared. In addition, trust in European reinsurers overall, including those of friendly nations' diminished due to the uncertainties of the war in Europe. Yet, it was a foreign company that seized the moment. Towards the end of the war, *Swiss Re* intensified its plans to create a second reinsurance company for the U.S. market. Research into the reasons for foreign companies' continued success may thus need to look at other factors besides regulation. Could the inactivity of U.S. investors be explained with the difficulty during the war to raise the large capital amounts necessary for reinsurance? Or were American businessmen otherwise reluctant to founding reinsurance operations? After a visit to the U.S. in 1918, a *Swiss Re* director reported that American insurance experts viewed reinsurance contracts as too volatile as they could be cancelled too easily.[15] Reinsurance, he continued, was seen as a business that could not really be owned due to its participative nature. Hence, American investors shunned the business. The idea that U.S. business was somehow not at ease with reinsurance practices would support Wright's theory that market solutions were preferred. Yet not out of necessity, but out of prejudice.

12.6 Special Risks

Takau Yoneyama's story of Japanese life insurance and reinsurance can be compared with the Dutch case. In both countries, the possibility to reinsure substandard risks expanded the life markets and increased or even created the need for life reinsurance. It may be important here to clarify that reinsurance in the life sector focused on biometric risks, especially mortality, not savings. The overwhelming bulk of life business was in savings while the mortality part was comparatively modest. Both in the Netherlands and in Japan, mortality business had been kept artificially low. Dutch and Japanese life insurers were cautious in their underwriting as the authors note.

In Japan, additionally, government had capped the maximum amount of mortality benefits to ¥ 250'000 for large companies and as little as ¥ 15'000 for smaller companies and introduced high self-retention rates. As

[15] SRCA 10.170 172.02.

these could not be passed on to reinsurers, life companies restricted their underwriting. This certainly helped keep the losses from the Spanish flu relatively modest. A main reason for the cautious underwriting may be attributed to the unreliability of mortality tables at the time. In Japan, this may have been more pronounced as using English tables until 1912 proved more than inadequate for an entirely different society. Japanese insurers then switched to the so-called "Three-offices-tables" established by *Meiji*, *Nippon*, and *Teikoku*. However, they were not unilaterally used. Only in 1931 did government-tables become available. While the Three-offices-tables had attributed close to fifteen per cent mortality to influenza during the Spanish flu, its actual toll was estimated at the time to be between thirty and forty per cent.[16]

On the one hand, the restrictions of life underwriting saved the Japanese life industry during the Spanish flu, but it also hindered growth and thus created a vicious circle. The life market was simply too small to be interesting for reinsurers as no sufficient aggregates of risks could be composed. We may assume that the same is true for the Dutch market. To break this vicious circle, Japan embraced Doctor Embden's proposal for substandard business. As the Japanese savings market was strong, fierce competition made the prospect of a new business field even more attractive.

The Netherlands had taken a different path and resorted to a cooperative solution already in 1905.[17] "Substandard lives" was a niche product, but it is a well-chosen topic as it nicely illustrates the need for risk spreading and the role that reinsurance can play. The difference between the Netherlands and Japan was that the former started insuring apparently uninsurable lives before the spread of actuarial innovations for substandard risks and collective risk theories in the Netherlands. Japan, on the other hand, relied on actuarial innovation. Both approaches worked. Gales thus raises the question how far actuarial evidence was relevant for life insurance and reinsurance. In the Netherlands, he argues, market forces appear to have proved actuaries irrelevant. Indeed, life actuaries had some difficulties replacing medical examinations. Although applying actuarial

---

[16] SRCA 10.170 649.01.

[17] The Netherlands appear to have had an overall larger number of cooperative or mutual reinsurers than other markets, cf. Gerathewohl et al. (1979, 1071–1072).

calculations from the second half of the eighteenth century on had continuously improved, the problem with many life insurance risk portfolios was that they were simply too small to behave according to actuarial theory. Life insurance, at least up until the early twentieth century had difficulties creating life risk pools large enough for the law of large numbers to function.

Hence, actuarial theory often proved inadequate despite its systematic accuracy. Most life insurers continued to trust medical examination more than actuarial evaluation. However, having to submit to medical examinations lowered the appeal of life insurance. Hence the experiment by *Sun Life* in Britain to do without examinations. How could this work? It required fixing premium rates far above the actuarially fair price. This was normal practice in life insurance anyway, just to be on the safe side. As Timothy Alborn (2009) has shown, substandard insurance functioned already in Victorian societies by simply "rating up" so-called inferior lives.

Yet, substandard lives were not only interesting as a field to expand business. In fact, they had an important statistical role to fulfil. They had the potential to overcome the dilemma of too careful underwriting which prevented forming a large enough portfolio for life insurance to function. Including riskier clients helped increase the aggregates towards a better functioning of the law of large numbers. Adding reinsurance, such portfolios could form even larger aggregates. The addition of actuarial methods did not necessarily create this possibility for insurers, as Gales rightly points out. But the extension of actuarial substandard calculations to reinsurance finally made such lives insurable on an actuarially fairer level. As a footnote in the Dutch chapter reveals, even the directors of *De Hoop* were not entirely relying on intuition.

12.7 What Difference Did Reinsurance Make?

Determining the impact of reinsurance is not easy. The US Federal Insurance Office (FIO), for example, sees a positive impact of the industry on "general economic prosperity" as it helps make insurance available and affordable. This is achieved by providing capital to the direct industry, providing balance sheet protection, and by distributing insured risks (quoted from Haueter, 2021).

Perhaps it is no coincidence, that the demand for the first modern reinsurance contracts came up in the 1820s, shortly after the end of the Napoleonic wars. Although the end of the wars led to a contraction of insurance costs, safer seas caused international trade and globalisation to boom. Reinsurance provided much of the capital for insurance to grow during this time as the business model aimed at extending insurance capacity. Historically, this was done by participating proportionally in insurers' business. Providing risk capital, allowed insurers to write more business than they could back with their own capital and thus expand also internationally. This early form of reinsurance, also called treaty reinsurance, led to a peculiar legal definition in that reinsurance agreements were regulated under company law rather than contract law. In other words, reinsurance was seen as a form of cooperation. As such, reinsurance provided an umbrella for a network of insurers. In addition to providing risk capital, reinsurance was designed to stabilise the insurance industry. It had an important function in spreading risk beyond their partners' markets. It thus balanced the risks of the direct industry on a global level. This is the main reason why the business needed to be global from the start. In turn, reinsurance also allowed direct insurance to globalise. Co-insurance spread globally as a principle but its application, in contrast, remained national or at best regional.

Reinsurance also served as a sort of think-tank. By having access to client data all over the world, it could establish best practices and support clients with contract design and financial management. This went to some lengths, as Kyrtsis (2017) argues. Reinsurers had access to their partners books, strategies, and close knowledge of the capability of their management. Such an intimate relationship was not possible with co-insurance. Kyrtsis therefore argues that treaty reinsurance and the accompanying services in financial and risk management made dedicated reinsurance companies a necessity.

Besides financial management, risk management became a core competency of reinsurers. In the case of many markets, such as Spain described here, reinsurance played an important role in developing risk management frameworks and strategies for clients. This largely happened in the area of risk engineering, implying that, for example, industrial risks were equipped with safety standards. Again, the global expertise of reinsurers predestined them to spread such best practices across markets.

The industry also promoted actuarial research. Theories of how to deal with substandard risks were mostly developed in the framework of reinsurance. Swedish actuary Filip Lundberg was the first to describe the problems of small insurers' life portfolios not behaving according to the law of large numbers. He created a theory that later came to be called collective risk theory. As it relied on aggregates, Lundberg published his theory under the title 'On the Theory of Reinsurance' (Bühlmann and

Lengwiler 2017). Such theories, however, go beyond their practical application. In fact, Lundberg's and his successors work radically changed the way risk was dealt with in financial services. In some ways, collective risk theory predated later portfolio theories in modern finance.

One of the possibly most important impacts of reinsurance was its ability to deal with large catastrophes. As the U.S. and other market histories here show, governments looked to reinsurance early on to assist them in handling catastrophes. The boom after the second world war created many new risks that were impossible for a single insurance company to carry. Tankers, amusement parks, space shuttles, airplanes and so on contributed to the demand for reinsurance. But perhaps the biggest impact was with natural catastrophes. Large parts of the losses from the San Francisco earthquake in 1906 were absorbed by London and continental reinsurers. At that time, the industry still had to rely on sufficient capital backing alone. The earthquake was one of a series of large events that contributed to the view that natural catastrophes are virtually not insurable. Storms and floods provided more proof that nature could not be insured. Such risks called for a different kind of contract as proportional participation was too risky. The business increasingly used so-called excess of loss, or XL contracts. These had already been invented in the nineteenth century but saw an exponential growth with the rise of large risks. The main difference to treaty reinsurance was that XL capped the liability of clients at a certain level from where on it carried losses up to a specified maximum. This implied a shift from mainly capital provision to clients' balance sheet protection. It also allowed for, at least partial, insurance of large risks as liabilities were capped.

This was combined with a new invention. In the 1970s and 1980s, reinsurance started developing computer-based risk modelling techniques. Maps of, for example, flood prone areas allowed calculating maximum losses and identify the insurable parts as well as fixing actuarially fair prices. Early models proved rather inadequate for some events but eventually the techniques became more sophisticated. In conjunction with the development of new alternative risk transfer products that Wright mentions, such risk modelling helped attract risk capital from outside the insurance and reinsurance community. Wright describes the interest of the U.S. government in such products developed by the reinsurance industry. Other players got interested as well. The World Bank, especially, as well as several UN organisations embraced reinsurance as an alternative to traditional practices that provided reconstruction loans to developing economies. These new products had the advantage that they did not create debt, one of the main issues with reconstruction finance.

There are many more impacts that are not mentioned in the chapters of this book. Perhaps the most important of these is risk governance. Climate change may be the most pressing issue where the reinsurance industry is advocating more severe measures.

12.8 Final Remarks

The main factors influencing the development of reinsurance identified in this volume include government interference in the form of regulation and nationalisation, different economic systems, path dependencies, and risk landscapes. In order to make reinsurance history relevant on a broader level, more research is required to investigate the industry in overarching theories on such economic systems, the historically changing role of governments in the economy and fiscal policies, and a so far still lacking comprehensive history of risk.

Literature on economic systems gives reinsurance fairly short shrift, if any at all. One main distinction, market-based versus bank-based systems, tellingly reduces the theory to banks. The theory may simplify matters somewhat as different economies combine elements of both and only show gradual tendencies towards either system. But it might profit from being applied to reinsurance. The main characteristics that reinsurance developed in the respective systems was an Anglo-Saxon tendency to look for a market-fair price for risk, while on the continent, price finding was negotiated and accompanied by additional risk management and financial consulting services. The two systems could also, although somewhat simplistically, be described as a market fair price model versus an actuarially fair price model. Continental reinsurance and Anglo-Saxon companies thus developed differing approaches that very much reflected their economic systems. Path dependency, as described here, might then have its roots not only within the reinsurance industry and its alternatives but in a broader context of financial services.

The politics of reinsurance offer a vast field for more research. In some way, reinsurance is a penultimate provider of risk protection. What cannot be covered by reinsurance goes to the government. Looking at the way different political systems dealt with reinsurance, be it through regulation or by direct intervention and nationalisation, may offer a new perspective on political agendas. The contradictory regulation and political approach to reinsurance in the U.S. may offer one of the most interesting backgrounds. What exactly the fiscal impact of foreign versus national reinsurance is has not been historically assessed. In this context, not only states should be looked at but also international organisations such as the United Nations and various World Bank organisations where reinsurance solutions have become ever more popular since the 1990s, replacing foreign aid schemes. In order to support recent developments towards a closer cooperation of state and private reinsurers, the past experiences should be researched in much closer detail.

Risk, finally, should embrace a wider perspective than reinsured risks. Company failures in reinsurance usually occurred due to the strategic errors, market shifts, as well as politics and regulation, but rarely as a consequence of large losses. Like possibly no other industry, reinsurance was exposed not only to the entire set of new risks that started emerging with the end of Bretton Woods, from currency fluctuations, high inflation to spiking interest rates. Additionally, the nature and value of insured risks changed, and risks became internationally interlinked. Risk management only features in one of the chapters here. More research into how reinsurers repositioned themselves as risk experts from the 1970s on may also benefit business history per se.

Bibliography

Alborn, Timothy. 2009. *Regulated Lives: Life Insurance and British Society, 1800-1914*. Toronto: University of Toronto Press.

Bühlmann, Hans, and Lengwiler, Martin. 2017. "Calculating the Unpredictable: History of Actuarial Theories and Practices in Reinsurance." In *Managing Risk in Reinsurance*, ed. Niels Viggo Haueter and Geoffrey Jones. Oxford: Oxford University Press.

Gerathewohl, Klaus, et al. 1979. *Rückversicherung. Grundlagen und Praxis*. Karlsruhe: Verlag Versicherungswirtschaft.

Haueter, Niels Viggo. 2021. *Reinsurance: Impact*. Oxford Research Encyclopedia on Business and Management. About | Oxford Research Encyclopedia of Business and Management.

Hotchkiss, W. H. 1914, 15 April. Reinsurance and Retrocession as Affecting and Affected by our American Insurance System: Extension of Remarks of William H. Hotchkiss, (former Superintendent of Insurance of New York) at the National Convention of Insurance Commissioners held at Chicago Ill. Original typescript, The Insurance Library Association of Boston (without archive identification number).

Kyrtsis, A. 2017. "The Rise and Decline of Treaty Reinsurance: Changing Roles of Reinsurers as Financial Service Providers." In *Managing risk in reinsurance:*

From city fires to global warming, ed. Niels Viggo Haueter and Geoffrey Jones. Oxford: Oxford University Press.
Swiss Re Company Archives (SRCA).

Index

A
Aachen and Munich Fire Insurance Company, 29, 30
Acemoglu, Daron, 174–176
A.F. Pearson and Company, 28
Africa, 93, 100, 109, 130, 221
AGARA, 189, 191
AGF, 137, 138
Agliardi, Antonio, 201
Agroasemex, 10, 232, 233, 246–252
Aikoku Life, 265
Algeria, 116
Alianza, 234, 275
Alien Property Custodian, 33, 34
Alleanza, 202
Altamirano, Rayes, 232, 235, 236, 239, 243, 245, 246, 249
Alternative Risk Transfer Mechanisms (ARTM), 5, 23, 24, 37–39, 271
Alternative Risk Transfer operations, 144
American, 5, 7, 19, 21, 25–28, 31–34, 37, 64, 68, 75, 79, 101, 107, 131, 133, 137–139, 145, 166, 182, 183, 233, 277, 281–283
American Marine Insurance Syndicates, 33
American Skandia, 106
American Society of Mechanical Engineers, 186
Ania-Associazione nazionale fra le imprese assicuratrici, 202
Annuario, 202, 203, 205
Anuario Financiero y de Sociedades Anónimas, 155–158, 160–162, 164
Arrow, Kenneth, 174
Aseguradora Nacional Agrícola y Ganadera, S.A. (Anagsa), 232, 239
Assicurazioni Generali, 154, 155, 165, 198, 199, 202, 205, 207–209, 212–214, 218
The Association, 47, 48, 54, 56, 65, 72, 75, 262, 264, 265

Association of Life Insurance Companies, 261, 262, 264, 266
Assonime-Associazione fra le società italiane per azioni, 202
Astrea Reinsurance, 96
Atanasio, Ernesto, 156
Atlántida, 157
Auburn German Mutual Fire Insurance Company of Campbellsport, 31
Auburn Mutual Insurance Company, 31
Ausonia, 216, 220, 221
Australia, 50, 93, 101, 139, 140
Austria, 19, 51, 71, 93, 97
Autarkic, 8, 78, 147, 150, 166, 168, 276
Automobile Liability, 121
Axa, 137
AXA Ré, 138, 141, 142
Axis Capital, 145

B

Baglioni, Roberto, 204
Balkans, 222
Banco de Crédito Agrícola, 178
Banco de Crédito Local, 178
Banco de México, 239
Banco Hipotecario de España, 178
Banco Nacional de Crédito Agrícola, 236
Banco Nacional de Crédito Ejidal, 235, 236
Banco Vitalicio de España, 155, 159, 160
Bank of Spain, 148, 178
Berkshire Hathaway Reinsurance Group, 26
Bermuda, 26, 36, 37, 101, 138, 139, 145
Besso, Giuseppe, 219
Besso, Marco, 213

Bico, Elena, 201, 226
Boletín Oficial de Seguros y Ahorro, 162
Boye, Edouard, 94
British, 1, 4, 13, 15–17, 28, 36, 47, 49–53, 63, 92, 93, 107, 126, 135, 141, 179, 182, 198, 233, 273, 278
British Airways, 182
Bungei Terumichi, 265

C

Caisse Centrale de Réassurances (CCR), 123, 273
Campbell sport Mutual Insurance Company, 31
Canada, 24, 25, 35, 36, 101, 128
Canofari, 162
Carreras, Albert, 174
Caruana, Leonardo, 1, 4, 5, 8, 9, 13, 16, 90, 91, 150, 154, 156, 161, 181, 182, 272, 274, 279
CASA, 182
Castellón Vital, 159
Catastrophe bonds, 39
Catastrophes, 18, 23, 34, 38, 39, 77, 178, 188, 193, 198, 219, 223, 272, 273, 279, 281, 282, 287
Cattolica, 207, 211, 212, 215
Centro Levantino de Seguros, 161
Chicago Board of Trade, 38
Chikutaro Nosaka, 265
China, 109, 140, 141
Chubb, 145
Chugai Shogyo News, 262
Cingolani, Giorgio, 9, 198, 271, 277
Ciocca, Pierluigi, 201, 202
Civil war, 8, 28, 149, 150, 168, 278
Clyman Town Mutual Fire Insurance, 31
Coinsurance, 2, 14, 15, 17, 27, 35, 37, 39, 184, 217, 226, 273

Cologne Re, 5, 18–20, 26, 274, 275
Coltorti, Fluvio, 202
Comín, Francisco, 148, 183
Comisión para el Estudio y Planeación del Seguro Agrícola Integral (CEPSAI), 236, 240
Commercial Risk Partners, 143
Common Market, 7, 125, 127, 175, 176
Compagnia di Roma Riassicurazioni, 207
Compagnie Havraise de Reinsurance, 128
Compañía Española de Reaseguros (CERSA), 156
Compañía General de Reaseguros, 155, 159
Compañía Hispano Americana de Seguros o Reaseguros (CHASYR), 159–161, 165
Compañía Vascongada de Seguros, 161
Conseil national de la résistance, 123
Consorcio Mexicano del Seguro Agrícola Integral y Ganadero, 237
Corena, 127
Corporate and Technical Risks Department, 135
Correu Toledo, Guillermo, 235–240
Covadonga, 155, 159
Credit Guarantee, 144
Credit Lyonnais, 142
Credito Italiano, 202
Croatian, 222
Cummins, J. David, 23, 26, 36–38, 50

D

Dai-ichi Mutual Life, 257–260, 265
Da Roit, Barbara, 223
Death bonds, 39
Deelstra, Griselda, 149

Del Angel, Gustavo, 10, 233, 234, 242, 272, 280
Denmark, 25, 51, 64, 78, 94, 97, 101
Deregulation, 7, 102–105, 108–110, 149, 272
De Simone, Ennio, 198
Diamond, 262
Diario Oficial de la Federación, 248
Direct writers, 24, 27–34, 36–39
Disasters, 3, 14, 94–96, 104, 136–139, 142, 179, 182, 247, 252, 256
Domovina, 222
Donau, 220
Dublin, 145

E

Earthquakes, 2, 4, 7, 23, 36, 95, 96, 137, 142, 219, 248, 282, 287
El Fénix Austríaco, 157
El Porvenir de los Hijos, 160
Emdem, Dr., 260
Empresa Nacional Siderurgica (ENSIDESA), 183, 186
ENASA, 182
E.N. Bazán–ASTANO, 182
ENDESA, 183, 186
Escamilla, Jesús, 236–243, 245
Escuela de Organización Industrial, 186
Europe, 16, 17, 20, 21, 27, 34, 51, 62, 78, 93, 97, 98, 100, 101, 109, 127, 133, 135, 136, 138, 141, 142, 144, 152, 173, 174, 179, 197–199, 218, 219, 222, 223, 226, 273, 278, 279, 283
European General, 25
European Union (EU), 37, 104, 109, 198
Everest Re, 145

F

Fairfax, 138
Falautano, Isabella, 202
Farm fire insurance mutuals, 28
Fascism, 221, 277
Favaretto, Tito, 198
Federación de Sociedades Mutualistas de Seguro Agrícola y Ganadero, 236
Feldman, Gerald, 217
Ferrera, Maurizio, 201
Fire division, 118, 121, 122
First Reinsurance Company of Hartford, 33
First World War, 15, 50, 51, 57, 58, 68, 72, 74, 80, 115, 116, 149, 205, 220
Fiumeter, 207, 213, 215
Folksamerica Reinsurance Company, 103
Folksam International UK, 103
Fondiaria, 202, 207, 214, 220
Fondo de Garantía y Fomento a la Agricultura, 238
Fondo Nacional de Garantía Agrícola, 236, 238
France, 2, 7, 15, 16, 19–21, 31, 51, 53, 63, 71, 77, 93, 101, 108, 115–118, 121–128, 130, 132, 133, 135, 139, 142, 144, 145, 148, 174, 180, 223, 226, 272, 273, 277, 279, 281, 282
France-Réassurances, 116
Franco, Francisco, 8, 147, 149
Francoist dictatorship, 149
Frankona Re, 31
Frederick W. Taylor, 186
Freja Reinsurance, 94, 96
French, 3, 7, 17–19, 52, 53, 63, 92, 93, 115–119, 121–129, 131–139, 141–143, 145, 163, 177, 179, 198, 205, 220, 233, 275, 282
Fuentes Quintana, Enrique, 177

G

Galli, Carlo, 222
Gan, 138
García Ruiz, José Luis, 150, 159
GE Global Insurance Holdings, 26
General Re, 19, 25, 26, 138, 273, 274
GenRe, 145
Gerling, 129
Germany, 1, 4, 5, 9, 13, 15–21, 25, 28–32, 51, 53, 56–58, 66, 71, 74, 80, 93, 94, 96, 97, 101, 108, 123, 125, 126, 128, 144, 174, 188, 189, 199, 202, 217, 220, 223, 226, 273, 282
Giannetti, Renato, 207
Gido, Maura, 265
Giichiro, Aso, 265
Gino, Gancia, 176
Gold standard, 35, 73, 148
Gómez, Fernández-Vegué, 189
González, Manuel Jesús, 177
Goshay, Bob, 38
Gota Bank, 103, 107
Grandine e Riassicurazione, 207
Great Depression, 34, 97
Great War, 33–35, 204, 205
Greece, 222
Groupama, 138, 141, 143
Gugerli, David, 199
Guipúzcoa Reaseguros, 161

H

Hamburg-Mannheimer, 101
Hannover Re, 39, 105, 107, 145
Hanse-Merkur (Hamburg), 101
Hans Grieshaber, Dr., 262

Hasbrouck, Frank, 32, 33
Hasler, Kurt, 199
Havre Reinsurance Company, 129
Hirasawa, Makoto, 265
Hochi Newspaper, 266
Hoken Ginko Jiho, 268
Holland, David M., 218
Home of New York, 103, 107
Hong Kong, 134, 139, 140
Host, Zeno M., 29
Hotchkiss, William L., 23, 28, 29, 32, 33, 274
Hudson Insurance Company, 97
HUNOSA, 183
Hurricane Andrew, 7, 108, 136, 139
Hurricane Catastrophe Fund, 38
Hurricanes, 2, 35, 234, 282

I
Iberia, 182, 186, 189
Illinois, 28
IMF, 177, 180
INA, 202, 204, 214, 220, 221, 226, 277
India, 141
Indiana Millers Mutual Fire, 30
Indonesia, 140, 141
Industrial revolution, 14–18, 20, 174, 182, 186, 191
Influenza, 257–259, 284
Instituto Español de Moneda Extranjera (IEME), 151
Instituto Nacional de Industria (INI), 8, 9, 180–185, 187, 188, 190, 191
Insurance-linked securities (ILS), 5, 24, 38, 39
International isolation, 147, 153
International Monetary Fund, 166
Italian, 8, 9, 93, 128, 138, 142, 197–202, 204–207, 213, 217–225, 233, 271, 277, 278

J
Japan, 2, 10, 23, 97, 106, 109, 140, 256–258, 260–262, 265, 268, 272, 273, 276, 283, 284

K
Kaufmann, 201
Kessler, Denis, 144
Kyoei Life, 10, 257, 262, 265–267
Kyoto Imperial University, 261

L
L'Abeille Fire, 31
La Catalana, 155, 159, 168
La Consorziale, 207, 213
La Equitativa–Fundación Rosillo, 154, 158, 159
La Equitativa Hispano Americana, 155, 158, 159
La Equitativa Nacional, 158
La Equitativa Reaseguros, 154, 155, 157–159
La Equitativa Riesgos Diversos, 154, 158, 159
La Fondiaria, 205, 208, 209, 211–216
L'Anonima Infortuni, 205
Länsförsäkringar Insurance Company, 99, 106
La Polar, 161
La Riassicuratrice, 207, 209, 210, 221
Lars F. Andersson, 148
La Unión Levantina, 161
La Unión y el Fénix, 152, 155–157, 168
La Vittoria, 204, 206, 213
Lencsis, Peter, 24, 27, 37
Levante, 207
Ley del Seguro Agrícola Integral y Ganadero, 239, 241

Ley del Seguro Agropecuario y de Vida Campesino, 242
Leyes de Crédito Agrícola, 235
Ley General de Instituciones de Seguros, 235, 236
Ley sobre el Contrato de Seguro, 236
Liljegren, J., 162
Lindert, Peter H, 201, 226
Lloyds, Edward, 1, 4, 15, 28, 38, 50, 58, 127, 132, 136, 137, 139, 145, 282
Long-tail risks, 36
Luxembourg, 145
Luzzato, Mario, 224

M
M&G, 35, 36
Madrid Agreements, 166
MAPFRE, 183
Martín Aceña, Pablo, 148, 178
Martínez Ruiz, Elena, 148, 150
Masato Isono, 261
Massachusetts, 29, 32, 34
Mayers, David, 149
Mediterránea, 159, 160
Meiji Life Insurance, 258
Mellinato, Giulio, 204
Merchants & Bankers Mutual Fire Insurance Company of Beloit, 30
Mercury Re, 34
Métropole, 220
Metropolitan Life, 34
Mexican Ministry of Finance, 232
Mexico, 2, 10, 100, 101, 231–236, 240, 241, 243, 246, 248, 252, 272, 275, 279
Middle East, 100, 144
Midland Union of Juneau, 31
Milano Assicurazioni, 205, 215
Millo, Anna, 198, 213, 217
Millo, Giovanni, 223

Minerva, 155, 156
Ministry of Finance (MOF), 222, 236, 251, 264, 268
Ministry of Labor, 116
Mitsui Life, 265
Miura, Dr., 260, 261
Mizruchi, Mark S., 153, 154, 161
Monoline, 27, 32, 33, 35
Münchener Rückversicherung, 121, 128
Munich Re, 1, 5, 9, 19, 25, 28, 29, 31, 33, 34, 37, 51, 66, 67, 72, 127, 132, 138, 145, 178, 179, 185, 188, 189, 191, 217, 224, 234, 266, 274
MUSINI, 9, 183–186, 188–191
Mutua General de Seguros, 159, 163
Mutualidad Comarcal de Seguros Agrícolas "La Laguna", 235

N
Nationale Ré, 128, 129
National Fund for Agricultural Calamities (FNGCA), 124
National reinsurance, 8, 72, 77, 127–129, 147, 165, 168, 179, 221, 272, 275, 276, 279, 281, 289
Natuji Natori, 265
Natural risks, 235
Nederlandse Reassurantie Group (NRG), 137, 273
Nervión Reaseguros, 161
New Jersey, 32, 37
New York state, 28
Nikka Life, 265
Nippon Life, 257, 258, 260, 262, 265, 267
Nordbanken, 103
Nordea, 103
North Africa, 222
North American Re, 25

Northwestern Mutual Life of
  Milwaukee, 30
Notizie statistiche, 202–205
Nullmeier, Frank, 201
NW Re, 137

O
Odaka, Jiro, 263
Odyssey Re, 145
Official Committee on Marine
  Insurance, 8, 151
Official Committee on Reinsurance, 8,
  152, 167, 275
*Oficina de Estudios del Seguro
  Agrícola*, 236
Old Mutual, 106, 109, 110
Öresund Group, 98
Orido, 262
Ortiz-Villajos, José María, 159
Osaka, 262
Osaka Jiji-Shinpo, 260
Osaka Mainichi News, 263
Otoine Tanaka, 265
Outflows of currencies, 150

P
Padoa, Fabio, 217
Parache, Manuel, 177
Partner Re, 138, 141, 143
Paternelle, 220
Patria, 234
Pearson, Robin, 15–17, 24, 25, 28,
  35, 36, 51, 90, 96, 151, 198,
  199, 202
Pegaso, 182
Penn State University, 186
Peripheral country, 173
Piedmont Management Company, 35
Pilot Life Re, 25
Piluso, Giandomenico, 9, 198, 199,
  217, 271, 277

Plan de estabilización, 177
Plantin, Guillaume, 149
Political unification, 197
Porri, Vincenzo, 219
Post-War, 75, 148, 200, 201, 204,
  221, 224
Powell, Lawrence S., 149
Prados, Leandro, 148
Pravidentia, 207
Prudential Financial, 106
Prussian Life, 34
Puerto Rico, 37
Putnam Re, 26

Q
Quitzaman, P.J., 236–240, 242, 243,
  245

R
Reale, 207
Reale di Riassicurazioni, 207
Reaseguradora Española, 155, 161
Regulation, 4–8, 14, 24, 27, 28,
  36, 37, 48, 53, 60, 99, 100,
  104, 108, 110, 141, 147,
  149, 151–153, 156, 161, 165,
  167–169, 178, 184, 189, 204,
  234, 236, 256, 264, 271, 276,
  280, 283, 288, 289
Regulation XXX, 27, 39
Regulators, 5, 27–32, 34, 36, 37,
  168, 274
Regulatory obstacles, 153
Reinsurance associations, 28, 54,
  71–73
Reinsurance bureaus, 28, 275
Reinsurance Company of America, 25
Reinsurance Corporation of New York
  (RCNY), 33–35, 37
Reinsurance Group of America (RGA),
  26, 145

Reinsurers, 3, 16, 25, 26, 30, 32, 33, 35, 36, 49, 54, 67, 72, 117, 123, 126, 129, 135, 137, 138, 140, 144, 145, 151, 154, 156–158, 160, 161, 163, 190, 219, 224, 225, 252, 263, 272, 274, 282, 286, 287
Report Toyo Life, 263
REPSOL, 183
Republican pesetas, 150
Retrocession, 19, 24, 27, 29, 32, 39, 117, 124, 129, 152, 276–278
Revista del Sindicato Vertical del Seguro, 155, 157, 162, 164
Risk-exchange, 148, 164, 165
Riunione Adriatica di Sicurtà (RAS), 198, 218
Rockoff, Hugh, 181, 182
Romano, Sergio, 222
Rosés, Joan, 148
Rossia, 25, 33
Rostow, Walt Whitman, 174
Royale, 220
Royal Insurance Company, 93
Royal Re, 137
Royal Sun Alliance, 107
Rück, Kölnische, 54, 56, 57, 68, 138
Russia, 31, 95, 115, 116

S
Sabatinelli, Stefania, 223
Sacerdoti, Piero, 200
SAFR, 127, 129, 138
SAI, 202
Sampo, 105–107
Sandor, Richard, 38
San Francisco, Earthquake, 4, 7, 91, 95, 96, 287
Santucci, Guido, 202
Sanzin, Luciano Giulio, 217
Sapelli, Giulio, 204

Saraceno, Chiara, 223
Sardá, Juan, 177
Schooling, 198
Schwepcke, Andreas, 218
Scientific Labor Organization, 186
Second World War, 76, 77, 122, 149, 150, 154, 168, 181, 199–201, 205, 223, 287
Second World War, 222
Semi-peripheral, 174
Severe Acute Respiratory Syndrome (SARS), 256
Shibusawa, Eiichi, 263
Shibusawa, Keizo, 263
Shigenao Kanai, 263, 265
Showa Seimei Hoken Shiryo, 265, 266
Sistema Alimentario Mexicano (SAM), 243
Sistema Nacional de Aseguramiento al Medio Rural, 249
Skandia America Reinsurance Corporation, 101
Skandia-Boavista, 101
Skandia Group, 98, 101, 104
Skandia Insurance Company, 92
Skandia International (SI), 102, 103, 107
Skandia Life, 106, 109, 110
Skandia Life UK, 101
Skandia Re, 101
Smith, Adam, 174
Social capabilities, 198
Sociedad Española de Automóviles de Turismo (SEAT), 182
Società Anonima Italiana di Assicurazioni, 207
Société anonyme de réassurances, 115
Societe Anonyme de Re-assurances de Paris, 28
Société Commerciale de Réassurance (SCOR), 7, 92, 115, 124, 125,

128–130, 133–145, 179, 205,
    273, 282
Solow, Robert, 176
Somner, David W., 149
Sorema, 135, 138, 141, 143, 145
South Carolina, 36
South Korea, 140
Spain, 2, 8–10, 31, 128, 144,
    148–155, 162, 165, 166,
    168, 173–191, 223, 271, 272,
    275–279
Spanish Flu, 6, 10, 257, 258, 260,
    267, 284
Stefani, Giuseppe, 204
Sterling Offices Limited, 28, 217
Stevenson and Kellogg, 35
Storebrand, 105, 107
Straumann, Tobias, 21, 217
Sumitomo Life, 265
Sweden, 2, 6, 7, 89, 93, 95, 98, 100,
    102, 104, 105, 107, 109, 110,
    116, 128, 272, 281
Sweden Re, 92
Swiss, 5, 21, 71, 115, 123, 126–128,
    138, 179, 198, 213, 219, 220,
    233, 266, 278
Swiss Re, 1, 3, 5, 21, 25, 26, 34–37,
    51, 54, 68, 123, 127, 129, 132,
    145, 153, 178, 179, 189, 191,
    198, 200, 217, 219, 220, 224,
    225, 234, 274, 275, 283

T
Tafunell, 174
Taiwan, 140
Takao Takada, 265
Takeshita, Kiyomatsu, 265
Tamesaburo Tamaki, 265
Tatuji Noe, 265
Taxes, 30, 34, 36, 37, 45, 46, 131,
    139, 145, 167, 248
Teikoku Life, 263, 265

Tellez, Luis, 243, 246, 247
Thailand, 140
Thule Group, 98
Tokyo, 139, 262
Tokyo Asahi News, 261, 266
Toro, 202, 207, 214, 217
Tortella, Gabriel, 159, 160, 184
Toshikazu Suzuki, 265
Towne, H.R., 186
Toyo Life, 262–265
Transatlantic Holdings, 26
Transcontinental Reinsurance
    Company, 127, 138
TransRe, 26, 145
TransRe Zurich, 26
Trygg-Hansa, 98–100, 103, 104, 107
Tsuneto Yamashita, 265
Turkey, 222, 275

U
UAP, 137, 138, 216
Unión, 234
*Unione Italiana di
    Riassicurazione-Uniorias*,
    207
Union Re, 262, 263, 266
Unistorebrand, 137
United American Fire Insurance
    Company of Milwaukee, 30
United Fire Reinsurance Company of
    Manchester, 28
United Kingdom, 7, 13, 15, 53, 125,
    137, 139, 148, 180
United States Lloyd Marine Insurance
    Underwriters of New York, 29
United States of America, 23
Utica Mutual Fire Insurance Company
    of Omro, 31

V
Vasta, Michelangelo, 207

Vec, Milos, 37
Vélez, Felix, 243, 246
Veracruz, 233, 236
Vittoria, 220
Volpi, Giuseppe, 222
Von Koch, Carl-Gustaf, 93

W
Wallerstein's, 174
Warman, Arturo, 243, 247
Warsaw Fire, 31
Watson Phillips y Cía, 233
Welfare state, 20, 198, 199, 226
Werner, Welf, 24, 26
Western General Insurance, 143
Wisconsin, 29–31
Wisconsin Town Mutual Reinsurance Company (WTMRC), 30, 31
World Bank, 177, 201, 287, 289
World War I, 5, 6, 91, 95, 97, 99, 281, 282
World War II, 25, 33, 35, 36, 39, 91, 97, 182, 273, 274, 282

X
XXX bonds, 24

Y
Yasuda Life, 265
Yataro Takahashi, 265
Yoneyama, Takau, 10, 260, 264, 272, 283
Yugoslavia, 222

Z
Zilibotti, Fabrizio, 176

CPSIA information can be obtained
at www.ICGtesting.com
Printed in the USA
LVHW081351260821
696158LV00002B/219